CW01329322

Global Regionalisms and Higher Education

Global Regionalisms and Higher Education

Projects, Processes, Politics

Edited by

Susan L. Robertson
University of Bristol, UK

Kris Olds
Department of Geography, University of Wisconsin-Madison, USA

Roger Dale
Graduate School of Education, University of Bristol, UK

Que Anh Dang
Graduate School of Education, University of Bristol, UK

Edward Elgar
PUBLISHING

Cheltenham, UK • Northampton, MA, USA

© Susan L. Robertson, Kris Olds, Roger Dale and Que Anh Dang 2016

All rights reserved. No part of this publication may be reproduced, stored in a retrieval system or transmitted in any form or by any means, electronic, mechanical or photocopying, recording, or otherwise without the prior permission of the publisher.

Published by
Edward Elgar Publishing Limited
The Lypiatts
15 Lansdown Road
Cheltenham
Glos GL50 2JA
UK

Edward Elgar Publishing, Inc.
William Pratt House
9 Dewey Court
Northampton
Massachusetts 01060
USA

A catalogue record for this book
is available from the British Library

Library of Congress Control Number: 2016938593

This book is available electronically in the Elgaronline
Social and Political Science subject collection
DOI 10.4337/9781784712358

ISBN 978 1 78471 234 1 (cased)
ISBN 978 1 78471 235 8 (eBook)

Typeset by Servis Filmsetting Ltd, Stockport, Cheshire
Printed and bound in Great Britain by TJ International Ltd, Padstow

Contents

List of figures	vii
List of tables	viii
List of contributors	ix
Acknowledgements	xiv
List of abbreviations	xvi

Introduction: global regionalisms and higher education   1
Susan L. Robertson, Roger Dale, Kris Olds and Que Anh Dang

1 Higher education, the EU and the cultural political economy of regionalism   24
Susan L. Robertson, Mário Luiz Neves de Azevedo and Roger Dale

2 Different regionalisms, one European higher education regionalization: the case of the Bologna Process   49
Susana Melo

3 Erasmus Mundus and the EU: intrinsic sectoral regionalism in higher education   65
Roger Dale

4 Inter-regional higher education arena: the transposition of European instruments in Africa   85
Jean-Émile Charlier, Sarah Croché and Oana Marina Panait

5 Harmonization of higher education in Southeast Asia regionalism: politics first, and then education   103
Morshidi Sirat, Norzaini Azman and Aishah Abu Bakar

6 Changing higher education discourse in the making of the ASEAN region   124
Roger Y. Chao, Jr

7 Shaping an ASEM (Higher) Education Area: hybrid sectoral regionalism from within   143
Que Anh Dang

8	Ir-regular regionalism? China's borderlands and ASEAN higher education: trapped in the prism *Anthony Welch*	166
9	Good friends and faceless partners: educational cooperation for community building in the Barents Region *Marit Sundet*	191
10	Transregionalism and the Caribbean higher educational space *Tavis D. Jules*	211
11	MERCOSUR, regulatory regionalism and contesting projects of higher education governance *Daniela Perrotta*	228
12	South–South development cooperation and the socio-spatial reconfiguration of Latin America–Caribbean regionalisms: university education in the Brazil–Venezuela 'Special Border Regime' *Thomas Muhr*	253
13	Higher education and new regionalism in Latin America: the UNILA project *Paulino Motter and Luis Armando Gandin*	272
14	Regionalization, higher education and the Gulf Cooperation Council *Tahani Aljafari*	289

Index 305

Figures

1.1	The formal structure of the Bologna Follow-Up Group	36
6.1	Emerging East Asian higher education policy architecture	133
7.1	ASEM education process in the ASEM institutional structure	151
8.1	China–ASEAN total trade, 1994–2009	169
9.1	Location of HEIs participating in educational cooperation	194
11.1	Results of MEXA, 2002–2006	233
11.2	Results of ARCU-SUR, 2008–2012	234
11.3	MARCA mobility flow, 2014	236

Tables

I.1	Old regionalism and new regionalism compared	8
3.1	Roles in the governance of the EU Erasmus Mundus programme, 2004–2008	72
6.1	ASEAN nations' economic status and focus on higher education	130
6.2	ASEAN'S 5-Year Work Plan in Education	131
6.3	Summary of ASEAN higher education actors and their mechanisms	135
8.1	The Dragon, the Tiger Cub	173
8.2	Summary, China–Viet Nam cross-border educational services	181
14.1	Main characteristics of the three projects	300

Contributors

Tahani Aljafari graduated with a PhD in Education from the University of Bristol, UK in 2013. Tahani's research interests include policy-making in higher education and regionalism, specifically in relation to the Gulf Cooperation Council. After graduation, she taught Global Citizenship at the King Fahad Academy in London, UK. She is currently Deputy Head of Academic Studies at the Primary School at the King Fahad Academy.

Mário Luiz Neves de Azevedo is Associate Professor at the State University of Maringá (UEM), Brazil. His research interests include internationalization, regionalization and globalization of higher education. Mário is also a researcher at the National Council for Scientific and Technological Development in Brazil.

Norzaini Azman is Professor of Higher Education at the Faculty of Education, Universiti Kebangsaan Malaysia. She is also an Associate Research Fellow at the National Higher Education Research Institute and a member of the International Association of Universities (IAU) Reference Group. Her main research interests include policy and governance of higher education, the academic profession, and higher education for sustainability. She has collaborated with the International Institute for Educational Planning, Paris, France; the Asian Development Bank, UNESCO Bangkok and the Malaysia–Australia Institute in research projects. She has published numerous scholarly articles in higher education journals, and numerous book chapters.

Aishah Abu Bakar is a Senior Lecturer at the Civil Engineering Department, the University of Malaya (UM). She is also the Director of the Academic Development Centre at UM and a member of a working committee for the Malaysian Qualifications Framework Review. She was actively involved in curriculum development and quality assurance, in higher education research specifically in assessment, curriculum design and delivery. Her research in e-assessment in tertiary learning has led to several national and international awards. She was the Director of Academic Development Management Division, Department of Higher Education, Ministry of Education Malaysia and has represented the Ministry at various forums in higher education policies and initiatives including student mobility programmes.

Roger Y. Chao, Jr is an independent international education consultant. Roger's research is engaged with higher education policies and reforms within national and regional contexts. He has written on the internationalization and regionalization of higher education and regularly writes commentaries on higher education developments in the Southeast and East Asia, and Asia Pacific regions. He has served as the international consultant for higher education with the United Nations Educational, Scientific and Cultural Organization (UNESCO) in Myanmar, and has been commissioned to write a number of technical reports for UNESCO including 'The Role and Effectiveness of Regional Recognition Conventions in the Asia and the Pacific Region'.

Jean-Émile Charlier has a PhD in Sociology. He is Professor at the Université catholique de Louvain-Mons, Belgium and co-tenured as UNESCO Chair in educational sciences at the University Cheikh Anta Diop of Dakar, Senegal. He has worked on a wide range of issues, including the sociology of religion and religious education in secondary schools in Africa. Over the last ten years his research has focused on concerns over the effects of the Bologna Process on European and African higher education systems and the resistances to international injunctions in education.

Sarah Croché has a PhD in Political and Social Sciences and a PhD in Educational Sciences. She is an Associate Professor at the University Picardie Jules Verne (UPJV), France. In her thesis, she studied the role of the European Commission in the Bologna Process. More recently, her research has taken two directions: truth discourses in competition in African education, and the effects of quality assurance mechanisms on academics.

Roger Dale is Professor of Education at the University of Bristol, UK. His academic interests centre around the sociology of education and education policy. He was from 2007 to 2010 Scientific Coordinator of the European Union (EU) Network of Experts on Social Science and Education, and he has been an editor of three collections of studies around aspects of European education policy. Together with Susan Robertson, he co-founded the journal *Globalisation, Societies and Education* in 2003.

Que Anh Dang is a Marie Curie Doctoral Researcher at the University of Bristol, UK. She has worked in the higher education sector for 15 years in Asia and Europe. Her research interests include mobility and mutation of higher education policies, the role of international organizations in policy-making, higher education and regionalism in Asia and Europe. She has published papers on higher education reforms, the role of the World Bank, foreign university campuses in Asia, and Association of Southeast

Asian Nations (ASEAN)–EU education cooperation. Her current research project is concerned with higher education in the knowledge economy and regionalism in Asia and Europe.

Luis Armando Gandin is Professor of Sociology of Education at the School of Education of the Universidade Federal do Rio Grande do Sul, Brazil. Among his publications are *The Routledge International Handbook of the Sociology of Education* (edited with Michael Apple and Stephen Ball). He is the editor of two journals: *Educação & Realidade* and *Currículo sem Fronteiras*. His research interests are sociology of education, curriculum and educational policy.

Tavis D. Jules is an Assistant Professor of Cultural and Educational Policy Studies at Loyola University Chicago, USA. His research focuses on the impact of regionalism upon (small and) micro-states and education in transitory space with a geographic focus on the Maghreb region. He is the book reviews editor, *Caribbean Journal of International Relations and Diplomacy* and author of *Neither World Polity nor Local or National Societies: Regionalization in the Global South – the Caribbean Community* (Peter Lang Press, 2012).

Susana Melo was awarded her PhD in Education by the University of Bristol, UK in 2013. Subsequently, she held a 21-month full-time position as Research Fellow at the University of Nottingham's School of Education, UK, where she contributed to a large EU-funded project (LLLight'in'Europe) with case study research on the multi-level governance of the EU's employment–lifelong learning policy nexus. Her doctoral research focused on the relations between the Council of Europe and the Bologna Process and informs her current main research interest in the nexus of European politics, higher education policies and theories on the societal role of (higher) education.

Paulino Motter has a PhD in Education awarded by the University of Wisconsin-Madison, USA. Paulino began his career as a journalist. Since the mid-1990s he has specialized in public policy and government management, and worked for the Brazilian Ministry of Education. Most of his academic research deals with the relationship between media, public discourse and policy formation. From 2008 to 2012, he was involved with the designing and implementation of the Federal University of Latin American Integration (UNILA) project, after spending many years on the so-called Triple Frontier, which connects Brazil, Paraguay and Argentina.

Thomas Muhr is Adjunct Lecturer in Sociology at Friedrich-Alexander University Erlangen-Nuremberg, Germany and Honorary Assistant

Professor at the Centre for International Education Research, University of Nottingham, UK. Thomas's research is concerned with the political sociology and geographies of globalization, development and education, especially post-school and non-compulsory education, with an area focus of Latin America–Caribbean in the context of global South–South cooperation. Thomas is the author of *Venezuela and the ALBA: Counter-Hegemony, Geographies of Integration and Development, and Higher Education for All* (VDM, 2011) and editor of *Counter-Globalisation and Socialism in the 21st Century: The Bolivarian Alliance for the Peoples of Our America* (Routledge, 2013).

Kris Olds is Professor in the Department of Geography, University of Wisconsin-Madison, USA. He also serves as a Senior Fellow with the Educational Innovation initiative in the Provost's Office. Kris's current research focuses on the globalization of higher education and research. This research agenda relates to his long-standing research interests in the globalization of the services industries (including higher education, architecture and property), and their relationship to urban and regional change. He has worked as an academic in England, Canada, Singapore (1997–2001), and the United States (2001 to present), and was also based at Sciences Po in Paris in 2007–2008.

Oana Marina Panait is a PhD researcher at the Faculty of Economics, Political, Social and Communication Sciences, Université catholique de Louvain-Mons, Belgium. Her research concerns the dissemination of international prescriptions in the field of education and the resistance of local actors.

Daniela Perrotta is a researcher at the National Council of Scientific and Technical Research based at the University of Buenos Aires, Brazil, where she is also a lecturer. Her courses are in the field of regional integration and Latin American thought. She coordinates the Latin American Evaluation System of the Latin American Council of Social Sciences. Daniela has a PhD in Social Sciences (FLACSO Argentina). Her research topic is the study of the policies of internationalization and regionalization of higher education, combining theoretical approaches and methodological tools in the field of education (critical sociology of higher education) and political science (studies of regional integration and comparative studies). Daniela is involved in community activities regarding the promotion of Latin American integration from the university in a project called 'Identidad MERCOSUR'.

Susan L. Robertson is Professor of Sociology of Education at the University of Bristol, UK. Susan's research is broadly engaged with transformations in the state, education and governance as a result of global, regional and national projects and processes. She has written extensively on the development of Europe as a regionalizing project, and Europe's inter-regional projects with Asia and Latin America. Susan is founding Director of the Centre for Globalisation, Education and Social Futures at Bristol, and is founding co-editor of the journal *Globalisation, Societies and Education*. Her recent books include *Public Private Partnerships and Global Governance*, and *Privatisation, Education and Social Justice*.

Morshidi Sirat is Professor in the School of Humanities, Universiti Sains Malaysia, and Founder Director, Commonwealth Tertiary Education Facility. He has served as the Director of the National Higher Education Research Institute and as Deputy Director-General, Department of Higher Education (Public Sector), Ministry of Higher Education, Malaysia. Between April 2013 and May 2014 Morshidi was Director-General of Higher Education/Registrar General, Private Institutions of Higher Education. Morshidi publishes widely on Malaysia's higher education policy and is very active in research and consultancy work for the Asian Development Bank (ADB), the World Bank, UNESCO Bangkok and the International Institute for Educational Planning (IIEP), Paris.

Marit Sundet is an Associate Professor at Nord University, Norway and a member of the UArctic academic leader team. Marit's research is broadly engaged with individual meaning structures in relation to the framework where they operate in terms of local, national and international conditions. In previous research Marit has been concerned with how institutions organize and act in relation to vulnerable groups of the population; she found that a given society's perception of normality affects the differentiation and classification of otherness. In international cooperation between higher education institutions her empirical studies reveal that the cooperation is rooted in very different political, social, economic and cultural conditions that are prerequisites for the individuals' participating in international networks.

Anthony Welch is Professor of Education at the University of Sydney, Australia. Anthony's research spans the sociology of education, policy studies, and international higher education, and he has written extensively on these developments, both in Australia and, particularly, in Asia, including China, Southeast Asia and Afghanistan. Anthony has won numerous awards, including as a Fulbright scholar, and most recently a national award as *Haiwai Mingshi* (Distinguished Overseas Scholar), China. He has a substantial consultancy record, and his recent books include *Education, Change and Society* (3rd edition), *Higher Education in Southeast Asia* and *Counting the Cost: Financing Higher Education for Inclusive Growth in Asia*.

Acknowledgements

This book is the outcome of a stimulating and highly fruitful collaboration over a decade between the authors of the chapters on global regionalisms and higher education. Like many intellectual endeavours, it was built upon a number of formally and informally organized encounters, conversations and exchanges between us as we tried to make sense of what was going on around us. Already several of us were collaborating on the changing spatial organization of higher education, and the ways this sector was being mobilized in the refashioning of cities, their regions, and nations and globally. We were also intrigued by the ways in which these disparate but often connected projects were increasing taking on a supra-regional form – the most obvious of course being Europe – but not only by this. Indeed there were other intriguing, novel, as well as imitatory developments under way, many of which are presented in this book.

The pathway to this book is more than ten years long, and draws upon research and dialogue in the United Kingdom and the USA. Our sustained engagement has been generously supported by the Worldwide Universities Network (WUN), the University of Wisconsin-Madison Center for European Studies (a US Department of Education National Resource Center), the UW-Madison European Union Center of Excellence (funded by the university and the European Commission), as well as the Division of International Studies and the Department of Geography. We are grateful for the background support of key UW-Madison faculty, staff, and students including Gilles Bousquet, Elizabeth Covington, Jason Nu and Noah Rost. Indirect support and valuable insights over this decade have been provided by some of the European architects of the Bologna Process (including Pavel Zgaga and Eric Froment), as well as key policy practitioners and analysts (including Anne Corbett and Michael Gaebel).

This volume is an outcome of this journey. But what makes it particularly remarkable is that it is one of the first systematic efforts to bring together this range of work on regionalizing projects and higher education from around the globe, and present it to a wider audience. There are huge gaps still to be filled, especially on emerging regionalisms and inter-regionalisms in regions such as Africa, the Mediterranean and North African region, and Oceania. But we see this as the start of an intellectual journey, and not its endpoint.

Acknowledgements

We have many people to thank for believing this was a worthwhile project; you know who you are. We would also like to thank many of our students, some not in this volume but nevertheless present, treading along fascinating paths researching global higher education regionalisms. All of us would like to thank our own institutions for providing intellectually challenging environments to work in, and for their support for this kind of academic endeavour. Finally, we would particularly like to thank Alex Pettifer and colleagues at Edward Elgar Publishing for all of their help in making sure we could bring this publication to fruition. Now, over to you.

Abbreviations

AACCUP	Accrediting Agency of Chartered Colleges and Universities
AAU	Association of African Universities
ACA	Academic Cooperation Association
ACC	Accreditation Committee of Cambodia
ACIA	ASEAN Comprehensive Investment Agreement
ACP	African, Caribbean and Pacific Group of States
ACRULAC	Association of Rectors of LAC Universities
ACTFA	Academic Credit Transfer Framework for Asia
ACTI	Association of Caribbean Tertiary Institutions
ACTS	ASEAN Credit Transfer System
ACTS	ASEM Credit Transfer System
ADB	Asian Development Bank
ADEA	Association for the Development of Education in Africa
AEC	ASEAN Economic Community
AFAS	ASEAN Framework Agreement on Services
AFTA	ASEAN Free Trade Area
AGU	Arabian Gulf University
AHEA	African Higher Education Area
AHEA	ASEAN Higher Education Area
AHELO	Assessment of Higher Education Learning Outcomes
AIA	ASEAN Investment Area
AIMS	ASEAN International Mobility for Students Programme
ALADI	Latin American Integration Association
ALALC	Latin American Free Trade Association
ALBA	Bolivarian Alliance for the Peoples of Our America
ALBA-TCP	ALBA – Peoples' Trade Agreement (Tratado de Comercio de los Pueblos)
ALFA	América Latina – Formación Académica
ANEAES	National Agency for Assessment and Accreditation of Higher Education (Agencia Nacional de

	Evaluación y Acreditación de la Educación Superior) (Paraguay)
APACET	Agency for the Promotion and Quality Assurance of Tertiary Education
APEC	Asia-Pacific Economic Cooperation
APEID	Asia-Pacific Programme of Educational Innovation for Development
APRU	Association of Pacific Rim Universities
APSC	ASEAN Political–Security Community
APT	ASEAN Plus Three
AQA	Academic Quality Agency
AQAN	ASEAN Quality Assurance Network
AQRF	ASEAN Qualifications Reference Framework
ARCU-SUR	Acreditación Regional de Carreras Universitarias del Sur
ARWU	Academic Ranking of World Universities
ASA	Association of Southeast Asia
ASC	ASEAN Security Community
ASCC	ASEAN Socio-Cultural Community
ASEAN	Association of Southeast Asian Nations
ASED	ASEAN Ministers of Education Meetings
ASEM	Asia–Europe Meeting
ASEM ME	Asia–Europe Meeting of Ministers for Education
AU	African Union
AUGM	Association of the Montevideo Universities Group
AUN	ASEAN University Network
AUN-QA	AUN Quality Assurance
AWCR	Arab World Competitive Report
BAN-PT	National Accreditation Board for Higher Education (Indonesia)
BCS	Bachelor of Circumpolar Studies
BEAC	Barents Euro-Arctic Council
BFUG	Bologna Follow-Up Group
CAFTA	China–ASEAN Free Trade Area
CAhPMM	MERCOSUR'S Mobility Programme Ad Hoc Commission
CAMES	African and Madagascan Council for Higher Education
CAN	Andean Community of Nations
CARICOM	Caribbean Community
CARIFTA	Caribbean Free Trade Agreement
CCP	Chinese Communist Party

CCR	Regional Coordinating Committee (MERCOSUR)
CELAC	Community of Latin American and Caribbean States
CEMAC	Central African Economic and Monetary Community
CEPES	European Centre for Higher Education (Centre Européen pour l'Enseignement Supérieur, UNESCO)
CHES	Caribbean higher educational space
CLMV	Cambodia, Lao PDR, Myanmar, Vietnam
CMC	Common Market Council (MERCOSUR)
CoE	Council of Europe
COMESA	Common Market for Eastern and Southern Africa
CONEAU	National Commission of University Evaluation and Accreditation (Argentina)
CRC	Regional Commission for Coordination
CRES	Regional Conference on Higher Education in Latin America and the Caribbean
CROSQ	Caribbean Regional Organization on Standards and Quality
CSME	CARICOM Single Market and Economy
CVQ	Caribbean Vocational Qualification
CXC	Caribbean Examination Council
DAAD	German Academic Exchange Service (Deutscher Akademischer Austauschdienst)
DGEAC	Directorate General of Education and Culture (EC)
DGHE, MOEC	Directorate General of Higher Education, Ministry of Education and Culture (Indonesia)
DIAC	Dubai International Academic City
EAC	East African Community
EACEA	Education, Audiovisual and Culture Executive Agency
EAS	East Asian Summit
EC	European Commission
ECQ	Education City Qatar
ECTS	European Credit Transfer System
EEA	European Economic Area
EFTA	European Free Trade Association
EHEA	European Higher Education Area
ELAM	Latin American School of Medicine
EM	Erasmus Mundus
EMA	Erasmus Mundus Alumni Association

EMMC	Erasmus Mundus Masters Course
EMU	European Monetary Union
ENLACES	Latin American and Caribbean Research and Higher Education Area
ENQA	European Association for Quality Assurance in Higher Education
ERA	European Research Area
Erasmus	European Region Action Scheme for the Mobility of University Students
ESU	European Students Union
EU	European Union
EUA	European University Association
EURASHE	European Association of Institutions in Higher Education
FDI	foreign direct investment
FEM	MERCOSUR Educational Fund
FOCEM	MERCOSUR Structural Convergence Fund (Fondo para la Convergencia Estructural del MERCOSUR)
FTA	free trade agreement
FTAA	Free Trade Area of the Americas
GATS	General Agreement on Trade in Services
GATT	General Agreement on Tariffs and Trade
GCC	Gulf Cooperation Council
GDP	gross domestic product
GMC	Grupo Mercado Común (MERCOSUR)
GTAE	Working Group of Specialists in Evaluation and Accreditation
GTPG	Working Group on Postgraduate Programmes
GTR	Working Group on Recognition of Degrees
GZAR	Guangxi Zhuang Autonomous Region
HE	higher education
HE&T	higher education and training
HEI	higher education institution
IAI	Initiative for ASEAN Integration
IAU	International Association of Universities
ICT	information and communication technology
IESALC	International Institute for Higher Education in Latin America and the Caribbean (UNESCO)
IFI	international financial institution
IIEP	International Institute for Educational Planning (UNESCO)

IIRSA	Initiative for the Integration of Regional Infrastructure in South America
IMEA	MERCOSUR Institute of Advanced Studies
IMF	International Monetary Fund
IMHE	Institutional Management in Higher Education
ISI	import-substituting industrialization
IUCEA	Inter-University Council for East Africa
KAUST	King Abdullah University of Science and Technology
LAC	Latin America and the Caribbean
LMD	Licence Master Doctorate
LO	learning outcome
Maphilindo	Malaysia–Philippines–Indonesia
MARCA	Programa de Movilidad Académica Regional
MERCOSUR	Southern Common Market (Mercado Común del Sur)
MEXA	Mecanismo Experimental de Acreditación de Carreras de Grado Universitario
M–I–T	Malaysia–Indonesia–Thailand
MOHE	Ministry of Higher Education (Malaysia)
MPI	Ministry of Planning and Investment (Viet Nam)
MQA	Malaysian Qualifications Agency
MRA	Mutual Recognition Agreements
NAB	national accreditation body
NAFTA	North American Free Trade Agreement
NDG	Narrowing the Development Gap
NQF	National Qualifications Framework
NRA	new regionalism approach
NUCLEO	MERCOSUR Centre for Studies and Research in Higher Education
OAS	Organization of American States
OECD	Organisation for Economic Co-operation and Development
OECS	Organization of Eastern Caribbean States
OEI	Organization of Ibero-American States
OHEC, MOE	Office of the Higher Education Commission, Ministry of Education (Thailand)
OMC	Open Method of Coordination
ONESQA	Office for National Education Standards and Quality Assessment (Thailand)
PAASCU	Philippine Accrediting Association of Schools, Colleges and Universities

PASEM	SEM Support Programme
PAU	Pan-African University
PKI	Partai Komunis Indonesia (Indonesia)
PMM	MERCOSUR Mobility Programme
PNAES	National Student Assistance Programme
PRC	People's Republic of China
PT	Partido Trabalhadores
QA	quality assurance
QF	Qatar Foundation for Education, Science and Community Development
R&D	research and development
RAM	Regional Accreditation Mechanism
RANA	Meeting of National Accreditation Agencies
RCEP	Regional Comprehensive Economic Partnership
REESAO	Network for the Excellence of the Higher Education of Western Africa
RIA	regional integration agreement
RIACES	Ibero-American Network for Quality Accreditation in Higher Education
RME	Meeting of Ministers of Education (MERCOSUR)
RSHE	Regional Space for Higher Education
RTA	regional trade agreement
SC	Supreme Council
SCME	Standing Committee of Ministers Responsible for Education
SEAMEO	South-East Asian Ministers of Education Organization
SEAMEO RIHED	SEAMEO Regional Centre for Higher Education and Development
SEATO	Southeast Asia Treaty Organization
SELA	Latin American and the Caribbean Economic System (Sistema Económico Latin-American y del Caribe)
SEM	MERCOSUR Education Sector (Sector Educativo del MERCOSUR)
SIDS	small island developing states
SINAES	National System of Higher Education Assessment (Sistema Nacional de Avaliação da Educação Superior) (Brazil)
SLAS	Society for Latin American Studies (UK)
SOM	Senior Officials' Meeting (ASEM)

TAC	Treaty of Amity and Cooperation in Southeast Asia
TVET	technical and vocational education and training
UAE	United Arab Emirates
UBV	Bolivarian University of Venezuela
UCTS	UMAP Credit Transfer Scheme
UdelaR	University of the Republic (Uruguay)
UEMOA	Monetary Union of Western Africa
UERR	Roraima State University (Universidade Estadual de Roraima)
UFAM	Federal University of Amazonas (Universidade Federal do Amazonas)
UFFR	Federal University of Roraima (Universidade Federal de Roraima)
UK	United Kingdom
UMAP	University Mobility in Asia and the Pacific
UNA	National Open University (Universidad Nacional Abierta)
UNASUR	Union of South American Nations
UnB	University of Brasília
UNDP	United Nations Development Programme
UNEFA	Universidad Nacional Experimental Politécnica de la Fuerza Armada Nacional
UNEG	National Experimental University of Guayana (Universidad Nacional Experimental de Guayana)
UNESCO	United Nations Educational, Scientific and Cultural Organization
UNESR	National Experimental University Simón Rodríguez (Universidad Nacional Experimental Simón Rodríguez)
UNIALBA	University Network for the Peoples of ALBA
UNICA	Association of Caribbean Universities and Research Institutes
UNICAMP	State University of Campinas
UNILA	Federal University of Latin American Integration (Universidade Federal da Integração Latino-Americana)
UNISUR	Experimental National University of the Peoples of the South
UPEL	Experimental Pedagogical University Liberator (Universidad Pedagógica Experimental Libertador)

USA	United States of America
UWI	University of the West Indies
VNU-HCM	Vietnam National University – Ho Chi Minh City
WTO	World Trade Organization

Introduction: global regionalisms and higher education

Susan L. Robertson, Roger Dale, Kris Olds and Que Anh Dang

INTRODUCTION

Over the past two decades, a growing number of researchers interested in transformations in world orders have focused their attention on the growth of supra-national (as opposed to sub-national) regions, and the role of education in this process. Indeed, just over a decade ago, two of us (Dale and Robertson, 2002) published a paper reflecting on such developments, arguing that state-created regional organizations were significant agents in powering and steering the forces that make up global capitalism. In the paper we pointed out that each of these organizations operates in a geographical 'regional' space that is itself constructed (for instance the 'Asia Pacific' or Latin America), that such regions are the deliberate creation of national governments ceding some authority and sovereignty to the bodies orchestrating and mediating their development, and that these global regionalisms differed from each other. These differences were not only the result of the kind of emphases they placed on the form of economic relations, but also because political, cultural and historical dynamics mediate the nature of their institutional forms and other social relations.

Our paper went on to examine in greater depth what were at the time three prominent regional groupings – the European Union (EU), the North American Free Trade Agreement (NAFTA) and the Asia-Pacific Economic Cooperation (APEC) forum – through an exploration of their form and purpose, the dimensions of power at work (such as decisions, agenda-setting, rules of the game), and the nature of the effects on national and sub-national education systems, whether directly on education policies (such as new curricula, discourses of inclusion, quality assurance mechanisms) or the broader politics of education (such as how social sectors like education were being recalibrated by, or indeed calibrating, bigger political projects).

Looking back at this period, it is clear a great deal has changed. APEC, for instance, heavily backed by the United States, Australia and Singapore, is now less significant as a regional organization, whilst the Association of Southeast Asian Nations (ASEAN) has become increasingly important. As 2015 came to a close, the ASEAN Economic Community was launched. It was also clear some forms of regionalizing are not (national) state-led but rather involve a range of other actors, with or without the state. It is also clear that, over this period of time, higher education has begun to play an increasingly more central role in different kinds of regional projects, for example through student and staff mobility programmes, the development of quality assurance mechanisms, regional qualifications frameworks, sharing best practice, and in some cases, introducing systems of credit transfer for students.

But one thing is also clear: our interest in region-building and novel forms of inter-regionalism, and the role that higher education is playing in this, has continued to grow. We were hooked. Regional projects and the spaces that they were creating beyond the national state – from Africa to Latin America, Europe, Central Asia, the Arab world, South East Asia and Oceana – are not just fascinating political developments. They also pose interesting intellectual challenges regarding how best to understand quite what they are, and how to research them. Were they spaces or 'areas', as in the European Higher Education Area or the African Higher Education and Research Space? But what kind of area, or space? Why have they emerged, and at this point in time? What is the source of their authority and legitimacy? How do the agendas of these higher education regional projects get set, and by whom? What is the relationship between different higher education regional projects and spaces, how are these brokered, and by whom?

Answers to some of these questions came as a result of a closer engagement with the EU's higher education and economic projects through workshops and conferences (including in Madison, Wisconsin), funded research projects, and contributing as experts to the European Commission and the European University Association. At close range, we could see and meet other key players who were instrumental in the rapid expansion of Europe's 'education space' through instruments like the Bologna Process launched in 1999 (Bologna, 1999). To change the degree architectures of its 29 signatory countries (expanding now to some 48 countries) through this Bologna Process was nothing short of astonishing, especially given the difficulties institutions inevitably present for any grand-scale reform initiative. And in this case, higher education was being enrolled in a regional integration project which had emanated from national governments: a proposal from Claude Allègre, then France's Minister of Education, Higher Education and Research to higher education ministers from Italy, Germany and the United Kingdom. His proposal, 'Towards a European University', culminated in the Sorbonne Declaration in 1998 (Corbett, 2005). This was state-led, to be sure, but was given energy and direction from below rather than above (Ravinet, 2008).

Histories, of course do not write themselves. They are made by actors under circumstances not entirely of their own choosing, to paraphrase the well-known line. Over the past decade and a half, higher education has been viewed by leaders of many developed economies as an important sector through which to resolve bigger challenges regarding global competitiveness through the creation of knowledge-based economies and societies. But we could also see very interesting new developments emerge, including forms of South–South cooperation especially in the Latin American region. Yet what is particularly intriguing, from our point of view, is the way this regional scale was being constituted as an important platform upon which solutions to the challenges facing governments and their higher education institutions were being sought. And what of the implications for (sub)national governments when their higher education institutions and efforts are being governed at a supra-national scale?

Much of our research effort went on to concentrate on Europe as a way of exploring these questions (see Robertson, 2006, 2008a, 2008b, 2010; Robertson and Keeling, 2008; Dale and Robertson, 2009). We were soon joined by a band of eager researchers, many of whom appear in this book, as keen as we were to look beyond the obvious – Europe – to already existing but under- or unstudied, newer, and novel forms of higher education regionalisms around the globe, from the Gulf Region to MERCOSUR, ASEAN, the Asia-Europe Meeting (ASEM), the Barents Region, Council of Europe (CoE) to the Bolivarian Alliance for the Peoples of Our America (ALBA), and new forms of inter-regionalisms. All include higher education in their agenda, albeit it in somewhat different ways, and at different levels of development.

REGIONS, REGIONALIZING, INTER-REGIONALISM

Encountering theoretical and empirical work on regions and region-making means encountering a bewildering lexicon (for example: regions, regionalism, regionalization, inter-regionalism, regionness) as researchers try to capture projects, processes, actors and institutions at work in the making of a more or less coherent regional territorial space. We might call this 'a region *in* itself'. But when a region acquires an identity, and acts 'as a region *for* itself' (Cammack, 2015), it has what Hettne (2005) calls 'actorness', for example when a region acts on the world stage as an entity.

Rather than provide an exhaustive account, we leave the various elaborations to the appropriate chapters in this volume. But a brief account will get the reader started. At its simplest, regions can be seen as the outcome of formal and/or informal arrangements to cooperate on economic, political and cultural affairs. Dent defines regionalism as the 'structures, processes and arrangements that are working toward greater coherence within a specific international regime in terms of economic, political, security, socio-cultural and other kinds of linkages' (Dent, 2008: 5).

Regionalism is often differentiated from regionalization, as the tangible material and human flows that cross borders within a region and in doing so generate an evident and usually deepening intra-regional integration pattern when viewed from a global perspective. For example, family firms in Southeast Asia trade heavily amongst one another, and help to bind together the region's economy. This form of regionalization, however, is differentiated from the regionalism associated with ASEAN; an institution with a reform agenda created by nation-states. Regionalization driven by private actors (investment flows including overseas university campuses) is often supported and reinforced by states (for example, Australian university campuses in different Southeast Asian countries). Furthermore, the density of interactions by non-state actors often leads to a demand for common institutions and formal institutional cooperation. For instance, when student mobility or worker mobility increases, states and their institutions may well sign agreements regarding mutual recognition of qualifications.

Clearly regionalism and regionalization are interdependent, though the nature of each phenomenon and their relationship varies across space and time. Indeed they are so interdependent that some scholars deliberately blur the terms with a focus on legal and regulatory dynamics at a variety of scales. As Breslin and Higgott (2000) put it, regionalism is an interactive process consisting of:

1. De facto economic integration on the one hand (at both global and regional levels) and *de jure* processes of regional institutionalized governance on the other.
2. Emerging (vertical) meso-levels of authority between the state and the global order (trans- or supra-national regionalization) on the one hand, and between the state and the local level (sub-national regionalization) on the other ('glocalization').
3. Emerging (horizontal) authority across extant territorial jurisdictions (natural economic territories or growth triangles).

While we agree broadly with this, we prefer to differentiate regionalism from regionalization in this text to help enhance our ability to communicate about some of their driving forces with greater clarity.

Inter-regionalism is a phenomenon obviously linked to regionalism (Gaens, 2011). Once a regional agenda and architecture is constructed (for example, the EU), regions often reach out to other regions to facilitate the development process via the building of linkages. Examples of inter-regional linkages include the European Union–Gulf Cooperation Council (EU-GCC), European Union–Latin America and the Caribbean (EU-LAC) and ASEM, which Que Anh Dang (Chapter 7 in this volume) examines. ASEM was established in 1996 by 25 countries from Asia and Europe, along with the European Commission, and has continued to morph into a very different kind of institution from the one its founding members launched. Indeed Dang argues that what has emerged is not simply a mix of Asia and Europe regionalism but a new set of social relations not reducible to the sum of its parts.

Inter-regionalisms are seen as a response to complex interdependencies caused by globalization (Rüland and Storz, 2008). It broadly consists of three strands: bi-regionalism, trans-regionalism and hybrid inter-regionalism (Rüland, 2010). Bi-regionalism denotes region-to-region dialogues between two more or less clearly defined regional entities and is organized in a hub-and-spoke relationship, mainly around the EU (ibid.), although that model is altering as partner regions, such as MERCOSUR, ASEAN and NAFTA, lead the charge to develop new hubs (Doidge, 2007). In bi-regional cooperation there are usually no common overarching institutions; both sides rely on their own organizational infrastructures (Rüland and Storz, 2008). Examples here include the EU–ASEAN, EU–MERCOSUR and EU–NAFTA.

Trans-regionalism refers to a process of dialogue with a more diffuse membership which does not include only regional organizations but also member states from more than two regions (Dent, 2004). Trans-regional forums tend to develop a modicum of organizational infrastructure, such as a secretariat (virtual or physical) or other (often informal) coordinating mechanisms. An example here is APEC which has a permanent secretariat in Singapore.

Hybrid inter-regionalism is a residual category that includes intercontinental forums, such as Africa–EU and EU–Community of Latin America and Caribbean States (EU-CELAC), or strategic partnerships of the EU with individual countries (EU–United States, EU–Russia, EU–China, EU–Japan, EU–India and EU–Mexico).

Many forms of regionalism are shaped by, and emerge out of, regional trade agreements (RTAs). The World Trade Organization (WTO) has a register of RTAs and it is useful to look at it to get a sense of their scope and scale. According to the WTO, an RTA is 'an agreement concluded between countries not necessarily belonging to the same geographical region' (WTO, 2016):

> The coverage and depth of preferential treatment varies from one RTA to another. Modern RTAs, and not exclusively those linking the most developed economies, tend to go far beyond tariff-cutting exercises. They provide for increasingly complex regulations governing intra-trade (for example with respect to standards, safeguard provisions, customs administration, etc.) and they often also provide for a preferential regulatory framework for mutual services trade. The most sophisticated RTAs go beyond traditional trade policy mechanisms, to include regional rules on investment, competition, environment and labour. (WTO, 2016)

As of 1 December 2015, some 619 notifications of RTAs (counting goods, services and accessions separately) had been received by the General Agreement on Tariffs and Trade/World Trade Organization (GATT/WTO). Of these, 413 were in force. These WTO figures correspond to 452 physical RTAs (counting goods, services and accessions together), of which 265 are currently in force (WTO, 2016). Amongst the best-known regions are the European Union, the European Free Trade Association (EFTA), NAFTA, MERCOSUR, the ASEAN Free Trade Area (AFTA), and the Common Market for Eastern and Southern Africa (COMESA).

RTAs have become increasingly prevalent since the early 1990s, though many regional agreements and their forms of organization have a longer history, including the League of Arab States (1945), the Organization of American States (1948), the Council of Europe (1949), the European Union (1957), the Association of Southeast Asian Nations (1967), and the Gulf Cooperation Council (1981).

Regional forms of cooperation and their agreements seem to have come in waves. They begin in the period immediately after the Second World War. In the 1960s a new wave follows with the rise of Asia. Later, in the 1990s, regions emerge again as a response to the globalizing of neoliberalism and a commitment to freer movement of trade over national boundaries. Most recently regional cooperation agreements are again a response to global processes, this time as a result of the collapse of the World Trade Organization's trade and services negotiations. In this most recent period, a huge number of bilateral preferential trade agreements have also been negotiated that include higher education as a services sector.

However, there are clearly very different speeds of integration (as well as disintegration or stalling, if we take the APEC case), with quite different degrees of: the ceding of authority from national states to these regional bodies; numbers of members and patterns of membership; accession agendas; spheres of competence especially in relation to social policy sectors such as higher education; and also institutional arrangements. Yet there are also some important similarities, especially when governance instruments, such as quality assurance mechanisms, are transferred or borrowed from one region to the next. These differences have presented researchers with major challenges regarding conceptualizing and theorizing regions.

CONCEPTUALIZING AND THEORIZING REGIONS

The expansion of inter-state activities at the regional level, and novel and new forms of regional cooperation and organization since the 1990s, have resulted in the proliferation of concepts and approaches. Börzel nicely captures this when she states:

> There is new and old regionalism, regionalism in its first, second and third generation; economic, monetary, security and cultural regionalism, state regionalism, shadow regionalism; cross-, inter-, trans-, and multi-regionalism; North, South and North–South regionalism; informal and institutional regionalism – just to name a few of the labels. (Börzel, 2011: 5)

Add to this mix different disciplines, from area studies to politics, international relations, anthropology, economics and sociology; and competing paradigms, such as functional, positivist, constructivist, neorealist, (neo) Marxist; and it is clear that there are many approaches to, or angles in on, the study of regions and regionalisms. In the next section we briefly sketch out the main contenders in the field, and show how those working on higher education have tended to position their work in relation to regions, regionalisms and regionalizing.

REGIONS AS FUNCTIONAL UNITS OF (MULTILEVEL) GOVERNING

Much of the early work on regions emerged in the mid-1950s and focused upon two things: Europe and integration, and building the region as an endogenous process through institutions aimed at using trade as a means for creating post-war security. Hettne (2002) coined this the 'old regionalism' in contrast to a 'new regionalism' which he argued characterized the state of the world in the last decade of the twentieth century onwards (see Table I.1).

Table I.1   Old regionalism and new regionalism compared

Old regionalism, post-1945–1990s	New regionalism, 1990s onwards
Bipolar world; Cold War; strong national states	Multipolar world made up of national, regional and global actors
Created from above through super-power engagement	Voluntary process from within the emerging region; cooperation to tackle global challenges
Inward and protectionist	Open and export-oriented
Specific and narrow objectives	More comprehensive, multidimensional societal processes
Concerned with relations between nation-states	New forms of special organization that are part of a global structural transformation that includes non-state actors

Source: Based on Hettne (2002).

What are the differences between old and new regionalism? For Hettne, they refer to differences in the state of world order (bipolar versus multipolar), the move from government to governance, from closed to open economies, from narrow regionalism to multidimensional regionalisms, and from concerns over relations between nation-states to new forms of global structural transformation. In short, they reflect the collapse of the post-Second World War rapprochement amongst Westphalian nation-states and their (in many cases) commitment to state-led Keynesianism or developmentalism to a post-Soviet, post-Cold War, neoliberal, globally competitive world. This shift to the 'new regionalism' has had huge and little understood implications for higher education; once the basis of post-war nation building projects, universities and higher education systems more generally have increasingly found themselves hitched as economic engines to the nation's strategies for economic survival, as many of our chapter authors show in great detail.

Theoretically, the dominant approach to what Hettne calls 'old regionalism' is neofunctionalism. To appreciate the distinction between functionalists and neofunctionalists we can say functionalists view integration as an inevitable and unpreventable result of those developments that impose more and more functions on national states, in turn pushing national states into cooperation with international functional institutions, such as the Asian Development Bank (ADB) or the Organisation for Economic Co-operation and Development (OECD).

Neofunctionalists, however, argue that the institutions that are created, and the 'spillovers' from economic integration to political unity, drive integration even further, and come to be seen as more powerful engines than national states. New elites and political alliances form at this new regional scale, giving rise to multiple levels of governing, with the end result that new competences are shifted to this level. As integration proceeds, a new centre is also created from which a 'new political community' arises. This kind of approach is quite popular amongst scholars interested in studying the governing of European higher education (see Enders, 2004 as one example).

The father of the neofunctionalist account of region-building is widely regarded as United States (US)-based Ernst Haas (see his 1958 book *The Uniting of Europe: Political, Social and Economic Forces 1950–1957*). Haas's aim was to provide an explanation for regional integration in Europe after the Second World War, and from there, to explain regional integration and development more generally, including in Latin America (Haas, 1958). However, over time Europe was to become the region where political and economic integration was the most fully developed. As a result, Europe has come to be closely associated with the study of regional integration and region-building, and as the archetypal region (Cini and Perez-Solorzano Borragan, 2004: 83).

Of course neofunctionalist approaches to the study of regions have not disappeared, and indeed it could be argued that this is the dominant perspective still to be found in the *Journal of Common Market Studies*, the flagship journal for EU scholars. Yet neofunctionalism has its limitations: not only does it tend to focus on integration (endogenous processes), but it finds it difficult to explain why Europe's national states tend to abandon collective problem-solving in times of crisis; an issue we again see following the global financial crisis of 2008 addressed by Robertson, de Azevedo and Dale in Chapter 1 in this volume, on European higher education and Europe's response.

REGIONS AS GOVERNING BLOCS IN A GLOBALIZING WORLD ORDER

In the context of a changing world order, together with a growing sense of the limitations of the functional accounts of regionalism, a 'new regionalism' approach has been developed by scholars such as Hettne and Söderbaum (2000) and James Mittelman (2000), amongst others. They argue that new regionalism has emerged out of major changes in world orders arising from globalization, with the region and its polity a Polanyian (1944) double movement against the advance of neoliberalism. As Hettne observes:

There are some conclusions from this contrasting of old and new regionalisms which are theoretically significant for the study of contemporary regionalism: the focus on the multitude of actors, the focus on the 'real' region in the making rather than the formal region defined by the list of member states, the focus on the global context as an exogenous factor not really considered by old regionalism theory, concerned as it was with regional integration as a merger of national economies through economic cooperation with nation states. (Hettne, 2002: 326)

Hettne's new regionalism combines endogenous with exogenous factors: those internal forces and motives that influence the process of integration (and are embedded in the concept of 'regionness') which we have called 'a region in itself', and the external challenges to which integration might be the answer (arising from the dynamics of globalization and regionalization projects in other parts of the world). This latter, 'inside-out', and not just 'inside', is particularly important to the study of higher education region-making activity, and helps to explain the evolving nature of higher education regional and inter-regional developments around the globe.

Hettne also argues that we can differentiate between regional arrangements by 'levels of regionness' (2002: 327). This is a staircase of regionness that makes up a 'natural history of regionness'. Here a region is conceptualized as evolving and changing; it is both a regional space in a geographic area, as well as a set of relations that can become more (or less) complex over time. A regional society can also emerge that has cultural, political and economic dimensions; perhaps anchored in a community that is an enduring framework for the creation of a transnational civil society. At its highest level of 'regionness' Hettne argues that it might have a regional institutional polity, much as the EU does, that arises out of attempts to control and promote globalization (ibid.: 329). For Hettne, these different stages of regions – from space to complex, community and polity – are a basis for comparative regional studies (ibid.: 327).

Work on the new regionalisms has been important, not least because it has moved conceptual work forward by viewing regions as made from both the inside and the outside. But the new regionalisms have also placed regions, as regional blocs, at the centre of the world order. Yet in reflecting on this, Cammack (2015: 2) argues this analytical push may well have been 'a step too far'. In putting 'regions' at the centre, what it failed to do is put regions in their place; as 'one means amongst others to achieve state or global transformation' (ibid.). He argues that it is important to 'focus analytical efforts primarily on the latter. Regionalism old and new has taken a wide variety of only loosely related forms embracing both security and political economy, and is not sensibly squeezed into a single frame or encompassed in a single theory' (ibid.).

In a paper published in 2005, Hettne returns to new regionalism as a concept and proposes its dissolution, largely because it has exaggerated the differences between 'old regionalism' and 'new regionalism'. His proposal is to move away from a focus on differences and look instead at the role of the regional in global transformations (Hettne, 2005: 543). In doing so, Hettne (ibid.: 554) brings into view a range of actors, other than the state, in regionalizing projects. Welch's Chapter 8, together with Motter and Gandin's Chapter 13 in this volume, highlight the importance of having a more open-minded way of thinking of regional projects and processes; in this instance, where shared borders create the conditions for certain kinds of exchanges.

The distinction Hettne makes between actors on the regional arena, and regions as actors in their own right, also enables us to see how some regions manage to acquire for themselves not only the resources but also the capacity to act, especially in different contexts. Inter-regional projects are one arena providing a stage, and enabling the capacity to act. In this volume, Chapter 7 by Dang on Asia–Europe, and Chapter 4 by Charlier, Croché and Panait on Europe–Africa, both explore these dynamics. In the case of Europe–Africa, Charlier, Croché and Panait point to the asymmetries in power between the two regions, as well as a high level of imposition by Europe on Africa regarding the Bologna Process, reinforcing old colonial relations.

But the question of for whom, how, with what purpose, and through which actors a regional project is being pursued is important, with the answer differing depending upon what social events and related phenomena are being analysed. As Motter and Gandin's Chapter 13 in this volume illustrates, the Federal University of Latin American Integration (UNILA) is a new regional university funded by the Federal Government of Brazil. Its mission is to develop a Latin American understanding of the world, and it is a novel form of regionalism. It is also largely a cultural and political, rather than economic, institutional project because of its location on the border between Brazil, Argentina and Paraguay, in Foz do Iguacu. Its academic staff, the students and the curriculum are all aimed at constructing a 'Latin American' and 'Latin American regional' understanding of the world, in contrast with a Northern hegemony centred on modernity and progress. Similarly, as Muhr (Chapter 12 in this volume) shows, a revamped MERCOSUR, along with the Bolivarian Alliance for the Peoples of Our America (ALBA) region promoted by the former President of Venezuela, Hugo Chavez, is a fascinating set of South–South political projects: to develop a very different form of regionalism which promotes both economic development and social welfare across the region as a contrast with, and counter to, neoliberal conceptions of the world. Sundet (Chapter 9 in this volume) also provides us with a unique insight into the ways in which higher education institutions in the Barents Region – from Russia to Norway – cooperate on developing governance structures in universities and in so doing broker a form of 'higher education diplomacy' as a means to ensuring ongoing relations in this region.

REGIONS AS SPATIAL FRONTIERS IN STATE PROJECTS OF TRANSFORMATION

But what if it is the national state pursuing a regionalizing project? Robertson, de Azevedo and Dale (Chapter 1) explore this regarding Europe; Jules (Chapter 10) examines this with regard to the Caribbean Community (CARICOM), Perrotta (Chapter 11) in relation to MERCOSUR, and Muhr (Chapter 12) with regard to ALBA. Much work on regions tends to privilege a particular – in this case, regional – level as discrete from, and thus separate, to other scales such as the national or the global. Yet if Hettne's new regionalism is concerned with grasping hold of the ways in which the 'inside out' or 'out there global' is implicated in region-making, what it does less well is focus attention on the dialectical relation between scales, and engage with the question of why it is that a regional scale or regional frontier emerges as a particular governing response to economic and political problems within the national arena.

'Regulatory regionalism' has emerged as a promising theoretical response to this conundrum. Jayasuriya (2003, 2009) and Hameiri (see Hameiri and Jayasuriya, 2011; Hameiri, 2013; Hameiri and Wilson, 2015) have sought to overcome an overemphasis on formal regional 'institutions' to the detriment of what they regard as an 'understanding of the *domestic* political mainsprings of regional governance' (Jayasuriya, 2003: 199). By domestic they mean sub/national challenges that need to be resolved through new spatial governing projects. They have thus adopted a 'political project' perspective, which:

> allows us to look at regions not as abstract identities but more or less as coherent projects of regional governance. Regional governance projects, in turn, embody particular constellations of power and interests – a framework that has the virtue of locating the dynamics of regional governance within the broader context of domestic political projects. (Jayasuriya, 2003: 201)

Furthermore, Jayasuriya (2009: 344) situates 'the process of state transformation – or rather the political topography of the state – at the centre of the study of regionalism'. In other words:

> the external imperatives are not to be located in terms of the changing dynamics of inter-governmental relations, but rather in the way the activities and

operations of domestic and foreign capital are restructured. It is this internal process of restructuring that creates the new dynamics of regionalisation, which, in turn, lead to the formation of new regional economic spaces of rule. (Jayasuriya, 2003: 205)

Yet as Hameiri (2013: 314) makes clear, 'states and regions are not identical and timeless phenomena; both are manifestations of struggles over the territorial, institutional, and functional scope of political rule'. That is to say, a region (as in this case, the supra-regional scale) is a socio-spatial manifestation of a particular organization of state rule, just as the national scale is. By focusing attention on a politics of regionalism that is simultaneously regional and national, with regional units deep inside national, and 'regional disciplines within national policy and political institutions', Hameiri and Jayasuriya (2011: 21) aspire to avoid a zero-sum approach typical of both the old and the new regionalisms.

However, Cammack (2013) points out that despite being a promising line of enquiry into regionalizing, regulatory regionalism only half-delivers on its analysis of the changing topography of the state because it does not single out a particular regional project as being more theoretically and practically important than others. Nor do Hameiri and Jayasuriya identify a particular logic at the heart of the national state's regionalization processes which, in Cammack's (2013) view, is the creation of the conditions for the expansion of an evolving world market. Regulatory regionalism as an approach would need to develop a more explicit account of the capitalist state and its relation to capital that does not simply invoke 'statecraft'. We argue that it is not just a question of the state and its capacity to 'govern' that is at issue, but that the state governs on behalf of capital to secure ongoing accumulation through the expansion of world market-making, although in doing so it also needs to manage the core problems that it faces: accumulation, legitimation and social cohesion (Dale, 1982). In the case of regions like the EU, this means developing mechanisms, such as the Open Method of Coordination to secure governing, and promoting ideas like the European dimension to help develop a shared set of values and social cohesion.

REGIONS AS SOCIALLY CONSTITUTED THROUGH IDEAS, INSTITUTIONS AND SOCIAL NORMS

A great deal of the work of regional actors and their institutions is to produce, or construct, new meanings about the region, including a regional identity, such as Europe and European, Bolivarian, the ASEAN way, and so on. This matters particularly in the study of education, as it is one of the key institutions and systems mobilized to help broker and create these new norms, and societal understandings. Scholars interested in the construction of the social have drawn upon social constructivism as a theoretical resource. Social constructivists draw on the work of conventional constructivist theorists, such as Martha Finnemore (1996), interested in the role of norms and identity in shaping political outcomes (Checkel, 2006: 58). In drawing attention to the socially constructed nature of regions, Checkel (2006) argues this highlights a particular analytic that can be applied across regions and not just the EU.

Social constructivists argue they are best-placed to study European integration as 'a process' because they are predisposed to think about how humans interact in ways that produce structures, such as norms (Rosamond, 2006: 130). Social constructivists are thus interested in how collective understandings and identities are created through the use of language, the development of ideas, powers of persuasion and the establishment of norms (Rosamond, 2006: 130). In other words, social constructivists study the ways in which European-level norms, ideas and discourses penetrate the various national polities which make up the EU (Rosamond, 2006: 131), whilst the EU itself acts as an arena for communication and persuasion (ibid.). Through the internalization of these norms, actors acquire their identities and establish what their interests are.

This view – that a region develops through the establishment of norms rather than changing as a result of external factors, such as the Cold War and increasing globalization – is core to social constructivism and can be contrasted with more rationalist views which place greater emphasis on these external factors. This body of work has had considerable influence on higher education scholarship around region-building. Dale's Chapter 3 in this volume on the development of Erasmus Mundus, as a means of developing not only a European Masters degree and joint doctorates, but also students and alumni whose identities are socially reoriented toward Europe, is a case in point. Similarly, research on programmes such as the EU's Erasmus Mobility scheme benefit from adopting a constructivist approach to understanding region-making through the ways in which ideas and institutions interact and have constitutive powers.

THIS VOLUME: VARIEGATED REGIONALISMS AND HIGHER EDUCATION

We began this Introduction by pointing out the growing role that higher education as a sector is playing in a range of different regional projects. As the chapters in this volume reveal, higher education institutions, think tanks, professional associations, international organizations, firms, student unions and civil society organizations, amongst others, are being enrolled in developing and constituting older and newer, or novel, forms of regionalisms, all showing considerable variegation as a result of their unique cultural political economies.

Higher education regional sectoral spaces are thus being made, higher education inter-regional spaces are being created, and new higher education institutions with regional identities are being shaped, to name a few of the processes at work. Yet, oddly enough, theorizing has tended to lag behind, and empirical work is curiously silent on these higher education regional and inter-regional developments occurring around the globe. Considering the role of higher education in the development of a more knowledge-based services economy, this is a problematic gap in ongoing analytical work.

In part this is because, as Warleigh-Lack and Rosamond (2010) and Söderbaum and Sbragia (2011) note, scholars on inter/regionalisms tend to speak past each other, with scholars opting for one camp over another rather than seeing each perspective as a 'take' on a more complex and varied whole. Scholars of regionalism have also paid insufficient attention to the role of higher education in regionalizing, whilst scholars of higher education have for their part given inadequate attention to the theoretical resources from the different intellectual fields concerned with understanding regions and regionalizing.

The outcome of this double gap (regionalism scholars not paying sufficient attention to higher education; higher education scholars not paying sufficient attention to regionalisms) is a missed opportunity in multiple ways: to see education as a particular kind of sectoral regional project and space, and from there, to appreciate how the study of higher education regional projects – sectorally and institutionally – generate new theoretical insights into regional projects, their cultural, political and economic dynamics, as well as logics, mechanisms and outcomes. And whilst functionalist explanations likely do not sit well with those offered by regulatory regionalists, in truth each of these perspectives offers important insights into processes of regionalizing for scholars of higher education.

Higher education regional projects are also spatial projects of governing at a regional scale; they are simultaneously cultural, political and economic, though not reducible to capitalist projects or indeed the products of 'Western' modernity, although there is a great deal of contestation as to whose ideas get traction. Higher education regional projects are also socially constituted and emerge out of the interaction between ideas and imaginaries, as well as strategies that are advanced and reproduced through new social norms. They can involve the whole sector on a grand scale, or be institution-to-institution projects involving several countries. They also vary across space and time. There is no single theory or methodological approach to capture this variety; rather, regionalizing projects and processes, and thus regions, are what we have elsewhere referred to as variegated regionalisms (see Robertson, 2014): the outcome of ongoing interactions with existing spatial, temporal, social and structural relations, norms and ways of making sense of the world.

This collection of chapters, which we sketch out briefly below, makes a unique contribution to these lacunae. Though incomplete in terms of representing the range and extent of regional projects under way, we hope this will stimulate the reader to delve into a rich set of chapters. Together they show the variegated nature of higher education regionalisms around the world as a result of diverse projects, processes and their politics, and what genuinely new insights can be revealed about our current world (Robertson, 2014).

The book begins with Susan Robertson, Mário de Azevedo and Roger Dale's Chapter 1 on Europe, and the creation of a European Higher Education Area and European Research Area. They trace out the detail of these political projects that are aimed at developing a globally-competitive Europe, on the one hand, and what they call a higher education regional sectoral space, on the other. Drawing upon and developing regulatory regionalism, they show how this regional space is an ongoing outcome of transformations of the state, its strategies of governing, and claims to statehood. They argue that over time, multiple spatial frontiers are strategically advanced and struggled over, and that more recently the regional frontier is losing rather than gaining greater governing capability as a result of governance changes within national state borders around higher education, as well as the ongoing politics of austerity projects.

The book then turns to Susana Melo's exploration of the Bologna Process (Chapter 2), widely regarded as the most prominent example of higher education (HE) regionalism. Employing new regionalism theory in order to go beyond the limitations of 'Bologna as model' approaches, she sets out the bases of the model it represents, and delves into its significance which she argues is rather different from that usually claimed for it: the harmonization of European HE systems. She discusses in detail how the 'informal regionalization' that Bologna represents contributes to the closer integration of European universities into the dynamic of globalization, and that this has taken precedence over de facto regionalism. She also asks about what new insights studying higher education regionalism might offer to the study of regionalisms more generally.

Roger Dale (Chapter 3) brings into view a rather different European regional project; the EU's Erasmus Mundus programme. Dale argues that Erasmus Mundus (EM) can be seen as an authentically (European) regional sectoral programme because it was irreducible to action at other scales, including the national. Fundamentally, the contract on which EM was based was made between the European Commission (EC) and the consortia of three universities in the different European countries which provided the courses. National states were at best only passively involved, and the programme was implemented through what is called by the European Commission 'comitology procedures', meaning sets of commitments against which progress is judged.

It is worth noting that the Bologna Process and the European Higher Education Area are the key drivers of global regionalisms and interregionalisms, hence our explicit decision to initially prioritize coverage of what has been happening in this part of the world.

A significant development in regionalisms is the emergence of inter-regionalism. Jean-Émile Charlier, Sarah Croché and Oana Marina Panait (Chapter 4) focus on EU–Africa inter-regionalism, and show how Africa is placed in an asymmetical relationship to global initiatives and policy-shaping actors, instruments, and spaces, such as the European Commission, the Bologna Process and the Bologna Policy Forum. Charlier and colleagues point out that the Bologna Process has not remained in Europe; rather, Africa has been the recipient of an explicit extra-regional strategy which Africa finds difficult to ignore. Using Foucault's work on governmentality and sovereignty, Charlier et al., argue that, paradoxically, Bologna exists in Africa in a purer form than it does in Europe, and that it is an instrument of imposition in the African case that has in turn given rise to a loss of African sovereignty. The chapter raises important questions concerning Africa's need to own its development agenda with the authors considering the role that a differently formed political project and governing strategy might play in shaping the region and what role higher education could play in this.

Morshidi Sirat, Norzaini Azman and Aishah Abu Bakar (Chapter 5) explore the way in which harmonization processes of higher education systems facilitate regional integration in Southeast Asia. They argue that regionalism in ASEAN was first driven primarily by political and security considerations, before being followed by economic justifications, and then other concerns. Although the idea of creating an ASEAN common space of higher education is inspired by the Bologna Process and the establishment of the European Higher Education Area, its implementation is constrained by a top-down approach, the wider political situation, the sovereignty of individual ASEAN member states, and the uniqueness of their higher education systems, which they identify as 'territorial constraints'. The authors call for more active participation of other stakeholder groups, particularly students and higher education institutions, in the regional harmonization process.

Roger Chao (Chapter 6) raises the role of ideas in region building, and explores the way in which economic rationales of higher education regionalization in Southeast Asia have shifted over time. Through analysing the activities of regional actors, such as the South-East Asian Ministers of Education Organization – Regional Centre for Higher Education and Development (SEAMEO RIHED) and ASEAN University Network (AUN), he shows that the changing ASEAN higher education discourse reflects the evolution of ASEAN regionalism, in turn shaping regional higher education policies and practices. ASEAN regionalism has evolved from its security rationale to economic regionalism, eventually incorporating the establishment of the ASEAN community in December 2015. Yet funding for the majority of ASEAN higher education regionalization initiatives tends to be from self-interested nations and extra-regional partners, including Australia, Japan and the European Union, all directing ASEAN initiatives toward increased linkages with their respective higher education systems.

Que Anh Dang (Chapter 7) draws on the concepts of 'emergence' and 'emergent properties' from critical realism to theorize the construction of regions. She argues that a region is an emergent entity whose existence depends on its constituent parts and the relations between them. Regionalizing is, therefore, a set of processes in which a set of constituent parts join together to constitute a new entity and new properties are produced. Dang's chapter explores the relationships between regionalism and the higher education sector, in turn offering an innovative conceptual understanding of the 'regional sectoral space' between Asia and Europe, designated an 'ASEM Education Area'. Her analysis of the ASEM case and its informal institutions – mainly meetings and joint projects – highlights the role of key actors (the senior officials and the secretariat) and their deliberate efforts at constructing a new entity with sufficient capability to change discourses and trigger changes to national higher education systems.

Novel forms of regionalization are also emerging. This is charted by Anthony Welch (Chapter 8) who discusses the merits of what he calls 'borderlands' research as a means of extending regionalism theory, focusing on the case of China–Vietnam relationships. He explores the complexity of Sino-Vietnamese via the 'pillars' of economy, knowledge mobility, Chinese regional diaspora, the regional perceptions of Chinese minorities, territorial disputes and, in particular, the history of Chinese–Vietnamese relations in higher education, especially their shared influence of Confucianism. On the basis of these arguments, Welch advances a conception of the differences between 'irregular' and 'regulatory' regionalism, based on the differences in the gap between claims and outcomes in much ASEAN-focused research, and the potential of borderlands research.

Marit Sundet's Chapter 9 is unusual in two respects: first, the region it addresses, the Barents Region is less well known than most of the others covered in the book; and second, it focuses in detail on the minutiae of the negotiation of region-building through the development of a Norwegian–Russian degree of Bachelor of Circumpolar Studies as a means of building bridges across international borders. Her major focus is on how the degree, and the region, are constructed through the activities of the network of coordinators – where 'the real internationalization takes place' – who develop and produce the degree.

The issue of different levels of 'regionness' over time is present in Tavis Jules's Chapter 10. He traces the nature and consequences of the shift he detects from 'immature' to 'mature' regionalism in the Caribbean, with the former characterized by the failure to implement regional decisions at national level, and the latter by local implementation. He shows that this shift arose from the increasing complexity of the demands placed on regional organizations. While the mechanisms of cooperation and collaboration have remained relatively consistent, Jules argues that the expansion of the range of regional blocs within the Caribbean has reached the point where it makes more sense to think in terms of 'pan-regional' or 'pan-hemispheric' integration.

Regional projects and their material form are also shaped by asymmetrical power relations and interests of participating states and other actors. Daniela Perrotta (Chapter 11) provides a deeply theorized and richly detailed account of the highly complex landscape of HE regionalism in Latin America. She distinguishes three contrasting historical projects: 'hegemonic regionalism', which essentially seeks to advance free trade; 'post-hegemonic' regionalism, seeking to reclaim welfarist projects; and 'counter-hegemonic regionalism', which seeks more far-reaching reforms. Following a broadly regulatory regionalist account, she addresses these issues through detailed accounts of MERCOSUR's 'birthmark' stage, characterized by the shift from development to competition; its 'brandmark' phase, through the development especially of quality assurance mechanisms; and the 'Bolognization of MERCOSUR', with a focus on mobility.

South–South cooperation refers to political projects that eschew the dominance of neoliberalism as an organizing politics. Here Thomas Muhr (Chapter 12) offers a fresh and insightful look at what he calls the 'changing geometries of Latin American–Caribbean regionalism' as a form of South–South cooperation. Muhr focuses specifically on the role of Brazil and Venezuela in the recent reinvention of MERCOSUR, and its relationship to the Bolivarian Alliance for the Peoples of Our America – Peoples' Trade Agreement (ALBA-TCP), where in both Brazil and Venezuela, university education is established as a fundamental right and state responsibility. His point throughout the chapter is that although South–South cooperation is often constructed as separate, incompatible, and competing, this form of cooperation reveals the commonalities, inter-relatedness, and convergence, of these third-generation regionalisms. This is largely because these are counter-hegemonic projects that have an explicit 'other': a neoliberal political project that has underpinned what more broadly is referred to as 'open regionalism'.

Many accounts of regionalizing focus on cross-national contexts. Here Paulino Motter and Luis Armando Gandin (Chapter 13) offer a unique insight into a novel form of institutional regionalism: the development of a 'regional university', the Federal University of Latin American Integration (UNILA), launched by Brazil in 2010. UNILA is an experimental higher education institutional space politically, academically and in terms of governance arrangements for the university. It draws staff and students from across Latin America and the Caribbean and teaches in both Spanish and Portuguese languages. Politically, it draws on the utopia of an integrated and united Latin America in its diversity and plurality. Yet, because Brazil is the main funder, questions are also raised about Brazil's motives around the development of a regional hegemony. Academically, the curriculum aims to research, and develop, a Latin American epistemology of knowledge. Finally, students, administrators and academics together engage in governing UNILA as a form of participatory democracy. Yet as Motter and Gandin argue, although this highly innovative experimental institution is not without its challenges, it is an important counter to hegemonic projects aimed at the regionalizing of the neoliberal university.

Tahani Aljafari (Chapter 14) examines a particular form of regionalism found in the Gulf States. She shows they find themselves put together in the face of inside and outside threats and challenges. These include issues of security both at home and in the region, and in more recent years, challenges over the development of their economies that do not depend on the extraction of oil and gas. However, as Aljafari also shows, the particular nature of their political economy, as rentier states, means their capacity to cooperate at the supra-regional level is limited by stronger commitments to domestic interests and innovations, including in the governance of higher education. She argues that whilst this is a region in a rather symbolic way, it is more useful to think of the Gulf Cooperation Council (GCC) as an arena where competition rather than cooperation tend to be the norm and thus shapes what is possible.

Ultimately, these chapters are designed to provide an array of insights on the variegated nature of higher education regionalisms in the global context. These regionalisms are both outcomes and drivers of structural change: they are political-economic programmes and projects that unleash processes designed to harness higher education to in some cases help build regional and globally-competitive knowledge economies, and in others to develop social and cultural cooperation and new forms of identity. The implications of these transformations are complex and worthy of much more attention that they have received to date.

REFERENCES

Börzel, T. (2011), Comparative Regionalism: A New Research Agenda. No. 28, August, KFG The Transformative Power of Europe, Freie Universitat Berlin.

Breslin, S. and Higgott, R. (2000), Studying Regions: Learning from the Old, Constructing the New. *New Political Economy*, **5**(3), 333–352.

Cammack, P. (2013), Exploring the Logic of Regulatory Regionalism: The Asian Development Bank and the World Market. Working Paper, Hong Kong: City University of Hong Kong.

Cammack, P. (2015), World Market Regionalism at the Asian Development Bank. *Journal of Contemporary Asia*, DOI: 10.1080/00472336.2015.1086407.

Checkel, J. (2006), Constructivism and EU Politics. In K.E. Jørgensen and B. Rosamund (eds), *Handbook of European Union Politics*, London: Sage, pp. 57–76.

Cini, M. and Perez-Solorzano Borragan, N. (eds) (2004), *European Union Politics*, Oxford: Oxford University Press.

Corbett, A. (2005), *Universities and the Europe of Knowledge: Ideas, Institutions and Policy Entrepreneurship in European Union Higher Education Policy, 1955–2005*, London: Palgrave Macmillan.

Dale, R. (1982), Education and the Contradictions of the Capitalist State. In M. Apple (ed.), *Cultural and Economic Reproduction in Education*, London: Routledge, pp. 127–161.

Dale, R. and Robertson, S. (2002), Regional Organisations as Subjects of Globalization. *Comparative Education Review*, **46**(1), 10–36.

Dale, R. and Robertson, S. (2009), *Globalisation and Europeanisation of Education*. Oxford: Symposium Books.

Dent, C. (2004), The Asia–Europe Meeting and Inter-regionalism: Toward a Theory of Multilateral Utility. *Asian Survey*, **44**(2), 213–236.

Dent, C. (2008), *East Asian Regionalism*, London: Routledge.

Doidge, M. (2007), Joined at the Hip: Regionalism and Interregionalism. *Journal of European Integration*, **29**(2), 229–248.

Finnemore, M. (1996), Norms, Culture and World Politics: Insights from Sociology's Institutionalism. *International Organization*, **50**(2), 325–348.

Gaens, B. (2011), The Rise of Interregionalisms: The Case of the European Union's Relations with Asia. In T. Shaw, A. Grant and S. Cornelissen (eds), *The Ashgate Companion to Regionalisms*, Farnham: Ashgate, pp. 69–87.

Haas, E. (1958), *The Uniting of Europe: Political, Social and Economic Forces 1950–1957*, Stanford, CA: Stanford University Press.
Hamieri, S. (2013), Theorising Regions through Changes in Statehood: Rethinking the Theory and Method of Comparative Regionalism. *Review of International Studies*, **39**(2), 313–335.
Hameiri, S. and Jayasuriya, K. (2011), Regulatory Regionalism and the Dynamics of Territorial Politics: The Case of the Asia Pacific. *Political Studies*, **59**(1), 20–37.
Hameiri, S. and Wilson, L. (2015), The Contested Rescaling of Economic Governance in East Asia: A Special Issue. *Australian Journal of International Affairs*, **69**(2),115–125.
Hettne, B. (2002), The Europeanisation of Europe: Endogenous and Exogenous Dimensions. *Journal of European Integration*, **24**(4), 325–340.
Hettne, B. (2005), Beyond the New Regionalism. *New Political Economy*, **10**(4), 543–571.
Hettne, B. and Söderbaum, F. (2000), Theorising the Rise of Regionness. *New Political Economy*, **5**(3), 457–472.
Jayasuriya, K. (2003), Introduction: Governing the Asia-Pacific – Beyond the 'New Regionalism'. *Third World Quarterly*, **24**(2), 199–215.
Jayasuriya, K. (2009), Regionalising the State: Political Topography of Regulatory Regionalism. *Contemporary Politics*, **14**(1), 21–35.
Mittelman, J. (2000), *The Globalization Syndrome*, Princeton, NJ: Princeton University Press.
Polanyi, K. (1944), *The Great Transformation*, Boston, MA: Beacon Hill Press.
Ravinet, P. (2008), From Voluntary Participation to Monitored Coordination: Why European Countries Feel Increasingly Bound by Their Commitment to the Bologna Process. *European Journal of Education*, **43**(3), 353–367.
Robertson, S. (2006), The Politics of Constructing (a Competitive) Europe(an) Through Internationalising Higher Education: Strategies, Structures, Subjects. *Perspectives in Education*, **24**(4), 29–44.
Robertson, S. (2008a), Embracing the Global: Crisis and the Creation of a New Semiotic Order to Secure Europe's Knowledge-Based Economy. In N. Fairclough, R. Wodak and B. Jessop (eds), *Education and the Knowledge-Based Economy in Europe*, Rotterdam: Sense Publications, pp. 89–108.
Robertson, S. (2008b), 'Europe/Asia' Regionalism, Higher Education and the Production of World Order. *Policy Futures in Education*, **6**(6), 718–729.
Robertson, S. (2010), The EU, Regulatory State Regionalism and New Modes of Higher Education Governance. *Globalisation, Societies and Education*, **8**(1), 23–38.
Robertson, S. (2014), Higher Education Regionalizing Projects in a Globalizing World: A 'Variegated Regionalism' Approach. Paper presented to ECPR, 3–6 September, Glasgow.
Robertson, S. and Keeling, R. (2008), Stirring the Lions: Strategy and Tactics in Global Higher Education. *Globalisation, Societies and Education*, **6**(3), 221–240.
Rosamond, B. (2006), New Theories of Integration. In M. Cini and M. Perez-Solorzano Borragan (eds), *European Union Politics*, 2nd edn, Oxford: Oxford University Press.
Rüland, J. (2010), Balancers, Multilateral Utilities or Regional Identity Builder? International Relations and the Study of Inter-regionalism. *Journal of European Public Policy*, **17**(8), 1271–1283.

Rüland, J. and Storz, C. (2008), Interregionalism and Interregional Cooperation: The Case of Asia–Europe Relations. In J. Rüland, G. Schubert, G. Schucher and C. Storz (eds), *Asia–Europe Relations: Building Block for Global Governance?*, London: Routledge, pp. 3–31.

Söderbaum, F. and Sbragia, A. (2011), EU Studies and the New Regionalism: What can be Gained from Dialogue? *Journal of European Integration*, **32**(6), 563–582.

Warleigh-Lack, A. and Rosamond, B. (2010), Across the EU Studies–New Regionalism Frontier: Invitation to Dialogue. *Journal of Common Market Studies*, **48**(4), 993–1013.

World Trade Organization (WTO) (2016), Regional Trade Agreements. Accessed 11 January 2016 at https://www.wto.org/english/tratop_e/region_e/scope_rta_e.htm.

1. Higher education, the EU and the cultural political economy of regionalism

Susan L. Robertson, Mário Luiz Neves de Azevedo and Roger Dale

INTRODUCTION

This chapter aims to make a substantive and theoretical contribution to the understanding of the role of higher education in regional governance projects. Substantively, through an exploration of two interlinked, ongoing regional governance projects – the creation of a European Higher Education Area (EHEA) by 2010, and a European Research Area (ERA) by 2014 – we will examine the ways in which higher education is mobilized in the constructing of Europe as a globally competitive region.

'What is new?,' one might ask, and at one level we agree. Researchers examining the ongoing Europeanization of once determinedly national higher education institutions and sectors have described in detail the launch of the Bologna Process in 1999 aimed at reforming degree architectures and systems of credit transfer amongst European universities, and its rolling out across the European Union (EU) and beyond (cf. Huisman and van der Wende, 2004; Keeling, 2006; Ravinet, 2008). They have also shown the ways in which the 2000 Lisbon Agenda, to make Europe a competitive region and society buoyed by good jobs and social cohesion, has been advanced by the European Commission, and have reflected on the central role that universities are expected to play in this (cf. Gornitzka, 2005). Yet at another level, what is missing in these accounts is a critical account of the way in which these higher education regional projects are tied to ongoing challenges facing national states as they manage crisis tendencies in their domestic economies, Europe's own claim to statehood, and the role that higher education regionalizing processes might play in this.

In this chapter we aim to offer a more complex reading of these regional higher education projects that we show have cultural, political and economic (Robertson and Dale, 2015) dynamics at play tied to the ongoing transformations of the state. In tracing out these projects over the period 2000 to 2015, we show the ways in which higher education is being drawn into the logic of capitalist expansion and world market-making. The 'region' – in this case two overlapping but distinct higher education regional projects – is not only dependent on, but has ongoing effects upon, the socio-political and spatial relations between domestic economies, the (supra-national) region, and the 'extra-regional', or global. In sum, these are novel, spatial strategies deployed by the state and allied social forces which in turn transform the state, the region, and overlapping higher education sectoral projects.

This leads to our second aim: to draw on our critical reading of these developments in order to contribute to current theorizing on regions. We are not alone in noting that conceptual work on regions is a minefield; this is in part because, as Hettne (2005: 543) observes, the approach to regionalisms varies as a result of different academic specialisms which means that 'regionalism means different things to different people'. Furthermore, as Cammack (2015: 3) points out: 'the diversity of regional projects and impulses towards them rules out a substantive theory of regionalism, as such, and makes it unlikely a single trend informs all contemporary manifestations of regionalism'.

But we also detect a further issue: in many cases work on regions tends to be driven by what Cammack (2015) calls 'regionalist ideology', fitting the case to the theory, rather than putting theories into a dialogue with facts and events. In the latter case we would expect to see variegation in regional projects and processes arising from the ways in which logics and mechanisms encounter the specificities of time, space and social arrangements (Robertson, 2014). Furthermore, it matters in important ways if regional projects are advanced by actors such as states (national, subnational), particularly in economic restructuring, as the state is a very particular kind of institution in capitalist societies and plays an important role in managing the challenges of ongoing economic development. By way of contrast, some regional projects, such as the one advanced by the Council of Europe in the fading shadow of the Second World War, might be viewed as a political and cultural project aimed at building regional cooperation within Europe and with its close neighbours.

At its most basic, and to avoid regionalist ideology, we take Ercan and Oguz's (2006), Hameiri's (2013) and Cammack's (2015) point, and suggest that one way we might approach regional projects and region-building is to pose a set of questions that in turn might reveal the logics and processes at work in producing regional space and its social relations: What underlying logics are at work? What is the ideational basis of these (political, cultural, economic) projects? How are meanings brokered, and by whom?

What processes, mechanisms and contradictions are at play? With what outcomes? For whom? How are multiple overlapping spatial projects managed? And so on. In our own response to these questions, we will argue for a way of researching regions conceptually and methodologically that focuses on a cultural political economy (Robertson and Dale, 2015) of regionalism; and in our case, higher education sectoral regionalism.

Our chapter is developed in the following way. We begin with some remarks on a cultural political economy of region-making. The six sections which follow trace out the development and ongoing recalibration of the EHEA and ERA as responses to political and economic crises, including the current challenges posed by the 2008 financial crisis. We conclude with a section on conceptualizing and theorizing regional projects as the ongoing manifestation of state–regions–frontier relations.

A CULTURAL POLITICAL ECONOMY OF REGION-MAKING

Why a cultural political economy of regionalism? A key argument we will be advancing here is that over time, and as a response to changing conditions (in this case, pressure to develop competitive services and knowledge-based economies), sectoral regions like the EHEA and the ERA, are the outcomes of territorially-based formal and/or informal arrangements arising from strategically selective socio-spatial projects and processes advanced by: (1) nationally-located states who strategize blockages to, and crises within, capitalist development trajectories by managing the governance of the territorial boundaries of the state – in this case, their regional mode – in turn transforming the nature of state space as simultaneously composed of regional and national frontiers (Jayasuriya, 2003; Hameiri and Jayasuriya, 2011); (2) regional state actors who mobilize power, resources, and the right to legitimate rule, enabling them to advance the region 'in and for itself' within and beyond the region (Cammack, 2015); and (3) 'extra-regional' or global actors and their institutions (neighbourhood economies; distant strategic domestic economies; old colonial relations and networks; emerging regions such as the Association of Southeast Asian Nations – ASEAN, the Southern Common Market –MERCOSUR and the Bolivarian Alliance for the Peoples of Our America – ALBA; new inter-regional formations) which are enrolled in, and transformed by, these regional state governance projects (Robertson, 2010; Azevedo, 2014). These dynamics are simultaneously cultural (meaning-making, subjectivities), political (power relations, state) and economic (logic of world market-making, capitalism).

It is worth reiterating here that just as the national scale and the state are not reducible to each other, so also 'states and regions are not identical phenomena; both are manifestations of struggles over the territorial, institutional, and functional scope of political rule' (Hameiri, 2013: 314). That is to say, a region (as in this case, at the supra-regional scale) is a socio-spatial manifestation of a particular organization of state rule, just as the national scale is. These state strategies and their spatial form also build upon, are challenged by, or replace, existing formal and informal state and other institutional, arrangements in a dynamic and changing way. However, what Hameiri (ibid.) underplays, and thus underestimates, is the underlying logic and role of the state in creating the conditions for the expansion of an evolving world market (now including higher education even more directly) (political economy) and the ideational (cultural) content of the state's political projects and their rule, including the ongoing work of the state in securing commitment and consensus through control over meaning-making and processes of socialization (cultural, political). And as we will see in this chapter, the spatial organization of state power, in particular its national, regional and global frontiers, and the ideational content of the state's project, are dynamic, shifting and contested.

The higher education regionalizing projects that we examine in this chapter are an outcome of political projects aimed at constituting and making governable a (competitive) European higher education space and knowledge-based economy. However, it is also clear there are distinctive phases in this project; the outcome of shifts in the balance of social forces and the subsequent recalibration and rearticulation of the socio-economic content of the political project as a result of the ongoing crisis tendencies within capitalism, issues of legitimation, and concerns over social cohesion. Focusing on the current moment of this project, we argue that 'regulatory regionalism' is only one form of territorial frontier, and that a global frontier is also evident, arising from Europe's claim to contingent territorial sovereignty (Elden, 2006) and statehood as a region 'in and for itself'; Europe's extension of its political project in relation to other geostrategic claims; the attractiveness to domestic actors in neighbouring and more distant economies and the usefulness of Europe's higher education tools for brokering the internal transformations; the desire of globally oriented export and import higher education institutions and domestic economies beyond the borders of Europe to align their architectures and regulatory frameworks to maximize market position; and the emergence of Europe's normative power on the global stage.

REGIONAL FRONTIERS AND THE MAKING OF POST-WAR EUROPE

The creation of a coherent and competitive Europe has its antecedents in the 1950s where higher education initiatives began to play a role (Corbett, 2005; Hingel, 2001). However, between the 1950s and early 1990s, the EU's higher education project was almost entirely intra-regional in its ontology and outcomes. With the notable exception of the United Kingdom (and to a lesser extent France and Germany), the internationalization of study programmes, curricula, student mobility and research career paths was primarily oriented towards European partners and Europeanizing processes. Key markers were the institutionalizing of regular meetings between the European education ministers, the eventual creation of the European University Institute in Florence in 1971, and the establishment of the EU's Erasmus mobility programme in 1987 to facilitate the movement of students and staff between universities of the member states.

The main policy aims embedded in these European-level initiatives were to produce European-minded citizens engaged with the expanding Community (and European Commission) and committed to the concept of European culture and values. EU President Jacques Delors 'had a highly developed idea of education and the part it could play in his strategy for advancing European integration via the single market' (Corbett, 2005: 121). Two concerns came together which it seemed higher education programmes could mediate: how to create a European single market, on the one hand, and a European citizen, on the other. Harnessing commitment to the European project was viewed as essential in order to combat narrow nationalism as an impediment to the advance of Europe as a political and cultural project.

In 1992, a single market and European Union were announced by the Treaty of European Union and signed at Maastricht by the heads of the European Community's member states. The Maastricht Treaty acknowledged the European Union's direct role in education whilst attempting to limit the European Commission's room for manoeuvre by restricting European-level action to 'supplementary' activities. Whilst the Maastricht Treaty appeared to suggest that the EU's role would be modest, under Delors the European Commission (EC) had ambitions to develop a more comprehensive policy for higher education at the European level.

The 1991 Memorandum on Higher Education shows that higher education 'had already become part of the Community's broader agenda of economic and social coherence' (Huisman and van der Wende, 2004: 350). The Commission quickly made an internal assessment of the EU's programmes and developed a new strategy to exploit the opportunities opened up by the Maastricht Treaty's acknowledgement of the 'European dimension' in education. The Commission also began to look outward, beyond the region. It established higher education collaborative programmes with non-EU countries through initiatives such as the América Latina – Formación Académica (ALFA) programme in Latin America; the development of the Tempus cooperation programme with the Western Balkans, Eastern Europe, Central Asia and neighbouring Mediterranean countries; and Asia–Europe relations through Asia–Europe inter-regional structures such as Asia-Link (Robertson, 2008b). However at this point these programmes tended to be based on cultural cooperation and exchange objectives, and were not well coordinated with the emerging policy programme for education within Europe.

To make sense of the politics behind the Memorandum and the events that followed, it is crucial to consider the changing nature of the wider economic and geopolitical context that Europe's member states found themselves in. In 1991–1992 the biggest economies (including Germany) experienced a recession which increased the number of unemployed graduates in Europe (Teichler and Kehm, 1995). This provided some legitimacy for the EC's higher education project. However, of greater significance were the wider changes taking place in the global economy as a result of economic globalization, the transnationalization of production and finance, and the ideological shift from Keynesianism toward neoliberalism (Cox, 1996: 259–260). These structural changes in the global economy had implications for the European project as they directly affected the restructuring of the EU. To be competitive in the global economy, Europe had to transform itself along free trade and free market lines. As Bieler and Morton (2001: 5) argue:

> the deregulation of the national financial markets was institutionalized in the Internal Market Programme ... while the shift toward neo-liberalism was expressed by the very nature of the Internal Market Programme and its drive for liberalization and the neo-liberal convergence criteria of EMU [European Monetary Union] focusing on low inflation and price stability.

EUROPE, GLOBAL COMPETITIVENESS AND THE CREATION OF KNOWLEDGE-BASED ECONOMIES

The imperative to advance Europe as a political and economic project more generally, and a knowledge-based economy most specifically, is linked to the United States of America (USA) and Europe's declining share of goods production globally. For this reason, both the USA and the EU have shared a common interest in expanding the global services economy including the restructuring of higher education as a market, as an engine for innovation, and as a key sector in developing new forms of intellectual property. And as Hartmann (2008: 210–211) notes, whilst the USA dominates world trade in commercial services, with 14.3 per cent of the world's share (WTO, 2007: 12), the combined share of European member states (now 27) generates around 46 per cent. This share has increased the aspiration and capability of the EU to also set standards in the emerging global service economy, giving further impetus to the struggle between Europe and the US in providing normative leadership over the development of a globally competitive, services-based economy.

In 2000, the European Union's educational activities were given a significant boost by the 'Lisbon Strategy' which famously declared: 'the European Union must become the most competitive and dynamic knowledge-based economy in the world capable of sustainable economic growth with more and better jobs and greater social cohesion' (European Council, 2000). The Lisbon Strategy provided a mandate and an agenda for extending the reach of Europe's policy responsibility deeper into national territory – education – and ultimately outwards to the rest of the world. The Strategy also confirmed a neoliberal understanding of higher education's contribution to the socio-economic well-being of the region; building and securing human capital for a knowledge-based economy.

In January 2000, upon the proposal of the European Commission, a decision was also taken to establish a European Research Area (ERA), with the principal explicit objective of supporting a knowledge-based economy on a European scale under the framing of a 'Europe of Knowledge'. The European Commission insisted on the urgency of the task, arguing:

> without a co-ordinated impulse and a determined effort to increase and better organise the European research effort, Europe might compromise its chances of taking full advantage of the potential offered by the transition to a knowledge-based economy and society. This will not be without its negative impact on growth and employment. (European Council, 2000)

The invoking of the idea of a European research effort here is important, as this also demands new forms of cultural identification for researchers and their research efforts.

Similarly, the Lisbon Summit in 2000, and the strategy that was articulated there, was intended to 'find a European way to evolve to the new innovation- and knowledge-based economy using distinctive attributes ranging from the preservation of social cohesion and cultural diversity to the very technological options' (Rodrigues, 2002: 14). Rodrigues's account of the Lisbon process is particularly important for she was not only a professor at the University Institute, Lisbon and president of the Social Sciences Advisory group to the European Commission, but also special adviser to the Portuguese Prime Minister, Antonio Guterres, in charge of preparing the Lisbon Summit.

The strategies that informed Lisbon drew self-consciously upon the expertise of European researchers, including evolutionary economist Bengte-Ake Lundvall, French regulation theorists Aglietta and Boyer, Gosta Esping Anderson's work on comparative systems of welfare, and Manuel Castells' concern with informationalism and emerging network societies. Taken together, their work was seen by the Lisbon architects to 'provide interesting tools with which to think about the role of structural policies and of institutional reforms in fostering growth and employment' (Rodrigues, 2002: 13).

Rodrigues's (2002: 10–13) account of the theoretical paradigm used to shape the Lisbon agenda is particularly interesting. She argues that there was a rejection of simple economic modelling and methodological individualism in favour of a more complex conceptual framework. This ideational moment represents an explicit rejection of a model of economic development based on *Homo economicus*. It also drew heavily on cultural ideas of learning and the importance of the socially embedded nature of economies. In wider political terms, this ideational agenda reflected the dominance, still, of centre-left governments in Europe and their respective politics (Collignon, 2006: 5), although this hold was increasingly tenuous and under pressure from social and political forces committed to neoliberalism and neomercantilism (Apeldoorn, 2001: 78).

The main strategic orientations of Lisbon 2000 thus combined supply-side economics with macroeconomic and social concerns: to develop information technologies, research and development (R&D) policy for institutions, enterprise policy, economic reforms that targeted job creation, macroeconomic policies that focused on employment and structural change along with education and training, a renewed social model, new priorities for school-based education, active employment policies focused on lifelong learning, new social protection politics, national plans to reduce social exclusion, and improved social dialogue between European civil society, the economy and structures of government (European Council, 2000). The European Council, however, faced a major challenge: of how to get the support of national governments. This is because member states want to keep control over their own agendas, and because national policy preferences, when taken together from across Europe, are much more heterogeneous. Yet delegating more power to the EU in order to undertake the tasks outlined above – particularly in those areas, like education, where the principle of subsidiarity invokes sensitivities around boundaries – is a highly political issue.

The Open Method of Coordination (OMC) was invented to overcome this problem. The OMC is an open intergovernmental process of policy coordination to enhance integration, where 'open' means soft governance (Zeitlen et al., 2005). Governments are urged to commit themselves to common policy objectives, while implementation is left to them. To ensure the direction of implementation, a series of structural indicators or benchmarks were developed which enabled member states to see their progress in relation to each other (benchmarking), backed up by peer learning, peer review and the exchange of good practice. Walters and Haahr (2005: 116, 120) argue that not only did benchmarking open new ways of historicizing and particularizing European integration, but also the OMC deployed a range of technologies to foster agency within and across the governmental apparatus of local, national and European institutions.

'NEW LISBON': RECALIBRATING REGIONAL PROJECTS AND SPATIAL FORM

However, by 2005, the 2000 Lisbon strategy was already in crisis. The Mid-Term Review (European Commission, 2005b), informed by the work of the High Level Group chaired by Wim Kok (2004), concluded that the Lisbon Strategy had failed to deliver satisfactory economic growth, and that Europe was falling far behind both the USA and Asia.

The spectre of China and India, as threat and opportunity (Kok, 2004: 12), now added a new level of threat from external challenges. For Europe to compete it needed to:

> develop its own area of specialisms, excellence and comparative advantage which inevitably must lie in a commitment to the knowledge economy in its widest sense ... Europe has no option but to radically improve its knowledge economy and underlying economic performance if it is to respond to the challenges of Asia and the US. (Kok, 2004: 12)

Europe was represented as a long way from achieving the potential for change that the Lisbon 2000 strategy had promised to deliver. The problems were seen to lie not only in difficult economic conditions which had faced the US and Europe with the dot.com collapse, but in 'a policy agenda which had become overloaded, and in failing coordination and sometimes conflicting priorities' within member states and across the region (European Commission, 2005a: 4).

The EC's 'new Lisbon' Communication argued that a new start was required, with investment, innovation and jobs at the centre (EC, 2005a: 4), whilst macroeconomic management and social cohesion – reflections of the dominance of centre-left governments in Europe at the time when the Lisbon agenda was negotiated (Collignon, 2006: 5) – were now represented in entirely economic, rather than in social terms (as a socially inclusive economy; see European Commission, 2005a: 26). This new ideational moment combined a Schumpeterian paradigm focused on innovation and entrepreneurship, human capital theory, supply-side economics, and freer conditions of trade; all considered important for world market-making advanced through regional frontiers. The Presidency Conclusions of the European Council acknowledged the mixed results of Lisbon, and called for urgent action in the relaunch of the Commission's proposed 'new' Lisbon Strategy (European Council, 2005: 3).

The 'new' Lisbon Strategy reflected an important shift in the nature of the political project driving higher education regionalism. This project now embraced a new imaginary as to how a European knowledge economy could be secured. While continuing many of the themes in the first Lisbon agenda, in a final Communication by the EC tabled in 2003, *The Role of the Universities in the Europe of Knowledge (TRUEK)* (European Commission, 2003), ideas such as innovation, knowledge and education, whilst present in the Lisbon 2000 and the TRUEK discourses, were now moved to centre stage, and given new meaning. For instance, with innovation, particular areas – digital technologies, biotechnology and the environment – were now regarded as key to 'making a reality of our vision of a knowledge society' (EC, 2005a: 8). In 2012 the ERA was again tasked with developing, by 2014, a:

> unified research area open to the world, based on the Internal Market, in which researchers, scientific knowledge and technology circulate freely and through which the Union and its Member States strengthen their scientific and technological bases, their competitiveness and their capacity to collectively address grand challenges. (EC, 2012)

BOLOGNA: REGIONAL GOVERNING OF NATIONAL HIGHER EDUCATION SPACES AND THEIR RELATIONS

The Lisbon 2000 agenda for higher education was paralleled by the Bologna Process, a distinctive and ambitious project driven by national governments and other key stakeholders to create a common degree architecture and a European area for higher education. The Bologna Process had its roots in a strategic articulation between domestic and regional agendas. Following a meeting in 1998 in Paris to celebrate the 800th anniversary of the Sorbonne, French Minister for Education Claude Allègre secured the agreement of the German, Italian and United Kingdom education ministers: to commit their countries to a new architecture for higher education (Ravinet, 2008). This architecture would build upon the Convention for the Recognition of Higher Education Qualifications in the European region (Lisbon Convention) which had been signed in 1997. Allègre argued that in order to develop a knowledge-based economy, Europe needed to both emulate the US system, and to stem the flow of European graduates to the US.

The following year the Bologna Declaration (1999) committed 29 signatory countries to six 'action lines' directed towards establishing a European Higher Education Area (EHEA) to be realized by 2010. Within this 'Area', staff and student mobility was to be enhanced by the alignment of national quality assurance mechanisms, compatible degree structures, the adoption of a credit transfer system, and a common way of describing qualifications to be outlined in a personal 'diploma supplement'. Taken together, these regulatory mechanisms were viewed as enabling Bologna to act as a vehicle for raising the attractiveness of Europe as a destination for study, and thus an education market worldwide (Zgaga, 2006: 10).

The Bologna Process is a voluntary international agreement, situated outside the European Union's formal governance framework, although it is driven by EU, and increasingly European Commission, interests and promotes many initiatives (such as the European Credit Transfer System, ECTS credit system) originally piloted by the European Commission (Keeling, 2006). 'Convinced that the establishment of the European area of higher education required constant support, supervision and adaptation to the continuously evolving needs' (Bologna Declaration, 1999), the European education ministers decided to meet regularly to assess progress, transforming the Bologna commitment into an ongoing policy process (via a Bologna Process Ministerial Conference held every two years).

Membership of the Bologna Process and the associated European Higher Education Area (officially launched in 2010) has since increased to include, by late 2015, 47 countries containing around 5600 public and private institutions with more than 16 million students. The European Higher Education Area includes Russia and Southeast Europe; it thus extends far beyond the European Union as a constitutional entity. New countries continue to be negotiated in as part of an ongoing process of expansion and integration of broadly European and neighbouring countries into the European Higher Education Area. In these cases, a broadly agreed roadmap is put into place, overseen by the Bologna Follow-Up Group, which in turn reports to the European Council of Ministers. In 2016, the latest country negotiating entry to the EHEA was Belarus.

Determining the ongoing basis of membership of Bologna has been an important geostrategic project. Initially, as Hartmann (2008) points out, membership of Bologna was based broadly on signatories to the Lisbon Convention (1997). For historical reasons this included the United States, Canada and Australia, via the United Nations Educational, Scientific and Cultural Organization's (UNESCO) definition of Europe (the US and Canada signed in 1975, Australia in 1986) (Hartmann, 2008: 213). This meant that these countries, most importantly the US, had a say in the drafting of the initial Bologna Process. Mindful that membership had to be more than Europe and the accession countries (in that it needed to include Russia but not its competitor, the US), some skilful political manoeuvring was required. The Lisbon Convention, as the basis for formal membership of the Bologna Process, was jettisoned in 2003 in favour of the Council of Europe's European Cultural Convention, thereby excluding the US, Canada and Australia. Hartmann (2008: 214) argues that this was one of a series of moves by Europe to challenge the imperial role of the US in standard-setting, turning it simultaneously into both a rival as well as a model. This dual-track membership of the EU, on the one hand, and the EHEA, on the other, also has a third track that includes countries with observer status, for instance China.

In 2009, at the Bologna Ministerial Meeting held in Leuven/Lourvain-la-Neuve, it was decided to establish the Bologna Policy Forum in recognition of its diverse, beyond-EHEA membership, with representatives from Australia, Brazil, Canada, China, Egypt, Ethiopia, Israel, Japan, Kazakhstan, Kyrgyzstan, Mexico, Morocco, New Zealand, Tunisia and the USA, along with the International Association of Universities. The Bologna Policy Forum, a wider group than the EHEA, committed itself to developing cooperation on a range of policy issues.

The Bologna Follow-Up Group (BFUG) has the main responsibility for advancing the ongoing policy agenda for the European Higher Education Area and its consolidation. It is composed of a BFUG Board, a Secretariat, working groups and activity groups (Figure 1.1). With Eurostat, Eurostudent and Eurydice, the BFUG collaborates on the *Bologna Process Implementation Report*, the first report released in 2012; the second in 2015. This report is currently published by the European Commission.

The BFUG has responsibility for organizing the activities of the Bologna Policy Forum, the ongoing Bologna Ministerial Meeting held every two to three years, along with ensuring the working and advisory groups continue to operate effectively. BFUG has a full-time permanent Secretariat (currently a head and four members who have been seconded from EHEA member countries) whose main tasks are to provide administrative and operational support to the BFUG and its Board, to support

Source: BFUG (2016).

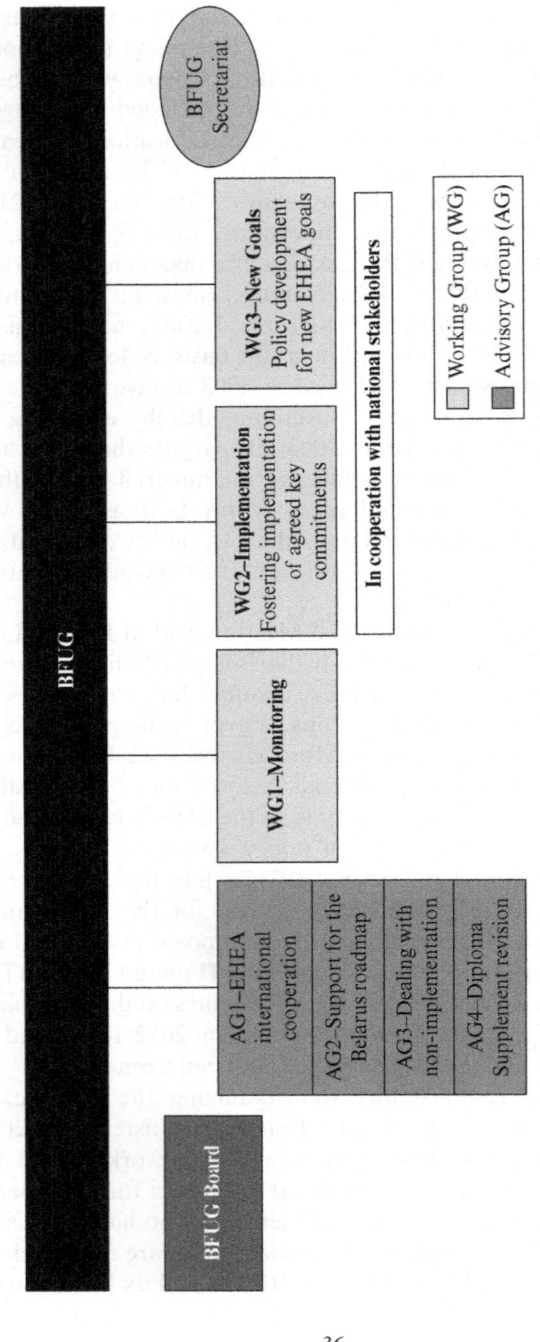

Figure 1.1 The formal structure of the Bologna Follow-Up Group

all working and advisory groups, to act as an internal and external contact for the EHEA, prepare both the Ministerial Conference as well as the Bologna Policy Forum, and maintain the EHEA website. Despite this thickening institutional structure at the level of the executive (if we can call the BFUG that), material support from the European Commission, the Council of Europe (see Melo, Chapter 2 in this volume), and national governments, there is increasing disquiet about levels of commitment and progress regarding the Bologna instruments; a question that we address below in the section on crisis and austerity and its impact on progress since 2010.

The EHEA has continued to expand, with multiple-track membership from the EHEA and beyond. This multiple-track membership is reflected in the ongoing structure of the BFUG; in the Leuven/Lourvain-la-Neuve Communiqué, it was decided to signal the equal footing of EU versus non-EU members of the EHEA. The Bologna Process is now co-chaired by the country holding the EU Presidency and a non-EU country, with the division of labour negotiated between the two co-chairs. This multiplicity of memberships and its evident spatial sprawl raises important questions about the overall coherence of the Bologna Process, and the ambiguous role it might play in a region 'for itself', as well as in creating further efficiencies for global competitiveness. However, as Harmsen (2013: 11) observes, this 'pick and choose' 'looseness' has its costs in that there are quite different levels of participation amongst member states. This is an issue for representatives in the Process. But perhaps what we also see here are the residues of other cultural and political projects: a post-war Council of Europe spatial form aimed at advancing European civility via academic cooperation and still visible in the Bologna Process, versus a market-oriented project tasked with making higher education institutions visible destinations for fee-paying students, as well as an attractive destination for researchers to remain in Europe.

The BFUG's Activity Group on International Cooperation continues to build upon an earlier mandate (from the London Ministerial Meeting held in 2007); to elaborate and agree upon a strategy for the external dimension in order to strengthen the attractiveness of the EHEA (Zgaga, 2006). But what is also interesting here are the ways in which these strategies work to advance the region not only in but also for itself on a global stage. This strategy, to be with other regions rather than with countries (BFUG, 2005), thus means developing regions of priority interest for Europe. The EC in particular has managed to advance this objective, often through financing meetings, providing expertise, and having ready-made governance mechanisms available for borrowing and use. We turn to these dynamics in the following section.

GLOBAL FRONTIERS AND EXTRA-REGIONAL DYNAMICS

If higher education had been oriented toward managing the territorial project and its politics within the expanding region as a result of different stages of accession, from around 2003 onwards the various political institutions of Europe, in particular the EC, began to pursue a more explicit extra-regional globalizing strategy. This has had direct and indirect effects on higher education as a sector. The direct effects are the outcomes, both within and outside of Europe, of explicit strategies to realize a competitive European higher education area and market following the launch of projects such as the Erasmus Mundus programme, the Neighbourhood Policy, and the mobilization of old colonial links to align with Europe's market interests. The indirect effects are the consequences of the reactions to this strategy in key domestic economies in the global political economy, where the Bologna architecture had become increasingly viewed as variously a threat (USA, Australia), as a model for domestic restructuring (USA, Brazil, China), and as the basis for new regional projects and higher education architectures around the globe (Africa, Latin America, ASEAN).

We discussed earlier one of the triggers for this change in strategy: the view of the Mid-Term Review that Europe was falling rapidly behind both the USA and Asia. This was added to by the spectre of the rise of China and India, as both threat and opportunity (Kok, 2004: 12). The EU Commission President Jose Manuel Barroso delivered a stirring speech at the European University Association convention in Glasgow entitled 'Strong Universities for Europe', complaining that the state of education in Europe compared to other world regions was nothing short of 'miserable' (Barroso, 2005: 25).

In a new departure, the Commission gave direct recommendations as to how universities' structures of governance, financing and research management (including performance measurements and incentives) should be 'modernized' to enable Europe to compete in the global competition for minds and markets (European Commission, 2005b, 2006). This included bringing 'third countries' into cooperation agreements to stem their flow to the US. Education also became an important area of sectoral dialogue with a number of Asian countries, including China. The EU's global talent strategy also sought to attract leading European researchers back to Europe by refining the Marie Curie policy and programme instruments.

Higher education thus became deeply incorporated into the European Union's drive to improve its economic position and influence around the globe. Crucial to this process was the remarkable unfolding, though uneven embedding, of the Bologna Process and its various instruments including the Tuning Programme (2003–) to translate existing disciplines of study into competencies, and the establishment of a European Qualifications Register (2008–) to ensure the quality assurance of higher education providers. These are simultaneously cultural, political and economic dynamics in the making of the HE region where new meanings and identities are being brokered, and new social relations pursued in efforts to bring higher education more directly into the making of world market-making.

In sum, the techniques of regional governance have their potency, not only in terms of internal regulation, but also as having the potential to challenge the basis of normative leadership in the education services sector. This has been given considerable impetus by the direct and indirect effects of Europe's higher education project on other domestic economies and nascent regional ambitions within the near region, and beyond.

In the United States, there has been growing interest in the European regional project. Admiration had been expressed for the rapidity of the European changes and the strength of the political will backgrounding them (Jaschik, 2006; Adelman, 2008). By implication, this would mean the loss of a competitive advantage for the US if it did not offer an internationally attractive model of higher education to power the US shift to a services-based economy. As Adelman noted: 'The core features of the Bologna Process have sufficient momentum to become the dominant global higher education model within the next two decades. We had better listen up' (Adelman, 2008: v). One effect was to fuel debate around a 'crisis' in US higher education, and specifically the need to review marketing, visa and admissions processes to stem the decline in share of international students that had followed in the wake of September 11 (Robertson and Keeling, 2008; Adelman, 2008). By 2009 more radical experiments were also under way in three US states (Utah, Indiana and Minnesota), drawing upon one of the Bologna Process's key instruments: 'Tuning Educational Structures in Europe'. Tuning is a project aimed at converting curricular into learning outcomes, enabling the translation of programmes offered in different institutions into a common learning metric.

The USA's response to Europe can be contrasted with the Australian response, which views winning market dominance more clearly as a numbers game. In April 2006, Julie Bishop, the then Australian Minister for Education, Science and Training, tabled a paper entitled 'The Bologna Process and Australia: Next Steps'. This official response to the Bologna Process claimed that Australia must ensure compatibility to Bologna or face the risks associated with being 'a Bologna outsider' (Bishop, 2006). Viewed in this way, the European higher education developments represent a major threat for a number of reasons. First, there is a steady flow of students from Europe; being Bologna-compatible enables and enhances these movements, as students would exit an Australian university with a qualification that is also acceptable in the European labour market. Second, the Australian government is well aware that the European Commission has used a number of instruments to create linkages and partnerships in the Asian and Latin American regions (Robertson, 2008a) in order to advance EU economic interests. If Europe were to become a desirable destination for Asian students because of its competitive fee structure, status of universities and the increasing tendency to teach in English at graduate level, then Europe might also threaten Australia's dominance in the market. By April 2007, Australia had signed a joint declaration with the EU to become Bologna-compatible and strengthen cooperation to cover issues of quality assurance, benchmarking and indicators, and qualifications frameworks (Figel and Bishop, 2007). These programmes are seen by the Australian federal government as being critical to developing the new 'globally aware' Australian worker and citizen.

The Bologna Process and its role in the creation of a European Higher Education Area has clearly inspired more strategic ways of thinking about regions and the value of creating and institutionalizing the role of education in regional relationships. Whilst education has been on the agenda in early regional forums such as the Asia-Pacific Economic Cooperation (APEC) (Dale and Robertson, 2002), Bologna offers a different kind of imaginary, creating a regional higher education architecture which offers the possibility for a single market for higher education services and the potential to improve future employability. These developments suggest that the national states and their domestic economies, such as Australia and the US, are involved in a complex set of strategic repositionings to manage the threat (and opportunities) posed by the rapid growth of the European Higher Education Area and the attempt to build a European Research Area. The entry of the EU into this sphere has clearly tipped the balance of the terrain in a different direction, though the slowing of the European sectoral project, which we address in the following section, will trigger interesting responses. It is not possible to ignore these pressures, given the multiple ways in which the EU has been engaged in inter-regional projects in both the Asian and Latin American regions (Robertson, 2010), and the long shadow cast by the rise of China.

CRISIS, AUSTERITY AND HIGHER EDUCATION GOVERNANCE CHALLENGES FOR EUROPE 2020: A RETURN TO NATIONAL FRONTIERS?

The global financial crisis in 2008 has generated major challenges for national governments and their higher education institutions on the one hand, and the EU and the legitimacy of its regional project, on the other. The scale of the crisis and the challenges ahead are evident in this statement from the European Commission:

> The recent economic crisis has no precedent in our generation... Our industrial production dropped back to the levels of the 1990s and 23 million people – or 10% of our active population – are now unemployed... Our public finances have been severely affected, with deficits at 7% of GDP on average and debt levels at over 80% of GDP – two years of crisis erasing twenty years of fiscal consolidation. Our exit from the crisis must be the point of entry into a new economy... What is needed is a strategy to turn the EU into a smart, sustainable and inclusive economy delivering high levels of employment, productivity and social cohesion. This is the Europe 2020 strategy... Policy instruments were decisively, and massively, used to counteract the crisis. Fiscal policy had, where possible, an expansionary and counter-cyclical role; interest rates were lowered to historical minima while liquidity was provided to the financial sector in an unprecedented way. Governments gave massive support to banks, either through guarantees, recapitalization or through 'cleaning' of balance sheets from impaired assets; other sectors of the economy were supported under the temporary, and exceptional, framework for State aid. (European Commission, 2010: 24)

It is no exaggeration to say that instances of local, regional or global power follow precepts of a global governance agenda compatible with phenomena of regional integration and economic globalization in order to preserve and promote the principles of the capitalist system.

In this section we review some of the early evidence of what this means for Europe's EHEA and ERA projects, and note growing anxieties about the uneven development unfolding across Europe (EC, 2014). One lens through which to view how the European Union sees the challenges facing its ongoing political project following the crisis and austerity measures is via its Europe's 2020 strategy, setting out its strategic priorities for the period 2010–2020. As the EC notes:

> Much like most other regions across the world, Europe is going through a period of transformation. The global economic crisis has wiped out years of economic and social progress and exposed structural weaknesses in its economy. Meanwhile, various long-term challenges such as globalization, pressure on natural resources and an ageing population are intensifying. If we are to adapt to this changing reality, Europe can no longer rely on business as usual. (EC, 2014: 3)

Once again, the European Union's state institutions are faced with major challenges: how best to move forward to boost sluggish economic growth, and to stem the rising social and economic inequalities that have cut even deeper into the social fabrics of the various countries making up the European Union. Smart, sustainable and inclusive growth is the new strapline (EC, 2014). Five key objectives now guide the Europe 2020 strategy, with renewed emphasis upon the 'social market': increasing employment for 20–64-year-olds; boosting innovation by targeting 3 per cent gross domestic product (GDP) for research and development; reducing school-drop-outs and ensuring social inclusion through education; a reduction in numbers living on or below the poverty line; and limiting greenhouse gas emissions, through climate and energy policy (EC, 2014).

The eurozone crisis – especially with the ongoing challenges posed by the Greek, Portuguese and Spanish economies – has raised new questions about increasingly deeper integration, and what this means for national sovereignty. The European Commission has sought to head off any suggestion that the direction of travel be reversed, and that national governments might selectively withdraw from their commitment to the development of the European project. They argue that:

> The crisis has shown us how interlinked our economies are. A housing bubble in one country can impact on neighbouring countries and indeed on all of the Union. This increased economic independence demands a coordinated response, including social partners and civil society. If we act together we can come out of the crisis stronger. In a globalized world, no country can effectively address the challenges it faces by acting alone. This is particularly true for Europe, where tackling such changes is most effective at the European level. (EC, 2014: 5)

The Commission's proposal is to further strengthen the regional coordination of national economic policies through a 'European semester': a specific time of the year when all member states work on the implementation of the Europe 2020 strategy through a national reform and a national convergence programme, on country-specific recommendations from the Commission, and the submission of a draft budget to comply with the Fiscal Compact. A scoreboard will be used to keep track of each member state and alert the EU institutions regarding potential problems. Taken together, these new governance initiatives suggest a much harder edge to the policing of policy implementation than in the past, such as through the use of sanctions. However, as writers such as Beckert (2013) have argued, this more pedagogical element, that is, socializing the member states into closer and ongoing self-assessment and reporting, does not in itself enable the better management of the future, in that the future by definition cannot be known.

It is also clear from data reported in the 2015 Trends Report commissioned by the European University Association (Sursock, 2015), from trends in the 2015 *Bologna Process Implementation Report* (European

Commission, 2015), and from the Eurostat 2015 Report on Indicators (Eurostat, 2015) supporting the Europe 2020 strategy, that from 2010 onwards there is considerable shortfall in meeting the EU's EHEA, ERA and Europe 2020 targets. In relation to the EHEA specifically, the Trends and Implementation Reports both note that in 2015 many countries were significantly further away from where they were in 2010. They point out that the move to new governance structures by many universities across Europe (often referred to as new forms of autonomy, but in truth this meant bringing in new public management as a mode of governing) meant new steering mechanisms were put into place, tied to new fiscal obligations. The financial crisis facing many national governments across Europe has, paradoxically, resulted in tighter bureaucratic control by national governments over their higher education sectors, in turn placing new limits on EU-level power and control. As Sursock (2015: 12) notes in the Trends 2015 Report: 'Although the scope of autonomy is respected, less funding and additional reporting requirements often increase the importance of institutional bureaucracies, limit the capacity of institutions to chart their own course, and erode collegial decision-making'.

With institutions pressed to do more with less following the 2008 financial crisis, institutions have sought to diversify their funding sources, whilst commercial firms, such as recruiters for for-profit providers, and quality assurers, have entered the sector. That Bologna has no funding and financial instruments, and that Europe 2020 and the ERA only address meeting R&D percentages, has thrown up the limits to the governing of the HE sector at the level of Europe. The crisis has also made visible new struggles over the cultural political economy of this regional sectoral project. Is a new national frontier again being advanced by the national state in this world market-making project? What activities continue to be located at the regional scale, and what ideational work is being done to secure it there? Are alternative spatial projects being mobilized by the state and capital – such as the current round of trade negotiations (for example, the Transatlantic Trade and Investment Partnership, Comprehensive Economic Trade Agreement, Trade in Service Agreement) – that might offer an alternative route forward for bringing higher education into a world market (Robertson and Komljenovic, 2015)?

CONCEPTUALIZING AND THEORIZING THE STATE–REGIONS–FRONTIER RELATION

In this final section, we return to the challenges and issues confronting researchers interested in studying the production of regions. We began by arguing for a more robust conversation between those who study higher education regionalism and the importance of this work to theoretical contributions on understanding regional governance.

In the chapter we have shown the value of developing a cultural political economy approach to region-making to explore the creation of a European Higher Education Area and a European Research Area. Specifically, we have argued that these can be understood as projects whose dynamics are shaped by ongoing transformations in the state and economy, and whose underlying logics at the current time can be better understood in terms of the making of world markets. Yet there is considerable political turbulence in this process as a result of ongoing crisis tendencies confronting the project, as well as ideational struggle over the shape and form of the project.

We also argued that higher education has been progressively drawn into these logics, and that the 'region' – in this case a higher education regional sectoral space – is not only dependent on, but has ongoing effects upon, the socio-political and spatial relations between domestic economies, the (supra-national) region, and the extra-regional, or global. These multiple frontiers – regional, national and global – as the state tries to advance these projects, suggests that theoretical contributions such as regulatory regionalism need to be further nuanced to think about the shifting strategies and frontiers of the state, including its consequent spatial and topological form over time. This means studying these dynamics over time and not only in a narrow temporal window.

We also explored the value of thinking about regions, not in terms of a regionalist ideology, but focusing on underlying logics, processes, mechanisms and outcomes which have socio-spatial manifestations – and in this case, as a result of a particular organization of state rule. They are simultaneously cultural (meaning-making, subjectivities), political (power relations, state) and economic (logic of world market-making, capitalism). They are also a form of sectoral regionalism: the outcome of territorially-based formal and/or informal arrangements arising from strategically selective socio-spatial projects and processes advanced by nationally located states, regional state actors that advance the region 'in and for itself', and the 'extra-regional' or global actors and their institutions. These different spatial frontiers are dynamic, shifting and changing, as a result of struggles over territory, institutions, networks and other forms of organization, and the meanings that they claim for themselves.

REFERENCES

Adelman, C. (2008), *The Bologna Club: What US Higher Education Can Learn from a Decade of European Reconstruction*, Washington, DC: Institute for Higher Education Policy.
van Apeldoorn, B. (2001), The Struggle Over European Order: Transnational Class Agency in the Making of 'Embedded Neo-liberalism'. In A. Bieler and A.D. Morton (eds), *Social Forces in the Making of the New Europe*, Basingstoke: Palgrave, pp. 70–89.
Azevedo, M.D. (2014), The Bologna Process and Higher Education in Mercosur: Regionalization or Europeanization? *International Journal of Lifelong Education*, **33**(2), DOI: 10.1080/02601370.2014.891884.
Barroso, J-M. (2005), Strong Universities for Europe. Speech given to the European Universities Association Convention, Glasgow, 2 April, accessed 8 January 2016 at http://www.eua.be/eua/jsp/en/upload/Barroso_speech.1112693429657.pdf.
Beckert, J. (2013), Capitalism as a System of Expectations: Toward a Sociological Microfoundation of Political Economy. *Politics and Society*, **41**(3), 323–350.
BFUG (2005), *From Berlin to Bergen. General Report of the Bologna Follow-up Group to the Conference of European Ministers Responsible for Higher Education*. Bergen, 19–20 May. Oslo, 3 May.
BFUG (2016), The Formal Structure of the Bologna Follow-Up Group. Accessed 8 January 2016 at http://www.ehea.info/
Bieler, A. and Morton, A. (eds) (2001), *Social Forces in the Making of the New Europe*, Basingstoke: Palgrave.
Bishop, J. (2006), *The Bologna Process and Australia: Next Steps*, Canberra: Australian Federal Department of Education, Skills and Training.
Bologna Declaration (1999), *The European Higher Education Area. Joint Declaration of the European Ministers of Education Convened in Bologna at the 19th June, 1999*.
Cammack, P. (2015), World Market Regionalism at the Asian Development Bank. *Journal of Contemporary Asia*, DOI: 10.1080/00472336.2015.1086407.
Collignon, S. (2006), *The Lisbon Strategy, Macroeconomic Stability and the Dilemma of Governance with Governments*, Boston, MA, USA and London, UK: Harvard University and London School of Economics.
Corbett, A. (2005), *Universities and the Europe of Knowledge – Ideas, Institutions and Policy Entrepreneurship in European Union Higher Education Policy, 1955–2005*, Basingstoke, UK and New York, USA: Palgrave Macmillan.
Cox, R. (1996), *Approaches to World Order*, Cambridge: Cambridge University Press.
Dale, R. and Robertson, S. (2002), Regional Organisations as Subjects of Globalisation. *Comparative Education Review*, **46**(1), 10–36.
Elden, S. (2006), Contingent Sovereignty, Territorial Integrity and the Sanctity of Borders. *SAIS Review*, **26**(1), 11–24.
Ercan, F. and Oguz, S. (2006), Rescaling as a Class Relationship and Process: The Case of Public Procurement Law in Turkey. *Political Geography*, **25**, 641–656.
European Commission (2003), *Communication from the Commission of 5 February 2003 – The Role of the Universities in the Europe of Knowledge*,

COM(2003) 58 final, accessed 23 April 2016 at http://eur-lex.europa.eu/legal-content/EN/TXT/HTML/?uri=URISERV:c11067&from=EN.

European Commission (EC) (2005a), *Communication to the Spring European Council. Working Together for Growth and Jobs. A New Start for the Lisbon Strategy*, accessed 8 January 2016 at http://europa.eu.int/growthandjobs/.

European Commission (EC) (2005b), *Mobilising the Brainpower of Europe: Enabling Universities to Make their Full Contribution to the Lisbon Strategy – European Higher Education in a Worldwide Perspective, Commission Staff Working Paper – Annex to the Communication from the Commission* [SEC(2005)518], European Commission: Brussels.

European Commission (EC) (2006), *Delivering on the Modernisation Agenda for Universities: Education, Research and Innovation (COM (2006) 208 final)*, 10 May, European Commission: Brussels.

European Commission (EC) (2012), *Communication from the Commission to the European Parliament, the Council, the European Economic Social Committee and the Social Committee of the Regions: A Reinforced European Research Area Partnership for Excellence and Growth*, COM (2012) 392 final, Brussels: European Commission.

European Commission (2014), *EU Annual Growth Survey 2015: A new Momentum for Jobs, Growth and Investment*, Brussels: European Commission, accessed 23 April 2016 at http://europa.eu/rapid/press-release_IP-14-2235_en.htm.

European Commission (EC) (2015), *Bologna Process Implementation Report, 2015*, Brussels: European Commission.

European Council (2000), *Conclusions of the European Lisbon Council*, 23–24 March, SN100/00, available at http://www.europarl.europa.eu/summits/lis1_en.htm.

European Council (2005), *Presidency Conclusions 22 and 23 March*, Brussels [DOC/05/1].

Eurostat (2015), Smarter, Greener, More Inclusive? Indicators to Support the Europe 2020 Strategy – 2015 edition, accessed 23 April 2016 at http://ec.europa.eu/eurostat/web/europe-2020-indicators/europe-2020-strategy/publications.

Figel, J. and Bishop, J. (2007), *Joint Declaration between the European Union and Australia. European Commission and the Government of Australia wish to reinforce co-operation in the fields of education and training*, Brussels: European Commission.

Gornitzka, A. (2005), Coordinating Policies for a 'Europe of knowledge': Emerging Practices of the 'Open Method of Coordination' in Education and Research. Working Paper 16, accessed 14 January 2016 at http: www.arena.uio.no.

Hameiri, S. (2013), Theorising Regions through Changes in Statehood: Rethinking the Theory and Method of Comparative Regionalism. *Review of International Studies*, **39**, 313–335.

Hameiri, S. and Jayasuriya, K. (2011), Regulatory Regionalism and the Dynamics of Territorial Politics: The Case of the Asia Pacific. *Political Studies*, **59**(1), 20–37.

Harmsen, R. (2013), The Bologna Process and New Modes of Governance: Logics and Limits of Arena Shaping. Presented at EUSA 13th Biennial Conference, Baltimore, MA, 9 May.

Hartmann, E. (2008), Bologna Goes Global: A New Imperialism in the Making. *Globalisation, Societies and Education*, **6**(3), 207–220.

Hettne, B. (2005), Beyond the 'New Regionalism'. *New Political Economy*, **10**(4), 543–571.
Hingel, A.J. (2001), *Education Policies and European Governance: Contribution to the Inter-service Groups on European Governance*. Brussels: European Commission, Directorate-General for Education and Culture (Unit A1: Development of Educational Policies), also published in the *European Journal for Education Law and Policy*, **5**, 7–16.
Huisman, J. and van der Wende, M. (2004), The EU and Bologna: Are Supra- and International Initiatives Threatening Domestic Agendas? *European Journal of Education*, **39**(3), 349–357.
Jaschik, S. (2006), Making Sense of 'Bologna Degrees'. *Inside Higher Education*. 6 November, available at http://insidehighered.com/news/2006/11/06/bologna.
Jayasuriya, K. (2003), Introduction: Governing the Asia-Pacific-beyond the 'New Regionalism'. *Third World Quarterly*, **24**(2), 199–215.
Keeling, R. (2006), The Bologna Process and the Lisbon Research Agenda: The European Commission's Expanding Role in Higher Education Discourse. *European Journal of Education*, **41**(2), 203–223.
Kok, W. (2004), *Facing the Challenge Ahead: The Lisbon Strategy for Growth and Employment, Report from the High Level Group*, Brussels: European Commission.
Ravinet, P. (2008), From Voluntary Participation to Monitored Coordination: Why European Countries feel Increasingly Bound By their Commitment to the Bologna Process. *European Journal of Education*, **43**(3), 353–367.
Robertson, S. (2008a), Embracing the Global: Crisis and the Creation of a New Semiotic Order to Secure Europe's Knowledge-Based Economy. In N. Fairclough, R. Wodak and B. Jessop (eds), *Education and the Knowledge-based Economy in Europe*, Rotterdam: Sense Publications, pp. 89–108.
Robertson, S. (2008b), 'Europe/Asia' Regionalism, Higher Education and the Production of World Order. *Policy Futures in Education*, **6**(6), 718–729.
Robertson, S.L. (2010), The EU, Regulatory State Regionalism, and Higher Education. *Globalisation, Societies and Education*, **8**(1), 23–37.
Robertson, S. (2014), Higher Education Regionalising Projects in a Globalising World: A 'Variegated Regionalism' Account. Paper presented to ECPR, Glasgow, 3–6 September.
Robertson, S. and Dale, R. (2015), Critical Cultural Political Economy of the Globalisation of Education. *Globalisation, Societies and Education*, **13**(1), 149–170.
Robertson, S. and Keeling, R. (2008), Stirring the Lions: Strategy and Tactics in Global Higher Education. *Globalisation, Societies and Education*, **6**(3), 221–240.
Robertson, S. and Komljenovic, J. (2015), Forum Shifting and Shape Making in Europe's Negotiations on (Education) Trade in Services Education. Presented to the Education and Trade Panel ECPR, Montreal, 26–28 August.
Rodrigues, M-J. (ed.) (2002), *The New Knowledge Economy in Europe*. Cheltenham, UK and Northampton, MA, USA: Edward Elgar.
Sursock, A. (2015), *Trends 2015: Learning and Teaching in European Universities*, Brussels: European Universities Association.
Teichler, U. and Kehm, B. (1995), Towards a New Understanding of the Relationships between Higher Education and Employment. *European Journal of Education*, **30**(2), 115–132.

Walters, W. and Haar, J. (2005), *Governing Europe: Discourse, Governmentality and European Integration*. London, UK and New York, USA: Routledge.
World Trade Organization (WTO) (2007), *International Trade Statistics, 2006*, WTO: Geneva.
Zeitlen, J. and Pochet, P. (eds) with Magnusson, L. (2005), *The Open Method of Coordination in Action*, Brussels: Peter Lang.
Zgaga, P. (2006), *Looking Out: The Bologna Process in a Global Setting – on the External Dimension of the Bologna Process*, Oslo: Norwegian Ministry of Education Research.

2. Different regionalisms, one European higher education regionalization: the case of the Bologna Process
Susana Melo*

INTRODUCTION

Standing for the governance of the project called the 'European Higher Education Area' (EHEA) since 1999, the Bologna Process has successfully become the main point of reference for a political and academic debate on the matter of governing a convergent transformation of higher education provision within and beyond the entire European continent. This chapter considers the circumstances under which the Bologna Process has gained such significance. In doing so, it focuses particularly on the consequences that the consolidation of the EHEA project during the 2000s has had for the diversity of views on the role of higher education in developing a 'united Europe'. The existing diversity, I argue, has increasingly been undermined by the way in which the mode of informal governance that characterizes the Bologna Process has implied the embedding of various higher education policy programmes and orientations developed in different formally institutionalized frameworks for European regional cooperation. This embedding forms the basis of the constitution of an overarching agenda for the steering of higher education regionalization in Europe, that is, the agenda for the EHEA.

I construct my argument theoretically, drawing upon the 'new regionalism approach' developed by Björn Hettne and Fredrik Söderbaum (Hettne and Söderbaum, 2000; Hettne, 2002, 2005, 2007; Söderbaum, 2007). The relevance of this approach will, I hope, be self-evident enough to encourage a discussion about the limitations of looking into the Bologna Process through the lenses of theories developed originally for the purpose of explaining the dynamic of regional integration within the framework of the European Union (EU).

THE NEW REGIONALISM APPROACH: THEORETICAL NOTES

Hettne and Söderbaum's (2000) conceptual framework and its subsequent variants (Hettne, 2002, 2005, 2007; Söderbaum, 2007) have been established as the new regionalism approach (NRA) in the discipline of international relations and the field of European studies (Soderbäum and Sbragia, 2010). Compared with other perspectives on regionalism in this scholarly context – such as realism, liberal institutionalism, neofunctionalism and regional economic integration theory – the NRA is built upon social constructivist tenets in a way that has been labelled 'critical' because it is in favour of a reflexive, dialectical and historical form of thinking (Söderbaum, 2007: 187). It is drawing upon the core constructivist ontological assumption, that the social world is made by humans in the course of their everyday lives, that the key concepts of 'region', 'regionalization' and 'regionalism' are defined in the NRA.

The NRA posits that a particular cross-national geographical area is a region when human actors ascribe a specific identity to it (in the most fundamental sense, when they name it a region) and can distinguish it as a relatively coherent territorial unit from the rest of the global geopolitical system (Hettne and Söderbaum, 2000: 461). A region therefore is not a predefined entity that exists 'out there' to be administered by groupings of nation-states. Rather, it is constructed by a variety of actors through regionalization. That is to say, through processes of inter- and/or transnational communication, cooperation, integration and identity formation that together create a regional space in specific sectorial areas (for example, education) or in general (for example, the urge for European unity based upon certain liberal democratic values and institutions). These processes are conceived as being geared towards making a region the organizing basis for social relationships and a coherent political and economic entity that has the capacity to act as a unit in world politics (Hettne and Söderbaum, 2000). This capacity in turn relates with what is described as 'regional actorness' (see below).

Importantly, a distinction is made between regionalization and regionalism in the NRA. Analytically, regionalism refers to particular regionalist projects, whereby state and non-state actors cooperate and coordinate strategy within a particular region (Söderbaum, 2007: 188). They relate with deliberate political efforts to create a supra-state regional order in a structured way. In the case of Europe, these efforts have historically led to the formation of what is termed as a 'regional institutionalized polity' constituted by a web of different state-led regional organizations with a specific mandate to promote a particular vision, programme and strategy for the region that is defined by the list of their member states (a *de jure* region). As some authors have noted, the constituents of this web and the relations among them are understudied largely because of the prevalence of a research fixation on the evolution of what today is the EU (Warleigh-Lack and van Langenhove, 2010: 553).

This does not mean that organizations such as the Council of Europe or Europe-focused institutions of the United Nations Educational, Scientific and Cultural Organization (UNESCO) play less of a role in construing and constructing Europe as a region (see Paasi, 2009). As noted below, with respect to higher education cooperation, the role of these organizations has actually been made clearly visible in the governance dynamic and agenda-setting of the Bologna Process since the early 2000s. The fact that they have often been ignored in research on the Process is not motivated by the lack of empirical evidence on this matter.

In any case, the point to be made here is twofold. On the one hand, the NRA does not assume that regionalisms are always formal in the sense that they lead to the creation of juridical institutions. Rather, it suggests that juridical regional institutions do not necessarily have to be the point of departure for a regional analysis; how and for what purposes state and non-state actors come together and deliberate on particular regionalist projects is a primordial starting point to explore whatever kind of evidence of a regionalism in the making. On the other hand, it emphasizes that attention to the interaction between various modes of regionalism and regionalization contributes to developing a comprehensive picture of region-building in the contemporary context of globalization (see Hettne, 2005: 550; Söderbaum, 2007: 188).

The last point stems from one of the core premises upon which the NRA is built: regionalism as a general phenomenon of dividing the world into regions is historically contingent and must be understood in the context of structural transformation of world order. It is from this perspective that a distinction between 'old' and 'new' regionalism is made. Whereas the former is placed in the period from the 1950s to the 1970s and seen as being shaped by the bipolar Cold War structure, the latter is historically located in the contemporary post-Westphalian era and linked with globalization. In this sense, 'new' regionalism denotes current regionalism.

To Hettne and Söderbaum, this periodization of regionalism helps above all in substantiating their argument that contemporary regional analysis needs to account for a particular trait identified with the new regionalism era: a stronger orientation of regional political forces towards establishing and maintaining political, economic, social and cultural links with the 'external' environment. This orientation is manifest in the proliferation of organized meetings aimed at fomenting inter-regional dialogues on a wide variety of matters. It is also evidenced in the expansion of formal agreements between regional organizations and other organizations and national governmental institutions around the world. Generally described as 'inter-regionalism', these various kinds of relations demonstrate what is termed as 'regional actorness' in the NRA (Hettne, 2007: 107–111). Succinctly, regional actorness denotes the political capacity of determining and sustaining a cohesive regional position in interactions and negotiation processes of global governance.

Such a capacity is associated with the internalization of a dialogue with globalization in the policy rationale and activities of current regionalist projects. In the NRA, globalization is seen to be predominantly driven by processes that are concerned about the achievement of a particular but also dominant globalist project at present: the extending of borderless industrial production and commerce worldwide. By relating with this globalist project, regionalisms in different parts of the world have increasingly become 'extroverted' in a wide range of policy areas. In this regard, Hettne claims that 'Regionalism is an approach to globalization, whether promoting it or trying to control it' (2002: 329). For research, this implies paying attention to purposive shifts towards the alignment of regional policy objectives with the sort of (de)regulation, marketing and standardization that goes alongside trade liberalization and market expansion at a global scale. And, more concretely, taking into account the analytical purposes of this chapter, it means to examine how the EHEA project can be understood as the taking on of a European regional standpoint with respect to the participation of the higher education sector in the dynamics of expansion of a global market in knowledge-based services and products.

To be clear, the concept of regional actorness entails the assumption that there is a regional society made up of actors which can take action in an orchestrated way and which are capable of representing the region as a coherent entity in different governance contexts (Hettne, 2007: 110–111; Hettne, 2005: 555–556); specifically, actors which can take action in accordance with the values, interests and identity of the regionalism that they represent externally. This suggests that a relatively high degree of political cohesion, ideational compatibility and policy coordination exists at the regional level, which in turn reinforces the credibility and the legitimacy of regional activities aimed at consciously playing a role in world politics. Yet, since this scenario is not taken as a given from the perspective of the NRA, it is an empirical question whether there is a shared position in relation to the policy orientation of the EHEA project.

In summary, the NRA offers a rather general framework that can be used for analysing contemporary regionalism in a wide range of fields and in diverse parts of the world. In this chapter, I use it for identifying the Bologna Process as a case of informal regionalism. Once identified as a regionalism, the conceptual lenses of the NRA are particularly helpful for examining: (1) the circumstances under which the Bologna Process has brought together various regional actors, and affected the sustainability of their different political positions and missions in relation to the direction of European regional cooperation in higher education; and (2) the consequences of seeking to articulate regionalist and globalist policy orientations in the development of the project that the Bologna Process sustains. Each of these cases is examined in the following sections.

THE BOLOGNA PROCESS: OUTSIDE AND INSIDE THE REGIONAL INSTITUTIONALIZED SPACE

The Bologna Process has its roots in the initiative that the British, French, German and Italian ministers for higher education took to draft and publicize their Joint Declaration on Harmonisation of the Architecture of the European Higher Education System on the occasion of the celebration of the 800th anniversary of the Sorbonne University in 1998. The Sorbonne Declaration communicates an agreement to adopt a common degree system of two cycles (undergraduate and postgraduate levels) for the purpose of 'improving external recognition and facilitating student mobility as well as employability'. The novelty of this statement lies not in the expressed purpose, but in the means of achieving it. Articulating the facilitation of student mobility and the enhancement of procedures for recognizing higher education studies undertaken abroad has been an oft-cited commitment since three Conventions on the recognition of foreign academic qualifications were opened for signature to members of the Council of Europe in the 1950s. In the 1990s, this line of reasoning expanded to accommodate a connection between the recognition of professional qualifications and transnational labour mobility within the EU. However, the idea of unifying higher education degree systems according to a model agreed at the European level went against a long-standing governmental concern with protecting education systems from the synergies of integration processes as regards the particularities of their organization and content (Corbett, 2005).

Closing with an invitation to other ministers from European countries, EU member states or not, to join the initiative, the Sorbonne Declaration suggests a willingness to enlarge the number of supporters for 'structural harmonization'. The response did not take long. The following year, 29 European ministers gathered at the University of Bologna to sign a revised version of the Sorbonne Declaration: the Bologna Declaration.

The Bologna Declaration draws on the power of ascribing an identity to the project. All of the measures that were agreed upon in Bologna were framed as serving the purpose of creating the European Higher Education Area (EHEA). While reaffirming the objective to adopt a degree system based on two differentiated cycles, ministers in Bologna also committed themselves to taking action towards: establishing a common system of credits; promoting cooperation in quality assurance; facilitating student and academic staff mobility by overcoming recognition issues; and promoting a 'European dimension' in higher education, particularly in regard to curriculum development. The common thread linking together the items of this agenda lies in the definition of the EHEA project as being about increasing the comparability and compatibility of higher education systems within Europe, and at the same time, about increasing the international competitiveness and worldwide attractiveness of what the Bologna Declaration states to be '*the* European higher education system' (my emphasis).

In contrast with the initiative at Sorbonne, the meeting in Bologna was well prepared and its preparation is reflected in subsequent decisions about how the governance of the EHEA would proceed, and define the Bologna Process as an informal regionalism (see Hackl, 2001; Croché, 2009). On the other hand, ministers in Bologna scheduled another summit for 2001, justified on the basis of a conception of the creation of the EHEA as a process that would involve regular revision of both progress and strategy. This settled the routine of the Bologna Process: ministerial summits held to take stock of the implementation of the agreed policies and to legitimate a revised agenda for the EHEA.

On the other hand, between the summits, a multi-actor group would be responsible for preparing the summits, drafting the ministerial communiqués, monitoring the achievement of objectives, disseminating the project, and so forth. In 2001, at the Prague summit, this group was named the Bologna Follow-Up Group. In its initial formation, it integrated representatives of the signatory states, the Council of Europe, the European Commission, the European Student Association, the European Association of Institutions in Higher Education and the European University Association. After 2001, the number of participating organizations enlarged with the inclusion of UNESCO and three other non-governmental organizations representing academic staff (Educational International), the labour market (Business Europe) and quality assurance agencies (European Association for Quality Assurance in Higher Education).

An interesting aspect of this development from a small-scale regional intergovernmental initiative into a large and hybrid coalition is that there have never been declared concerns about the material sustenance of the Bologna Process.[1] However, research has shown that the participation of the European Commission has been critical with respect to endowing the process with financial capabilities (Croché, 2009). Moreover, aside from financial sponsorship, the organizations participating in the Bologna Follow-Up Group have put at the service of the Process their premises and staff. For example, the Council of Europe has been a Bologna Process meeting place and provided administrative and technical support in different ways. Furthermore, all of these organizations have contributed to publicizing the project of Bologna within their respective (local, national, regional and global) spheres of influence and, moreover, to promoting mutual understanding of its technical specificities. Hence, whilst none of the conditions that facilitate trans- and international interactions and decision-making have been formally created for the governance of the EHEA, the Bologna Process has operated on the basis of a strong dependence on the material capabilities of the regional institutionalized polity and on the organizational skills of experienced actors of the regional higher education society.

These circumstances of dependence have arguably had important consequences for the dynamic of European cooperation in higher education as well as for the evolution of the EHEA project. The involvement of the Council of Europe, the European Commission and UNESCO in the Bologna Follow-Up Group is of particular relevance for illustrating this point. Broadly, these organizations take part in the Bologna Process on the basis of the historical role that they have had in differently framing the steering of higher education regionalization in Europe.

Since the 1950s, cooperation in higher education at the Council of Europe has been legally framed by the European Cultural Convention and shaped by the historical understanding that the mission of the Council of Europe is to promote European unity on the basis of agreements on any other issues than security and economics (Robertson, 1956: 15). Entering into force in 1954, the European Cultural Convention was a statement of the understanding that cultural cooperation should be aimed at facilitating the mutual understanding among the peoples of Europe, and dissociated from the politico-ideological differences dividing Europe at the time. Accordingly, the Convention was opened to signature to any country, member or not of the Council of Europe, committed to the promotion of the 'European civilization' via facilitating cross-cultural exchanges (educational exchanges included) and history learning.

Moreover, it was established that parties to the Convention could participate on an equal basis in the structures for cultural cooperation of the Council of Europe, including higher education. In sum, this means that interactions and decision-making in higher education at the Council of Europe have been marked by a sense of participating in a process of construction of pan-European unity. Following the integration of the Council of Europe in the Bologna Process in 2001, the European Cultural Convention was taken as the main criterion to judge the eligibility of new participating countries in the Bologna Process in 2003. It is the legal instrument that explains why the EHEA today affects the entire European continent, including Belarus (which has conditional access, pending on completion of the Roadmap), Kazakhstan and the Russian Federation. In 2015, the total of EHEA member countries was 47.

In contrast with the Council of Europe, it is well documented that the European Commission has since the 1970s sought to justify the development of EU higher education policies and student exchange programmes according to a rationale that emphasizes the notion that higher education plays an instrumental role in the achievement of regional economic integration and development objectives (Corbett, 2005; Papatsiba, 2005, 2009; Tzortzis, 2007). While elements of this rationale will be mentioned in the next section, for reasons of space it is sufficient to highlight here that two of the main standardizing policy instruments that the European Commission developed in the 1990s, with the view of advancing a solution to the simplification of processes of recognition of qualifications completed during periods of study abroad, the European Credit Transfer System (ECTS) and the Diploma Supplement, were introduced in the agenda for the making of the EHEA in the early 2000s.

Finally, there is UNESCO. Through its decentralized office established in Bucharest in 1972, the European Centre for Higher Education – CEPES (Centre Européen pour l'Enseignement Supérieur), UNESCO developed a strong diplomatic presence in Eastern and Southeastern Europe largely focused on organizing discussion fora as well as on promoting networking with Western European regional actors and organizations (Maassen and Vabø, 2006). In addition, in the 1990s, UNESCO joined the Council of Europe in a revision of the various Conventions that were both part of its legal framework and of the Council's; and that aimed at establishing convergent attitudes and practices with respect to the recognition of foreign academic qualifications across Europe (for details, see Jorge de Melo, 2013: Ch. 6; Hartmann, 2010). The outcome of this revision was in 1997 the Council of Europe–UNESCO Convention on the Recognition of Qualifications Concerning Higher Education in the European Region, best known as the Lisbon Recognition Convention. This legal text establishes that UNESCO and the Council of Europe are to permanently collaborate in the follow-up to the implementation of the agreed measures. UNESCO joined the Bologna Follow-Up Group in 2003, when the ratification of the

Lisbon Recognition Convention was explicitly stated to be a measure for the making of the EHEA (EHEA, 2003).

All of the above points to the dynamic of establishing the Bologna Process in the first half of the 2000s. Traditional facilitators of an institutional setting for the promotion of higher education regionalization became implicated as actors in a systematic process of entanglement of visions, policies and instruments. The entanglement represents a homogenization of different European higher education agendas; or at least a shift wherein agenda-setting processes in higher education at the Council of Europe, the European Commission and UNESCO became conditioned by the shared aim to contribute to defining what makes the EHEA.

This shift has over time tended to bring into question the value of developing a higher education-specific programme within the framework of the institutionalized polity: if decisions and outcomes are primarily intended to be directed to be potentially constitutive of a unified agenda for regional higher education integration in Europe, why engage in developing a particular institutional positioning? There is no evidence that this question was formulated in these terms in European political circles. However, the fact is that UNESCO-CEPES was closed in 2011, and in the same year the Council of Europe's Steering Committee for Higher Education and Research was merged with the Steering Committee for Education. Furthermore, Gornitzka (2010) remarks upon a growing tendency throughout the 2000s to a non-differentiation of higher education from other policy areas within the framework of the EU.

Yet, the shift has also resulted in an increasing capacity to orchestrate ideas and priorities in European higher education politics, and above all in the emergence of regional actorness in this field. The latter is something that has been consciously developed and explored by actors in the Bologna Process, in particular by the European Commission (Croché, 2009; Hartmann, 2008; Robertson and Keeling, 2008). Furthermore, it has become explicitly articulated as a Bologna Process strategy (Zgaga, 2006) and specifically advanced through the Bologna Policy Forum, which was set up in 2009. Organized in conjunction with the ministerial summits, this Forum brings together representatives of non-European countries and non-governmental organizations for the purpose of worldwide cooperation and partnership in higher education. Ultimately, it stands for disseminating the norms, policies, policy instruments and mode of governance of the EHEA as constituting a model for regionally integrating diverse higher education systems, and a model that could be adopted at the global scale (see European Commission, 2013; EHEA, 2012, 2015a).

THE PURPOSE OF MAKING THE EHEA: REGIONALIZING FOR GLOBALIZING

The creation of the Bologna Policy Forum corresponds to a clear manifestation of the dominance of the outward orientation of the EHEA project and of its underpinning aspirations to facilitate and participate in the expansion of global trade in higher education services. Several studies coincide in noting that the 1998 Sorbonne Declaration was of particular relevance for the French and German ministers (Charlier and Croché, 2007; Corbett, 2005: 195–199; Ravinet, 2005; Hackl, 2001: 16–17). Apart from pursuing the shortening of the length of higher education studies, they sought to make the EHEA more competitive with the US and Australian degree systems. These differences were viewed as a disadvantage of French and German universities with respect to competing in the recruitment of foreign students at the global scale. The agreement that was reached focused precisely on making higher education systems compatible with a regional model on the one hand, and competitive with main Anglo-Saxon countries in the sector on the other. However, apart from particular governmental reasons for initiating the EHEA project via the Sorbonne Declaration, it is important to consider the broader context of readjustments of the political economy of European regional integration in the 1990s in order to make sense of the swift adherence to the proposal advanced at Sorbonne.

When the Sorbonne Declaration was drafted, the depth of economic regionalization encompassing the completion of the single market programme and monetary union (with effect from 1 January 1999) among the majority of EU member states had increased and included a shift toward neoliberalism, which went hand in hand with a further economic globalization of the EU *de jure* region (van Apeldoorn, 2001: 79). Whilst the construction of the single market institutionalized the deregulation of national financial markets and the end of states' barriers to free trade, it did not create external barriers. It therefore created a regional market that is not 'protected'. Alongside the restructuring of the EU project, a discursive strategy was developed by the European Commission in the early 1990s.

The Commission drew on an image of Europe as needing to be competitive in the face of exogenous shifts, detailed as: the growing market interdependence resulting from global liberalization of capital movements; the emergence of new technologically advanced rival economic spaces; the new skills revolution; and the shift to a knowledge-based economy (Rosamond, 1999: 662). In relation to this portrayal, the recognition emerged during this period in EU political circles that higher education was fundamentally implicated in the aspiration of making the single market coherent with respect to the identified trends in the global economy; as a service that could be traded and 'internationalized', as a key centre for research and innovation, as a producer of new forms of intellectual property, and as a developer of an idealized transnational highly qualified and mobile labour force (Gornitzka, 2010: 537–540; Robertson, 2008: 3).

Notwithstanding contestation of these ideas in the context of relations between the Commission and national governments, the 1990s witnessed a widespread tendency in EU member countries to adopt policies that were in line with the neoliberal globalist rationale which informed the setting up of the single market and monetary union (see Huisman and van der Wende, 2004: 350). Thus, the emergence of the Bologna Process in 1999 can be seen as a first sign of a consensual way of reasoning regionalization as instrumental to globalizing higher education, attuned to the vision of the making of a European common market.

It was soon followed by the adoption of the strategy for the EU to become the world's most dynamic and competitive knowledge-based economy, declared at the 2000 European Council in Lisbon. In the Lisbon Strategy, the 'knowledge' policy areas – (higher) education and research – were pushed towards the centre of the EU agenda and these sectors were opened to a wide range of articulations with political and economic objectives to construct Europe as a leader in world trade in commercial services. As Huisman and van der Wende argue (2004: 353), the Bologna Process and the Lisbon Strategy came to converge in their aims, and this convergence explains the prominence of the latter in the formulation of the EHEA project to be realized by 2010.

In this context, there are two aspects that need to be underscored. Firstly, as mentioned, it was agreed in 2003 that parties to the European Cultural Convention would be eligible members of the EHEA. As a result, the membership of the EHEA is not in total committed to the EU project. Secondly, as discussed above, besides the presence and influence of the agenda for the EU in the Bologna Process, other European-level agendas interact and are entangled in the context of the workings of the Bologna Follow-Up Group. This means that the Bologna project is best understood as being to a great extent in accord with the strategy for the EU, but not as being a reproduction of that strategy. Above all, it is a project that coincides with its orientation towards global competition in higher education more generally, and towards generating income out of universities' recruitment of foreign students more particularly.

Certainly, in parallel to this convergence, there exists the permanence of some 'old' concerns with promoting student and academic staff exchanges, and with keeping the rate of participation in higher education high within

Europe. Since the late 2000s, 'new' concerns with a various number of crises developing in Europe have equally been articulated in a discourse that is continuously reformulated when it comes to depicting how higher education is to contribute to social cohesion and well-being. However, the prevalent tendency has been to make the process of creating the EHEA a highly technocratic matter and to use it as a joint platform to promote European higher education in the rest of the world.

The initial proposal at Sorbonne was that of implementing a higher education degree structure that was clear to all, within and outside Europe. As mentioned, it implied a need to take action towards restructuring higher education studies into two cycles defined in accord with an unambiguous description of each cycle. This proposal became more complex in the course of the continuous updating of the agenda for the EHEA. In 2003, the model became one of three cycles (Bachelor, Master and Doctorate), with each cycle and course units partitioned into credits based on the ECTS. In taking credits as the frame of reference, variance in the schemes that may be adopted became acceptable.

In addition to the issue of regionalizing degree structures, a set of policy instruments was introduced in 2005: the use of the EHEA qualifications framework as a model for describing the various qualifications that can be obtained within a national higher education system; the adoption of quality assurance procedures and standards; and the Lisbon Recognition Convention. Taken together, they constitute a concrete response of the Bologna Follow-Up Group to the objectives that were defined in the Bologna Declaration regarding the comparability of higher education systems (see above). Specifically, they are means to standardizing and 'industrializing' higher education in Europe enabled by the impregnation of a particular notion of academic qualifications: qualifications have a value which ought to be recognized worldwide and certified against intermediary agencies' assessments of the quality of the universities where they were obtained.

According to Croché (2009: 495), these policy instruments reinforce pan-European regional cooperation and maintain outside Europe 'the illusion of a "European Higher Education Area" functioning as its promoters had imagined'. By 'illusion' Croché alludes to the little impact these instruments have had so far on a coordinated and convergent higher education transformation. There now exists vast empirical evidence that the outcome of the Bologna Process over the past decade was not after all the envisaged harmonization of national higher education systems, but rather the production of new kinds of cross-national systemic variation (for an overview, see Westerheijden et al., 2009; Vögtle, 2014). In this respect, I would like to emphasize that the instruments in question require a preliminary normalization of the technical knowledge that has been developed at the regional level, but not evenly transferred to national and local agencies involved in the implementation of the EHEA. Furthermore, the instruments themselves are viewed as in the process of being finalized by their developers. For example, the quality assurance standards agreed in 2005 were revised and updated in 2015.

Yet, their ongoing development has enabled the worldwide promotion and valorization of European higher education provision and an increase in overall percentage terms of enrolments of students from non-EHEA countries everywhere within the EHEA (Croché, 2009: 497). Indeed, the European Commission continues to highlight the contribution of these enrolments to economic growth, suggesting that income generated from charging these students high fees is not the only factor to take into consideration: remittances and the increase of local consumption also count (European Commission, 2013: 4). In sum, the exercise of regional actorness in light of the original idea that the EHEA project would be a way to ensure that 'the European higher education system acquires a world-wide degree of attraction' (1999 Bologna Declaration) has tended to be justified less for the proved internal regionalizing impact of the EHEA, and more for the expectation of good economic results deriving from a global marketing of European higher education provision.

CONCLUSIONS

To conclude, it can be said that the Bologna Process is a case of informal regionalism where the capacity to act as a regional unit has been further developed amongst a particular constellation of actors whose expertise is higher education policy. Moreover, it is a regionalism which implies a concerted way of engaging in the transformation of views on the role of higher education in the European political and economic project. In particular, the Bologna Process policies have been orientated towards adjusting the European higher education sector to market-dominated forms of globalization, and supported by a communication strategy in which the idea of a 'united Europe' is used to enhance the competitiveness of European universities in the global market for international students. Within this framework, facilitating the integration of European universities into the dynamic of globalization has preceded de facto regionalization.

In this analysis, in accordance with the new regionalism approach, I have paid particular attention to the questions of by whom and for what purposes the Bologna Process became established as an informal regionalism. This has helped to identify change and tensions in the current dynamic of European regional cooperation in higher education. Focusing on the participation of the Council of Europe, the European Commission and UNESCO in the governance of the EHEA, I have sought to emphasize that the constitution of the Bologna Process as the overarching framework for higher education transformation and policy in Europe has been accompanied by compromises between different historical positions and structures. These compromises might explain an increase in the compatibility of ideas and coordination that facilitates regionalisms acting as global actors. However, a reflection upon their consequences for a comprehensive and pluralist debate about higher education change is a pressing matter.

NOTES

* I would like to thank the Economic and Social Research Council (ESRC) for Doctoral funding (Award number EDUC.SC1802.6525), without which the empirical research informing this chapter would not have been possible. The analysis builds on the contextual insights I gained as a participant observant at the Council of Europe, semi-structured interviews with participants in the Bologna Follow-Up Group and archival research.
1. In 2015, the Bologna Follow-Up Group reported on the EHEA website several debates about the possibility of terminating the Bologna Process without ever mentioning why these debates are taking place. The economic crisis and its associated social and political consequences could be a motivation, as it has become more difficult to argue with and for the construction of a pan-European region (see, e.g., EHEA, 2015b).

REFERENCES

Apeldoorn, B. van (2001), 'The struggle over European order: transnational class agency in the making of "embedded neo-liberalism"', in Bieler, A. and Morton, A.D. (eds), *Social Forces in the Making of the New Europe*, Basingstoke: Palgrave, pp. 70–89.

Bologna Declaration (1999), 'The Bologna Declaration of 19th June 1999. Joint Declaration of the European Ministers of Education', available at http://www.ehea.info/Uploads/about/BOLOGNA_DECLARATION1.pdf (accessed 23 April 2016).

Charlier, J.E. and Croché, S. (2007), 'The Bologna Process: the outcome of competition between Europe and the United States and a stimulus to this competition', *European Education*, 39(4), 10–26.

Corbett, A. (2005), *Universities and the Europe of Knowledge: Ideas, Institutions and Policy Entrepreneurship in European Union Higher Education Policy, 1955–2005*, New York: Palgrave Macmillan.

Croché, S. (2009), 'Bologna network: a new sociopolitical area in higher education', *Globalisation, Societies and Education*, 7(4), 489–503.

EHEA (2003), 'Realising the European Higher Education Area', Communiqué of the Conference of Ministers Responsible for Higher Education, Berlin,

19 September, available at http://www.ehea.info/Uploads/about/Berlin_Communique1.pdf (accessed 23 April 2016).
EHEA (2012), 'Beyond the Bologna Process: creating and connecting national, regional and global higher education areas', Background paper for the Third Bologna Policy Forum, Bucharest, 27 April.
EHEA (2015a), 'Statement of the Fourth Bologna Policy Forum', Yerevan, 14–15 May.
EHEA (2015b), 'Yerevan Communiqué', EHEA Ministerial Conference Yerevan 2015, Yerevan, 14–15 May, available at http://www.ehea.info/Uploads/SubmitedFiles/5_2015/112705.pdf (accessed 23 April 2016).
European Commission (2013), *European Higher Education in the World*, COM(2013) 499 final, Brussels: European Commission.
Gornitzka, Å. (2010), 'Bologna in context: a horizontal perspective on the dynamics of governance sites for a Europe of Knowledge', *European Journal of Education*, **45**(4), 535–548.
Hackl, E. (2001), 'Towards a European Higher Education Area: change and convergence in European higher education', EUI Working Papers, Working paper RSC No. 2011/09, San Domenico: Robert Schuman Centre for Advanced Studies, European University Institute.
Hartmann, E. (2008), 'Bologna goes global: a new imperialism in the making?', *Globalisation, Societies and Education*, **6**(3), 207–220.
Hartmann, E. (2010), 'The United Nations Educational, Scientific and Cultural Organisation: pawn or global player?', *Globalisation, Societies and Education*, **8**(2), 307–318.
Hettne, B. (2002), 'The Europeanisation of Europe: endogenous and exogenous dimensions', *European Integration*, **24**(4), 325–340.
Hettne, B. (2005), 'Beyond the "new regionalism"', *New Political Economy*, **10**(4), 543–571.
Hettne, B. (2007), 'Interregionalism and world order: the diverging EU and US models', in Telò, M. (ed.), *European Union and New Regionalism*, Farnham: Ashgate, pp. 107–126.
Hettne, B. and Söderbaum, F. (2000), 'Theorising the rise of regionness', *New Political Economy*, **5**(3), 457–473.
Huisman, J. and van der Wende, M. (2004), 'The EU and Bologna: are supra- and international initiatives threatening domestic agendas?', *European Journal of Education*, **39**(3), 349–357.
Jorge de Melo, S. (2013), 'Regionalising higher education transformation in Europe: what kind of positionality for the Council of Europe in relation to the Bologna Process, 1999–2010?', PhD thesis, University of Bristol.
Maassen, P. and Vabø, A. (2006), 'Evaluation of the UNESCO-CEPES, IOS/EVS/PI/42/REV', Paris: UNESCO.
Paasi, Anssi (2009), 'Regions and regional dynamics', in Rumford, C. (ed.), *Handbook of European Studies*, London: Sage, pp. 464–484.
Papatsiba, V. (2005), 'Political and individual rationales of student mobility: a case study of Erasmus and a French scheme for studies abroad', *European Journal of Education*, **2**, 173–188.
Papatsiba, V. (2009), 'European higher education policy and the formation of entrepreneurial students as future European citizens', *European Education Research Journal*, **8**(2), 189–203.
Ravinet, P. (2005), 'The Sorbonne meeting and declaration: actors, shared vision

and Europeanisation', Third Conference on Knowledge and Politics, 18–19 May, University of Bergen.

Robertson, A.H. (1956), *The Council of Europe: Its Structure, Functions and Achievements*, London: Stevens & Sons.

Robertson, S.L. (2008), 'The Bologna Process goes global: a model, market, mobility, brain power or state building strategy?', Invitational paper to ANPED's Annual Conference, October, Brazil.

Robertson, S.L. and Keeling, R. (2008), 'Stirring the lions: strategy and tactics in global higher education', *Globalisation, Societies and Education*, **6**(3), 221–240.

Rosamond, B. (1999), 'Discourses of globalization and the social construction of European identities', *Journal of European Public Policy*, **6**(4), 652–668.

Söderbaum, F. (2007), 'African regionalism and EU–African interregionalism', in Telò, M. (ed.), *European Union and New Regionalism*, Farnham: Ashgate, pp. 185–202.

Söderbaum, F. and Sbragia, A. (2010), 'EU studies and the "new regionalism": what can be gained from dialogue?', *European Integration*, **32**(6), 563–582.

Tzortzis, K. (2007), 'Higher education policy in the European Union: an institutional account', PhD thesis, University of Nottingham.

Vögtle, E.M. (2014), *Higher Education Policy Convergence and the Bologna Process: A Cross-National Study*, Basingstoke: Palgrave Macmillan.

Warleigh-Lack, A. and van Langenhove, L. (2010), 'Rethinking EU studies: the contribution of comparative regionalism', *European Integration*, **32**(6), 541–561.

Westerheijden, D., Beerkens, E., Cremonini, L., Huisman, J., Kehm, B., et al. (2009), 'The first decade of working on the European Higher Education Area. European Commission', accessed 12 November 2011 at http://www.ond.vlaanderen.be/hogeronderwijs/bologna/2010_conference/documents/IndependentAssessment_executive_summary_overview_conclusions.pdf.

Zgaga, P. (2006), *Looking Out: The Bologna Process in a Global Setting. On the 'External Dimension' of the Bologna Process*, Oslo: Norwegian Ministry of Education and Research.

3. Erasmus Mundus and the EU: intrinsic sectoral regionalism in higher education
Roger Dale*

INTRODUCTION

There is a very wide range of literature that addresses the nature and impact of a range of claims to, and strategies for, the construction of a European regional form of higher education (HE). However, the intention and purpose of this chapter is not to draw attention to the heterogeneity of institutions and practices carried out in the name of HE regionalism. Instead, the approach taken in this chapter problematizes these different representations and performances of European HE, which effectively assume and construct quite different conceptions of Europe and of regions, even in such a small field as higher education. It does this by setting them against what is the most intrinsically European project in the area of HE, Erasmus Mundus ('Erasmus' is the European Region Action Scheme for the Mobility of University Students). Originally launched in 2004, and still in operation, Erasmus Mundus will be taken as an extreme case[1] of regionalism. By 'intrinsically European', I mean not just in its purpose but also in its design, and especially the forms of governance through which it is shaped and delivered, which are irreducibly (European) regional and (HE) sectoral rather than international, or 'cross-member'.

The chapter is based on intensive research into the origins and development of the Erasmus Mundus programme, on archival research, and interviews with key figures in the programme's development. It will seek to sketch in the wider contexts from which the programme emerged and was developed, discuss briefly some of its major features, and conclude by outlining the distinctive features of its governance and the nature of its contributions. It will be suggested that these features collectively add up to the European Commission (EC) acting as a region for itself, rather than a region in itself.

The chapter first looks at the claim to uniqueness of the Erasmus

Mundus (EM) programme. It then discusses the wider political contexts of HE in Europe in which the EM emerged – what made it *desirable* – which shaped the terrain it was to occupy. This is followed by a brief account of what made it *possible*; that is, how various elements and mechanisms of governance were assembled to construct a new, irreducibly regional, programme at the regional level. The chapter then analyses the nature and implications of the governance of the programme, in terms of its funding, provision, regulation, implementation and ownership, and of the nature and distribution of its benefits across its various constituencies.

A UNIQUE PROGRAMME

The claim to uniqueness of the Erasmus Mundus programme can be established by comparing it with the two main institutional and programmatic icons of HE regionalism – the Bologna Process and the Erasmus mobility programme – and also with the European Commission's broader policy for HE. In a nutshell, the argument is that whilst it is widely, readily, and correctly, acknowledged that both Bologna and Erasmus have clear and necessary European origins and scope, and despite their considerable differences from each other, the role and place of Europe in both cases is as a space of, and for, the promotion and coordination of joint activity between members. In both cases, Europe provides the geographical and political arena for a shared institutional infrastructure as the basis for individual member state benefit, without infringing the treaty status of education (as a national responsibility). The broader ambition driving both Erasmus and Bologna – again in very different ways – is the establishment of a European Higher Education Area, which might also act as a model of intra- and inter-regional cooperation.

The first and best-known European project aimed at extending a sense of common regional attachment across at least the university students of Europe was the Erasmus programme of European Union (EU)-subsidized academic (student and staff) mobility, which has often been trumpeted as the most popular EU programme ever. Erasmus's main purpose has always been the construction of European identity through the modality of intra-European mobility programmes. The experience of living and studying in other European countries was seen as a key means of augmenting young people's understanding – and practising – what it means to be European. Most importantly in this context, it created a precedent for Community funding of student and academic mobility.

By contrast, the Bologna Process is an international agreement, between European countries, whose membership is not confined to EU members (see Melo, Chapter 2 in this volume). It can be seen as constructing a model of regional governance of HE that can be transferred on a region-to-region basis as a means of a constructing a framework of equivalences between EU and other regional organizations. This could both reduce transaction costs, and act as a means of opposing and curbing the power and attraction of the United States system. It is governed by the Bologna Follow-Up Group (BFUG), of which the European Commission is an important and influential member (see Robertson et al., Chapter 1 in this volume). It covers a number of aspects of higher education, with formal rules through a quality assurance framework. Countries' adherence to the Bologna Process is monitored by the BFUG. Its major aim was the creation of a European Higher Education Area, which it achieved and celebrated by 2010. It has an increasing extra-European presence based originally on the development of its 'external dimension', which acts as a means of extending its scope and influence through the development of associations such as Bologna Global. This very brief account does indicate that Bologna's chief aim and purpose is extending the space of European influence on HE globally; as Melo (Chapter 2 in this volume) also points out.

A third element of the context consists of the European Commission's policy proposals for HE (see Dale, 2005). These were largely contained in three major Communications in the 2000s, which focused very heavily on the need for enhanced contributions from the HE sector to economic growth, in very hortatory tones. Here, problems are identified as national, and solutions as (necessarily) regional, for the purpose of HE regionalism is to extend and intensify HE's contribution to Europe as an economic region.

Although EM shares many of the aims of both programmes, its substance and modus operandi represent a very significant departure from them. That difference can be captured most effectively by seeing it as inhering in its intrinsically European substance and form of governance. It was designed and framed by, and is governed by, the European Commission, and the nature and consequences of this can be substantiated through a very brief sketch of the nature of EM as a programme.[2]

The major strand of the Erasmus Mundus is based on providing two-year Masters degree programmes for 'third country' (that is, non-EU, rather than 'Third World') graduates, whose academic, travel and subsistence costs are covered through the provision of scholarships by the Commission. The crucial 'Europeanizing' element is that these courses are to be provided by consortia of three universities from different EU countries, with scholarship students spending parts of the period of study in at least two different universities of the consortium. All European universities are eligible to take part in bids to be part of consortia and to provide such programmes.

However, the key governance and processual basis of the programme is that the European substance mentioned above inheres in the fact that the contracts for the successful applicant consortia are agreed between each separate consortium and the European Commission. One consequence of this process is that, national governments have effectively very little involvement in the process; nevertheless, while there have been different responses to the programme from different national ministries, most notably in the case of fees, no member state has prevented its universities from taking part. The programme is, then, essentially governed in what can be understood as a non-national, irreducibly European regional sectoral space.

THE CONTEXTS OF ERASMUS MUNDUS: WHAT MADE IT DESIRABLE?

It is useful here to consider both the demand- and the supply-side framing of the conditions that led to the emergence of Erasmus Mundus. The demand for such a programme was rooted in a very particular set of circumstances. The challenges framing the problems that EM would address were those brought into prominence by the EU's Lisbon Agenda, and possibly more directly and in different ways by the Sorbonne Declaration and the initiation of the Bologna Process, both of whose objectives included enhancing the global competitiveness of European HE.

From the supply side, its history can be traced back to earlier Commission initiatives in higher education, especially the Erasmus programme. The familiarity of the name, and its association with one of the Commission's most popular initiatives, seems to have been very useful in enabling EM's very rapidly apparent wide acceptability. At least equally importantly for what would become EM, the 'Erasmus programme set a precedent for the mechanism of incentive funding to stimulate student exchanges, (through which, in the case of Erasmus) the Community [was enabled to] encourage(d) [sic] individual academics to set up networks' (Corbett, 2004: 11).

Both these elements were to become crucial in the development of EM. Corbett also notes that the Erasmus Declaration 'insisted that there should be academic recognition for the diplomas involved and for periods of study spent abroad' (Corbett, 2004). This, too, of course, relied on EC coordination, providing an entrée for the Commission into areas of national discretion from which it had until then been excluded. The original Erasmus programme, then, removed potential obstacles to EM by providing precedents for a central coordinating role for the Commission in academic mobility programmes, and for particular mechanisms that EM would adopt – especially incentive funding that followed students and encouraged academics to operate in networks.

We may then conclude that the EU's political response to globalization and neoliberalism, via Lisbon, Sorbonne and Bologna, shaped the context from which EM emerged in three main ways. First, Sorbonne and Bologna provided the context of a perceived urgent need to improve and internationalize Europe's universities, and to provide instruments for bringing them closer together, which EM could develop and extend. Second, Lisbon supplied the broader political economic aims that were to steer all EU activity over the first decade of the new millennium (though this was radically reoriented in 2005, and later in 2010), and in particular prioritizing the need to enhance the competitiveness of European higher education. Third, together they provided a major opportunity for Commission intervention in the HE sector, essentially through its ability to fund activities such as, eventually, a significant amount of Bologna Process activity, and via EM.

These broad concerns became the object of considerable brainstorming within the Directorate General of Education and Culture (DGEAC). This eventually resulted in their commissioning the Academic Cooperation Association (ACA),[3] with which DGEAC had considerable previous experience of cooperation, 'to provide the European Commission with recommendations concerning a coherent future European Union cooperation policy with non-Union countries ("third countries") in the field of education and training, which would contribute to enhance the quality of education and training inside the Union' (Reichert and Wachter, 2001: 1).

The basic aim was to produce 'a set of recommendations for future EU third country cooperation, as a result of a comparison of present EU practice in third country cooperation with the international state of the art' (ibid.: 14), which would 'contribute to the formulation of a future EU third country cooperation policy which would respond in a coherent and meaningful way to the challenges posed by the ongoing process of economic globalization and the need for an enhancement of the quality of education and training inside the Union' (ibid.: 11).

Some of the main 'systemic measures', 'aimed at improving the general framework conditions for the third country cooperation of European higher education institutions', proposed in the report, clearly constituted a basis for the conceptualization of EM:

- to encourage Europe's higher education institutions to better promote themselves and their services globally through a variety of measures,

amongst them the marketing of genuinely European 'flagship products' (joint/double degrees developed through SOCRATES/ERASMUS . . .) . . .
- to face the challenge of 'transnational education' by supporting the creation and development of European educational alliances and their products which would be competitive on a global scale. (Reichert and Wachter, 2001: 10–11)

The most directly relevant recommendation was that, in the wake of the Sorbonne and Bologna declarations:

Institutions of higher education are now challenged to . . . create Masters Degrees in environments where there were no short, or separate, programmes at this level in order to meet the needs and expectations of the mobile students from the rest of Europe and the world. The main benefit one would expect from the development of such independent master's courses would be to have a much wider redistribution of students entering the postgraduate level than we currently have, which could also pave the way for a new type of mobility. (Reichert and Wachter, 2001: 41)

Interestingly, what became EM could be seen as a product of the marriage of the last two recommendations: the formation of European educational alliances, and the creation of specific Masters degrees for students from the rest of the world as well as from Europe. The first seeks to go beyond national to international (intra-EU) provision, and the second calls for intrinsically European-governed projects of a quite different kind from Bologna, and associated with the kinds of mobility found in the Erasmus programme.

THE CONTEXTS OF ERASMUS MUNDUS: WHAT MADE IT POSSIBLE?

While the ACA report thus provided both a clear warrant for action in the field of international higher education and a digest of what was already available, and also foreshadowed some of the directions it might take, that was only the beginning of the story. A small team was assembled in DGEAC to develop the proposal, and it was also building up support within the Commission. In addition, it received the support of the European University Association (EUA) and individual university rectors who had been consulted (Informant Interview 1), leading the same informant to suggest that 'it was [seen as] an idea whose time was right'.

One further comment that might be seen as having presaged key features of the eventual EM programme came from the Communiqué of the Prague BFUG meeting in 2001, which suggested that:

In order to further strengthen the important European dimensions of higher education and graduate employability Ministers called upon the higher education sector to increase the development of modules, courses and curricula at all levels with 'European' content, orientation or organization. This concerns particularly modules, courses and degree curricula offered in partnership by institutions from different countries and leading to a recognized joint degree. (European Ministers of Education, 2001)

Further impulsion came in the form of a European Commission Communication on Strengthening Cooperation with Third Countries in the Field of Higher Education (European Commission, 2001). This Communication effectively signalled an intention on the part of DGEAC to develop and advance the work of the ACA report. The communication had a double agenda: developing university exchanges between the Community and third countries; and promoting the Community as a centre of excellence attracting more students, teachers and researchers from those countries.

Most significantly, the Communication was jointly launched by the Commissioner for Education, Viviane Reding, and the Commissioner for External Relations, Chris Patten. Patten's presence was extremely important, and possibly crucial, in the history of EM. He was keen to devolve some of the activities of his Directorate to 'thematic' Directorates, such as Education (Informant Interviews 1 and 3; former DGEAC officials), and this 'quite deliberate nod towards Education' (Informant Interview 1) lent powerful support to the idea of educational cooperation with third countries. Indeed Patten's interest eventually became the basis of the external windows element of EM, as indicated below.

In concrete terms, the Communication (EC, 2001: 4) put forward a twofold strategy: 'develop[ing] high quality human resources in partner countries and within the EC, through reciprocal human resource development, and promot[ing] the EC as a world-wide centre of excellence for study/training as well as for scientific and technological research'. One way of doing this is 'To promote, in conjunction with the Member States, the Union's teaching and training assets by concentrating on third countries which have a high proportion of prospective exchange [sic] applicants' (EC, 2001: 4).

Whilst this document does frame, and foreshadows, some of what was to follow in EM, it does not do so in a detailed way. Its real importance lay in the acceptance and promotion of the idea that European higher education could benefit from having a role to play in developing high-quality human resources in third countries through teaching as well as research, and placing that objective very firmly on the agenda of DGEAC.

One further important feature was the external political climate. A key

Table 3.1 Roles in the governance of the EU Erasmus Mundus programme, 2004–2008

Activities Actors	Funding	Provision	Regulation	Implementation	Ownership	Benefits
EU	Scholarships contribution to administrative costs of consortia	Programme administration	Programme as a whole	Programme management (comitology)	Overall	Prestige; 'soft power': thickened inter-regionality, via Erasmus Mundus Alumni Association (EMA) funding student living costs
Member states	Wider university activities					
Individual universities	Additional fees (in some cases)	Wider institutional services	Individual degree rules	Contribution to course	Within consortium	Prestige; access to good international students: enabling viability of existing courses
University consortia	Admin costs above €15 000 (2004)	EM course construction and details	Contract between consortium and EU: joint degree rules	Courses; consortium management; student support	Contract consortium/EU	Prestige; networking
Individuals	Non-funded costs	Cooperative involvement; feedback	Feedback	Involvement at course level, and via EMA	Via EMA	International degrees from three European universities; EMA membership and activities

72

element here was the events of September 11, 2001 which in the opinion of one former senior official of DGEAC 'changed everything' in terms of the climate for EM. It clearly enhanced sensitivity to what was happening outside Europe, and in particular led to an increased emphasis on the importance on promoting cultural understanding. This was especially strongly supported by the President of the European Commission, Romano Prodi (Interview 1 with former DGEAC official, who also suggested that tough negotiations about the fledgling EM with DG Budget may have been resolved in favour of the EM proposal as a result of 'a political signal from on high'). The whole process thus took place against the backdrop of the renewed impetus given by the European Commission to the dialogue between peoples and cultures, placing it among high political priorities, and the recognition of the potential of cooperation in higher education in promoting understanding and tolerance.

A second significant climate was that within the Directorate General for Education itself. Here, the idea did have the strong support of the DGEAC Commissioner Viviane Reding and her cabinet, who 'needed a high profile political project' (Interview 1 with former DGEAC official) and were attracted by one with an external dimension and which advanced the possibility of a European Masters degree. I have already noted the particularly important support of External Relations and its Commissioner, Chris Patten. This was to take a more concrete form in shape of money earmarked by DG RELEX for projects in India and China becoming the basis of the funding 'windows' that greatly supplemented DGEAC funding of EM, and put it on a 'region-to-region' basis.[4]

Finally, the climate in the academic community turned out to be positive and propitious. This may have occurred for a number of reasons. One was that the higher education sector, and individual universities, were feeling increasingly starved of funds and were being forced to look wherever they could for new sources of income especially for research, where funding was becoming much more concentrated and important, leading to much more funding for far fewer universities and people. The second reason is that the regime proposed for EM, with transnational networks and consortia at its heart, was one that many universities and academics had become used to, enjoyed, and benefited from, through the Framework Programmes.

THE ERASMUS MUNDUS PROPOSAL

The details of the Erasmus Mundus programme were based on three basic arguments, centring on regional influence, regional attractiveness and regional commerciality. The argument went something like this:

- in an era of globalization, Europe's response to emerging needs in higher education could not be confined only to the geographical limits of the European Union or the wider Europe; and
- following the Bologna Declaration, Europe's higher education sector must acquire a degree of attractiveness equal to Europe's cultural and scientific achievements, and be made known to students from Europe and other parts of the world; the sector's potential to contribute to the Europe of knowledge should be further exploited through its synergies with the European Research Area; as a result,
- higher education is becoming globalized through both its contributions to development and its commercial potential (EC, 2002).

A key point in the proposal is that:

> European higher education institutions have so far failed to combine individual strengths, educational diversity and wide experience in networking to offer courses unique to Europe and of world class and which would enable the benefits of international mobility simultaneously to be maximized and shared more widely within the EC and partner countries. (EC, 2002: 4)

This might be taken as the essence of 'the European HE offer' that fulfils the aims of EM to improve the quality and embed the identity of European HE and to make it more attractive globally, while recognizing that 'Europe's political and commercial success in the world is dependent on future decision-makers in third countries having a better understanding of, and closer ties with, Europe' (ibid.). Indeed, this argument gets to the core of the shift from European HE as a sector in itself, to a sector for itself.

What Made Erasmus Mundus Intrinsically European?

The argument here is that EM's uniqueness and significance can be explained in terms of the combinations of activities and agents of its governance. Here, I draw on an approach developed in the education field by Dale (1997). This presented a governance diagram based on the interaction of two axes: the activities of education governance, which were reduced to the categories of funding, provision, regulation and ownership; and the agents of education governance, classified into state, market, community and household, which are involved (typically in combination) in carrying out those activities. I have extended and specified the categories of both actors and activities for the case of the governance of EM, which produces Table 3.1, enabling the identification, at a very broad level, of the (unique) pattern of forms of governance represented in EM.

Funding

One of the most conspicuous features of EM is that the EC is the overwhelmingly dominant source of its funding. Most of that funding goes into the scholarships provided to EM students. EM can then be seen as an example of *trans*national funding of *sub*national institutions (the members of the consortia) that operate *inter*nationally. And of course, this funding is at the core of the incentive structure that is the source of the EC's control over the programme and its mechanisms. However, the Commission is not the sole funder of EM. Each consortium may set a common tuition fee. One consequence of this is that the value of EM scholarships to the student varies across consortia.

At the same time, the majority of higher education institutions (HEIs) participating in the programme considered the amount of €15000 per year for each EM Consortium to cover the cost of administering Masters courses as 'failing to reflect the true cost of administering a fully integrated high quality transnational Master, notwithstanding the lack of any reporting mechanism' (European Commission, 2007: x), which clearly represents an additional funding contribution from the consortium.

However, this may also have been compensated somewhat by the fees received from non-EM students on courses designed for EM students, while there is evidence from some universities that the addition of EM students to an existing programme clinched the programme's viability. There is no direct contribution from member state governments, although it is, of course, clear that the universities providing the EM courses could not exist without funding from their states. The crucial importance of the EU funding is underlined by the fact that while the first batch of funded courses were all considered academically sustainable, none could be sustained beyond the duration of the funding period (one attempted to do so, but was unsuccessful) (see EACEA, 2012).

Provision

Courses are devised, managed and implemented by the consortia consisting of at least three higher education institutions from different eligible countries (EU members, European Economic Area – EEA, candidate members), with at least one partner from a EU member state. Partners from 'third countries' are also eligible. In terms of Table 3.1, provision of EM courses is carried out at subnational levels (by individual university members of the consortium) and coordinated at an international scale by consortium members.

The consortium is a key element of the delivery of EM courses. The required composition of members goes some way to ensuring that the benefits of membership go beyond the 'usual suspects'; one central aim of EM was to address the dominance of France, Germany and the United Kingdom (UK) in internationalizing HE. In fact, evidence from the Interim Evaluation of the first phase of EM shows that from 2004 to 2006 approximately 1 in 7 applications were successful. In that time, France, Spain, the UK, Germany and Italy collectively accounted for 55 per cent of all HEIs involved in Action 1 EM Masters consortia. This compares with approximately 1 per cent for Estonia, Slovenia and Slovakia combined.

A key feature of EM provision was that the various consortia programmes did not concentrate on, or cluster around, European issues to any great degree. Although some courses focused on aspects of Europe, the overall programme could be seen not so much as teaching a European curriculum as demonstrating that Europe can provide first-class graduate courses across a very wide range of subjects, while building cadres of scholars committed and able to act as ambassadors for Europe. Consortia, thereby, both constitute European value added in their composition, and construct it through their activities. And collectively, the range of EM offerings could be seen to demonstrate and embellish the scope and attractiveness of the European Higher Education Area (EHEA).

The selection of courses to be included in the EM programme, and of the students who will receive scholarships to follow the courses, presents an intriguing balance of strategies. On the one hand, selecting the students who are to receive EM scholarships is a key role of the consortium to whom potential students must apply. The selection of courses is the responsibility of the Commission. It requires the development of a joint programme, with common – or at least compatible – curricula, pedagogy and assessment. This is at the core of the provision element of EM. While the consortia provide all the trappings of the courses to be followed, they do so under strict rules, laid down by the Commission, which they are effectively taught by the Commission, and in the neglect of which they will be declared ineligible. Evaluation of eligible courses is carried out through two stages. The first involves evaluation by subject experts, and the second comprises selection from those recommended by subject experts by the EM Selection Committee, which is made up of senior figures with wide experience of HE in Europe, either as politicians (the committee includes a number of former national ministers of education) or as senior academic leaders.

One further, particularly important, element of the funding of EM is that the EC funds the Erasmus Mundus Alumni Association (EMA), which is based on a wide range of regional chapters. This enables the extension of the reach of the programme in an additional, 'diplomatic' direction, with graduates expected to take part in promotional activities. This was to a degree anticipated from the start of the programme by a former Director of Education at DGEAC, who pointed out that in respect of Erasmus Mundus:

> The educational aims are obvious; but the potential political gain is obvious too, and it is that which motivates a number of our Member States to support it. So, if our internal programmes are currently running at cruising speed, education is taking on a diplomatic role it did not have before, and growing with it. (Coyne, 2004: 18)

Regulation

The central issues at stake here revolve around the questions of: which body regulates what, and according to which rules? The 'what' question is crucial here: it is clearly not national higher education systems that are being regulated. EM has little direct effect on national HE policies, which are, of course, formally a national responsibility, and not an area where the Commission has discretion (notwithstanding its significant role as a member of the Bologna Follow-Up Group). The answer to the crucial 'what' question is a *distinct subsector* that has been created by the EC in the interstices of transnational, national and institutional policies in a unique, shared, institutional regulatory space. It affects the cross-national collectivities of institutions that it has created and that to a degree depend on there being others also involved for them to be involved, for the idea to be possible; to have EM in one country is not possible.

Some of the key issues involved have also been identified by Ase Gornitzka et al. (2007: 31). She writes:

> There are also legal side effects ensuing from university participation in EU education programs. These are not instances where the national legal and regulatory order is penetrated by the legal system developed at the European level, but where such changes are implications of European integration
>
> The case of joint Master degree programmes selected by the EC's Erasmus Mundus initiative is a telling example of this. These programmes operate in a grey zone between national legal frameworks and European-level integration ambitions. National participation in the establishment of a joint Masters degree programme and the issuing of joint diplomas have de facto implied regulation changes at national level and changes in local rules. This is a consequence of an indirect pressure on national regulations from the institutions that are participating in this scheme, as well as from the Commission and transnational actors, notably the European University Association (EUA) that actively promotes the

development of joint degree programmes, amongst other things, as part of its participation in the Bologna process. (Gornitzka et al., 2007: 32)

What this suggests is that in a sense national legislations may have been presented with a fait accompli, in that it was difficult on the one hand not to recognize the potential benefits of EM, and on the other, to find convincing obstacles to put in its way. Indeed, the Interim Evaluation of the first EM programmes suggested that 'the absence of a legal framework does not appear to have been a significant inhibiting factor to participating in EM since in countries such as Sweden and the Netherlands, where there is not currently the possibility of issuing joint degrees, there are high participation rates in Erasmus Mundus' (European Commission, 2007: 12).

The Interim Evaluation also indicated that potential involvement in EM has also:

> had a positive impact on those EU countries where there was previously no legal framework for the accreditation of joint, double or multiple degrees involving partners in different EU countries. Even where joint degree accreditation problems remain, EM Masters Courses have implemented effective double or multiple degree structures that have permitted genuine integration and co-operative study to take place. Joint degrees also help make the EU labour market more transparent and accessible to European students. (EC, 2007: iii)

The fundamental mechanism in the regulation of EM, however, is that the basic contract upon which it rests is constructed between the Commission and the providing consortia. This perhaps locates EM not so much in a 'grey zone' as in a new and distinct space of regional educational governance, created by the Commission.

Ownership

The question of the ownership of the programme is quite as complex. At one level, the overall programme is clearly a product of, and owned by, the Commission. However, the individual EM programmes are owned by the consortia who designed them (as is evident in the possibility that they could continue without EC funding), while the contributions of the members of the consortia might be seen as elements of their intellectual property (albeit enabled by their individual universities). Thus there is multiple but fragmented ownership of the programme, with all elements necessary, but not sufficient. Hence, ownership is not reducible to any of the partners, but is enabled and coordinated by the EC. Some of the ways in which this occurs are evident in the ways that the programme was implemented and evaluated.

Implementation and Evaluation

Such fragmented ownership could create problems of implementation and evaluation, but in fact this seems to have been one of the more straightforward aspects of the programme. This is because these issues became subjects of the comitology[5] procedures, with the Education, Audiovisual and Culture Executive Agency (EACEA) as the executive agency responsible for its administration and management, making and enforcing its rules. The EACEA was in a sense the public face of EM; it was the first point of contact for applicants (both potential consortia and potential students) and set out the rules and procedures under which they could become affiliated to the programme. It was to the EACEA that EM consortia were responsible for carrying out their contributions to the programme, and who carried out evaluations of them. However, as might be expected of responsibility for such roles, it is in the areas of definition, administration and management that the most apparent criticisms of the programme are to be found.

Beneficiaries

Finally, it is important to ask who benefited from the programme, and how. Overall, it is clear that Europe has benefited from the prestige which the programme generates, and its contribution to the attractiveness of European HE. This is not confined to the academic success of the programme, though the opportunity to work in a consortium of like-minded colleagues is very positive. At the level of individual universities, the ability to attract outstanding graduate students has been a clear bonus, especially perhaps through the possibility of earning joint graduate degrees from consortia of European universities. However, there seem to be few benefits accruing to national education systems, beyond those accruing to the programme as a whole, though it is clear that the profile of some HE systems has been lifted in some cases.

Individual universities have been, in a sense, 'secondhand' beneficiaries of the programme, essentially benefiting from the success of the programme as a whole, and especially of the consortium of which they are part, and which they have been involved in supporting, administratively, academically and financially. Involvement in the programme can enhance their prestige, and not only in the areas relevant to the courses they are involved in.

Students

Fundamentally, what EM provides for students is the academic, social and cultural capitals that are embedded in the programme. However, it is very easy to take for granted the ways in which such opportunities may be valorized, for instance through an assumption that the embedded cultural capital accruing from the programme will be recognized and rewarded, for instance by employers, quasi-automatically. What I want to suggest here is that such conversion cannot be taken for granted, or seen as a natural outcome of the programme, but is better seen as produced by particular forms of social organization, and in particular, social capital and networks which are intrinsic to the programme. In this case, one might argue that EM itself provides the crucial conversion factor, through at least three levels. First of all, EM is not only intrinsically a unique European network, but more importantly in this context, one that is given deeper substance and extended opportunity by EU funding of the Erasmus Mundus Alumni Association. In a very real sense, then, the EU provides not only the incentives but also a network to help realize them in a range of forms.

Second, it is a unique form of degree, backed up by the prestigious nature of the programme. More than that, it is not left to speak for itself: it also needed to be recognized – which it was, for instance through other EU activities boosting its importance and success. And third, it is a programme that is experienced as part of a multinational, multicultural group, from whose collective cultural capital each individual benefits. The network thus delivers two effects: one from the extension of the value of the support it provides, and the other from its existence as a network that may in itself have desirable attributes to which each individual member can offer access.

Consortia Members

The consortia members are able to valorize EM through the mechanism of the double value of the networks they are part of, for instance including membership of the programme itself. They both contribute to and benefit from the European basis of the programme. Beyond the institutional and national prestige that come with EM selection and participation, and the experience of novel forms of collaboration, they are exposed to more international arenas, and to more opportunities of networking. In addition, as I have already noted, even the consortia whose applications were not successful are being 'educated' in this particular form of European cooperation. According to the *Ex Post Evaluation*, 'the process of establishing and implementing EMMCs [Erasmus Mundus Masters Courses] appears to have strengthened a twin process of "Europeanization" on the supply side [as higher education institutions from different countries worked together] and "internationalization" on the demand side (as institutions sought to attract more students from abroad and respond to their needs)' (Ecotec, 2009: v).

The European Commission

For the EC, the valorized benefits are even greater than for the other two parties, because all the benefits they accrue also increase the aggregate benefit of the EC. They are, in a sense, the return to the EC on its very considerable investment in the programme, and they contribute powerfully to the basis of success of the programme, and its vindication as a novel form of HE regional collaboration. More specifically, first, EM does appear to have been successful in achieving the first objective of the programme, to improve the quality of European HE (this cannot be taken for granted as an outcome of the programme; it contained a number of novel elements), as shown, for instance by the increasing number of applications from consortia of universities, and the rising percentage of them deemed eligible for selection.

Second, it has enabled much greater access for the EC to influence over university curricula, setting rules for the consortia that both stretch national rules and constitute the basis which future consortia will have to follow. Through requiring all applicants to follow the same complex and demanding procedures, it has also been able to 'socialize' even those institutions which were not successful in the competition. It has been able to set up a further generation of European networks, greater than and different from the sum of their national parts, and quantitatively and qualitatively different from earlier HE networks such as the Socrates thematic networks.

And third, it seems well set to achieve the broader objective, referred to by David Coyne (2004: 18), of contributing to Europe's public diplomacy, especially through its sponsorship of the EMA, and its ambition to create European (rather than national) 'ambassadors'; that the EMA is organized on a regional basis greatly strengthens the inter-regional aspect of the cooperation. It appears to be considered a mark of prestige, and its popularity with potential providers seems to have remained high, not least in the kinds of inter-institutional networking opportunities it has opened up.

CONCLUSIONS

The main purpose of this chapter has been to show how and with what consequences the EM programme can be seen as an intrinsic, and irreducibly regional, programme in HE. As such, it represents an extreme case of forms of HE regionalism, which can stand as a template against which the 'regionality' of other programmes may be compared. Three main sets of conclusion can be drawn from this chapter.

The first is that the claim that EM represents a distinct form of 'irreducibly regional' HE can be sustained on the basis of the evidence. The second is that methodologically this 'extreme case' approach may provide us with a new governance analysis tool, and means of refocusing on what we understand by governance. Taken together, these point to different ways of developing regional HE programmes.

In terms of the first of these, the arguments presented here resonate with arguments about the nature and significance of 'regionalism for itself'. This rests on the dual claims that, on the one hand, this is implicit in the assumption of regional irreducibility, and on the other that the region is the main beneficiary, as the region's global reach and influence is extended in and through a particular programme, which extends both its institutional 'thickness' and its political reach. As far as the EU involvement is concerned, it may be useful to consider the forms of power that it is based on and able to deploy, in this case using Lukes's (1993) three faces of power approach. One might say that the EU's capacity to shape preferences (third face) is in this case both very intense and extensive, as it is able both to set criteria of involvement, and to select the programmes for funding; this is to do with the power of the purse (Batory and Lindstorm, 2011), but is by no means confined to it. Alongside this flows the power to set the agenda (second face) very precisely, in the form of the structure, governance, organization and evaluation of the programme. And in terms of decision-making (first face), as we have seen, it is able to deploy the power of comitology in controlling the conditions of implementation.

In terms of the second, the approach through the method of combining actors and activities of governance does enable the development of greater clarity in locating the bases of the institutional process, and outcome, in terms of distribution of benefits, of forms and practices of HE governance that contribute to the development of an aspect of 'region-ness for itself'. The significance here comes not in the form of possible emulation, but as a case that reveals the limitations of key elements of 'typical' – unrecognized and understudied – assumptions about regions, for instance those revealed through Table 3.1 linking benefits to processes of governance. Furthermore, these benefits are to a degree cumulative, for the 'local' benefits – to consortia and students – also act as elements of, and contribute to, the regional success. The regional organization is the main beneficiary, and the programme represents an opportunity for the extension of the EU's political and diplomatic reach. The case of EM illustrates the possibility of intrinsically sectoral regionalism, in HE.

NOTES

* This chapter draws on work carried out under the UK ESRC project, LLAKES (Learning and Life Chances in Knowledge Economies and Societies) Project number RES-594-28-0001.
1. By 'extreme case', I mean a case which, by highlighting particular unusual elements of an area of investigation, enables us to shed light on the 'normal', or typical case. In this instance, my intention is to draw attention to aspects of regional HE governance that might otherwise remain taken for granted. Here, focusing on the irreducibility of the governance of EM may enable problematizing regional HE governance in different, and productive, ways.
2. It should be noted that this account is based on the experience of the first phase of the programme, which ran from 2004 to 2008. It also focuses mainly on Action 1 of the programme, Erasmus Mundus Masters courses (the other actions are: Action 2 – scholarships for third-country students; Action 3 – partnerships with third-country HEIs; Action 4 – awareness-raising projects for the worldwide promotion of European HE. The programme was modified somewhat in its second phase (2009–2013), particularly in the addition of a Doctoral strand, and the eligibility of EU-based students for EM.
3. The Academic Cooperation Association (ACA) is a federation of national organizations from Europe and beyond – including the British Council, the German Academic Exchange Service (Deutscher Akademischer Austauschdienst; DAAD) and EduFrance – which all fund and encourage the internationalization of their higher education systems.
4. In addition to the core EM programme budget, additional funding of €57 million was made available through the 'Asian windows' programme. The 'windows' are financial envelopes from the Community's external relations budget, which provide additional financing for students and scholars from Asian countries to study on an EM Masters course in the EU. The following Asian windows were set up: the China Pilot Window €9 million (2005–2007), the India Window €33 million (2005–2007), the Thailand Window €3.2 million (2005–2006), and the Malaysia Window €2.1 million (2005–2006). A further €10 million was provided for an 'Other Asian Countries' window (DG EAC, 2007: 11, 22).
5. The term 'comitology' is shorthand for the way the Commission exercises the implementing powers conferred on it by the EU legislator, with the assistance of committees of representatives from the EU member states (http://ec.europa.eu/transparency/regcomitology/index.cfm?do=FAQ.FAQ). It is essentially the EU's means of implementing and managing programmes that have been agreed. EM has its own comitology committee. 'The following measures necessary for the implementation of the programme and of the other actions of this Decision shall be adopted in accordance with the management procedure referred to in Article 8(2) in accordance with the principles, general guidelines and selection criteria laid down in the Annex: (a) the annual plan of work, including priorities; (b) the annual budget, the breakdown of funds among the different actions of the programme, and indicative grant amounts; (c) the application of the general guidelines for implementing the programme, including the selection criteria as laid down in the Annex; (d) the selection procedures, including the composition and the internal rules of procedure of the selection board; (e) the arrangements for monitoring and evaluating the programme and for the dissemination and transfer of results. The selection decisions shall be taken by the Commission, which shall inform the European Parliament and the Committee referred to in Article 8(1) thereof within two working days.'

REFERENCES

Batory, A. and Lindstrom, N., (2011), 'The power of the purse: Supranational entrepreneurship, financial incentives, and European higher education policy'. *Governance*, **24**(2), 311–29.
Corbett, A. (2004), 'Europeanisation and the Bologna Process: a preliminary to a British study', paper presented to conference co-sponsored by the ESRC and UACES, Sheffield Town Hall, 16 July.
Coyne, D. (2004), 'From regional integration to global outreach: the education policies of the European Commission', in Wächter, B. (ed.), *Higher Education in a Changing Environment: Internationalisation of Higher Education Policy in Europe*, Bonn: Lemmens, pp. 13–24.
Dale, R. (1997), 'The state and the governance of education: an analysis of the restructuring of the state–education relationship', in Halsey, A.H., Lauder, H., Brown, P. and Wells, A. (eds), *Education, Culture, Economy and Society*, Oxford: Oxford University Press, pp. 273–282.
Dale, R. (2005), 'Globalisation, knowledge economy and comparative education', *Comparative Education*, **41**(2), 117–149.
Directorate-General Education and Culture (DG EAC) (2007), 'Interim evaluation of Erasmus Mundus – case studies', Centre for Strategy and Evaluation Services, Brussels: European Commission, available at http://ec.europa.eu/smart-regulation/evaluation/search/download.do;jsessionid=H0tpTTWGmxWGgRW0TwPnm2119pLqqYQg6xFZPJWJ2RyLBKbp512F!1601440011?documentId=703 (accessed 23 April 2016).
EACEA (2012), 'Experience and lessons learned from first generation of EMMC: EACEA Synthesis Evaluation Report', Brussels: EACEA.
Ecotec (2009), *Ex Post Evaluation of Erasmus Mundus: A Final Report to DGEAC*, Brussels.
European Commission (EC) (2001), *Communication on Strengthening Cooperation with Third Countries in the Field of Higher Education*, Brussels, 18.7.2001 COM (2001) 385 final.
European Commission (EC) (2002), *Proposal for a European Parliament and Council Decision Establishing a Programme for the Enhancement of Quality in Higher Education and the Promotion of Intercultural Understanding through Co-operation with Third Countries (Erasmus World) (2004–2008)*, COM/2002/0401 final – COD 2002/0165, *Official Journal* 331 E, 31/12/2002 P. 0025 – 0049.
European Commission (EC) (2007), *Report from the Commission to the Council, the European Parliament, the European Economic and Social Committee and the Committee of the Regions of 2 July 2007 – Report on the Interim Evaluation of the Erasmus Mundus Programme 2004–2008*, Brussels: European Commission.
European Ministers of Education (2001), 'Towards The European Higher Education Area': *Communiqué of the meeting of European Ministers in charge of Higher Education*, Prague, 19 May, Brussels: European Commission.
Gornitzka, Å., Maassen, P., Olsen, J.P. and Stensaker, B. (2007), '"Europe of Knowledge": search for a new pact', Arena Working Paper no. 3, University of Oslo.
Lukes, S. (1993), 'Three distinctive views of power compared', in Hill, M. (ed.), *The Policy Process – A Reader*, 2nd edn, Prentice Hall: London, pp. 45–52.
Reichert, S. and Wachter, B. (2001), *The Globalisation of Education and Training: Recommendations for a Coherent Response of the European Union*, Brussels: ACA.

4. Inter-regional higher education arena: the transposition of European instruments in Africa

Jean-Émile Charlier, Sarah Croché and Oana Marina Panait

INTRODUCTION

If Western countries filter global references through their national preferences, and particularly so in the education sector, this is not the case for African countries, whose references are largely drawn from the global context (Khelfaoui, 2009; Copans, 2001). African countries are developing their education policies within the framework of global references or frames, held to be universal, set out by specific norm setting instituions. The access to the definition and the negotiation of global references in education will be provided only through participation in, or membership of international organizations, such as the European Commission (EC), the United Nations Educational, Scientific and Cultural Organization (UNESCO), and the Organisation for Economic Co-operation and Development (OECD). National and local actors will no longer have influence downstream of the decision-making process. The only option left to them, when confronted with the constraints of implementation, is to use cunning to circumvent global references (Imaniriho, 2015). Attention has been drawn to the role of organizations such as the Pôle de Dakar of the International Institute for Educational Planning (IIEP-UNESCO), in the definition of educational policies in primary education in Africa (Lewandowski, 2011). This chapter looks at the ways in which global references in the higher education (HE) sector, which have impacts at global, regional and local levels, are set by organizations such as the Bologna Policy Forum and the European Commission.

Taking the Bologna Process as a case study, this chapter examines both the manner in which global normative references are disseminated in the HE sector in Africa and their future effects on the local HE landscape. The impact of the Bologna Process as a HE governance mechanism has not been limited to Europe. It has been impossible to ignore the so-called success story of the Bologna Process amongst both Western and non-Western actors (Robertson, 2010). Since 2003, the EC has been deploying an 'explicit "extra-regional" globalizing strategy' (ibid.) from which African HE institutions, faced with the risk of being excluded, cannot escape. African HE institutions are forced to undergo structural reforms, whose immediate effects are perhaps not as powerful as the longer-term effects on the local HE landscape.

Several comparative researchers have analysed the contemporary convergence patterns of HE systems, and specifically the transfer of global educational reforms and their appropriation at local level, particularly through what writers refer to as either policy-borrowing (Eta, 2015; Brøgger, 2014; Steiner-Khamsi, 2004; Phillips, 2005; Phillips and Ochs, 2003) or policy transfer (Dolowitz and Marsh, 2000). However, significant criticism can be made of the policy-borrowing approach, whose sequential analysis seems to reach an impasse when it comes to considering dynamics such as: local peculiarities: the case of developing, postcolonial and post-conflict countries; power relations in the global, national and local education arenas including the role of leading countries and the weight of international organizations and donors; and the gap between discourse and practices (Fan, 2007). This chapter departs from the two main approaches discussed above by using the Foucauldian approach of 'apparatus' (Foucault, 1994) to illustrate how global references in HE are elaborated and are recognized as unquestionable. The following three sections cover: a brief history of the institutionalization of the Bologna Process's 'external dimension'; the analysis of the reappropriation of the Bologna Process in Europe and in Africa through Foucault's (1978) concepts of 'governmentality' and 'sovereignty'; and the effects of the Bologna Process instruments on Africa, with a final concluding section.

THE INSTITUTIONALIZATION OF THE 'EXTERNAL DIMENSION' OF THE BOLOGNA PROCESS

In this section we focus our attention on the history, as well as the ongoing institutionalization, of what the Bologna Follow-Up Group (BFUG) referred to as the 'external dimension' of the Bologna Process (Zgaga, 2006).

Brief History of the External Dimension of the Bologna Process

Designed to enhance 'the attractiveness of European higher education' worldwide (Prague Communiqué; EHEA, 2001) and to organize resistance against the growing influence of United States universities (Charlier and Croché, 2009), the Bologna Process has progressively stabilized its 'domestic' and 'external' dimensions. If 1998–2001 was a period dominated by a Eurocentric perspective on the process, the following period was marked by a change of focus (Croché and Charlier, 2012; Charlier and Panait, 2015). Originally projected in order to reform and harmonize European HE systems, after 2001 the Bologna Process began to slowly capitalize on what was referred to as the 'external dimension' of the Process.

Cautiously suggested by the Prague Communiqué (EHEA, 2001), the change become explicit with the Berlin summit in 2003. The 2001 summit opened the Bologna Process only to those countries which were beneficiaries of European Community programmes, such as Socrates, Leonardo da Vinci and Tempus-Cordis (Prague Communiqué; EHEA, 2001). In 2003, however, the Berlin summit explicitly marked an evolutionary change in the Bologna Process, as the European HE ministers, for the first time, focused their attention on the 'external dimension'. The Process was to be open to the 48 countries who had signed the European Cultural Convention of the Council of Europe. The final Communiqué of the 2003 Berlin summit highlighted the European HE ministers' interest in other regions, with representatives from Latin America being invited to participate as observers (Berlin Communiqué; EHEA, 2003).

The progressive focus on the external dimension was crystallized in the 2005 summit in Bergen, and the 2007 summit in London. In Bergen, the European ministers reaffirmed that 'the European Higher Education Area must be open and should be attractive to other parts of the world' (Bergen Communiqué; EHEA, 2005). They stressed the importance of establishing cooperation and dialogue with other continents, by 'stimulating balanced student and staff exchange and cooperation between higher education institutions' (ibid.). Representatives from Australia, the International Association of Universities (IAU), the OECD and the United States (USA) also participated in this summit.

During the 2005 Bergen summit, the Bologna Follow-Up Group was asked to elaborate a clear strategy regarding the external dimension of the Process. This became concrete two years later when the European ministers gathered at the London summit and adopted the European Higher Education Area in a Global Setting strategy (London Communiqué; EHEA, 2007). At the same summit they announced that future activities would aim at 'improving information on, and promoting the attractiveness and competitiveness of, the EHEA [European Higher Education Area]; strengthening cooperation based on partnership; intensifying policy dialogue; and improving recognition' (ibid.). Partners from Australia,

Canada, Chile and New Zealand were also invited to participate in the London summit.

Another key stage in the construction of the external dimension was the creation in 2009, in Louvain-la-Neuve, of the Bologna Policy Forum, a body which demonstrated the strong commitment of European partners to establishing a space for dialogue with other regions of the world (Leuven/Louvain-la-Neuve Communiqué; EHEA, 2009). The Forum invited 46 countries, among which African countries were included for the first time, to participate in a debate on 'worldwide cooperation and partnership in higher education' (ibid.). Three follow-up forums took place in 2010, 2012 and 2015 in Vienna, Bucharest and Yerevan, where cooperation between Europe and other regions was reiterated. The Bologna Policy Forum was progressively institutionalized and opened to an even bigger number of countries (61 countries were included during the Vienna Forum; Belarus gained access in the Yerevan Forum; and partners, such as the regional university associations of each continent, during the Bucharest Forum).

Gradually Redrafting the European Higher Education Policy for Africa

The progressive institutionalization of the Bologna Process's external dimension initially went hand in hand with Europe's disregard for African countries and the lack of dialogue with these countries, whose HE systems were created as mirrors of those in Europe. As previously shown, the European partners initially targeted emerging countries of Asia and South America, 'whose economic growth is strong and which open up a wealth of commercial, financial, and industrial opportunities' (Charlier and Croché, 2009: 44).

A number of researchers have drawn attention to the initial lack of dialogue with African partners during the negotiations that preceded the elaboration of the Bologna model. Ignoring African partners has led to Europe being considered as a (new) hegemon in the global HE sector, which seeks to consolidate its influence in Africa. Similarly, the effects of the Bologna Process in Africa have been interpreted as a return to a past set of colonial relations (Charlier and Croché, 2011; Khelfaoui, 2009).

Having resolved inner conflicts, such as the control of the Bologna Process and its territorial borders, and having established new collaborations with partners from Asia and South America (Espinoza Figueroa, 2008), the EC focused also on Africa. The HE partnership with Africa began only in 2007 within the framework of the Joint Africa–European Union Strategy, and not as part of the Bologna Process. The next year, the conference on Developing Links: EU–Africa Cooperation in Higher Education through Mobility gathered representatives from African and European universities, the EC, the Commission of the African Union, and the Secretariat of the African, Caribbean and Pacific Group of States (ACP). Yet it was only in 2009, during the Bologna Policy Forum in Louvain-la-Neuve, that African partners participated for the first time in the Bologna Process follow-up ministerial conferences. The fourth Bologna Forum held in Yerevan in May 2015 focused in particular on strengthening cooperation between the EHEA and North Africa.

The French-speaking African countries were once more 'forgotten' and left out of the discussions on the future of the Bologna Process, although since 2009 a series of European HE tools have been transferred to Africa. This oversight becomes even more problematic inasmuch as the fourth EU–Africa summit, held in Brussels in May 2014, underlined that: 'In an ever changing world, one thing is sure: Africa and Europe will remain each other's closest neighbours. Africa's 54 countries and the European Union's 28 Member States have a shared neighbourhood, history and future' (European Union, 2014: 6). The objective of the Africa–EU Partnership, 'to overcome the traditional donor–recipient relationship, and to develop a shared long-term vision for EU–Africa relations in a globalised world' (ibid.: 7), could be undermined if the French-speaking African countries continue to be left out of any discussion on the evolution of the Bologna Process, as happened in Yerevan, where the focus was on North Africa.

'GOVERNMENTALITY' VERSUS 'SOVEREIGNTY' IN THE REAPPROPRIATION OF THE BOLOGNA PROCESS

The early interactions of the European partners with non-European actors suggest a contradiction between the universalization claims of the Bologna Process, and the lack of dialogue with African actors. The lack of dialogue with African partners is reflected in the impossibility of their expressing their concerns about the HE reforms contained by the Bologna Process, which now affect them to a very large degree (Charlier and Croché, 2011).

Europe's Reappropriation of the Bologna Process

In the domestic arena, 'the Bologna Process is still marked by push and pull, steps backwards, trial and error' (Charlier and Croché, 2009: 48). Adjustments made in Europe show that if an agreement was achieved on some major principles, European countries would still continue to enjoy a great flexibility in pursuing national objectives. If the initial objective was to achieve the convergence of HE national systems, each academic

European system could define its own modalities of integration (Éyébiyi, 2011). Even if a consensus was reached between European countries on 'the creation of an European higher education area as an essential condition to ensure the competitiveness of European education systems', a gap would remain between the political discourse and countries' practices (Croché, 2006: 92).

For example, local variations to national Bologna practices can be observed in many European countries (Crosier and Parveva, 2013), such as in the initial objective of standardizing the degree structure on the '3-5-8 model' of a three-year Bachelor's degree, a two-year Master's degree and a three-year Doctoral degree. This was abandoned as soon as it was proposed, following objections by European countries (Charlier and Croché, 2009). As a result, although this goal was promoted at a discursive level, the existence of a plurality of national practices around study cycles demonstrates forms of reappropriation of the Bologna Process amongst many European countries (Charlier and Croché, 2011).

The harmonization of degree structures was later sought through the adoption of a qualifications framework in the EHEA. This framework includes three cycles: generic descriptors based on learning outcomes (LOs), competences associated with each cycle, and credit ranges (Bergen Communiqué; EHEA, 2005). The work on the qualifications framework was followed up at the meeting in London (2007), where their importance as tools for achieving comparability and transparency within the EHEA was underlined. In order to improve the recognition of qualifications, the HE institutions were to be encouraged to develop modules and study programmes based on learning outcomes and credits (London Communiqué; EHEA, 2007).

The qualifications framework fixes the number of minimum and maximum credits for each study cycle, and reflects the flexibility that in turn characterizes the Bologna model (Croché, 2006). A European Credit Transfer System (ECTS) was established in order to enable the comparability and compatibility of programmes, and to validate learning achievement within the EHEA. 'Credits reflect the total workload required to achieve the objectives of program-objectives which are specified in terms of the learning outcomes and competences to be acquired – and not just through lecture hours' (Gebremeskel, 2014: 91). The ECTS instrument facilitates the comparability of learning outcomes, and thereby both mobility and academic recognition (EUA, 2003). All these compatible and complementary instruments – the ECTS, the learning outcomes and the qualification framework – set out the direction of reforms that HE institutions should follow in order to attain the comparability of HE systems.

Africa's Reappropriation of the Bologna Process Norms

Even if the standardization of the degree structure on the 3-5-8 model did not become a reality in Europe, paradoxically it is fast becoming one in Africa. European countries (especially France) and international organizations (the EC, World Bank, OECD and UNESCO) have very effectively sold the illusion of a homogenous EHEA to the Southern partners through the so-called 'Bologna myth' (Croché, 2009).

Africa is one of the world's regions that has taken up the Bologna Process on the basis of the 'Bologna myth'. African universities began reforming the academic year into two semesters and the degree structure into Licence, Masters and Doctoral (Sall and Ndjaye, 2007). The 3-5-8 model, presented in Attali's (1998) report ordered by the French Minister for Education Allègre (which, as we noted above, was rejected by EU members) is now the model structuring the HE institutions in French-speaking Africa. Indeed the LMD (Licence Master Doctorate) model was presented to French-speaking African partners as the only possible expression of the Bologna project.

While the adoption of semesters and the 3-5-8 model were not subjected to any reappropriation by the African countries, the ECTS instrument has undergone some local reappropriation. In Europe a credit is equivalent to 25–30 working hours, but in Africa the equivalent of a credit is 20–25 hours. This means that the workload necessary for a European and an African student to master skills sanctioned by the first-cycle diploma is quite different: 5400 hours versus 3600 hours. The difference of 1800 hours makes it more difficult to achieve the recognition of equivalences, given the different weightings of the credits and the system of compensation.

The Bologna Process: 'Governmentality' versus 'Sovereignty'

In this subsection we develop a different reading of the movement of the Bologna Process into other territorial spaces based upon Foucault's concept of 'apparatus'. Foucault (1994: 299) proposes that an 'apparatus' is 'a thoroughly heterogeneous ensemble consisting of discourses, institutions, architectural forms, regulatory decisions, laws, administrative measures, scientific statements, philosophical, moral and philanthropic propositions' (Peltonen, 2004: 213–214). Elsewhere we have argued (see Croché, 2010) that a 'European higher education apparatus' was activated by France's Minister for Education, Claude Allègre, at the Sorbonne meeting. A 'network [was] established after 1998, between the European higher education systems, and the programs, instruments and initiatives that structured the landscape of higher education previously, to which one assigns specific and political objectives' (Charlier and Panait, 2015). The instruments, such as the ECTS, the LOs and the qualifications framework, contribute to further 'tighten(ing) the apparatus' (Souto Lopez, 2015), and de facto, its normative effects.

As has been argued, the Bologna Process 'does not offer to any country, region or continent any prescriptive one-jacket-fits-all approach' (Cio, 2014: 2093). Its institutionalization has been subject to lengthy processes through which European actors have negotiated, resisted and redefined the goals of the Process, the manner of achieving them, its territorial borders, and the bodies that would drive the domestic and the external dimension of the process. The institutionalization of the Bologna Process in Europe could be read as a good example of Foucault's (1994) 'governmentality', through which 'no element of the apparatus was imposed, each one of them was the object of negotiations, exchanges, and debates, which explains the variations observed in the durations of the cycles or in the numbers of hours of credits' (Croché and Charlier, 2012: 469).

Its flexibility is strongly based on the principles of the Open Method of Coordination (OMC) (Croché, 2006; Dale, 2004). The OMC was a new form of governance introduced at the 2001 Lisbon summit; it favours the flexibility of norms and their national reappropriation whilst framing it through a series of instruments (especially evaluative tools) to obtain convergence and the progressive alignment of resistant partners to the European standard. Although the Bologna Process showed the limits of this method in achieving convergence, the OMC also facilitated compromises even with those partners whose positions were quite opposed.

In contrast, the transfer of the Bologna Process in Africa was achieved 'without significant consultation of local social agents' (Khelfaoui, 2009: 25). The Bologna Process common framework and tools, which are still expanding, were established without a substantive discussion with the African partners. As shown above, the African partners became involved in the project only after the first Bologna Policy Forum held in Louvain-la-Neuve in 2009. The transposition of certain norms of the Bologna Process into the various countries of the African region, especially the 3-5-8 norm, has been undertaken without much renegotiation or readjustment. The flexibility that the Process presented domestically was lost at the global level (Charlier and Croché, 2009).

The common framework and instruments structuring the Bologna Process appeared neither as negotiable for the African partners, nor any longer negotiable for any new partners wanting to join the EHEA. The common framework includes the Framework for Qualification of the EHEA, the common credit system, student-centred learning, the European Standards and Guidelines for Quality Assurance, a common Register of Quality Assurance Agencies, a common approach to recognition, and the different common methodologies of European HE institutions. The EHEA's common tools include the *ECTS Users' Guide* (European Commission, 2015), the Diploma Supplement and the Lisbon Recognition Convention (Bologna Policy Forum, 2015). These initially flexible common framework and tools, integrating a variety of heterogeneous European practices, were gradually transformed into binding tools for non-European actors (Croché and Charlier, 2012).

EHEA's common framework and tools will be henceforth referred to as key references and will 'offer to the rest of the globe an imperative synergy' (Cio, 2014: 2093) from which African countries will not be able to pull out. This is despite the fact that many African HE institutions still struggle with major challenges, including a lack of capacity to manage the high influx of students, a lack of (qualified) professors, and the lack of adequate infrastructure (Croché and Charlier, 2012). Although the university authorities from Central and Western Africa are well aware of the fact that the implementation of the Bologna model does not respond to their urgent local needs, 'they are forced to accept it as a reference point' (ibid.: 468). Not only that, but despite French-speaking African countries having a long tradition of cooperation with French universities, they are now unable to find self-sustaining bonds with their Northern equivalents.

The transfer of the Bologna Process common framework and tools into Africa moves away from one characterized as 'governmentality' to one that is closer to Foucault's notion of 'sovereignty' (Foucault, 1978). The unequivocal nature of rule and its legitimacy now no longer lie in its power to reach consensus between all stakeholders, but in the authority of the one who enacts it – the sovereign. The Bologna Process becomes, therefore, an interesting study case which illustrates what Foucault (1978) identified as the coexistence of two distinct forms of power: on the one hand, 'governmentality'; and on the other hand, 'sovereignty', or what Butler (2004) has argued is the anachronism which refuses to die. The forms that the Bologna Process takes in African countries and the lack of space for response left to them in the reappropriation process bear a strong resemblance to a 'bubble of sovereignty' (ibid.). Throughout the institutionalization process, the operating procedures of the 'European higher education apparatus' were based on one best described as 'governmentality', here understood as the conduct of conduct (Foucault, 1994). Once the Bologna Process began to expand and extend out into global space, its governmentality specific to the domestic dimension of the process in Europe now created the conditions for its sovereignty in Africa. Bologna now displayed a dual face, of both governmentality and sovereignty, as a result of its territorial extension from Europe into Africa.

EFFECTS OF THE BOLOGNA PROCESS INSTRUMENTS ON AFRICA

The creation of the EHEA has produced several African initiatives seeking to ensure the convergence of HE systems at continental, regional and national level. In this section we examine these processes.

Continental Initiatives to Harmonize HE Systems in Africa

In 2007 the Association of African Universities (AAU) launched the initiative to create the African Higher Education Area (AHEA) (Cio, 2014). Nevertheless, Africa as a single entity does not currently present a unified position on this subject. This was also the case in Europe at the beginning of the Bologna Process.

The impact of the Bologna Process is perhaps felt most strongly in French-speaking Africa, and more precisely in Western Africa. HE institutions in English-speaking Africa came into contact with external references in HE much sooner. Indeed, they had already begun to establish tools, such as quality assurance mechanisms, as a result of their relationship with Anglo-Saxon and the US HE institutions which have integrated similar instruments into their operations, even before the Bologna Process spread.

At the continental level, several attempts had been made by joint committees of Ministers of Education of the African Union (AU), representatives of HE institutions in Africa, and other stakeholders in order to achieve the harmonization of African HE (Cio, 2014). The AU identified HE as a central sector in the Plan of Action for the Second Decade of Education for Africa (2006–2015), aimed at enhancing both the quality of, and the global competitiveness in, its HE institutions as well as the attractiveness of the African HE area (AU, 2006). The actions included by this Plan were: the creation of the Pan-African University (PAU), the African Quality Rating Mechanism, the AU Strategy for Harmonization of HE, and the Nyerere student mobility programme. The PAU was launched in 2010 and aimed 'to develop and retain world-class human resources in areas essential to Africa's development, by stimulating fundamental and applied research in these key areas' (EU, 2014).

The African Union Commission engaged in both the promotion of quality assurance and the adoption of a framework for the harmonization of HE programmes in Africa. One example of this is that the African partners 'agreed to use the *Tuning Educational Structures and Programmes* methodology as an instrument for implementing parts of the African Harmonisation agenda' (ibid.). A Tuning Project (Tuning Africa I), launched in December 2008 and financed by the European Commission, was completed in 2014. The Tuning Project was first launched in Europe and has subsequently been promoted as a model in the South American region, in Russia and also in the United States (Croché and Charlier, 2012).

It was preceded by the Erasmus-Nyerere programme, approved in October 2005 and supported by the EC, which aimed to facilitate the mobility of students both within Africa, and between Africa and Europe. The EC supports also two other initiatives: the Erasmus Mundus programme (student mobility between Europe and other world regions) and EDULINK (university cooperation projects for Africa, Caribbean and Pacific countries). The EU–Africa 2014 summit in Brussels reiterated the intention 'to further strengthen the cooperation between the EU and African Higher Education Areas, to address the key features of the African Higher Education Harmonisation Strategy and to enable closer ties between higher education policy makers' (EU, 2014: 27).

The Tuning Africa Project aims to contribute 'to the transparency of curricula as well as the development of learning outcomes and quality assurance' (ibid.). The first phase of the Tuning Africa initiative was focused on five subject areas: medicine, teacher education, agriculture, mechanical engineering and civil engineering. Each of these was led by a region: Northern Africa, Southern Africa, Western Africa, Central Africa and Eastern Africa. Sixty African universities were involved in this first phase of the initiative. This initiative will now enter into a second phase (Tuning Africa II), which aims to affect more universities and more African countries. It will also be focused on more subject areas, such as applied geology, economics and higher education management.

Regional and National Initiatives to Harmonize the HE Systems in Africa

Apart from the EU–AU joint programmes to harmonize the African HE systems, concrete initiatives have been launched by various regional organizations in different parts of the continent aimed at achieving the harmonization of practices and policies in HE systems. For instance, the ECTS and the European Qualification Framework, two European instruments, have already inspired African regional and national initiatives of the same type.

Since 2000, several African organizations – the African and Madagascan Council for Higher Education (CAMES), the Monetary Union of Western Africa (UEMOA), the Central African Economic and Monetary Community (CEMAC), the Network for the Excellence of the Higher Education of Western Africa (REESAO), the Association of African Universities (AAU) and the Association for the Development of Education in Africa (ADEA) – have encouraged African HE institutions to adopt the Bologna model (Croché and Charlier, 2012).

In 2005, the heads of state of the CEMAC undertook to build a Space for Higher Education Research and Professional Training through the Bologna Process (Libreville Declaration, 2005; Eta, 2015). From 2007 the UEMOA has followed the same path as the CEMAC, which aims to implement the project to support higher education and research, with the goal of improving the quality of both in West Africa (Éyébiyi, 2011). Strong foundations for a Euro-Mediterranean Higher Education and Research Area have been set by several countries of the Maghreb region, such as Algeria, Morocco, Tunisia, to which adhered Egypt and Jordan (Cio, 2014).

Established in 1999 between Kenya, Tanzania, Uganda, Burundi and Rwanda, the East African Community (EAC) has created a common curriculum for all the HE institutions within the EAC in the areas of medical, technical and agricultural training. In March 2011, the Inter-University Council for East Africa (IUCEA) launched a *Quality Assurance Handbook* which aims 'to enhance the quality of higher education across the region [the EAC], and to promote a harmonised quality assurance system' (IUCEA, 2011).

A high-level forum on quality assurance in HE in East Africa, organized by the IUCEA in collaboration with the German Academic Exchange Service (DAAD), took place in February 2013, in Nairobi. One year later, during the IUCEA's meeting in Kampala, the President of Kenya urged the IUCEA 'to expedite the development of the Regional Qualifications Framework' (President Kenyatta Statement, 2014). The IUCEA proposed a regional HE qualifications framework and a credit transfer system to start in the EAC in 2015. The credit transfer system's goal was to enable the transfer of students' credits from one university to another across the EAC and to enhance African students' mobility across the region. The success of this framework is still to be verified given that the EAC's countries remain unwilling to transfer a part of their sovereignty in the education field to a regional entity. Yet important discrepancies in terms of curricula structures, credit hours and learning outcomes continue to characterize the HE systems of the EAC's countries.

If the initiatives at the regional and continental level are driven and supported financially by international organizations, such as the EC or the AU, the initiatives at the national level are a priori 'voluntarily' undertaken by African countries. In some countries, the implementation of the Bologna Process is related to the openly expressed wish of a particular European country (such as France) to see its ex-colonies adopting the Bologna model (Sall and Ndjaye, 2007). In other countries, such as in Ethiopia, an adaptation of the previous credit system according to the ECTS Users' Guide has been carried out (Gebremeskel, 2014). Finally, in still others, such as South Africa, quality assurance mechanisms have already been implemented (the South African Qualification Agency and the Council on Higher Education) (Cio, 2014).

Harmonization of Quality Assurance and its Consequences for African HE Systems

The alignment of African countries to the European norms underlying the Bologna Process is often presented as 'taking the good practices' developed in the North (Gebremeskel, 2014: 95), or 'an opportunity to introduce [locally] elements of the Bologna Process' (ibid.). Failure to critically question this alignment means turning a blind eye to the impact that this process will have on longer-term developments. Once regional or continental harmonization is reached in terms of curricula in Africa – a goal that remains, for the moment, distant – the next step will be to evaluate the HE institutions' quality, and more specifically the LOs. 'Evaluation has become an essential tool of new regulation forms of higher education policies' (Croché, 2006: 106). Once the global race for quality assessment affects Africa's HE institutions, African countries will be caught in their own trap. Countries' learning results will be compared without taking into consideration the fact that a number of necessary conditions for comparison have not yet been reached. African HE systems are still far from being homogenous in terms of HE curricula, volumes and levels of learning, as well as the comparability and compatibility of qualifications.

On top of this, a global cross-countries initiative, the Assessment of Higher Education Learning Outcomes (AHELO), was launched by the OECD in 2015 (Altbach, 2015; Morgan, 2015). Its purpose is to test students' achievement across a number of fields, in order to compare learning outcomes cross-nationally, at a global level. The OECD's Institutional Management in Higher Education (IMHE) originally launched a pilot AHELO project in 2010, but the same body recommended in 2012 that the project should no longer be continued. However, three years later in 2015 the OECD proposed to launch a global AHELO. Comparing achievements on a range of disciplines in quite different countries remains at the level of a 'myth of measurement and comparability' (Altbach, 2015). This disregards the fact that HE programmes and courses vary greatly not only from region to region, but also across countries in the same region. As always, the institutions likely to be most affected by the initiative will be the mass universities, whose marginal status will be further exacerbated (Altbach, 2015).

What will be the role to be played by African HE institutions and governmental authorities in the conceptualization of this project? Once again, it will be those actors closely connected to international organizations who will define a global project in which African HE institutions will have little option but to participate. The assessment instruments will once more be developed outside Africa, only to be transferred and implemented by African HE institutions.

It seems highly likely that the global AHELO assessment instruments will not take contextual differences and the plurality of institutional arrangements into account, and that the project is not going to be beneficial to African countries. The skill needs of African countries are primarily local needs. A global AHELO might threaten to leave African countries far behind in terms of the results of the learning outcomes.

CONCLUSIONS

The above analysis leads us to several questions. Could one hope to find in Africa nowadays a similar form of 'regulatory state regionalism' (Robertson, 2010) to that which exists in Europe? Could Africa act in a 'state-like way' (ibid.), like Europe which is able both to choose its cooperation partners, and to exert domination in the inter-regional arena through the HE instruments it has created in the last decade and that claim the right to become universal? We question the ability of the AU to become a key player in the inter-regional HE arena by pulling together the fragmented HE national policies and systems. Could the AU truly propose a continental approach fitting the variety of local needs of African HE systems or countries? Might the AU propose an alternative HE approach to counterbalance the European model?

Our view is that when the development challenges for Africa are confronted, it leads us to conclude that the reform of the African HE systems should be an African common reaction to African problems (Charlier and Croché, 2010) rather than an embrace of a European solution. Submitting external references and protocols to national forms of reappropriation is extremely important not only for the African countries in particular, but also for many countries more generally. We should not forget that the efficacy of the Bologna Process relies on the fact that it was initially conceived as a European response to national crises in the European economies (Robertson, 2010). The African forms of reappropriation of Bologna Process, whatever they might be, should first of all take into account the necessity of finding local solutions to the acute and urgent problems with which African universities are being confronted. These solutions cannot be found in a mechanical adoption of the European model as 'good practice'. In 2011, the Association for the Development of Education in Africa underlined the importance of adapting the Bologna Process in accordance to the African context (culture, values) (Gebremeskel, 2014).

The AU's ability to propose a counterbalancing African model in the HE sector is hindered by its very nature, which prevents it from playing the same role and having the same weight that the EU has in Europe. In this context, the AU still has a long road ahead in order to become a supra-national organization able to guide African development in any powerful, over-determining way (Fagbayibo, 2008). The main challenge is to elaborate the instruments and programmes in HE with the same normative power as the ones that exist within the EU. The African countries have so far been unwilling to transfer a part of their sovereignty to a regional entity in general, not only in the education field. However, even in the absence of a supra-national dimension, the AU remains a regional space under construction, and the preferred contact of the EU in terms of HE. Moreover, even in Europe, the HE sector was initially the responsibility of member states. It was only progressively and after lengthy negotiations that the European Commission acquired such influence in this sector, to orient the European higher education apparatus and to 'conduct its conduct'.

REFERENCES

African Union (AU) (2006), *Second Decade of Education For Africa (2006–2015) Plan Of Action*, Addis Ababa.

Altbach, P.G. (2015), 'AHELO: The Myth of Measurement and Comparability', *University World News*, 367, 15 May, http://www.universityworldnews.com/article.php?story=20150515064746124.

Attali, Jacques (1998), *Dictionnaire du XXIe siècle*, Paris: Fayard.

Bologna Policy Forum (2015), 'The Bologna Process Revisited: The Future of the European Higher Education Area', Yerevan Ministerial Conference, 14–15 May.

Brøgger, K. (2014), 'The Ghosts of Higher Education Reform: On the Organisational Processes Surrounding Policy Borrowing', *Globalisation, Societies and Education*, 12(4), 520–541.

Butler, J. (2004), 'Détention illimitée. Guantanamo, ou la gouvernementalité souveraine', *Vacarme*, 29, 124–131, www.cairn.info/revue-vacarme-2004-4-page-124.htm. DOI: 10.3917/vaca.029.0124.

Charlier, J.É. and Croché, S. (2009), 'Can the Bologna Process Make the Move Faster towards the Development of an International Space for Higher Education where Africa would find its place?', *JHEA/RESA*, 7(1–2), 39–59.

Charlier, J.É. and Croché, S. (2010), 'L'inéluctable passage au LMD des universités africaines', *Revue française de pédagogie*, 172, 77–84.

Charlier, J.É. and Croché, S. (2011), 'The Bologna Process: A Tool for Europe's Hegemonic Project on Africa', *Power and Education*, 3(3), 304–316.

Charlier, J.É. and Panait, O.M. (2015), 'The Bologna Policy Forum: A New Voice in the Harmonisation of Higher Education Policies at Global Level', in Olson, J.R., Biseth, H. and Ruiz, G. (eds), *Educational Internationalisation, Academic Voices and Public Policy*, Rotterdam: Sense Publishers, pp. 59–76.

Cio, O. (2014), 'Learning from "Good" Practice: What Could African (Universities) Possibly Learn from the Bologna Process and European Students' Mobility?', *Mediterranean Journal of Social Sciences*, **5**(23), 2092–2102.

Copans, J. (2001), 'La situation"coloniale" de Georges Balandier: notion conjoncturelle ou modèle sociologique et historique?', *Cahiers internationaux de sociologie*, PUF, no. 110, pp. 31–52.

Croché, S. (2006), 'Qui pilote le processus de Bologne?', *Education et Sociétes*, **18**, 203–217.

Croché, S. (2009), 'Le mythe de Bologne', in Charlier, J.É., Croché, S. and Ndoyé, A.K. (eds), *Les universités africaines francophones face au LMD*, Louvain-la-Neuve: Academia Bruylant, pp. 89–112.

Croché, S. (2010), *Le pilotage du processus de Bologne*, Louvain-la-Neuve: Academia Bruylant.

Croché, S. and Charlier, J.É. (2012), 'Normative Influence of the Bologna Process on French-Speaking African Universities', *Globalisation, Societies and Education*, **10**(4), 457–472.

Crosier, D. and Parveva, T. (2013), *The Bologna Process: Its Impact in Europe and Beyond*, Paris: International Institute for Educational Planning UNESCO.

Dale, R. (2004), 'Forms of Governance, Governmentality and the EU's Open Method of Coordination', in Larner, W. and Walters, W. (eds), *Global Governmentality: Governing International Spaces*, New York: Routledge, pp. 174–194.

Dolowitz, D.P. and Marsh, D. (2000), 'Learning from Abroad: The Role of Policy Transfer in Contemporary Policy-Making', *Governance: An International Journal of Policy and Administration*, **13**(1), 5–23.

Espinoza Figueroa, F. (2008), 'European Influences in Chilean and Mexican Higher Education: The Bologna Process and the Tuning Project', *European Education*, **40**(1), 63–77.

Eta, E.A. (2015), 'Policy Borrowing and Transfer, and Policy Convergence: Justifications for the Adoption of the Bologna Process in the CEMAC Region and the Cameroonian Higher Education System through the LMD Reform', *Comparative Education*, **51**(2), 161–178.

European Commission (2015), *ECTS Users' Guide 2015*, Brussels: European Commission.

European Ministers in Charge of Higher Education (2001), 'Towards the European Higher Education Area: Communique on the Meeting, Prague', 19 May, http://www.ehea.info/article-details.aspx?ArticleId=43 (last accessed 23 April 2016).

European Ministers in Charge of Higher Education (EHEA) (2003), 'Realising the European Higher Education Area', http://www.ehea.info/Uploads/Declarations/Berlin_Communique1.pdf (accessed 23 April 2016).

European Ministers in Charge of Higher Education (EHEA) (2005), 'The European Higher Education Area – Achieving the Goals', http://www.ehea.info/Uploads/Declarations/Bergen_Communique1.pdf (accessed 23 April 2016).

European Ministers in Charge of Higher Education (EHEA) (2007), 'Towards the European Higher Education Area: Responding to Challenges in a Globalised World', 18 May, http://www.ehea.info/Uploads/Declarations/London_Communique18May2007.pdf (accessed 23 April 2016).

European Ministers in Charge of Higher Education (EHEA) (2009), 'The Bologna

Process 2020: The European Higher Education Area in the New Decade', 28–29 April, http://www.ehea.info/Uploads/Declarations/Leuven_Louvain-la-Neuve_Communiqu%C3%A9_April_2009.pdf (accessed 23 April 2016).
European Union (EU) (2014), *The Africa–EU Partnership. 2 Unions, 1 Vision*, Summit Edition 2014, Luxembourg: Publications Office of the European Union.
European University Association (EUA) (2003), 'Key Features of ECTS as the European Credit Transfer and Accumulation System', http://www.eua.be/eua-work-and-policy-area/building-the-european-higher-education-area/bologna-basics/Bologna-an-overview-of-the-main-elements.aspx.
Éyébiyi, E.P. (2011), 'L'alignement de l'enseignement supérieur ouest-africain. La construction des savoirs entre intranéité et extranéité au Bénin', *Cahiers de la recherche sur l'éducation et les savoirs*, Hors-série, no. 3, mis en ligne le 15 juin 2013, consulté le 21 mai 2015, http://cres.revues.org/109.
Fagbayibo, B. (2008), 'A Supranational African Union: Gazing into the Crystal Ball', *De Jure*, **3**, 493–503.
Fan, P. (2007), 'Educational Policy Borrowing's Past, Present, Future: A Literature Review', MSc dissertation, University of Oxford.
Foucault, M. (1978), 'La "gouvernementalité"', in Foucault, M. (2001), *Dits et écrits II. 1976–1988*, Paris: Gallimard, pp. 635–657.
Foucault, M. (1994), *Dits et écrits*, Paris: Gallimard.
Gebremeskel, H.H. (2014), 'Influence of the Bologna Process on African Higher Education: Ethiopian Higher Education in Focus', *International Journal of Research Studies in Education*, **3**(4), 85–98.
Imaniriho, D. (2015), *Appropriation des politiques éducatives dans un contexte de dépendance économique. Réflexion sur le fonctionnement du réseau d'acteurs éducatifs au Rwanda*, Thèse de doctorat en sciences psychologiques et de l'éducation, Louvain-la-Neuve: Collection de thèses de l'Université catholique de Louvain.
Inter-University Council for East Africa (IUCEA) (2011), *Quality Assurance Handbook*, 4 vols, http://www.iucea.org/index.php?option=com_content&view=article&id=106&Itemid=238 (accessed 23 April 2016).
Khelfaoui, H. (2009), 'The Bologna Process in Africa: Globalization or Return to "Colonial Situation"?', *Journal of Higher Education in Africa*, **8**(1–2), 1–20.
Lewandowski, S. (2011), 'Politiques de lutte contre la pauvreté et inégalités scolaires à Dakar: Vers un éclatement des normes éducatives', *Autrepart*, **3**(59), 37–56.
Libreville Declaration (2005), *The Libreville Declaration on the Building of the CEMAC Zone for Higher Education, Research and Professional Training*, Libreville, 11 February.
Morgan, J. (2015), 'OECD's Ahelo Project could Transform University Hierarchy', *Times Higher Education*, 7 May, http://www.timeshighereducation.co.uk/news/oecds-ahelo-project-could-transform-university-hierarchy/2020087.article.
Peltonen, M. (2004), 'From Discourse to *Dispositif*: Michel Foucault's Two Histories. Citation Historical Reflections', *Réflexions Historiques*, **30**(2), 205–219.
Phillips, D. (2005), 'Policy Borrowing in Education: Frameworks for Analysis', in Zajda, J. (ed.), *International Handbook on Globalisation, Education and Policy Research*, pp. 23–34.
Phillips, D. and Ochs, L. (2003), 'Processes of Policy Borrowing in Education: Some Explanatory and Analytical Devices', *Comparative Education*, **39**(4), 451–461.
President Kenyatta Statement (2014), 'The President of Kenya. The Development

of the Regional Qualifications Framework', Inter-University Council for East Africa (IUCEA), Kampala, 30 March.
Robertson, S.L. (2010), 'The EU, "Regulatory State Regionalism" and New Modes of Higher Education Governance', *Globalisation, Societies and Education*, **8**(1), 23–37.
Sall, A.N. and Ndjaye, B. (2007), 'Higher Education in Africa: Between Perspectives Opened by the Bologna Process and the Commodification throughout of Education', *European Education, the Implications of Competition for the future of European Higher Education*, **39**(4), 43–58.
Souto Lopez, M. (2015), 'Resserrer le dispositif européen de l'enseignement supérieur par les acquis d'apprentissage, Thèse de doctorat en sciences politiques et sociales', Université catholique de Louvain, École Normale Supérieure de Lyon.
Steiner-Khamsi, G. (ed.) (2004), *The Global Politics of Educational Borrowing and Lending*, New York: Teachers College Press.
Zgaga, P. (2006), *Looking Out: The Bologna Process in a Global Setting. On the 'External Dimension' of the Bologna Process*, Oslo: Norwegian Ministry of Education and Research.

5. Harmonization of higher education in Southeast Asia regionalism: politics first, and then education

Morshidi Sirat, Norzaini Azman and Aishah Abu Bakar

INTRODUCTION

Regionalism exists in many different forms and contexts (IPPTN, 2008). Following Olds and Robertson (2011), regionalism is a state-led initiative to enhance integration among countries within a defined region towards better security and trade. Since the end of the Cold War, however, the areas in which regionalism seems most salient have included institutional structures, relationships between institutions and national governments, the academic profession, and student mobility (Forest, n.d.). Based on the post-Cold War situation and European experience, it is argued that educational policy has become linked in many specific forms to economic policy, and thus must follow in the direction economic policies go (ibid.). But politics has not featured in recent discussion on regionalism in Asia, though in reality, regionalism is also about politics, followed by economic justifications and then other concerns. Such has been the development of regionalism since the 1950s.

In this respect, it is important to examine the Association of Southeast Asian Nations, or ASEAN, which was established on 8 August 1967 in Bangkok, Thailand, as a case study to illustrate the relationship between regionalism and higher education development. ASEAN was established with the signing of the ASEAN Declaration (Bangkok Declaration) by the founding states of ASEAN, namely Indonesia, Malaysia, the Philippines, Singapore and Thailand. It is important to note that ASEAN was established when communist ideology was spreading in Indochina during the Indochina War, and the fall of South Vietnam to North Vietnam led to the idea that the 'domino theory' would become a reality in Southeast Asia. Furthermore, in the 1960s, communist parties were also very active in Malaysia and Southern Thailand, lending credence to the 'domino theory' that after Indochina, Malaysia and Thailand would be overwhelmed by communist insurgencies.

When politics and ideology took a different turn and economic competitiveness in the global market took precedence, Brunei Darussalam joined ASEAN on 7 January 1984, and more significantly, Vietnam joined ASEAN on 28 July 1995, Lao PDR and Myanmar on 23 July 1997, and Cambodia on 30 April 1999, making up what is today the ten member states of ASEAN (ASEAN Secretariat, n.d.). Vietnam, Lao PDR, Myanmar and Cambodia are noted for their different political ideologies and systems compared to those of the other six member countries of ASEAN. So in the context of ASEAN, politics and security were the initial building blocks of regionalism. Currently, economic competitiveness, cultural understanding and education are increasingly becoming important for this regional grouping.

It is noteworthy that, since the 1990s, as ASEAN expanded, regional cooperation and collaboration have been emphasized while differences in political ideology and governments have been increasingly deemphasized (Hassan et al., 1997). ASEAN is about regional collaboration to promote political stability, socio-economic development and cultural awareness among member states and with East Asia partner countries such as China, Japan and South Korea. In their relations with one another, primarily in the political sphere, the ASEAN member states have subscribed to the fundamental principles as contained in the Treaty of Amity and Cooperation in Southeast Asia (TAC) of 1976. TAC 1976 underlined the importance of mutual respect for the independence, sovereignty, equality, territorial integrity and national identity of all nations, and non-interference in the internal affairs of other member countries (ASEAN Secretariat, n.d.). Thus, Myanmar was left alone to deal with its internal political circumstances. It is the only country within ASEAN where a visa is required for all visitors including those from other member states within ASEAN. There are also many unsettling geopolitical issues affecting several member states within ASEAN. But the principle of non-interference in the political affairs of member states remains.

At the 12th ASEAN Summit in January 2007, the leaders of ASEAN affirmed their strong commitment to accelerate the establishment of an ASEAN Community by 2015 and signed the Cebu Declaration on the Acceleration of the Establishment of an ASEAN Community by 2015 (ASEAN Secretariat, n.d). The ASEAN Community vision is supported by three pillars, namely: the ASEAN Political-Security Community, the ASEAN Economic Community and the ASEAN Socio-Cultural Community. Each pillar has its own Blueprint, and, together with the Initiative for ASEAN Integration (IAI) Strategic Framework and IAI

Work Plan Phase II (2009–2015), they form the Roadmap for an ASEAN Community 2009–2015 (ASEAN Secretariat, n.d.).

Based on the experience of Europe and the Bologna Process, it was envisaged that higher education would play a crucial role in supporting the continued economic integration of ASEAN that was launched at the end of 2015 (Zhang, 2013). Since 2009, the South-East Asian Ministers of Education Organization Regional Centre for Higher Education and Development (SEAMEO RIHED) has been coordinating the implementation of a roadmap aimed at creating a systematic mechanism to support the integration of universities across Southeast Asia through student mobility and other exchanges. This initiative is strongly influenced by developments in Europe, in particular the Bologna Process and the establishment of the European Higher Education Area (Yavaprabhas and Dhirathiti, 2008). Important initiatives towards the harmonization of higher education systems within ASEAN were subsequently implemented together with related programmes of the ASEAN Plus Three and the ASEAN University Network. The latter coordinates matters relating to quality assurance and qualifications frameworks critical to facilitating student mobility within ASEAN.

In a general context, the harmonization of higher education is essentially a process that recognizes the significance of regional education cooperation and the importance of establishing an 'area of knowledge' in which activities and interactions in higher education, mobility and employment opportunities can be easily facilitated and increased. It is a process that acknowledges diversity of higher education systems and cultures within a region, while simultaneously seeking to create a 'common educational space' (Wallace, 2000; Enders, 2004). Clearly, the region of a supranational organization with different cultures, religions, languages and educational systems must develop a harmonized system of education so that it can foster a higher level of understanding, a sense of shared purpose and common destiny in a highly globalized world. This system could be developed or constructed on the basis of common, but not identical, practices and guidelines for cooperation in education. But the main point is that this agenda can only be moved forward with strong political will over and above differences in political structures and systems of government.

Regionalism in the European context is primarily driven by an economic agenda. Economic considerations have come to play a prominent role in higher education policy; as one Eastern European scholar notes, 'the relationship between higher education and industry has changed fundamentally in Western Europe since the 1970s, showing rapid increases in the influence of the latter in the policies of the former' (Cerych, 1985; cited in Forest, n.d.). But regionalism in Southeast Asia as manifested in the form of ASEAN was driven by political and security considerations, only to be expanded later to include trade and economic cooperation. With globalization and internationalization of higher education, a common education space has been given due consideration. In this recent development, and in light of the ASEAN Community 2015 vision, the question is whether development of a common higher education space will take precedence over the political situation and sovereignty of individual member states within ASEAN. One may also hypothesize that political will towards harmonization of higher education systems has already been made clear by the ASEAN Secretariat and SEAMEO, and that what is holding back its progress is the higher education sector and players within ASEAN themselves, who are slow to decide on a regional qualifications framework and quality assurance issues that would facilitate harmonization.

REGIONALIZATION FOR EDUCATION: HARMONIZATION OF HIGHER EDUCATION SYSTEMS WITHIN ASEAN

The general idea about a common space or higher education area excludes any intention of creating a uniform or standardized system of higher education. The primary goal is to create general guidelines in areas such as degree comparability through similar degree cycles and qualifications frameworks, quality assurance, lifelong learning or credit transfer systems (Armstrong, 2009; Clark, 2007). These general guidelines will facilitate international student mobility, lifelong learning and hassle-free movement of talented workers within the region, which will strengthen the regional economy in the long run. The regional higher education area is the space in which students, faculty members and higher education institutions (HEIs) are the key players promoting similar or equivalent standards of higher education activities. In other words, in a region with a harmonized system of higher education there will be continuous opportunity for interactions and mobility for students, faculty members and talents which are seen as essential in enhancing the ASEAN grouping.

Arguably, the most important factor that contributes to the success of the process of harmonization in higher education is the participation and consensus-building at the level of national agencies, the public as well as other stakeholders. The key element of harmonization in higher education will be the establishment of a mutually accepted roadmap that will consist of a vision of future goals (such as the establishment of a higher education space or area), areas to develop common frameworks (identified by key stakeholders such as credit transfer systems, quality assurance guidelines, regional qualifications frameworks or comparable degree cycles, and so on), methods and the key players who will be responsible for framework development and information dissemination to the public. According to Hettne (2005), harmonization is cyclical, and a policy process (functional cooperation) and policy tools (lesson-drawing, policy externalization and policy transfer) anchor it. Arguably, these need clear and strong policy direction from policy-makers and political masters if the agenda is to move forward.

Admittedly, the idea of a harmonized higher education system in Southeast Asia which covers all ASEAN member states was inspired by the development of regionalism in higher education in Europe, specifically the establishment of the European Higher Education Area (EHEA) (Yavaprabhas, 2009). The idea of regionalism in higher education in the context of ASEAN is a very exciting idea, seeing that regionalism in the European context has dismantled obstacles to student and staff mobility through the mechanism of the Bologna Process (Morshidi, 2009). ASEAN has been integrating rapidly, mainly through trade and investment (Hassan et al., 1997), and it is also witnessing increasing mobility of people in the region and between regions. This new context places higher education in a pivotal role in developing human resources capable of creating and sustaining ASEAN as a regional entity with a vision towards regional prosperity. Harmonizing the highly diverse systems of higher education in the region is seen as an important step towards the regional integration objective where, even now, differences in systems of government, political and market structures are increasingly blurred.

Arguably, regionalism and higher education have political, economic, social and cultural dimensions, similar to globalization (Terada, 2003; Hawkins, 2012). As a political lever, regional and inter-regional cooperation provides opportunities for regions and individual nations to contribute to international quality assurance policy discussions. As an economic lever, regional integration and inter-regional collaborations open up the possibility for smaller higher education systems to compete and cooperate on an international or regional scale. As a social or cultural lever, regional activities build solidarity among nations with similar cultural and historical roots (Yepes, 2006). Therefore, higher education regionalization is perceived differently, depending on the dimensions, actors and values involved in the process.

Political Commitments towards Harmonization of Higher Education Systems

In Southeast Asia, the status of integration of higher education in ASEAN is being studied and promoted by three main bodies, namely SEAMEO

RIHED, ASEAN Plus Three and the ASEAN University Network (AUN). All of these entities were established and sanctioned by the highest policy-making body within ASEAN. Their aim is to promote education networking at various levels of educational institutions and to continue university networking to enhance and support student and staff exchanges and professional interactions.

In fact, as far back as 1997, the ASEAN Community had begun creating organizations within its framework with the intention of achieving their regional and extra-regional goals. ASEAN Plus Three, the first of the extra-regional set-ups that were designed to improve existing ties with the People's Republic of China, Japan and South Korea, developed a 'Plan of Action on Education: 2010–2017' which emphasizes the need to develop and implement strategies related to quality assurance and the promotion of mobility. Subsequently, the ASEAN Plus Three Working Group on Mobility of Higher Education and Ensuring Quality Assurance of Higher Education among ASEAN Plus Three countries was created. The working group's main objectives are to analyse credit transfer systems within the ASEAN Plus Three region, and to explore ways to improve student mobility programmes in the ASEAN Plus Three region.

Another high-level set-up, SEAMEO is an international organization established in 1965 among governments of Southeast Asian countries to promote regional cooperation in education, science and culture in Southeast Asia. Members of SEAMEO include Malaysia, Brunei Darussalam, Cambodia, Indonesia, Lao PDR, and Republic of the Union of Myanmar, Philippines, Singapore, Thailand, Timor-Leste and the Socialist Republic of Vietnam. SEAMEO RIHED was later developed under the umbrella of SEAMEO, working for 11 member countries in Southeast Asia. Specifically, its mission is to foster efficiency, effectiveness and harmonization of higher education in Southeast Asia through a system of research, empowerment, and development of mechanisms to facilitate sharing and collaborations in higher education (Yepes, 2006; Nguyen, 2009). Programmes under SEAMEO RIHED serve the following five main objectives:

1. Empowering higher education institutions via study visit programmes to the United States, the United Kingdom, Australia and People's Republic of China; training courses for International Relations Offices in Southeast Asian HEIs; and workshops on governance and management for HEI.
2. Developing a harmonization mechanism which includes internationalization Awards (iAwards), workshops on Academic Credit Transfer

frameworks from Asia, and the Southeast Asian Quality Assurance Framework.
3. Cultivating globalized human resources via the ASEAN International Mobility for Students (AIMS) Programme.
4. Advancing knowledge frontiers in higher education system management through policy action research, and building an academic credit transfer framework for Asia.
5. Promoting university social responsibility and sustainable development via seminars on university social enterprise.

The main focus of the five objectives is cultivating globalized human resources through the Malaysia–Indonesia–Thailand (M–I–T) Student Mobility Project, which has been expanded to become the ASEAN AIMS Programme. Student mobility has always been one of the key strategic elements of cooperation leading to the development of a harmonized higher education environment among countries in Southeast Asia.

Thus, in more recent years, Southeast Asian countries through ASEAN and SEAMEO have shown commitment towards deepening connections and interactions by viewing their rich regional diversity (ASEAN and Asian) as an important basis for regional cooperation and collaboration rather than as a stumbling block. It was envisioned that the ASEAN Community 2015 would be the outcome of cooperation and collaboration in ASEAN in areas relating to regional understanding and economic integration. There is indeed a high level of political commitment towards achieving this vision.

From the ongoing discussion, in terms of political will and direction, ASEAN leaders have a shared vision to build an ASEAN Community with three pillars: the ASEAN Economic Community (AEC), the ASEAN Socio-Cultural Community (ASCC) and the ASEAN Political–Security Community (APSC). The primary goal of ASCC is to create an ASEAN Community that is people-centred and socially responsible, based on shared values. Education, particularly higher education, has been treated as the core action line in promoting the ASEAN Socio-Cultural Community and in supporting the continued economic integration of ASEAN by 2015. Higher education in the region has been mentioned in many official declarations as one of the important steps towards enhancing human resource development in the region. In order to realize this vision, an ambitious plan was drawn up in 2009 aimed at creating a systematic mechanism to support the integration of universities across Southeast Asia. Student mobility, credit transfers, quality assurance and research clusters were identified as the four main priorities to harmonize the ASEAN higher education system, encompassing 6500 higher education institutions and 12 million students in ten nations (ASEAN Secretariat, n.d.).

The ultimate goal of the plan is to set up a Common Space of Higher Education in Southeast Asia. The strategic plan calls for the creation of the ASEAN area of higher education with a broader strategic objective of ensuring the integration of education priorities into ASEAN's development. The education objectives are to:

1. advance and prioritize education and focus on creating a knowledge-based society;
2. achieve universal access to primary education;
3. promote early childcare and development; and
4. enhance awareness of ASEAN to youth through education and activities to build an ASEAN identity based on friendship and cooperation, which is key to promoting citizens' mobility and employability and the grouping's overall development.

It is interesting to note that the declaration advocates specific reforms focusing on harmonization in the higher education system with the objective of increasing the international competitiveness of ASEAN higher education. Thus, as argued earlier, the new building block of ASEAN is internationalization of higher education, in addition to security and trade within ASEAN.

Since the declaration, individual ASEAN governments have increased public investment in universities to support the ASEAN Higher Education Area, and the region's burgeoning knowledge economy. Measures have been established to strengthen the performance of Southeast Asian universities across a wide range of indicators such as teaching, learning, research, enterprise and innovation. These initiatives also pave the way for further collaboration and integration among universities in the region, enhancing the overall reputation of ASEAN universities compared to their competitors in the West and elsewhere in the world. It is not surprising to see the improved performance of several ASEAN universities in the 2014 QS University Rankings: Asia.

Arguably, from the discussion above, there seems to be no lack of political will and commitment in the progress of initiatives towards harmonization of higher education systems within ASEAN. Progress in harmonization is highly dependent on other players, in particular the AUN, SEAMEO RIHED, ministries supervising and regulating higher education, and individual universities within ASEAN. National qualifications agencies or similar institutions in each of the ASEAN member nations have a crucial role in promoting harmonization by encouraging active movement towards the development of quality assurance collaboration and sharing. While there is already a network of quality assurance agencies among Southeast Asian countries, known as the ASEAN Quality Assurance Network (AQAN), progress is still very slow. AQAN was introduced to develop and recognize strength and commonalities in academic practices without losing individual country identity, as well as ensuring compatibility of qualifications and learning outcomes within the ASEAN countries. The main problem for harmonization is the fact that higher education systems in Southeast Asia are very diverse, and even within each nation some degree of incompatibility is to be expected. However, it is important to appreciate that in the context of Southeast Asia, with its diverse systems, harmonization is about comparability, not standardization or uniformity of programmes, degrees and the nature of higher education institutions.

Benefits and Advantages

Admittedly, there are benefits in creating a common higher education space in Southeast Asia, the more obvious ones being greater mobility, widening access and choices, academic and research collaborations, enhanced collaboration on human capital investment, and the promotion of ASEAN and/or Southeast Asian higher education within the fast-changing global higher education landscape. The immediate advantage of such harmonization of higher education systems is presented as easier exchange and mobility for students and academics among member nations within Southeast Asia, in addition to the availability of access to systems, tools and best practices for quality improvement in higher education. For some countries, harmonization serves as a jump-start for keeping up with globalization.

Arguably, the goal that is most desired and considered most feasible is that which does not require all higher education systems to conform to a particular model. The general consensus is that such a system would serve as a reference, or that it can be fitted into without jeopardizing cultural diversity and national identity. This consensus is very much in line with the successful approach used by early Muslim scholars (during the Renaissance in Europe), whose methodology involved taking all ideas which are non-contradictory to their religious values and faith. The scholars not only borrowed ideas from others but they went on further to expand and introduce innovative ideas (Abbas, 2011). This approach has led to the development of a unique learning culture, which is the basis of a stronger community. Harmonization would result in differing national standards coming closer together. However, it has been very difficult for nations to agree on common standards, mainly because issues of sovereignty usually become points of contention, and also because it is not, in itself, an easy process.

It is worthwhile considering the idea of finding commonalities in practices rather than imposing uniformity when developing standards, and that such initiatives should be undertaken in stages, taking into consideration the various levels of higher education development in ASEAN.

Plan of Action

Having secured political commitments from the ASEAN heads of government, the following actions are deemed necessary in achieving the desired goal in harmonizing higher education among the ASEAN Community.

Regional accreditation
Accreditation is very important in higher education. It is viewed as both a process and a result. It is a process by which a university or college or technical and vocational training institution evaluates its educational activities, and seeks an independent judgement to confirm that it has substantially achieved its objectives, and is generally equal in quality to comparable institutions. As a result, it is a form of certification, or grant of formal status by a recognized and authorized accrediting agency to an educational institution as possessing certain standards of quality over and above those prescribed as minimum requirements by the government.

Unified education framework
Intergovernmental organizations need to establish ASEAN standards for HEIs, including those for the curriculum. Consequently, the curriculum and delivery modes in all programmes are still in the process of revision to meet labour market needs. Thus, a unified curriculum in the ASEAN region is highly recommended to achieve the desired goal of one community. The focus should be on learning outcomes.

Improved quality of education
ASEAN countries need to improve the quality of their education systems as many graduates lack the skills needed in today's rapidly changing workplace. The shortage of skilled workforce in the Asia-Pacific region, male and (even more so) female, has been a major bottleneck in economic and social development. There is a need for greater emphasis on technical and vocational education and training (Liang, 2008; Kehm, 2010).

Scholarships for students and faculty exchange
More programmes with scholarship grants for students from all the regions are now being offered in most ASEAN countries. The scholarships are aimed at providing opportunities to the young people of ASEAN to

develop their potential and equip them with skills that will enable them to confidently step into the wider community at large. Another way of improving the quality of education is by enhancing the education of teachers, academics and other educational personnel and by upgrading their professional competency. Programmes that focus on talent management and leadership selection could be introduced. Teachers' and lecturers' workloads should also be reviewed. Various initiatives, from faster promotion prospects to awards, can be introduced to acknowledge the role teachers and academics play and to raise their morale, which would also enhance the image of the teaching and academic profession.

Regional skills competition
Higher education institutions, and technical and vocational education and training (TVET) institutions, could be encouraged to participate in skills competitions such as the ASEAN Skills Competition to support workforce development and to achieve regional standards competency. This will contribute towards raising the quality and enhancing the skills of workers in all ASEAN member countries.

Increase usage of the English language
Language is key in the development of a global community. Workers should realize the importance of being able to communicate in English as an important tool that helped towards the realization of the ASEAN Community 2015 so that they would not be disadvantaged, but instead be able to benefit from the fruits of the ASEAN Community.

TOWARDS A HARMONIZED HIGHER EDUCATION SYSTEM: CRITICAL SUCCESS FACTORS

In this section we examine a series of regional initiatives so as to make visible the critical success factors that are associated with each programme.

The ASEAN International Mobility of Students (AIMS) Programme

In the first three years of the AIMS Programme, the number of participating students grew from a total of 260 in 2011 to more than 500 in 2013, exceeding the target set in 2009 (Ratanawijitrasin, 2013). The five disciplines involved were hospitality and tourism, agriculture, language and culture, international business, and food science and technology. Two additional disciplines, engineering and economics, were included in 2013. The implementing partners are:

- Department of Higher Education, Ministry of Higher Education (MOHE), Malaysia.
- Directorate General of Higher Education, Ministry of Education and Culture (DGHE, MOEC), Indonesia.
- Office of the Higher Education Commission, Ministry of Education (OHEC, MOE), Thailand.
- Department of Higher Education, Ministry of Education and Training, Vietnam, recently joined in 2012.
- The Philippines, Brunei and Japan joined the programme in 2013.

The AIMS Programme set targets to involve ten member nations with ten fields of study and 500 students by 2015. The programme aims to make temporary student mobility a regular feature of higher education in Southeast Asia, since dedicated academic and administrative measures for internationalization of students' experiences are generally viewed as essential features of dynamic institutions of higher education.

So far, the AIMS Programme has only involved undergraduates (of any year) in the programme from disciplines that have been determined collectively by participating countries. The duration of the mobility programme as agreed by the SEAMEO RIHED Governing Board is a minimum of one semester, but no longer than six months. The host government funds undergraduates participating in the AIMS Programme, whilst their education ministries nominate the HEIs involved in the AIMS Programme. Only flagship and leading universities are selected to assist in credit transfer, matching of course syllabi, accreditation and promoting the programme to students. The number of students involved in the exchange programme and the AIMS administrative arrangements are decided through the HEIs' bilateral agreements. However, while the AIMS Programme marks the emergence of student mobility in ASEAN higher education institutions, what needs to be highlighted for further review is the issue of recognition, not only of periods of study but also of academic qualifications obtained in another country.

To ensure the effectiveness and sustainability of the AIMS Programme, semi-annual review meetings involving the government agencies and HEIs' representatives from member countries are carried out each year. At the review meetings, member countries are updated on the development of the programme; experiences and good practices are expanded; exchanges on policy-making are made; student mobility data are verified; and future mobility activities are planned and organized (SEAMEO RIHED, 2012).

There are a number of challenges that the AIMS Programme needs to manage. The programme has been rapidly expanding from three countries in 2010 to seven countries in 2013 and to ten by 2015. As the number of students increases, the programme needs to move its focus from numbers and percentages of students involved in each country to the content and quality of the regional experience. After all, student mobility and internationalization of higher education is not a goal in itself, but a means of enhancing the quality of the educational experience and the international learning outcome of the students.

The ASEAN Qualifications Reference Framework

In order to facilitate student mobility, the region's diverse higher education systems need more harmonized standards and mechanisms for permeable and transparent quality assurance and credit transfer among institutions. Encouraging and supporting students to study abroad is a major strategy to develop a well-trained regional workforce, which can improve the quality and quantity of human resources in the ASEAN economy as well as the national education sector.

A common reference framework, the ASEAN Qualifications Reference Framework (AQRF), functions as a device to enable comparisons of qualifications across participating ASEAN countries, while at the same time supporting and enhancing national qualifications frameworks or qualifications systems that are currently at varying levels of development, scope and implementation. The AQRF addresses education and training sectors and the wider objective of promoting lifelong learning. The framework is based on agreed understandings between member countries, and invites voluntary engagement from countries. Therefore it is not regulatory and binding on member countries.

The AQRF aims to be a neutral influence on the national qualifications frameworks of participating ASEAN countries. The process for endorsing the AQRF is by mutual agreement of the participating countries. Countries will be able to determine when they will undertake the processes of referencing their qualifications framework, systems or qualification types and quality assurance systems against the framework. The purpose of the AQRF is to enable comparisons of qualifications across countries that will:

- support recognition of qualifications;
- facilitate lifelong learning;
- promote and encourage credit transfer and learner mobility;
- promote worker mobility; and
- lead to clearer and higher-quality qualifications systems (AQRF, 2013).

Currently chaired by the Malaysian Qualifications Agency (MQA), the AQRF will also provide a mechanism to facilitate comparison and transparency of regulatory agreements and harmonize them. It will link the participating ASEAN National Qualifications Frameworks (NQFs) or qualifications systems and become the ASEAN mechanism for recognition of its qualifications against other regional and international qualifications systems. To promote quality assurance of education and training across the region, the AQRF is underpinned by a set of agreed quality assurance principles and broad standards related to:

1. the functions of the registering and accrediting agencies;
2. systems for the assessment of learning and the issuing of qualifications; and
3. regulation of the issuance of certificates.

The AQRF utilizes the East Asia Summit Vocational Education and Training Quality Assurance Framework quality principles, agency quality standards and quality indicators, as the basis for the agreed quality assurance standards. The East Asia TVET Quality Assurance Framework is to be used as the benchmark for evaluating the quality assurance processes (for all education and training sectors). The referencing process will include member countries referencing their education and training quality assurance systems against the Framework (AQRF, 2013).

A board, or managing committee, was established by the ASEAN Secretariat for the maintenance, use, evaluation and review of the AQRF, including a mechanism for assessing whether the Framework is providing an enabling function for member countries. The board or managing committee responsible for the on-going management of the AQRF is to be made up of national representatives (from an NQF or responsible body) in each country and an independent expert. The board or managing committee shall also be tasked with providing a central repository for member country referencing documents, and with providing access to information and guidance to other countries external to the ASEAN region on the AQRF.

Based on the current status, the development of a comprehensive AQRF still has a long way to go. To move forward, there is a need to identify major obstacles including reaching a mutual understanding between the sending and the receiving countries, and identifying key players in the taskforce. It requires strong and long-lasting commitment by the participating countries and entails strong collaborations within and across ministries, and other stakeholders in the participating countries. Nevertheless, there have been significant steps towards an AQRF that will facilitate student and labour mobility in the region.

Credit Transfer System

To date, there have been two attempts at developing a credit transfer system in Southeast Asia. The first was by University Mobility in Asia and the Pacific (UMAP), a network of voluntary associations of government and non-government representatives of the higher education (university) sector in the region. UMAP's major contribution to the formation of a harmonized regional approach to higher education in the Asia Pacific region was the development of the UMAP Credit Transfer Scheme (UCTS), a mechanism to satisfy one of the key concerns of most proponents of a regional approach to higher education (mobility for students seeking transfer of credits within the region). Founded in 1994 with 35 countries and more than 359 HEI members, UMAP has developed a trial programme to promote student mobility in the Asia Pacific. Similar to other endeavours in many parts of the world, the UCTS aims at creating a more sustainable mobility programme that enables students to earn credits during their studies in other universities. According to UMAP, host and home universities are required to complete a credit transfer agreement in advance of the enrolments, at both graduate and postgraduate levels. Participating universities are now voluntarily taking part in the trial process of implementing the UCTS. According to Nguyen (2009), very few institutions have utilized UCTS and nor have they clearly understood the system (Japan, a major proponent of receiving students from Asia, had only 6 per cent of its HEIs utilizing UCTS as a tool). She notes that the programme lacks not only identity in the region, but also financial support.

Somewhat more successful in terms of usage is the AUN's credit transfer system known as the ASEAN Credit Transfer System (ACTS). The AUN was established by ASEAN in 1995 to embark on a programme of strengthening relations and activities among higher education institutions. As of 2011, it had about 26 members. According to ACTS, credit transfer is the award of credit for a subject in a given programme for learning that had taken place in another programme completed by a learner prior to the programme they are undertaking or about to undertake. When the institution recognizes a subject or a group of subjects that have been completed at a different institution as equivalent to the subject or a group of subjects in the programme that the student is about to undertake, the credit from the subject or group of subjects is transferred to the programme the student is about to undertake. The equivalence between the subjects completed prior to the subject to be taken by the student is assessed based on the credit value, the learning level and the learning outcomes of the two subjects in question (Asia Cooperation Dialogue, 2016).

While ACTS is open to all HEIs in the region, it has in fact become primarily an elite programme, as 'elites prefer to cooperate with elites' (Nguyen, 2009: 80). Therefore, it is somewhat self-limiting (Hawkins, 2012). More interesting is the AUN sub-regional networking on quality assurance (QA) practices, which seeks to establish some common standards for the region. In particular, the AUN Quality Assurance (AUN-QA) programme has the goal of enhancing education, research and service among its members. AUN-QA, complemented with a set of guidelines and manual for implementation, reaches out to all institutions in the region that wish to get the AUN-QA label. In the last decade, AUN-QA has been promoting, developing and implementing quality assurance practices based on an empirical approach where quality assurance practices are shared, tested, evaluated and improved. The AUN-QA activities have been driven not only through increasing collaboration among member universities, but also with the ASEAN Quality Assurance Network (AQAN), SEAMEO RIHED, the German Academic Exchange Service (DAAD) and the European Association for Quality Assurance in Higher Education (ENQA). The collaboration efforts are expected to further hasten the harmonization of the AUN-QA framework within and outside ASEAN.

In addition, SEAMEO RIHED, through policy action research funded by the Asian Development Bank, created an Academic Credit Transfer Framework for Asia (ACTFA). The framework reviews different credit transfer systems. Unlike UCTS, which used conversion, ACTFA addresses credit earned in a course regardless of the total number of credits required by the programme. It is applicable to courses in a module, a semester or a quarter and is managed at the level of system component (Ratanawijitrasin, 2013). ACTFA's four key components are mutual recognition, credit transfer, grade transfer, and supporting mechanisms and system context. Mutual recognition is considered at three levels: institution, programme and course. This implies that both participating institutions have to recognize one another's programmes and courses. The main concerns regarding this credit transfer system include course equivalence, the variety of core or elective courses, number of credits per course, the 'workload' principles used for credit transfer, and also maximum allowable credit to be transferred, which depends on the decision of the institutions. ACTFA also allows flexibility in how the home university determines students' grades and whether they are included in the grade point average calculation. Additional measures taken under this flexible system include the requirement for criteria and rules to be made transparent and public, and to be available beforehand.

CHALLENGES

The implementation of the harmonization concept is not without challenges. Steps need to be taken to improve student readiness. Barriers to language and communication must be overcome, and there should be serious efforts to reduce constraints that are essentially 'territorial' in nature. Admittedly, students participating in a mobility programme may face adjustment problems, particularly with respect to instructional practices, curriculum incomparability and cultural diversity. Then there is the language problem: differences in languages pose a great barrier for inward and outward mobility of students at the macro level. 'Territorial' constraints, by which each country hopes to safeguard the uniqueness of their educational programmes, and in turn which may ultimately constrain the implementation of regional harmonization efforts, are a major consideration to be factored in.

Generally speaking, the stakeholders have favourable views regarding the credit transfer system for ASEAN. Nevertheless, there is the issue of quality, since the role of the AQA (ASEAN Qualifications Agency) as a reliable monitoring body is being questioned. The AQA needs to exist, and links need to be built among the different national quality assurance systems. The number of significant issues associated with quality assurance would require resolution facilitated by the AQA so that local, regional and national autonomy is not compromised by an external credit system. Nevertheless, ASEAN needs a system that guarantees the quality of credits associated with education gained under any national system. Most importantly, mutual trust and confidence between different systems have to be developed. Without greater transparency and knowledge about the quality of one another's system, the development of a credit transfer system within ASEAN will be very slow.

In the context of cooperation in quality assurance, the region still possesses a few structural impediments, the most important of which is the problem of the disparity in QA development. While it may not be argued that the level of disparity of HEIs and QA development in this region is extremely high, it could be said that the current stage of QA development in Southeast Asia is more or less similar to that in other developing countries, in the sense that most of the QA systems have originated or operated as a national formal mechanism. Half of the countries in the region, including Cambodia (Accreditation Committee of Cambodia, ACC), Indonesia (National Accreditation Board for Higher Education, BAN-PT), Malaysia (Malaysian Qualifications Agency, MQA), the Philippines (Accrediting Agency of Chartered Colleges and Universities, AACCUP; Philippine Accrediting Association of Schools, Colleges and Universities, PAASCU, and so on), Thailand (Office for National Education Standards and Quality Assessment, ONESQA) and Vietnam (Department of Education Testing and Accreditation) have national QA systems operating either under the umbrella of the ministries of education or partly funded by the government. Although the majority of Southeast Asian countries in this region have already established and developed their national QA mechanisms, such as Indonesia, Thailand, Malaysia and the Philippines, the rest, namely Myanmar, Cambodia and Lao PDR, are still at the stage of developing a quality assurance infrastructure. Such disparity has fundamentally contributed to the inefficiency in developing a formal or common QA cooperation within the region. However, this does not mean that it is impossible for Southeast Asia to promote mutual development of QA systems within the sub-region. In fact, it has developed the ASEAN Quality Reference Framework as a guideline for an effective quality assurance mechanism.

ASEAN countries are rich in culture, and diverse in languages and religions, but share one common goal, which is to be united as one. The language barrier has been a constant problem among the people of the member countries. This is a great challenge to the ASEAN Community to further create programmes to address this issue that is highly relevant to higher education development. Regardless of all those differences, ASEAN and Southeast Asian countries share a similar emphasis on human resource development as key in developing the region as one, which is developing towards a knowledge-based economy.

CONCLUSIONS

The drive towards harmonization of ASEAN higher education appears to be on track, and member signatories of the ASEAN community are determined to move forward. The increased cooperation in education evidenced by all of the combined actions detailed here provides an important background for the next phase in the process of ASEAN higher education integration. The ASEAN Community recognizes the need to create a common but not an identical or indeed standardized ASEAN Higher Education Area (AHEA) that would facilitate the comparability of degrees and the mobility of students and faculty within Southeast Asia. While recognizing the fact that national and institutional variations in curricula, instruction, programmes, and degrees resulting from different historical, political, and socio-cultural influences are bound to exist, it has managed to create a common ASEAN Credit Transfer System (ACTS), degree structure, credit and quality control structures.

In conclusion, familiarization with the idea and concept of harmonization, as opposed to standardization, of higher education systems in Southeast Asia is indeed an initial but a critical step towards the implementation of a meaningful and effective harmonization of higher education systems in the region. While managers of higher education institutions and academics are not ignorant of the idea of harmonization, they tend to talk about it with reference to the Bologna Process in Europe and the creation of the EHEA. We argue that other stakeholders (particularly students), however, are not very clear as to how this concept could be realized in the context of Southeast Asia, which is culturally and politically diverse. Generally, students fail to appreciate the positive aspects of harmonization affecting their careers, job prospects and, of equal importance, cross-fertilization of cultures.

The task of creating a common higher education space appears insurmountable in view of the vast differences in the structure and performance of the various higher education systems and institutions in Southeast Asia. Admittedly, the internal structure of the higher education systems needs to be harmonized in the first instance before a region-wide initiative is attempted. More importantly, the determination to realize this idea of harmonizing higher education in Southeast Asia should permeate and be readily accepted by the regional community. Typical of Southeast Asia, directives need to come from the political masters. Thus, the role of South-East Asian Ministers of Education Organization (SEAMEO) is highly critical to a successful implementation of this idea of harmonization of the higher education systems. Although other regional bodies such as the AUN and UMAP play important roles, in the final analysis it is the nations and the individual HEIs which are the actors determining the progress of the idea of harmonization in the region. Equally importantly, national prejudices and suspicions need to be put aside if regional aspirations and goals are to be realized.

REFERENCES

Abbas, M. (2011), 'Globalization and Its Impact on Education and Culture', *World Journal of Islamic History and Civilization*, 1(1), 59–69.

AQRF (2013), 'ASEAN Qualifications Reference Framework for Education and Training Governance: Capacity Building for National Qualifications Frameworks (AANZ-0007)', Consultation Paper, accessed 7 February 2014 at http://ceap.org.ph/upload/download/20138/27223044914_1.pdf.

Armstrong, L. (2009), 'The Bologna Process: A Significant Step in the Modularization of Higher Education', *World Education News and Reviews*, 22(3), accessed 7 February 2014 at http://www.wes.org/ewenr/09apr/feature.htm.

ASEAN Secretariat (n.d.), 'ASEAN', accessed 26 September 2014 at http://www.asean.org/asean/about-asean.

Asia Cooperation Dialogue (2016), 'Asian Credit Transfer System', available at http://www.acd-dialogue.org/Areas-of-Cooperation/e-Education/ACTS.pdf.

Cerych, L. (1985), 'Collaboration between Higher Education and Industry: An Overview', *European Journal of Education*, **20**(1), 7.

Clark, N. (2007), 'The Impact of the Bologna Process beyond Europe, Part I', *World Education News and Reviews*, **20**(4), accessed 7 February 2014 at http://www.wes.org/ewenr/07apr/feature.htm.

Enders, J. (2004), 'Higher Education, Internationalisation, and the Nation-State: Recent Developments and Challenges to Governance Theory', *Higher Education*, **47**(3), 361–382.

Forest, J.J.F. (n.d.), 'Regionalism in Higher Education: An International Look at National and Institutional Interdependence', accessed 26 September 2014 at http://www.higher-ed.org/resources/JF/regionalism.pdf.

Hassan, N.K., Abibullah, S. and Morshidi, S. (1997), *Penubuhan dan Perkembangan Semasa ASEAN. Persepektif Geografi* (The establishment and current development of ASEAN. A geographical perspective), Pulau Pinang: Penerbit Universiti Sains Malaysia.

Hawkins, J. (2012), 'Regionalization and Harmonization of Higher Education In Asia: Easier Said Than Done', *Asian Education and Development Studies*, **1**(1), 96–108.

Hettne, B. (2005), 'Beyond the New Regionalism', *New Political Economy*, **10**(4), 543–571.

IPPTN (2008), 'Regionalism in Higher Education (Part 1) Trends and Examples', Updates on Global Higher Education No. 27, 15 March.

Kehm, B.M. (2010), 'Quality in European Higher Education: The Influence of the Bologna Process', *Change*, **42**(3), 40–46.

Liang, Y. (2008), 'Asian Countries Urged to Improve Education Quality', *China View*, accessed 8 Febuary 2014 at http://news.xinhuanet.com/english/2008-06/17/content_8388460.htm.

Morshidi, S. (2009), 'Trends in International Higher Education and Regionalism: Issues and Challenges for Malaysia', GIARI working paper, 2008-E-17, Tokyo: Waseda University Global COE Program, Global Institute for Asian Regional Integration.

Nguyen, A.T. (2009), 'The Role of Regional Organizations in East Asian Regional Cooperation and Integration in the Field of Higher Education', in Kuroda, K. (ed.), *Asian Regional Integration Review*, I, Tokyo: Waseda University, pp. 69–82.

Olds, K. and Robertson, S. (2011), 'Regionalism and Higher Education', *Trends and Insights for International Education Leaders*, October, accessed 26 September 2014 at http://www.nafsa.org/Explore_International_Education/Trends/TI/Regionalism_and_Higher_Education/.

Ratanawijitrasin, S. (2013), 'Vision and Current Trends of Students Mobility – from ASEAN Perspective', *The Proceedings of ASEAN+3 Higher Education Quality Assurance Forum*, Tokyo, 1 October, pp. 7–17.

SEAMEO RIHED (2012), *ASEAN International Mobility for Students (AIMS) Programme: Operational Handbook*, Bangkok: SEAMEO RIHED.

Terada, T. (2003), 'Constructing An "East Asian" Concept and Growing Regional Identity: From EAEC to ASEAN Plus 3', *Pacific Review*, **16**(2), 251–277.

Wallace, H. (2000), 'Europeanization and Globalisation: Complementary or Contradictory Trends?', *New Political Economy*, **5**(3), 369–382.
Yavaprabhas, S. (2009), 'Experiences of Asian Higher Education Frameworks and their Implications for the Future', GIARI Working Paper, 2008-E-19, Tokyo: Waseda University Global COE Program, Global Institute for Asian Regional Integration.
Yavaprabhas, S. and Dhirathiti, N.S. (2008), *Harmonisation of Higher Education: Lessons Learned from The Bologna Process*, Bangkok: SEAMEO RIHED.
Yepes, C.P. (2006), 'World Regionalization of Higher Education: Policy Proposals for International Organizations', *Higher Education Policy*, **19**(2), 111–128.
Zhang, C.Y. (2013), 'The Rise of Glocal Education: ASEAN Countries', accessed 26 September 2014 at http://www.topuniversities.com/where-to-study/region/asia/rise-glocal-education-asean-countries.

6. Changing higher education discourse in the making of the ASEAN region
Roger Y. Chao, Jr

INTRODUCTION

Although the Association of Southeast Asian Nations (ASEAN) was officially established in 1967, its regional integration initiatives only started to take off in the early 1990s. In this chapter I will argue that how ASEAN perceives, utilizes and engages higher education in its regionalization processes, including ASEAN's higher education discourses, is influenced by historical regional development, power asymmetries and policy dynamics within the diversity of its member nation-states. ASEAN higher education discourses, however, are also located within parallel processes of globalization and regionalization.

Global regionalisms are influencing the nature, scope, direction and pace of key public policies, such as higher education. As the most advanced regionalism project to date, the European project's influence is particularly prominent in shaping other emergent regions, including the Southeast Asian regional integration project, and the regionalization of higher education. Key aspects of the Bologna Process, and the various initiatives leading to the establishment of the European Higher Education Area, can be seen across a range of regional projects that are currently under way. This influence has been advanced by Europe and other nations through funding of projects via organizations, such as the ASEAN University Network (AUN), and the South-East Asian Ministers of Education Organization – Regional Centre for Higher Education and Development (SEAMEO RIHED).

As the Southeast Asian region advanced towards the establishment of the ASEAN community by late 2015, key questions needed to be, and were being, asked. Who are the core actors in regionalization of ASEAN higher education? What are the implications of the changing ASEAN higher education discourse to the regionalization of higher education in the ASEAN region? To what extent does a study of ASEAN shed light on the broader mechanisms and policy instruments used to influence regional higher education policies?

This chapter traces the changing ASEAN higher education discourse within the ASEAN regionalism project over the past decade, and links this to key regionalization of higher education initiatives, to better understand the nature and shape of this project. External (inter-regional) and internal (intra-regional) influences will be highlighted in order to highlight the policy dynamics and influences in regional higher education policy-making, and the implications for the regionalizing of higher education for the ASEAN region.

LOCATING ASEAN REGIONALISM

The emergence of ASEAN regionalism can be contextualized by a series of events that took place prior to its formal establishment in 1967. These events include ongoing developments in the Asia Pacific region itself, the Cold War, and increasing regionalism across the world, especially in Europe. Later global developments within the multilateral liberalization of trade initiatives of the World Trade Organization in the 1990s have also influenced the shape and form of ASEAN regionalism. It follows that changes in ASEAN higher education discourses over time thus need to be understood within this context. This section is thus a brief discussion of ASEAN regionalism and its initiatives over time that in turn led to the establishment of the ASEAN (Economic) Community on 31 December 2015.

The centrality of ASEAN regionalism in Asian (especially East Asian) regionalism is evident in contemporary Asia. Its influence on Asian (East Asian) regionalism, however, remains in question and it mainly serves as a platform for the broader regionalization initiative in the region. It should be noted that there were a number of failed Asian and Southeast Asian regionalization initiatives prior to ASEAN's establishment in 1967. These initiatives include the Asian Relations Conferences in the 1940s–1950s, the establishment of the Southeast Asia Treaty Organization (SEATO) in 1954, and the failed Southeast Asian regionalization initiatives in the 1950s–1960s.

The lack of legitimacy or capacity among the leading contenders for Asian regional leadership – the United States (US), Japan, India and China – since the 1940s–1950s, and the multiple and conflicting ideas for Asian regionalism, have paved the way for an ASEAN-led Asian regionalism and the multiple frameworks that have been established since 1967[1]

(He, 2004; He and Inoguchi, 2011; Acharya, 2012). Unlike the US-led SEATO which focused on preventing the spread of communism in the region, these multiple frameworks centred on regional economic integration within a slow-paced multilateral trade liberalization on the one hand, and as a reaction to the Asian Financial Crisis in the late 1980s and 1990s on the other.

ASEAN regionalism, however, was built on two earlier, failed South East Asian regionalization initiatives: the Association of Southeast Asia (ASA) and Malaysia–Philippines–Indonesia (Maphilindo). ASEAN's establishment should be seen as a result of a series of political negotiations among its founding member countries[2] aimed at finding a balance between nation-building, regional security needs, and as an alternative to Asian regionalism (Chao, 2014a). In fact, the so-called 'ASEAN way' – of prioritizing discussion, consensus-building and non-interference in other member countries' internal affairs – is central to ASEAN policy-making, and has become a requirement for all future ASEAN members and ASEAN-led frameworks.

With the end of the Cold War and the rise of China and India in the late 1980s, ASEAN regionalism started to focus on economic regionalism primarily to maintain its competitiveness with bigger non-ASEAN neighbours. The ASEAN Free Trade Area (AFTA), the ASEAN Framework Agreement on Services (AFAS), the ASEAN Investment Area (AIA) and the ASEAN Comprehensive Investment Agreement (ACIA) were established in 1992, 1995, 1998 and 2009, respectively. Furthermore, various ASEAN plus one or two countries,[3] and even inter-regional (ASEAN–European Union) free trade agreements, have proliferated since the mid-1990s, increasing the significance of ASEAN economic regionalism within the East Asian network of nations and other economic and political actors. The expansion of economic trade agreements beyond ASEAN, however, has increased the complexity of ASEAN policy-making. This has important implications for public policies, including ASEAN higher education policy within the region as well as the respective member states.

In relation to the ASEAN Vision 2020, and the Declaration of ASEAN Concord II made in Bali, Indonesia, and adapted in 1997 and 2003, respectively, ASEAN regionalism proposed the establishment of the ASEAN Community by 2020 (later advanced to 2015) anchored on three pillars: (1) the ASEAN Security Community (ASC); (2) the ASEAN Economic Community (AEC); and (3) the ASEAN Socio-Cultural Community (ASCC). This is intended to facilitate the free movement of goods, services, investment and skilled labour, and freer flow of capital, within the ASEAN region;[4] in turn transforming the dynamics within and across the region. It is also likely to have a major impact on regional projects elsewhere, including Europe and Latin America.

With the accession of Vietnam (1995), Lao PDR (1997), Myanmar (1997) and Cambodia (1999),[5] collectively known as CLMV, over the 1990s ASEAN experienced increased political, socio-economic and cultural diversity, and increased the complexity of the 'ASEAN Way'[6] of regional policy-making. This increased diversity created challenges for ASEAN that saw projects such as the Initiative for ASEAN Integration (IAI),[7] Narrowing the Development Gap (NDG),[8] and the ASEAN Minus X formula,[9] in turn facilitating multitrack liberalization in the ASEAN region. Indeed the adaption of the ASEAN Charter in 2007 was based on the need to increase ASEAN institutionalism, and its international legitimacy in the international community.

Overall, ASEAN regionalism has evolved from embracing a largely 'security' rationale to an economic rationale, in turn moving it forward as a particular kind of regional community-building. It has also engaged in increased institutionalization at the regional level, with the adoption of the ASEAN Charter that now grants formal authority and responsibilities to the ASEAN Secretariat. ASEAN, however, is divided in terms of political and policy influence with the ASEAN6 leading developments, and the CLMV having a sub-regional initiative to catch up with the former. These ASEAN developments are also influenced by ongoing developments in the European regional project and partner countries within the ASEAN Plus Three (APT) and the East Asian Summit (EAS) frameworks, through their economic and political relationship, on the one hand, and funding provided for particular policy directives, including higher education, on the other.

SHIFTING ASEAN HIGHER EDUCATION DISCOURSE

The changing ASEAN higher education discourses can be seen in the ongoing shifts within the various ASEAN policy documents and declarations, the establishment and evolution of regional organizations working on higher education (for example, the AUN and SEAMEO RIHED), and the various regional higher education initiatives. This section focuses specifically on the changing ASEAN higher education discourses in relation to ASEAN regionalism, while the following section presents the various regional higher education initiatives, discussions and conclusions on the impact of ASEAN's changing higher education discourse on the regionalization process itself.

From manpower planning to the commercialization of higher education, ASEAN's role in regional community-building through higher education has changed a great deal since its establishment in 1967. With higher education increasingly seen as a global market within the knowledge-based economy discourse, it is not surprising that ASEAN has embraced a human capital rationale towards economic development.

As early as 1977, higher education had been seen by ASEAN as supporting regional economic integration and community-building, especially within manpower development objectives more generally, and teacher education and the education system (ASEAN, 1977) specifically. However, it was only with ASEAN's focus on economic regionalism in the early 1990s that higher education cooperation was seriously considered. At the policy level AFTA and AFAS, adopted in 1992 and 1995 respectively, set the guidelines for regional economic integration, created the means for the establishment of a regional market for goods, and provided the guidelines for trade in services and the basis for the mutual recognition of qualifications. Human resource development thus became one of ASEAN's key strategies aimed at employment generation, poverty alleviation, narrowing socio-economic disparities and ensuring equitable growth through investment in education, training and development in science and technology (ASEAN, 1997, 2003, 2004).

Given the common challenges across the ASEAN nations, such as increasing student enrolments, economic restructuring, financial constraint, and equity, quality and relevance issues (Lee and Healy, 2006; Umemiya, 2008), a general consensus emerged on the benefits and necessity for higher education cooperation. This included the production of highly qualified graduates to contribute to the region's competitiveness and sustainable development, and growing acceptance of the need for increased liberalization to secure a regional knowledge-based economy. In fact, the need to harmonize ASEAN higher education systems, and improve quality and initiative regional quality assurance initiatives, was driven by ASEAN's policy of reducing its member nations' economic gap so as to realize the creation of a single market (community), and its member nations' policy objective: to internationalize higher education (Umemiya, 2008).

The influence of multilateral trade liberalization initiatives on ASEAN economic regionalism, however, should not be forgotten. In addition to the fact that the ASEAN6 were founding members of Asia-Pacific Economic Cooperation (APEC), AFTA and AFAS especially mentioned ASEAN's (then the ASEAN6) commitments to the General Agreement on Tariffs and Trade (GATT) and General Agreement on Trade in Services (GATS), while APEC was established to support and fast-track the slowing multilateral trade liberalization project (Ravenhill, 2001). ASEAN's commitment to the multilateral liberalization project and its focus on economic regionalism resulted in the following key, but largely unimplemented, policy documents:

1. Framework Agreement on Enhancing ASEAN Economic Cooperation (1992).
2. ASEAN Framework Agreement on Services (1995).
3. ASEAN Framework Agreement on Visa Exemption[10] (2006).
4. ASEAN Agreement on the Movement of Natural Persons[11] (2012).
5. A number of Mutual Recognition Agreements: engineering services (2005), nursing services (2006), surveying and architectural services (2007), dental, accountancy and medical practitioners (2008), and tourism professionals (2012).[12]

These policy documents show not only ASEAN's increased focus on regional economic integration, but also its increasing interest in trade in services. In fact, amendments to the original agreements have been made to facilitate what can be called 'two-track liberalization' between the ASEAN6 and the CLMV countries, including the ASEAN Minus X arrangement to generate service liberalization.

The Mutual Recognition Agreements, however, are basically guidelines and are thus non-binding, with the final decision to recognize qualifications and entry to national labour markets still anchored in individual countries. Furthermore, this also shows the challenges in key areas of ASEAN regionalism, including the free movement of people, and the actual implementation of the various Mutual Recognition Agreements (MRAs).[13]

An Asian Development Bank (2011) study shows that the economic status of nations has implications for the status and focus of higher education in the respective nation-states (see Table 6.1). Lower-income nations tend to focus on policy reforms, and on expansion and infrastructure developments, whilst lower-to-middle-income nations tend to focus on quality improvements. High-income nations, however, tend to be more independent, and are more engaged with global partners, and in gaining international recognition. As revealed with this observation, the wider disparities between the ASEAN partners economically were also mirrored in their higher education sectors.

Higher education and the recognition of ASEAN qualifications gained increased visibility in ASEAN policy-making circles, beginning with the ways in which policy supported ASEAN economic regionalism, and more recently through their role in helping to establish the ASEAN sociocultural community. In fact, the ASEAN 5-Year Work Plan in Education

Table 6.1 ASEAN nations' economic status and focus on higher education

Economic Status	Countries	Higher education focus
Lower income	Cambodia, Lao PDR, Myanmar, Vietnam	Policy reform and system expansion; Increasing enrolment; Infrastructure development
Low–middle income	Indonesia, Malaysia, Philippines, Thailand	Quality improvement
High income	Brunei, Singapore	More independent with global partnerships; Well developed with high international recognition

Source: Asian Development Bank (2011).

(2011–2015) focused on both the ASEAN Economic Community (AEC) and the ASEAN Socio-Cultural Community (ASCC) (see Table 6.2). Its priorities include promoting ASEAN awareness, increasing access to quality primary and secondary education, increasing the quality of education performance, standards, lifelong learning and professional development, cross-border mobility and internationalization of education, and supporting other sectorial bodies with an interest in education.

Table 6.2 also reveals that ASEAN's higher education agenda is still located in an economic rationale although its focus is also on promoting an awareness of an ASEAN identity, and placing education on ASEAN's development agenda. This shows how ASEAN's higher education agenda has moved from a more simple economic rationale to one that now incorporates regional community-building.

The ASEAN higher education agenda, thus, can be seen as constructed by its member nation-states[14] through regional organizations, including ASEAN, SEAMEO RIHED and the United Nations Educational, Scientific and Cultural Organization (UNESCO) regional office for Asia and the Pacific (UNESCO Bangkok). However, it is also informed by more global higher education discourses, promoted by international organizations such as the World Bank, the World Trade Organization and the Asian Development Bank, along with the practices and developments of key nation-states, and other regional developments, especially the European Union. In particular, the General Agreement on Trade in Services has not only redefined higher education as a commodity and part of a services industry to be framed by the rules of trade but has also facilitated the establishment of a global higher education market.

Table 6.2   ASEAN'S 5-Year Work Plan in Education

ASEAN Economic Community	ASEAN Socio-Cultural Community
Enhancing cooperation among the ASEAN University Network to increase the regional mobility of students and faculty	Putting education on ASEAN's development agenda and creating a knowledge-based society
Developing core competencies and qualifications for job/occupational and trainer skills required in priority and other service sectors	Achieving universal access to primary education
Strengthening the research capabilities of each member state by promoting skills, job placements and information networks	Promoting early childcare and development
	Raising youth awareness of an ASEAN identity rooted in friendship and cooperation

Source: http://www.asean.org/resources/publications/asean-publications/item/asean-5-year-education-work-plan; and partly adapted from Gajaseni (2014).

SHAPING THE ASEAN HIGHER EDUCATION REGION

I have been arguing that the ASEAN higher education agenda is not stagnant. Rather, it has evolved according to developments related to ASEAN regionalism, and also as a result of the influence of key economic and political partners. In fact, the regionalization of ASEAN higher education is a complex web of political and economic influences and policy dynamics, involving not only ASEAN member nations, but also external partners. In particular, the role of Japan, Australia and the European Union in the ongoing regionalization of ASEAN higher education has influenced and shaped this process. In this section I discuss the various initiatives related to the regionalization of ASEAN higher education, and the power dynamics that have inevitably accompanied this process.

Understanding the ongoing regionalization of ASEAN higher education also requires understanding the role of key regional organizations involved in the process. These include ASEAN, the AUN, SEAMEO RIHED and UNESCO Bangkok. SEAMEO RIHED was established in 1965 with the purpose of promoting regional cooperation in education amongst its 11 member nations and intra-regional cooperation. Its programmes are focused on five interconnected objective areas: empowering higher education institutions, promoting university social responsibility and sustainable development, cultivating globalized human resources, developing harmonization mechanisms, and advancing knowledge frontiers in higher education system management.[15]

By way of contrast, the AUN was established by ASEAN in 1995 (paralleling other regional initiatives in the 1990s) with its current mandate being to: (1) strengthen the existing network of cooperation among universities in ASEAN; (2) promote collaborative study, research and educational programmes in ASEAN identified priority areas; (3) promote cooperation and solidarity among scholars, academicians and researchers in ASEAN member states; and (4) serve as the policy-oriented body in higher education in the ASEAN region. As of 2008, the AUN became one of ASEAN's ministerial bodies responsible for higher education cooperation and development. With 30 current AUN member universities, it also serves as a policy laboratory where successful policies are disseminated to other ASEAN universities.

UNESCO Bangkok was established in 1961. UNESCO's interest in Southeast Asia stems from its wider United Nations mandate: that is, to promote education and development globally, and in specific regions. UNESCO Bangkok is thus a regional education bureau in the Asia and Pacific region. It is widely seen as providing a neutral platform for policy dialogues, strategic advice, and for the monitoring and assessment of the Asia Pacific region's schooling and higher education sectors, involving 48 member states and two associate members. Aside from working with governments, UNESCO Bangkok also works with UNESCO national commissions and other government and non-government partners, and supports UNESCO field offices and UN country teams in the area of education (Chao, 2014b).

In fact, the possible emergence of the East Asian (and Southeast Asian) higher education policy architecture was recently suggested, as seen in Figure 6.1 (Chao, 2014b), highlighting the various influences of key Southeast Asian and non-East Asian nations, regional and international organizations in ASEAN higher education policy-making.

Although at one level SEAMEO RIHED is regarded as at the core of the East Asian higher education policy architecture, it should also be noted that the AUN is increasingly gaining greater prominence in ASEAN, and thus in East Asian higher education policy discussions and its regionalization. Furthermore, with SEAMEO RIHED not having a full-time director since late 2013, its momentum and impact on the regionalization of ASEAN higher education, and its core place within the East Asian higher education policy architecture, may shift and be replaced by the

Higher education discourse in the ASEAN region 133

ANS = ASEAN nation-states
B-N/S = East Asian Summit nation-states
C-N/S = Other nation-states

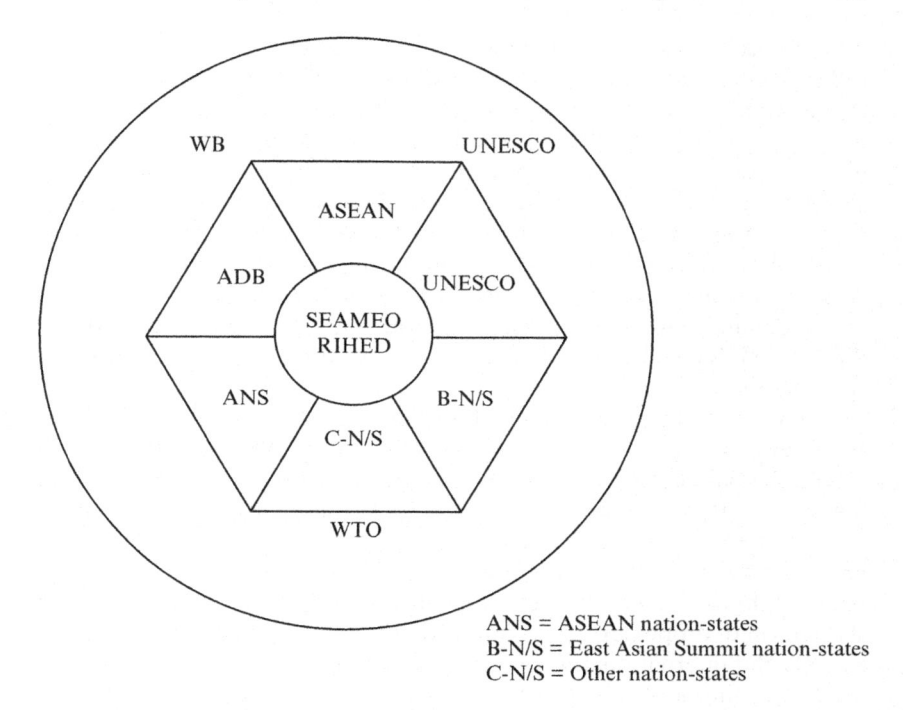

Note: WB = World Bank; WTO = World Trade Organization; ADB = Asian Development Bank; ANS = ASEAN nation-states; B-N/S = East Asian Summit nation-states; C-N/S = other nation-states.

Source: Chao (2014b).

Figure 6.1 Emerging East Asian higher education policy architecture

AUN. Added to this is the increased influence of the European Union's EU-SHARE project, which has focused attention upon, and given support to, ASEAN higher education harmonization in the AUN, and supported initiatives to develop mechanisms that link ASEAN with European higher education, such as intra-student mobility with scholarships, and ASEAN Credit Transfer System (ACTS)–European Credit Transfer System (ECTS) linkages and harmonization.[16]

Discussions on regionalization of ASEAN higher education was started by SEAMEO RIHED in mid-2007 with its Japan Foundation-funded 'Raising Awareness: Exploring the Ideas of Creating a Higher Education Common Space in Southeast Asia', aimed at raising awareness of the various issues and benefits in establishing a regional framework for higher education harmonization and the establishment of a future common space in higher education, in the form of the ASEAN Higher Education Area, influenced by the Bologna Process and eventually the Brisbane communiqué (Chao, 2011; SEAMEO RIHED, 2009). This discussion evolved into an agreement to develop mechanisms or frameworks for regional higher education harmonization in five key areas: quality assurance, closer connection between existing education and research areas (clusters), credit transfer systems, mobility systems and lifelong learning systems (SEAMEO RIHED, 2009). Participation, however, was limited to five ASEAN country cases (Malaysia, Indonesia, the Philippines, Thailand and Vietnam), with participation of Australia, Japan, New Zealand and the United Kingdom presenting their views and experiences with the Bologna Process.

In fact, a significant number of higher education initiatives from the four key organizations – the AUN, ASEAN, SEAMEO RIHED and UNESCO Bangkok (see Table 6.3) – resulted from these discussions. These higher education initiatives are presented in different categories: quality assurance, qualifications framework, accreditation, credit transfer system, harmonization and the establishment of the ASEAN Higher Education Area, diploma supplement and student mobility. Hidden within, though shaping and propelling these initiatives, is the involvement of various nations and international organizations in funding, and in providing technical assistance and expertise, in turn shaping and directing the nature of ASEAN higher education, and enhancing processes of regionalization of ASEAN higher education.

The AUN was initially focused on increasing AUN member universities collaboration at an institutional level and in enhancing internal quality assurance through the AUN Quality Assurance network. However, SEAMEO RIHED-led discussions on regionalization of ASEAN higher education have set the pace and direction of the process in the ASEAN region. This is seen with the establishment of the ASEAN Quality Assurance Network in 2008, and the development of various frameworks, including the ASEAN Qualifications Reference Framework (AQRF), the ASEAN Quality Assurance Framework for Higher Education, and the ASEAN Credit Transfer Framework Agreement in 2010, 2011 and 2013, respectively.

ASEAN initiatives towards economic regionalism, and eventually its ASEAN Framework Agreement on Services (AFAS), together with the various Mutual Recognition Agreements (MRAs), have provided the focus for higher education recognition, including credit transfer and mutual recognition. UNESCO Bangkok's 1983 recognition convention in the Asia Pacific was revised and implemented in 2011, taking into consideration contemporary developments in global higher education,

Table 6.3 Summary of ASEAN higher education actors and their mechanisms

	AUN	ASEAN	SEAMEO RIHED	UNESCO – Bangkok
Quality assurance	AUN Quality Assurance (AUN-QA) (1998) AUN-QA Guidelines (2004) AUN-QA Manual (2006) IAI QA – Training Manual (2009) Guide to AUN Actual Quality Assessment at Program Level (2010) ASEAN Quality Assurance Framework for Higher Education (2011)[1]		ASEAN Quality Assurance Framework Higher Education (2011)	
Qualifications framework		ASEAN Qualifications Reference Framework (started 2010)		
Accreditation			ASEAN Quality Assurance Network (AQAN) (2008)	

Table 6.3 (continued)

	AUN	ASEAN	SEAMEO RIHED	UNESCO – Bangkok
Credit transfer system	ASEAN Credit Transfer System (2010)		Harmonizing CTS in Greater Mekong sub-region and beyond (started 2009) Academic Credit Transfer Framework Agreement (ACTFA) (2013)	
Mutual recognition		ASEAN Framework Agreement on Services (AFAS) (1995) Various Mutual Recognition Agreements (since 1995)		Mutual Recognition Convention – Asia and Pacific (1983, 2011)
Harmonization and establishment of an ASEAN Higher Education Area			Envisioned and increased awareness of the benefits and challenges of an ASEAN Higher Education Area (since 2007)	

Diploma supplement[2]		
Student mobility	Various AUN-linked scholarships	ASEAN International Mobility for Students Programme (AIMS) (2012) (formerly M-I-T, 2010)

Notes:

1. The ASEAN Quality Assurance Framework for Higher Education was developed by the ASEAN Quality Assurance Network in collaboration with the AUN and SEAMEO RIHED with support from the German Academic Exchange Service (DAAD), German Rectors Conference (HRK) and the European Association of Quality Assurance in Higher Education (ENQA).
2. Initiatives to establish a diploma supplement are located within APEC's initiative to apply the diploma supplement in the Asia Pacific region, and Australia's initiative to link Australian and ASEAN higher education within the ASEAN–Australia–New Zealand Free Trade Agreement. See http://ienews.minedu.govt.nz/apec-diploma-supplement-workshop/.

Source: Compiled from AUN, SEAMEO RIHED, UNESCO, ASEAN and other websites.

and its regionalization initiatives. ASEAN Credit Transfer Systems[17] and student mobility programmes were also developed. AUN student mobility programmes, however, are focused between its member universities and their institutional partners, whilst SEAMEO RIHED's ASEAN International Mobility Scheme (AIMS) has evolved from its focus on Malaysia, Indonesia and Thailand, to the broader ASEAN region.

Amidst all of these developments the involvement of interested parties, specifically Australia, Japan, Germany and the European Union has increased. Australia's determined efforts to harmonize the Asia Pacific's higher education sector through the Brisbane Communiqué and the ASEAN–Australia–New Zealand Free Trade Agreement, which includes higher education, provides the drive to support ASEAN harmonization, and increasingly link higher education sectors. Japan supported SEAMEO RIHED's initiative to establish the ASEAN Higher Education Area. Germany and the European Association for Quality Assurance in Higher Education (ENQA) supported the development of the ASEAN Quality Assurance Framework for Higher Education; and the European Union, through the EU-SHARE project, is increasingly supporting AUN initiatives towards the regionalization of ASEAN higher education and increasing ASEAN–EU higher education linkages.

Given that the AUN and SEAMEO RIHED's financial capacities to undertake projects are limited, external partners provide a platform to support, direct and shape the regionalization of ASEAN higher education, and in doing so, enhance linkages between ASEAN and their respective countries and region. Stimulating these partnerships is an assumption that economic and political benefits will flow in terms of mutual recognition of higher education qualifications, increased student and academic mobility, increased access to the global labour market in an increasingly competitive global higher education and labour market, and the demographic challenges across the developed nations. Although economic interest may still be the driving force for such support by ASEAN's partner nations, it does facilitate the development, and eventual establishment, of an ASEAN Higher Education Area.

The regionalization of ASEAN higher education, however, is not only an ongoing project but is also a challenging process. The diversity of ASEAN higher education systems is not limited to size, access, quality and relevance, but also involves international stature and recognition. Furthermore, the predominance of private higher education in some ASEAN nations (for example, the Philippines, Thailand, Indonesia and Malaysia) adds to this diversity. This very diversity, as with ASEAN's socio-economic status, presents development challenges for ASEAN member nations.

A SEAMEO RIHED (2012) scoping study of ASEAN higher education quality assurance shows the diversity of quality assurance systems, and even of the development or establishment of quality assurance agencies and national qualifications frameworks. The Philippines has at least five privately led quality assurance agencies; Myanmar and Singapore[18] do not have a quality assurance agency at all; whilst the development of national qualifications frameworks are still under construction in Cambodia, Lao PDR, Myanmar and Vietnam, with Singapore having no intention of developing one.

The CLMV higher education systems are still focused on policy development, expanding their higher education sectors and developing infrastructures, whilst low- and middle-income nations focus on quality improvements, and high-income nations are increasingly gaining international recognition and global partnerships. Furthermore, even among middle-income countries, national higher education initiatives to increase internationalization have seen diverse effects, with Malaysia rapidly becoming a regional higher education hub, and Thailand, the Philippines and Indonesia struggling to attain international recognition. Such diversity within ASEAN higher education systems remains a huge challenge for region-building. But the various ASEAN frameworks and guidelines aim to narrow the gap, and lead to the establishment of an ASEAN Higher Education Area.

CONCLUSIONS

This chapter has focused attention on ASEAN regionalism, and the changing ASEAN higher education discourses that are shaping the region. I have argued that this is a complex and diverse project, though there are signs that there is a thickening of regionalism as its core actors, as well as range of mechanisms and policy instruments, are being advanced to influence, and thus shape, regional higher education policies and practice. ASEAN regionalism has evolved from its security rationale to economic regionalism, eventually incorporating the establishment of the ASEAN Community by December 2015.

At least three key regional actors are involved in the regionalization of ASEAN higher education as presented in the emerging and evolving East Asian (and Southeast Asian) higher education policy architecture. And it is these distinct initiatives, both separately and in combination, which give form and content to this region-building project and the ways in which it both mediates and is mediated by higher education. The three main players are ASEAN, the AUN and SEAMEO RIHED, with

UNESCO Bangkok's engagement limited to its Asia Pacific recognition convention, though increasingly working towards regionalization projects focused on the Asia Pacific region.[19] Yet funding for the majority of regionalization initiatives tends to be from self-interested nations and regions, including Australia, Japan, Germany and the European Union, all directing ASEAN initiatives toward increased linkages with their respective higher education systems.

ASEAN diversity, including its higher education systems, however, poses a challenge to the regionalization of ASEAN higher education. The different socio-economic and higher education development of ASEAN nation-states significantly impacts upon ASEAN higher education harmonization, although the development of regional frameworks provides the impetus and direction towards the establishment of a future ASEAN Higher Education Area. ASEAN regionalism and its challenges in narrowing the development gap among ASEAN member nations are reflected in the different levels of development of the ASEAN higher education sector, quality assurance systems, their private sector participation, quality and international recognition.

The changing ASEAN higher education discourse reflects the evolution of ASEAN regionalism, which has in turn been influenced by global regionalisms within a changing world order. Its early stages of enhancing ASEAN higher education cooperation were focused on the institutional levels through the AUN, while increased economic regionalism, the acceptance of the human capital and knowledge-based economy discourses, and the establishment of higher education common spaces or areas (especially the European Higher Education Area) provided the impetus to start discussions and initiatives to establish the ASEAN Higher Education Area. The increased focus on establishing the ASEAN Community in the mid-2000s, however, has incorporated a community-building and identity formation rationale within the ASEAN higher education discourse, and resulted in the focus on higher education's role in increasing awareness of and building the ASEAN identity along with its core economic rationales.

There is little doubt that the future of regionalization of ASEAN higher education will evolve over time, and as a result of the development of ASEAN economic regionalism itself, the establishment of the ASEAN Community, and the external assistance and involvement of its core economic partner nations and regions. It will influence not only the ideational basis of ASEAN higher education discourses, but also the ongoing development of the future ASEAN Higher Education Area.

NOTES

1. ASEAN, the Asia-Pacific Economic Cooperation (APEC), ASEAN Plus Three (APT) and the East Asian Summit (EAS) were established in 1967, 1989, 1998 and 2005, respectively.
2. ASEAN's founding members are the non-socialist countries of Indonesia, Malaysia, Singapore, Thailand and the Philippines.
3. ASEAN–China, ASEAN–Japan, ASEAN–Korea and ASEAN–Australia–New Zealand, to name just a few.
4. http://www.asean.org/archive/5187-10.pdf.
5. Brunei Darussalam actually joined ASEAN in 1984 shortly after its independence.
6. The 'ASEAN way' is focused on intensive dialogue and consensus-building, and non-interference of member countries' internal affairs.
7. Launched in 2000, the Initiative for ASEAN Integration (IAI) focuses on collective efforts to narrow the development gap within ASEAN, and between ASEAN and the rest of the world.
8. NDG is an ASEAN initiative focused on addressing various forms of disparities among and within member states (http://www.asean.org/communities/asean-economic-community/category/overview-ndg-iai-iai-work-plan-iai-task-force-idcf).
9. ASEAN Minus X facilitates ASEAN countries that are ready to push forward with liberalization to move forward with other ASEAN countries joining later.
10. Not in force.
11. Not in force.
12. The Mutual Recognition Agreement on Tourism Professionals was signed in Bangkok, Thailand on 9 November 2012 but is still not in force.
13. The actual implementation of these MRAs is still in the development phase with key national regulations being one of the key obstacles.
14. Other stakeholders including industry and civil society also contribute to the ASEAN higher education agenda, especially within national dialogues; however, it is through nation-states that these are brought forth to the ASEAN level.
15. http://www.rihed.seameo.org/about-us/objective-areas/.
16. http://www.aunsec.org/aseanqaeuproject.php.
17. There are two ASEAN-based credit transfer systems: one by the AUN (AUN-ACTS, commonly referred to as ACTS, the ASEAN Credit Transfer System), and the University Mobility in Asia and the Pacific (UMAP) Credit Transfer Scheme (UCTS).
18. Singapore's Council for Private Education is only responsible for the private education sector.
19. Informal discussion with Dr Libing Wang, Chief of the Asia-Pacific Programme of Educational Innovation for Development (APEID), UNESCO Bangkok, on 4–5 July 2014 in Yangon, Myanmar.

REFERENCES

Acharya, A. (2012), 'Foundations of Collective Action in Asia: Theory and Practice of Regional Cooperation', ADBI Working Paper Series 334, Tokyo: Asian Development Bank Institute.

Asian Development Bank (ADB) (2011), *Higher Education Across Asia*, Manila: Asian Development Bank.

Association of Southeast Asian Nations (ASEAN) (1977), *Joint Communique of the First ASEAN Education Ministers Meeting*, accessed 15 May 2012 at www.aseansec.org.1443.htm.

Association of Southeast Asian Nations (ASEAN) (1997), *Hanoi Plan of Action*, accessed 15 May 2012 at www.aseansec.org/8754.

Association of Southeast Asian Nations (ASEAN) (2003), *Bali Concord II*, accessed 15 May 2012 at www.aseansec.org/15159.htm.

Association of Southeast Asian Nations (ASEAN) (2004), *Vientiane Action Programme*, accessed 15 May 2012 at www.aseansec.org/VAP-10th%20ASEAN%Summit.pdf.

Chao, R.J. (2011), 'Reflections on the Bologna Process: The Making of an Asia Pacific Higher Education Area', *European Journal of Higher Education*, **1**(2–3), 102–118.

Chao, R.J. (2014a), 'Pathways to an East Asian Higher Education Area: A Comparative Analysis of East Asian and European Regionalization Processes', *Higher Education*, **68**, 559–575.

Chao, R.J. (2014b), 'Regionalization, International Organizations and East Asian Higher Education: A Comparative Study of East Asian Higher Education Reforms', PhD thesis, City University of Hong Kong, China.

Gajaseni, N. (2014), 'ASEAN – a Regional Overview for Higher Education: The Current Roadmap: Case of the ASEAN University Network', presented at the Global Education Dialogue – Myanmar, 4–5 July, Yangon.

He, B. (2004), 'East Asian Ideas of Regionalism: a Normative Critique', *Australian Journal of International Affairs*, **58**(1), 105–125.

He, B. and Inoguchi, T. (2011), 'Introduction to Asian Regionalism', *Japanese Journal of Political Science*, **12**(2), 165–177.

Lee, M.N. and Healy, S. (2006), 'Higher Education in South-East Asia: An Overview', in Lee, M.N. and Healy, S. (eds), *Higher Education in South-East Asia*, Bangkok: UNESCO Asia and Pacific Regional Bureau for Education, pp. 1–12.

Ravenhill, J. (2001), *APEC and the Construction of Pacific Rim Regionalism*, Cambridge: Cambridge University Press.

South East Asian Ministers of Education Organization – Regional Centre for Higher Education and Development (SEAMEO-RIHED) (2009), *Raising Awareness: Exploring the Ideas of Creating a Common Space in Higher Education in Southeast Asia: A Conference Proceeding*, Bangkok: SEAMEO RIHED.

South East Asian Ministers of Education Organization – Regional Centre for Higher Education and Development (SEAMEO RIHED) (2012), *A Study on Quality Assurance Models in Southeast Asian Countries: Towards a Southeast Asian Quality Assurance Framework*, Bangkok: SEAMEO RIHED.

Umemiya, N. (2008), 'Regional Quality Assurance Activity in Higher Education in Southeast Asia: Its Characteristics and Driving Forces', *Quality in Higher Education*, **14**(3), 277–290.

7. Shaping an ASEM (Higher) Education Area: hybrid sectoral regionalism from within

Que Anh Dang*

INTRODUCTION

There is now a growing literature on regions and regionalisms, and on the role of the higher education sector in regional projects, such as Europe. The main thrust of this chapter is to bring these two into conversation with each other through examining how a region and sector relate to each other in terms of the consequences of sectoral cooperation for the region, on the one hand, and of regional cooperation on the sector, on the other. My entry point is the construction of a new 'regional sectoral space' between Asia and Europe, designated as an Asia–Europe Meeting (ASEM) Education Area by the ASEM Ministers of Education in 2011. In particular, the chapter seeks answers to the following questions: How and through what process has the ASEM education process emerged as a region-building project? How and why was higher education made a key priority on the ASEM education agenda?

Three aspects to this distinctive regionalizing process will be developed in this chapter. The first is that the ASEM Education Area is a *hybrid* in that it develops traits from novel combinations of the Bologna Process, on the one hand, and Asian experiences on the other, through its regional educational cooperation activities. The second is that it is *sectoral*. That is, it refers to those processes in the higher education sector which are distinct from, and thus different to, ASEM cooperation in other sectors (such as trade, public health, environment, transport or security). The third, *regionalism from within*, is used to explain the distinct features of the ASEM education process that have been shaped by the national interests of member countries and the inter-subjective knowledge which has emerged from within the community of actors who are endogenous to the higher education sector.

Taken together, I will argue these can be regarded as a form of 'hybrid sectoral regionalism from within'. My understanding of this as a form of sectoral regionalism draws on my direct observations in, and field notes on, five ASEM Education Ministers' Meetings and ten Senior Officials' Meetings (SOMs) between 2008 and 2015, related policy documents, and more than 20 personal interviews with key actors between 2013 and 2015.

The chapter is organized in the following way. I begin with a discussion of the concepts of 'emergence' and 'emergent properties' as a means to explain 'hybrid regionalism' and to explore ASEM education processes as a series of emergent properties. Using a process tracing method, I then test this idea by analysing the complex processes of institution-building and agenda-setting from 2008 to the beginning of 2015 to enhance understanding of how a hybrid region is created in practice, and what effects it has on its constitutive parts. Finally, I reflect on the concept of emergence as a tool for helping to explain the construction of ASEM as a distinctive regional form.

EMERGENCE, EMERGENT PROPERTIES AND REGIONALISMS

In a recent study of the intellectual history of regionalism over the last 60 years, De Lombaerde and Söderbaum (2013) acknowledge the continuing ontological confusion about the object of enquiry: 'what exactly it is we study when we study regionalism'. In essence, scholars are dealing with different parts of a 'metaphoric elephant'; some are focused on regional subsystems, regions and region-building, whereas others are concerned with regional integration and regional organizations. Most studies base their explanations on international relations or economic theories (Camroux, 2010; Dent, 2003, 2004; Doidge, 2008; Mansfield and Solingen, 2010; Rüland and Storz, 2008; Rüland, 2010; Väyrynen, 2003) leaving open the question of how best to study a sector like education whose cultural, political and economic features are distinctively different.

At one level, then, this chapter is about two constituent regions – Asia and Europe – being put together. Yet at another level, methodologically it is more than a question of juxtaposition and comparison. Since the two regions are obviously not equivalent constituent parts, comparison would make less sense than analysing hybrid features of the new region in order to address the questions at hand. Moreover, the ASEM cooperation process is not one of regional integration in the sense of being led by formal agreements or treaties between governments (Breslin and Higgott, 2003) requiring some degree of shared sovereignty (Fioramonti, 2012) and involving the setting-up of supra-national institutions to make collectively binding decisions (Börzel, 2011). So far, ASEM has not been characterized by these features. Hence, it is an intriguing form of region-building to be studied. But the question is, how?

It is widely agreed that integration theories continue to be heavily influenced by the European Union's history and experience (Breslin and Higgott, 2003). This can lead to underestimating the possibilities of many different forms of region-making projects, and thus entities, and the approaches to their study. This chapter is an exploration of region-building in a particular sector, and I begin with the proposition that the idea of emergence, as developed in critical realism, offers a way of explaining how a new regional education space arises from its constituent components.

A key idea in critical realism is that the world is characterized by emergence; that is, where the conjunction of two or more components gives rise to new phenomena whose properties are not reducible to their constituent parts (Sayer, 2000). For example, the power to extinguish fires and slake thirst are properties of water, not of the individual atoms (hydrogen and oxygen), of which water is composed. Martin and Sunley (2012: 340) define emergence as a process in which lower-level components of a system interact so as to produce effects (for example, properties, patterns, functions, powers) at a higher level of the system, so that the latter becomes 'supervenient' on the former, and is not reducible to those individual components.

Conversely, downward causation refers to the idea that a higher-level emergent property, pattern or phenomenon causes, determines, regulates or influences, lower-level properties and parts, either in those component entities or in their interactions (Martin and Sunley, 2012). Lewis (2012) argues that downward causation may take different forms. It could include the conformity of lower-level entities that are constrained to act in accordance with the laws governing the emergent higher-level entities. A more robust version of downward causation allows for the possibility that lower-level entities may be reconstituted rather than merely being restrained, by the emergent causal powers of higher-level entities. For example, people make or adopt social rules and norms, and behave in conformity with them. These social rules, in turn, have powers to structure how people interact with each other and to change people's dispositions to conceptualize and respond to their circumstances in certain ways (ibid.: 339).

Lewis (2012) also emphasizes the significance of the relations between constituent components. He adopts the definition of emergence that states, 'when certain elements or parts stand in particular relations to one another, the whole that is formed has properties – known as "emergent properties" – that are not possessed by those elements or parts taken in isolation' (ibid.: 368). According to his argument, the existence of emergent properties depends not only on the presence of its constituent components but also on their standing in certain relation to one another. Sayer (2000) calls these relations 'structures' or 'mechanisms', which suggest that the parts are arranged in a particular way to form the whole and generate emergent properties. Thus, the emergent property or causal power is a qualitatively novel and *sui generis* property of the whole, not of the individual parts taken in isolation or as an unstructured aggregate. This understanding will shed light on the questions of what mechanisms organize countries together to construct the ASEM education process and what new policy tools emerge from the ASEM higher education cooperation.

Furthermore, Lewis (2012) examines the 'spontaneous (non-planned or non-imposed) character' of emergence and argues that not all emergent properties arise spontaneously. The distinction between 'emergence' and 'spontaneous order' is of particular relevance for explaining the roles of actors and their deliberate actions in the creation of an ASEM Education Area.

Martin and Sunley (2012) distinguish 'strong' from 'weak' emergence. A 'strong emergence' (also known as second-order emergence and third-order emergence) implies that new properties are real and distinct; they not only come into existence at higher levels, but also exert their influence on the lower-level constituents that produce them. In contrast, 'weak emergence' (also known as first-order emergence) does not entail the introduction of new processes or mechanisms that causally influence lower-level components. The authors also argue that an increase in the number of lower-level components increases iterative interaction possibilities. With every iteration of interactions, relational properties are multiplied with respect to each other. When the number of elements and chances for interactions grow, emergent properties are more likely to emerge. In the case that I will examine here, this prompts questions about the consequences of the evolving and extensive membership on the hybridization of ASEM as a higher education region, and its properties.

The theory of emergence suggests a region is an emergent entity whose existence depends on its constituent parts and the relations between them. Regionalizing, therefore, is a set of processes whereby a set of constituent parts are joined together to constitute a new entity (the whole) in which new properties are produced. According to Elder-Vass (2010), both wholes and parts are entities, and the terms 'whole' and 'part' describe roles played by particular entities in particular contexts. An entity can be a whole in one context, and a part in another context. Any entity must be structured in some way, in the sense that the relations between the parts are more than merely aggregative. This is to distinguish an entity from a collection of parts that does not form an entity, like a pile of vegetables is still not a soup

(Elder-Vass, 2010: 16). Furthermore, an entity must sustain its existence over a significant period of time.

ASEM: AN ENTITY WITH EMERGENT PROPERTIES

Building on the theory of emergence and Elder-Vass's concept of entity, a region may be defined as a persistent whole, constructed by a set of parts that is structured by the relations between these parts. The parts in ASEM refer to the Asian and European member countries and the regional entities such as the European Union, the European Commission, the Association of Southeast Asian Nations (ASEAN) Secretariat, and other regional non-governmental organizations who are essential to the existence of ASEM. The regional institutions (for example, ministerial meetings, working groups, soft rules such as the chair's conclusions, joint projects and other norms) are the mechanisms which bring these members together by establishing the pattern of their interactions and the relations between them. Seen from this perspective, the Bologna Process, or more formally the European Higher Education Area (EHEA), is an example of a strong emergence. Through various mechanisms (for example, Ministers' Communiqués, the Bologna Follow-Up Group, action lines, standards, benchmarks, guidelines, stocktaking and implementation reports, and so on) the Bologna Process has gained the capacity to coordinate higher education reforms, as well as to standardize and converge policies across 48 countries with regard to degree structures, quality assurance, student mobility, and so on. This coordinating capacity, or 'downward causation', is an emergent property which becomes an intrinsic element of the EHEA, in turn affecting the behaviour of its members. Therefore, emergent properties and causal powers may be regarded as synonyms (Elder-Vass, 2010).

On the Asian side, there is a series of emergences: for example, two identifiable regional institutions, the ASEAN Ministers of Education Meetings (ASED) and the South-East Asian Ministers of Education Organization (SEAMEO), and the cooperation between these two organizations and several countries or a single country, such as ASEAN + China, Japan and South Korea, ASEAN + Australia, or SEAMEO and China. These two organizations are concerned with all levels and sectors of education, not only higher education. SEAMEO has set up issue-based centres for knowledge exchange in tropical biology, teacher training, mathematics and science, special needs education, higher education, and so on. Both SEAMEO and ASED can also be seen as emergent entities because they are the results of regional cooperation. However, they are examples of 'weak emergence', at least in the higher education sector, because so far there has been little evidence of them generating mechanisms that causally influence policies in their member countries. Nevertheless, this fact has been changing in recent years, and will change in the foreseeable future owing to the establishment of the ASEAN Community, and to the launch of the ASEAN Community Vision 2025 which took place at the end of 2015.

ASEM is a political construct at a higher level of the global system constituted by two world regions, Asia and Europe, as the name suggests. In essence, the evolution of ASEM consists of a series of emergent hybrids, including those that occur within and across the two constituent regions. Although ASEM does not include all the countries in Europe and in Asia, it still exemplifies an extensive region with its borders stretching eastward from the Atlantic coast of Europe to Oceania, and this distance does not seem to hinder the development of the region.

New regionalism theory argues that the social construction of regions matters more than geographical proximity (Acharya, 2009; Katzenstein, 2005). Regions are constructed through purposeful social, political, cultural and economic interactions amongst states which often, though not always, inhabit the same geographical space (Acharya, 2007, 2012). Stated differently, these interactions constitute emergent entities. The ASEM education process could, therefore, be seen as a form of hybrid regionalism that emerges from a series of social and political interactions between Asia and Europe. This, in turn, creates a new regional sectoral space for developing higher education policies. Thus, the next section sets out to examine what institutions in place are key mechanisms that generate hybridization between Asian and European higher education systems, and what powers this ASEM hybrid region obtains and exercises.

HIGHER EDUCATION IN ASEM: A NEW REGIONAL SECTORAL SPACE

Higher education has been deliberately selected to construct ASEM through the development of a new regional sectoral space shaped by domestic interests of member countries and their senior officials. This argument is supported by the analysis of regional institutions or mechanisms that enable ASEM to set agendas and generate hybrid forms of the discourse of higher education. The following sections trace and explain the resulting hybridization as a series of interactions of distinct activities (for example, ASEM joint projects), and the outcomes of negotiations to create inter-subjective understandings and hybrid identities.

Emergence: Institutions and Membership of ASEM Education Process

From its origin, ASEM was conceived as an informal platform for dialogue between the European Union (EU) and ASEAN (Camroux, 2006; Dent, 2004; Yeo, 2002). ASEM was initiated in 1994 by Singapore, supported by France[1] and launched in 1996 by Thailand with 26 members.[2] Today ASEM involves 53 partners,[3] consisting of 30 European and 21 Asian countries, the European Union and the ASEAN Secretariat. After the establishment of the Asia-Pacific Economic Cooperation (APEC) in 1989 between Asia and North America, ASEM has been seen as an act to strengthen the link between Asia and the European Union and to balance the powers in the triad of Asia, North America and Western Europe (Dang, 2013; Yeo, 2003).

The economic pillar, being the main purpose of ASEM, has been the most developed and substantive form of cooperation. Education is a subtopic in the ASEM socio-cultural pillar, which aims at achieving a deeper understanding between Asia and Europe through intellectual exchange and student mobility (Dang, 2015). Although the ASEM Vision Group (1999) urged the leaders to issue a declaration on education with an aim to increase student exchange between Asia and Europe and create a high-profile ASEM scholarship scheme, education was less prominent than trade and security on the leaders' agenda.

In the early 2000s, and especially after the 9/11 event, there was an incoming tide of Asian students going to Europe, both as self-funded students and via scholarship schemes funded by individual Asian and European governments, as well as the European Commission through the Asia-Link and Erasmus Mundus programmes. At the same time, the Bologna Process gathered pace and developed its global dimension to intensify the exchange of ideas and experiences with other regions, not least to attract students to Europe (Bologna Process, 2005). Despite these developments, the ASEM 1999 Vision Group's ambitious projection of a fivefold increase in the number of students mobile between Asia and Europe was far from realized. Against this background, at the sixth ASEM Summit of Heads of State and Government in 2006, the German Chancellor proposed to host the first ASEM Education Ministers' Meeting, hence making education a strategic and high-level cooperation.

It is worth noting that Germany is a Western European country without colonial relations with Asia in the past. Moreover, German higher education was not regarded as an aggressive export industry. Therefore the proposal was generally seen as a diplomatic endeavour emphasizing the value of dialogue and exchange in education between Europe and Asia. Subsequently, Berlin hosted not only the first ASEM Education Ministers'

Meeting but also the first ASEM Rectors' Conference[4] in 2008, which brought together education leaders from over 40 countries and marked the beginning of the so-called 'ASEM education process'. The very phrase first appeared in the minutes of the Senior Officials' Meeting (SOM) in January 2009 and the word 'process' was chosen to denote a sense of continuity and progressive development.

Two mechanisms generating the ASEM hybrid education area are institutions and evolving membership. This education area is a whole in the sense that it is an outcome of a sectoral cooperation between ASEM members, but it is a part in relation to the overall multisectoral ASEM process. This regional institutional design is illustrated in Figure 7.1, but the chapter focuses on the education sector including actors and agenda captured in the lower left corner only.

The reason for focusing on the higher education sector is twofold. Firstly, ASEM cooperation in this sector has grown very fast, and secondly, it manifests a novel combination of non-Bologna and Bologna experiences. The European members have unique expertise and success particularly in the regionalization of higher education. Drawing on this expertise, within a relatively short period of seven years to early 2015, the ASEM education process has been able to establish its own norms and institutions consisting of biennial ministerial meetings, biannual meetings of senior officials, a rotating secretariat, numerous working groups, joint projects, expert seminars, Rectors' conferences and student forums. Adopting the ASEAN way, these institutions are based upon informal rules and normative values, such as mutual respect, mutual learning, and decisions by consensus not by voting. Informality is one of the major strengths of these institutions, which generate open interactions between members and can over time change the context (Solingen, 2008), create shared understandings that direct the behaviours of individual actors, as well as to develop their sense of collective identity (Zhang, 2008). These institutions are, in essence, the mechanisms for constructing an ASEM higher education regional sectoral space.

The evolving membership of ASEM is an integral part of the institution-building process. ASEM membership is voluntary and inclusive. It does not require political criteria or structural reform of higher education systems. Unlike the EHEA, it is not decided by the ministers of education but by heads of state and government, based on proposals from the ministers of foreign affairs. Once a country becomes a member of ASEM, it automatically has the right to participate in all sectoral cooperation under the ASEM framework, including the ASEM education process. The 'Europe' in ASEM today consists of 28 EU member states and the European Union,[5] and Norway and Switzerland. All are the EHEA

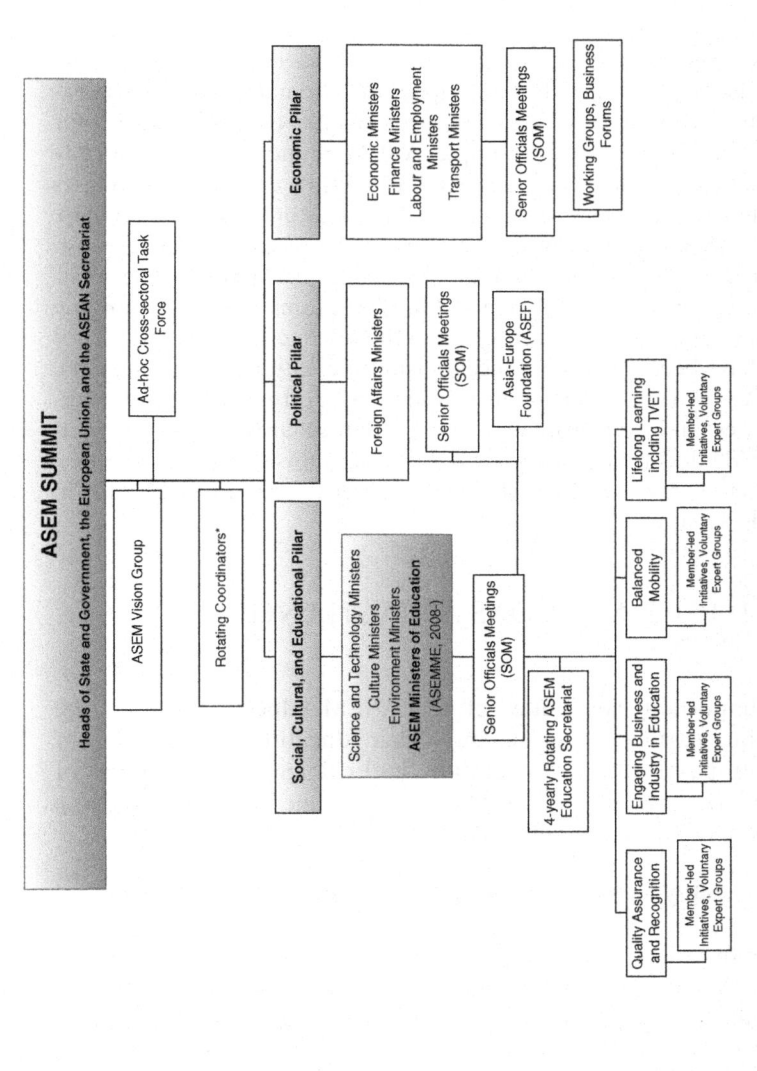

Note: * ASEM process has no permanent secretariat, but it is assisted by a group of four coordinators: the European Union through its External Action Service (the only permanent coordinator), EU Presidency country, an ASEAN country and a non-ASEAN country.

Source: Author.

Figure 7.1   ASEM education process in the ASEM institutional structure

members.[6] In terms of higher education, this Europe is an organized and homogenous region. On the contrary, the 'Asia' in ASEM is a dispersed group of countries.[7] Broadly speaking, ASEM higher education is constructed through a process of hybridization between European and Asian ideas of higher education; and in a narrower sense, between Bologna and non-Bologna higher education systems.

The size of membership has made ASEM the world's largest region of higher education, which also has an impact on internal regional cooperation because there are greater status rewards at stake (Ravenhill, 2012) for any members to cooperate (for example, ASEM countries enthusiastically volunteer to host meetings and the secretariat[8]) thus creating possibilities of more extensive emergent properties. Along with growing membership, over 50 ASEM education meetings between 2008 and early 2015 have also created plentiful opportunities for inter-regional interactions. The bilateral partnership meetings and signed Memorandums of Understanding between Asian and European countries on the sidelines of each ministerial conference have become another mechanism for creating this new regional sectoral space. In sum, informal institutions, which themselves are emergent properties, and extensive membership are mechanisms for constructing the ASEM education process. How these mechanisms work in practice, what powers they produce, and who drives the processes, are elaborated in the following section.

POWER TO SET AGENDAS AND CHANGE DISCOURSES

The most important capabilities of the ASEM education process are agenda-setting, particularly in making higher education a key priority of the Asia–Europe education cooperation, and changing the meanings of the discourse around cooperation. These have changed over time, and as a result of the actions of particular actors.

2008: Employability and Mobility Overshadow Cultural Understanding

In March 2008 some 50 senior officials from 31 ministries of education in Asia and Europe and the European Commission gathered in Bonn to identify agenda items for the first Asia–Europe Meeting of Ministers for Education (ASEM ME1) to be held in May that year. The meeting tabled two issues, employability and mobility, based on the assumption that mobility creates the relevant social capital that improves employability. The focus is on higher education exchange, but the new meaning is distant from that of the first ASEM summit statement that intends 'to foster exchange of students and scholars with a view to developing better understanding of the cultures, histories and business practices of both regions' (ASEM, 1996: 19).

The new meanings of the ASEM education cooperation are shaped by the background documents 'EU–Asia Higher Education Cooperation' and 'Education and the Labour Market' which were prepared by the German Academic Exchange Service (DAAD). The director of German National Agency of EU Higher Education Cooperation at the DAAD – who later became the director of the ASEM Education Secretariat – presented the summaries of the papers to the senior officials. This director has extensive experience with the Bologna Process and was heavily involved in the organization of the 2003 Bologna Ministerial Meeting in Berlin. He brought to ASEM his expertise accumulated from many national and European projects, the Bologna working group on mobility, and the European Commission's working group on the future of Erasmus. Being the lead author of the two background papers and acting as a coordinator at the first SOM, undoubtedly this director had the opportunity to shape the discussion and frame the first concepts for the ASEM education process. The SOM minutes recorded consensus on two plenary sessions with the same titles as the background papers; each has two sub-themes that define scope, purposes and activities of cooperation. In a nutshell, mobility and employability were presented as two common issues of higher education, for which the Asian and European ministers need to forge strategic partnerships and find solutions.

At the ASEM Ministers' Meeting in May 2008, mobility was placed at the top of the agenda for the first day, and it was also seen as opening up opportunities for other areas, such as quality assurance, because it 'has been considered important to improving the attractiveness of higher education institutions and to attracting the best "brains"' (ASEM SOM, 2008). Mobility was deemed so important and relevant for ASEM that the chair's conclusions devoted five out of nine clauses to the concrete activities that would promote mobility between Asia and Europe, including the recommendation to set up a working group on 'strengthening the mobility of students, teachers and researchers . . . and improving the framework conditions for bi-regional exchanges with special regard to recognition of qualifications and degrees' (ASEM ME1, 2008).

Subsequently, the German Federal Ministry of Education and Research, in collaboration with the DAAD, organized a follow-up meeting in December 2008 in Frankfurt on 'enhancing mobility by removing obstacles' to set up a 'working group' involving not only senior officials but also regional stakeholders active in the Bologna Process (for example, ENQA,

EUA, ESU, EURASHE[9]). The working group also put forward a set of recommendations to the second Ministers' Meeting in Vietnam the following year. They coined many new phrases, such as 'the ASEM quality assurance and recognition systems should be designed', 'to develop ASEM Quality Assurance Networks', 'to establish an ASEM university information clearinghouse', 'to develop an ASEM Credit Transfer System (ACTS) in line with ECTS [European Credit Transfer System]', 'ASEM University Platform', 'to organize joint ASEM Higher Education Fairs', 'to introduce an ASEM Mobility Quality Charter', 'to establish a bi-regional ASEM University–Business Forum'.

The acronym 'ASEM' has become a prefix, rather like a signature or a new identity of the joint initiatives. These initiatives constitute an ensemble of hybrid regional institutions which add up to an ASEM regional higher education sectoral space. Although these grand (or even 'alien' to some delegates) concepts are borrowed from the Bologna Process vocabularies, they are the emergent properties that exist at the ASEM level, not in Asia or in Europe, alone. Also they are not created spontaneously, but rather by specific people and their deliberate actions in the right contexts. Consequently, the regional issues of mobility and employability are turned into new joint regional projects combining European and Asian capacity and expertise. Such hybridity is expected to advance the new 'strategic Asia–Europe education partnership', although there is no mention of financial resources.

2009–2011: From Matching Domestic Interests to Fixing ASEM Education Agenda

The second Ministers' Meeting in Hanoi made higher education an exclusive topic. This is reflected in the official title of 'ASEM Meeting of Ministers Responsible for Higher Education' and the theme of 'Sharing Experience and Best Practices on Higher Education'. Hosting this event and selecting these titles were seen as matching the domestic interests of the host country, which was undergoing a profound reform of its higher education system. During this period, Vietnam established a joint Vietnamese–German university[10] with full support of the then Minister of Education cum Deputy Prime Minister who earned both his Bachelor and Doctorate degrees in Germany. Against this backdrop, ASEM ME2 focused primarily on 'Quality assurance, credit recognition and transfer among ASEM members'. This idea led to the ministers' endorsement in 2013 of the 'ASEM Recognition Bridging Declaration' combining the spirit of the Lisbon and Tokyo Conventions on recognition of qualifications. Having generated a series of ASEM expert meetings and developed a new website, this project itself is a distinct emergent property. Furthermore, quality assurance, being a subtopic under mobility in the previous meeting, was made to be the top item on the agenda which matched domestic interests and generated various initiatives, such as an ASEM expert group on credits and learning outcomes, an ASEM working group on mutual recognition of higher education qualifications, meetings of ASEM quality assurance agencies hosted by France, Korea, Thailand and Cyprus, and the ASEMundus project to promote joint programmes and mobility. These initiatives, which are hybrids, become the mechanisms to actualize the Frankfurt recommendations.

The Hanoi meeting had also decided to establish the ASEM Education Secretariat, which was to become an important institution. The secretariat, led by a director and a deputy director from the DAAD higher education unit and supported by seconded experts from Indonesia, China and Benelux, began its operation in September 2009 under the auspices of the German Federal Ministry of Education and Research. The first status report on the ASEM education process was presented by the secretariat as an input for the SOM in Copenhagen in January 2011. The interval between the Ministers' Meetings also changed from annual to biennial and there were now new member countries,[11] so that some institutional memory was lost. The status report was the most official source of information.

Consequently, the Danish-proposed agenda on mathematics and science at school level[12] has disappeared; instead, a four-point agenda exclusively on higher education was decided for ASEM ME3: (1) balanced mobility; (2) quality assurance and recognition; (3) lifelong learning; and (4) university–business cooperation. Since these four topics reflected common interests, they became fixed items on the agenda for the ASEM education process, although the order of priority and some wording have changed. The fixed agenda also had the power to guide the countries to select the relevant ministers and delegates to meetings, identify experts to working groups, and sponsor activities that fit the topics. In summary, it was evident that member countries and their interests were essential elements in constructing ASEM education cooperation and its secretariat. Once this relationship was established, this means of acting, in turn, gave it the power to act upon its constituent parts, and set in train the introduction of changes.

2013–2015: Negotiation and Key Actors

By analysing the agenda-setting processes above, I have explained how and by whom higher education has been drawn into the construction of the ASEM education region. Now I shall turn to the question of why higher education was made the key priority, and what hybrid meanings it takes on over time. To answer the 'why' question, it is essential to examine the ASEM regional institutions, particularly the ASEM Ministers' Meetings and their outcomes. This is because those institutions are purposive agents which have authority to allocate responsibilities among actors (Acharya, 2011; Solingen, 2008). Obviously the ministers' interactions at meetings and their conclusions are the highest-level justification for why higher education is a key priority. The ASEM ME1 chair's conclusions in Berlin state:

> Ensuring the quality and competitiveness of higher education systems and institutions is a key element for educating qualified and employable citizens and promoting economic growth in Asia and Europe. Higher education is therefore regarded as an important area of exchange and cooperation. The internationalization of education in general, and of higher education in particular, is an important factor for making education systems and institutions more attractive and competitive worldwide. (ASEM ME1, 2008: 3)

'Internationalization' in the ASEM context encourages inter-regional cooperation; or in other words, hybridization. This statement also has the tone of the European Commission Communiqué 'Mobilising the brainpower of Europe: enabling universities to make their full contribution to the Lisbon strategy' (EC, 2005) which brought higher education onto the European competitiveness agenda. Universities were viewed as key institutions in the development of a knowledge economy in Europe (Dale, 2008; EC, 2006). Subsequently, the global dimension of the Bologna Process was employed to attract talent from around the world, people who potentially become the innovators, entrepreneurs and value creators for the European economy (Robertson, 2008).

In this context ASEM ME1 was organized in Europe and hosted by a 'pro-EU' country; thus the ASEM chair's statement above simply mirrors the prevailing instrumental view and economic discourse on higher education. However, as the ASEM process progressed, people become more open, and the exchange of viewpoints more reciprocal. The third meeting in Copenhagen emphasized humanistic values, such as 'sustainable Asia-Europe education partnership on the basis of mutual respect and benefit for democracy and social cohesion', and 'investment in all education and training sectors is of utmost importance' (ASEM ME3, 2011). The fourth meeting in Kuala Lumpur added, 'for the development of highly qualified and active citizens who have a strong sense of social responsibility, are open-minded and respect cultural diversity' (ASEM ME4, 2013). At the meeting in Riga in 2015, the ministers devoted a special session to reviewing the agenda and developing a vision of the future of the ASEM education process. The question was raised whether or not to focus only on higher education or to broaden the scope and topics. Many Asian countries and two Nordic countries were in favour of adding other topics, such as primary and secondary education, education for sustainable development, post-2015 education goals, and research cooperation. However, most European countries were very keen on higher education and highlighted the importance of achievements and continuity of the process. There was no voting, only open discussion and persuasion at the meeting. The final decisions were drawn on consensus.

In response to the Asian proposals for primary education, a European delegate expressed her view:

> It is sensible to focus on higher education because it is easier to get the mobility work and we have all knowledge in place for quality assurance. We have already some established procedures, common guidelines and standards. So, that would be the easiest way to achieve results. I think we need some very specific and sort of visible signs that we are actually accomplishing something. (Intervention from a European Minister, ASEM ME5, 2015)

Although the phrase 'Bologna Process' was not mentioned, the delegates around the table could immediately identify the familiar vocabularies referring to the body of the Bologna knowledge and experience. Mobility was again stressed as a key and achievable goal. Another European minister commented:

> The influence of government on research is much lower than on higher education. Primary and secondary education is still culturally and nationally bound. If we change our focus, perhaps we should change the format of our meeting and the format of preparation because in the government there are different people involved. So, we could have a discussion at the next SOM, or even before, about whether we enlarge the scope, how we can do it and how we can achieve results without neglecting what we have achieved in the field of higher education which we have to cherish and carry forward. (Intervention from a European Minister, ASEM ME5, 2015)

The role of 'people', specifically senior officials, was emphasized, and tangible results were seen as a source of motivation. In response to the above views, an Asian minister stated:

> One area I would like to propose that we should network around is the issue of teacher preparation. Many countries struggle with this. My country with 8 million teachers is very concerned about how standards of teacher preparation should be. There are excellent examples in many countries where we could learn from, and this is the bridge which enforces the connectivity between higher education and the benefits to primary and secondary education. (Intervention from an Asian Minister, ASEM ME5, 2015)

Although this proposal expressed a specific national interest, it did hint at a common problem and tactfully linked higher education to other levels of education. It was delivered in an open and sincere manner. It brought out many nods around the table and reminded the ministers of how central this 'learning' is to the ASEM cooperation. Consequently, the chair's conclusions resolved the negotiation by adopting a proposal from the SOM in order to accommodate diverse national interests:

> [T]he Ministers expressed their willingness to build the ASEM education cooperation on a two-pillar system. The first pillar would represent the dialogue-oriented cooperation, providing a platform for mutual learning and exchange of experiences strengthening mutual understanding ... The second pillar would represent the result-oriented cooperation composed of tangible activities and measures. The Ministers supported the commitment of ASEM member countries to specific themes or result-oriented activities depending on different national targets and interests. (ASEM ME5, 2015: 10)

This new institutional model is itself another form of hybridity combining different approaches to cooperation. On the one hand, it creates a space for testing new ideas, but on the other hand, it filters them through concrete joint projects representing levels of commitment of countries.

This proposal also shows that the senior officials and their conceptions of an ASEM Education Area are at the heart of the process, where the actual region-making activities occur. Although many of the ministers have changed, a majority of the senior officials are still in post, and continue to carry the ASEM education process forward. There were five Ministers' Meetings,[13] whereas there were 12 SOMs. The senior officials not only devise the agenda, but also craft the chair's conclusions documenting political viewpoints, common goals, a list of achievements, new initiatives and a vision of future. Furthermore, ministers' speeches are written by the senior officials and substantive ideas for ministers' interventions during meetings were whispered over the shoulders or via note-passing from the senior officials sitting in the back row. A European senior official who has been participating in the ASEM process since 2008 shared his experience:

> Dang: Why higher education?
> Official: [smile] A lot of people around the table are also involved in the Bologna Process.
> Dang: What topics and activities are to be included in the chair's conclusions? And why?
> Official: Well, it depends, perhaps not so much on the ministers, but on the wishes and interest of the people around the table. I think the ministers ... tend to look at 'what is the image of my country, whether my country is involved in any activities', but in this topic or other topics, it doesn't matter so much. For

example, the commitments my minister made in Kuala Lumpur actually came from me. And why? . . . [repeated the question and laughed] . . . I don't know . . . Honestly, I am very much involved in the Bologna Process, and from that experience came the ideas.
Dang: Your view on the role of SOM?
Official: Absolutely important. Of course I have talked with my minister but just 'these are the proposals, do you agree?' Often there is no objection. Of course we need to have a kind of endorsement . . . a broad endorsement. I think this is the case also for many other countries. (Interview with a European senior official, April 2015)

Although the roles of SOMs are very similar to the roles of the Bologna Follow-Up Group, the major difference is that SOMs initiate many pilot projects. They are the main activities between meetings and each project involves from five to 12 Asian and European countries volunteering to work together on a specific theme, in many cases under the leadership of, and with a budget allocated by, the senior officials. Whereas most common projects in the Bologna Process are launched and financed by the European Commission, including the stocktaking reports, there is no 'ASEM budget': individual governments are willing to take part and sponsor the projects, be it a joint curriculum programme, a comparative study, or a website on recognition of qualifications. These joint projects, in turn, generate more *sui generis* hybrids, such as inter-subjective knowledge, hybrid meanings of discourse, and group identities that will be elaborated in the next section.

A NEW FORM OF REGIONAL OUTCOME: AN ASEM HIGHER EDUCATION SECTORAL SPACE

I have shown that the ASEM higher education area, though still in the making, is not simply the extension of a European or Asian model. As a European minister said: 'ASEM is more than the sum of its parts'; the ASEM education space possesses its own 'emergent properties' that have powers in their own right. For example, ASEM developed a vision of an 'ASEM Education Area' in 2011 which was affirmed in 2013: '[the Ministers] renewed their commitment to strengthen the Asia–Europe education process and shape an ASEM Education Area' (ASEM ME4, 2013), and it was specified in 2015 as 'a single higher education area linking Europe and Asia';[14] 'an area where mobility of students, teachers, researchers, ideas and knowledge would be the core common goal' (ASEM ME5, 2015).

'Mobility' on the ASEM agenda seems to resemble the Bologna Process action line, but the real meanings are constructed differently over time. The idea of 'balanced mobility' is no longer about the balance between the number of Asian students studying in North America and those who study in Europe (that is, an aim to attract more Asian students to Europe); in today's context it is about motivating more European students to study in Asia and creating more joint programmes (ASEM ME3, 2011; ASEM ME4, 2013). Moreover, 'balanced mobility' is a way to conceal the brain drain issue, where ASEM meetings make policies aimed at improving reciprocal exchange.

The physical space (meetings) and virtual space (newsletters, website updates from the secretariat) are important components in discursive construction of an ASEM Education Area. Such regular interactions also build a sense of togetherness (He, 2012) and co-opt the members to adopt collective patterns of behaviours (Gilson, 2002). This hybrid is reflected in the language of the participants when they say 'we' at ASEM meetings. Sometimes it means 'we Asians', at other times 'we Europeans', and increasingly, 'we ASEM'. In essence, this is a process of constructing collective identities, which form a defining trait of a region (Acharya, 2009, 2012; Mansfield and Solingen, 2010).

Collective identities are also layered, with local identities not replaced by national ones, national identities coexisting with, and even complementing, emerging regional identities (Katzenstein, 2005). It is thus possible for former enemies to become friends, and former colonial countries to become partners, in a higher education region. Indeed, the increasing number of joint projects over the past years has created more commingling between the Asian and European countries and less of an 'us-and-them' feel at meetings.

CONCLUSIONS

This chapter set out to understand ASEM higher education cooperation through examining the question of how and by whom the ASEM education process has been constructed as a region-building project, and how, why and with what outcomes higher education has been made to be a key priority on the ASEM education agenda.

The main conclusion is that a key outcome of the mobilization of higher education in ASEM has been the construction of a new educational space derived from matching and combining elements of Asian and European capacity and experience, giving rise to a new set of spatial relations and regional form. ASEM activities in higher education are grouped around the issue of mobility, which is specified as 'the core common goal' and realizable through the creation of what might be called an ASEM higher education regional sectoral space.

The theoretical analysis in this chapter suggests that regionalizing is a process in which a set of constituent parts is joined together to constitute a new entity, and where new emergent properties are produced. These emergent properties are possessed by the whole, and are not reducible to the parts. Moreover, they can exert their downward influence on the parts that constitute them. The empirical data analysis in this chapter supports the proposition that the concepts of 'emergence' and 'emergent properties' are an effective theoretical tool to explain the concept of hybrid regionalism.

The data have provided insights into a series of ASEM informal institutions; mainly meetings and joint projects, which are the mechanisms for generating emergent properties and causal powers. These powers manifest themselves in the capacity of ASEM to set its own agenda, to decide which agenda items and discourses should be made politically relevant (Neumann, 1994) and to initiate joint projects. Moreover, it has been argued that these mechanisms are shaped by domestic interests and are consciously designed and adjusted from within the ASEM region by deliberate actions of the key actors, especially the senior officials and the secretariat. Thus, the region is being constructed from within.

Taken together, we can see that the ASEM higher education area has emerged from, but is not reducible to, its constituent parts; the outcome is a new form of regional space, one that I am calling an ASEM higher education regional sectoral space.

NOTES

* I am grateful to Professor Roger Dale, Professor Susan Robertson, Professor Takao Kamibeppu, Daniel Couch and Janja Komljenovic for their comments on earlier drafts of this chapter. This research is funded by the EU Marie Skłodowska-Curie Scholarship as part of the 'Universities in the Knowledge Economy' (UNIKE) project.
1. France, especially President Jacques Chirac, worked to secure the support of other EU members during the French presidency of the EU in 1995. Meanwhile, Singapore was able to secure the commitment from East Asian countries.
2. The initial ASEM partnership in 1996 consisted of 15 EU member states, the European Commission and seven ASEAN member states plus China, Japan and Korea.
3. 53 ASEM partners as of May 2015 include: 28 EU member states, Norway and Switzerland, 10 ASEAN countries, China, Japan, the Republic of Korea, Russia, India, Mongolia, Bangladesh, Pakistan, Australia, New Zealand, Kazakhstan, the European Union (represented by the European External Action Service) and the ASEAN Secretariat.
4. Unlike the European context where a rectors' conference is often the name of the national organization of higher education institutions' leaders, the ASEM Rectors' Conference is a biennial forum, attended by rectors of one or two leading universities

from each ASEM country. The list of invited rectors at each event changes according to the priority and level of funding raised by the main organizer (Asia–Europe Foundation) and the rotating host university.
5. From the tenth ASEM Summit in 2014, following a decision on aligning the status of the European Union in the ASEM process with the provisions of the Lisbon Treaty, a conversion was made from the 'European Commission' to the 'European Union' (EU). The permanent coordinator for the European Union in the ASEM process is the European External Action Service. At the recent ASEM Education Ministers' Meetings there was double representation of the EU, with participation of high-level representatives from the Directorate General of Education, Culture, Youth and Sports, and representatives from the External Action Service (see http://eeas.europa.eu/asem/index_en.htm).
6. The membership of the European Higher Education Area is not confined to EU member states.
7. The Asian side of ASEM consists of 21 countries and the ASEAN Secretariat. Alongside ASEAN, ASEAN+3 and the ASEAN Secretariat, the accession of India, Pakistan, Australia, New Zealand, Russia, Mongolia, Bangladesh and Kazakhstan has made the 'Asia' that meets Europe in ASEM increasingly broad and diverse. Additionally, the Bologna members Turkey, Serbia and Ukraine might be joining ASEM at the summit in 2016. Russia, Kazakhstan and the three potential members are the EHEA members.
8. In April 2015 a list of host countries was already confirmed for the Ministers' Meetings until 2019. In May 2013, Belgium had already volunteered to take over the secretariat from 2017 to 2021.
9. The E4 group consisting of the European Association for Quality Assurance in Higher Education (ENQA), European Students Union (ESU), European University Association (EUA) and European Association of Institutions in Higher Education (EURASHE). All four organizations are consultative members of the Bologna Process.
10. Vietnamese–Germany University, http://www.vgu.edu.vn.
11. Australia, New Zealand and Russia joined ASEM in 2010 and participated in ASEM ME3 for the first time.
12. At ASEM ME2, the Danish minister, as the host of the next meeting, announced three topics: (a) innovation; (b) entrepreneurial competences; and (c) maths, information and communication technology (ICT) and natural sciences. These topics were high on the national school reform agenda in Denmark and within his responsibility. The minister was in charge of schools and colleges, but not universities. In 2010, he left for another position, while his colleagues were preparing for ASEM ME3 with the support from the new ASEM education secretariat.
13. ASEM ME: 2008 in Berlin, 2009 in Hanoi, 2011 in Copenhagen, 2013 in Kuala Lumpur, 2015 in Riga.
14. Keynote speech by a European minister at ASEM ME5, April 2015.

REFERENCES

Acharya, A. (2007), 'The Emerging Regional Architecture of World Politics', *World Politics*, **59**, 629–652.

Acharya, A. (2009), *Whose Ideas Matter? Agency and Power in Asian Regionalism*, New York: Cornell University Press.

Acharya, A. (2011), 'Dialogue and Discovery: In Search of International Relations Theories Beyond the West', *Millennium: Journal of International Studies*, **39**(3), 1–19.

Acharya, A. (2012), 'Comparative Regionalism: A Field Whose Time Has Come?', *International Spectator*, **47**(1), 3–15.

ASEM (1996), The first ASEM Summit Chair's Statement, issued by the Prime Minister of Thailand in Bangkok, 1–2 March.
ASEM ME1 (2008), Conclusions by the Chair of the 1st ASEM Conference of Ministers Responsible for Education 'Education and Training for Tomorrow: Common Perspectives in Asia and Europe', 5–6 May, Berlin, Germany.
ASEM ME3 (2011), Conclusions by the Chair of the 3rd Asia–Europe Meeting of Ministers for Education 'Shaping an ASEM Education Area', 9–10 May, Copenhagen, Denmark.
ASEM ME4 (2013), Conclusions by the Chair of the 4th Asia–Europe Meeting of Ministers for Education 'Strategizing ASEM Education Collaboration', 13–14 May, Kuala Lumpur, Malaysia.
ASEM ME5 (2015), Conclusions by the Chair of the 5th Asia–Europe Meeting of Ministers for Education 'ASEM Education Collaboration for Results', 27–28 April, Riga, Latvia.
ASEM SOM (2008), Chair's Minutes of the Senior Officials Meeting (SOM) in Bonn, 10–11 March 2008 in preparation of the ASEM Conference of Ministers responsible for Education in Berlin, 5–6 May.
ASEM Vision (1999), 'For a Better Tomorrow: Asia–Europe Partnership in the 21st Century', Report presented at the third ASEM Summit in Seoul, South Korea in 2000.
Bologna Process (2005), Bergen Communique 'European Higher Education Area – Achieving the Goals', accessed 15 May 2015 at http://www.ehea.info/Uploads/about/050520_Bergen_Communique1.pdf.
Börzel, T. (2011), 'Comparative Regionalism: A New Research Agenda', KFG Working Paper Series, No. 28, Kolleg-Forschergruppe (KFG) 'The Transformative Power of Europe', Freie Universität Berlin.
Breslin, S. and Higgott, R. (2003), 'New Regionalism(s) in the Global Political Economy. Conceptual Understanding in Historical Perspective', *Asia Europe Journal*, **1**, 167–182.
Camroux, D. (2006), 'The Rise and Decline of the Asia–Europe Meeting (ASEM): Asymmetric Bilateralism and the Limitations of Interregionalism', Sciences Po Working Paper, no. 04, Paris: Centre d'études européennes at Sciences Po.
Camroux, D. (2010), 'Interregionalism or Merely a Fourth-Level Game? An Examination of the EU–ASEAN Relationship', *East Asia*, **27**, 57–77.
Dale, R. (2008), 'Conclusions: Shifting Discourses and Mediating Structures in the Co-construction of Europe, Knowledge and Universities', in Jessop, B., Fairclough, N. and Kodak, R. (eds), *Education and the Knowledge-Based Economy in Europe*, Rotterdam, Netherlands and Taipei, Taiwan: SensePublishers, pp. 193–206.
Dang, Q.A. (2013), 'ASEM – The Modern Silk Road: Travelling Ideas for Education Reforms and Partnerships between Asia and Europe', *Comparative Education*, **49**(1), 109–117.
Dang, Q.A. (2015), 'Why Does ASEM Education Cooperation Matter?', *ASEM Education Gazette*, **1**(2015), accessed 20 May 2015 at http://asem-educationsecretariat.kemdikbud.go.id/wp-content/uploads/2015/04/ASEM-Gazzete-Vol-1.pdf.
De Lombaerde, P. and Söderbaum, F. (2013), 'Reading the Intellectual History of Regionalism', in De Lombaerde and Söderbaum (eds), *Regionalism*, 4 vols, SAGE Library of International Relations, London: SAGE Publications, pp. xvii–xlviii.

Dent, C. (2003), 'From Inter-Regionalism to Trans-regionalism? Future Challenges for ASEM', *Asia–Europe Journal*, **1**, 223–235.
Dent, C. (2004), 'The Asia–Europe Meeting and Inter-regionalism: Toward a Theory of Multilateral Utility', *Asian Survey*, **44**(2), 213–236.
Doidge, M. (2008), 'Regional Organisations as Actors in International Relations: Interregionalism and Asymmetric Dialogues', in Rüland, J., Schubert, G., Schucher, G. and Storz, C. (eds), *Asian–European Relations: Building Blocks for Global Governance*, London, UK and New York, USA: Routledge, pp. 32–54.
Elder-Vass, D. (2010), *The Causal Power of Social Structures: Emergence, Structure and Agency*, Cambridge: Cambridge University Press.
European Commission (EC) (2005), *Mobilising the Brainpower of Europe: Enabling Universities to make their full Contributions to the Lisbon Strategy*, COM 152 Final. Brussels 25 April.
European Commission (EC) (2006), *Delivering on the Modernisation Agenda for Universities: Education, Research and Innovation*, Communication from the Commission to the Council and the European Parliament. COM 208 Final. Brussels 10 May.
Fioramonti, L. (2012), 'Conclusion – Building Region from Below: Has the Time Come for Regionalism 2.0?', *International Spectator: Italian Journal of International Affairs*, **47**(1), 151–160.
Gilson, J. (2002), 'Defining Inter-Regionalism: The Asia–Europe Meeting (ASEM)', SEAS Electronic Working Papers, Vol. 1(1), School of East Asia Studies, University of Sheffield.
He, B. (2012), 'A Concert of Power and Hybrid Regionalism in Asia', *Australia Journal of Political Science*, **47**(4), 677–690.
Katzenstein, P. (2005), *A World of Regions: Asia and Europe in the American Imperium*, Ithaca, NY, USA and London, UK: Cornell University Press.
Lewis, P. (2012), 'Emergent Properties in the Work of Friedrich Hayek', *Journal of Economic Behavior and Organization*, **82**, 368–378.
Mansfield, E. and Solingen, E. (2010), 'Regionalism', *Annual Review of Political Science*, **13**, 145–163.
Martin, R. and Sunley, P. (2012), 'Forms of Emergence and the Evolution of Economic Landscapes', *Journal of Economic Behavior and Organization*, **82**, 338–351.
Neumann, I. (1994), 'A Region-Building Approach to Northern Europe', *Review of International Studies*, **20**(1), 53–74.
Ravenhill, J. (2012), 'The Numbers Game in Asia–Pacific Cooperation', in Dent, C. and Dosch, J. (eds), *The Asia-Pacific, Regionalism and the Global System*, Cheltenham, UK and Northampton, MA, USA: Edward Elgar Publishing, pp. 75–93.
Robertson, S. (2008), 'Embracing the Global: Crisis and the Creation of a New Semiotic Order to Secure Europe's Knowledge-Based Economy', in Jessop, B., Fairclough, N. and Kodak, R. (eds), *Education and the Knowledge-Based Economy in Europe*, Rotterdam: SensePublishers, pp. 89–108.
Rüland, J. (2010), 'Balancers, Multilateral Utilities or Regional Identity Builder? International Relations and the Study of Inter-Regionalism', *Journal of European Public Policy*, **17**(8), 1271–1283.
Rüland, J. and Storz, C. (2008), 'Interregionalism and Interregional Cooperation: The Case of Asia–Europe Relations', in Rüland, J., Schubert, G., Schucher,

G. and Storz, C. (eds), *Asian–European Relations: Building Blocks for Global Governance*, London, UK and New York, USA: Routledge, pp. 3–31.
Sayer, A. (2000), *Realism and Social Science*, London, UK; Thousand Oaks, CA, USA; New Delhi, India: Sage Publications.
Solingen, E. (2008), 'The Genesis, Design and Effects of Regional Institutions: Lessons from East Asia and the Middle East', *International Studies Quarterly*, **52**, 261–294.
Väyrynen, R. (2003), 'Regionalism: Old and New', *International Studies Review*, **5**, 25–51.
Yeo, L.H. (2002), *ASEM, The Asia–Europe Meeting Process: From Sexy Summit to Strong Partnership?*, Copenhagen: Danish Institute of International Affairs.
Yeo, L.H. (2003), *Asia and Europe: The Development and Different Dimensions of ASEM*, London: Routledge.
Zhang, J. (2008), 'EU in ASEM: Its Role in Framing Inter-Regional Cooperation with East Asia Countries', *Asia–Europe Journal*, **6**, 487–505.

8. Ir-regular regionalism? China's borderlands and ASEAN higher education: trapped in the prism

Anthony Welch

> ASEAN [Association of Southeast Asian Nations] has a lot riding on the success of China's peaceful development. There is no question that our future, our prosperity, will be strongly linked to China. (Susilo Bambang Yudhoyono, 2014)

REGIONALISM AND ITS LIMITS

The fact that China–ASEAN relations are conventionally viewed through the prism of economics and trade is misleading in at least two senses. Firstly, even within the trade portfolio, the emphasis is conventionally on goods, obscuring swiftly rising service sector trade in areas such as finance, tourism and education. Secondly, the emphasis on trade is itself misleading, in that China–ASEAN relations are far richer, of longer duration, and more varied than mere trade relations indicate.

In this chapter I will show that China's southern borderlands, selected as an illustration of wider China–ASEAN regionalism in higher education, reveal a rich and complex tapestry of relations extending over more than a millennium, and that crucially embrace forms of higher learning and knowledge mobility. Six pillars of China–ASEAN relations are sketched below: economics, knowledge mobility, historical background, Chinese regional diaspora, territorial disputes and regional perceptions of Chinese minorities; before turning to a specific focus on China's southern borderlands region that has long featured close relations with Viet Nam. This might be considered an asymmetric relationship. Yet Chan has argued that, whilst Viet Nam has maintained its independence, China will have to buy its way into Southeast Asia, via Viet Nam (Chan, 2013: 121–122; *South China Morning Post*, 2015a, 2015b).

The re-establishment of formal diplomatic relations after the Sino-Vietnamese War of 1979, and the reopening of the border in 1991, together with the increased priority accorded Southeast Asia by China, has issued in an intensification of regionalism, including in higher education. Despite a series of obstacles outlined below, some of which persist, the last three decades or so of reform, instigated by the inception of the Reform and Opening era initiated by Deng Xiaoping in 1978, and its equivalent *Doi Moi* in Viet Nam from 1986, has *inter alia* deepened and widened cross-border flows of knowledge and educational personnel, enriching and extending the character of regionalism.

As a number of scholars have pointed out, borderlands – by definition peripheral – represent a good litmus test of the (limits of) regionalism. The notion of limit is arguably inherent. At one and the same time, borderland regions function as a marker of the limit of state sovereignty – 'the boundary which marks the name of the state' (Chan, 2013: ix) – but also as a site that tests and at times defies the power and authority of the state, and where cross-currents of people, languages, cultures, currencies and ways of life interweave and collide, constituting quotidian realities. Well captured in the traditional Chinese idiom 'The mountains are high and the Emperor far away' (*Shan gao, huangdi yuan* 山高皇帝远),[1] the southern provinces of Yunnan and Guizhou and Guangxi Zhuang Autonomous Region (GZAR) neatly illustrate both the tensions and options that borderlands spaces embody (Eimer, 2014; Chan, 2013). The porosity and liminality of borderland regions harks back to earlier eras characterized as 'territorial nonchalance in the peripheries of states' (Chan, 2013: 90).

While, as illustrated below, the currency of both commerce and ideas between China and Viet Nam is at least a millennium old (one illustration of which is that some centuries ago both Chinese and Vietnamese coins circulated simultaneously in what is now Viet Nam), the era since the end of the Sino-Vietnamese War of 1979, and more particularly since the implementation of structural economic reforms to each economy since the 1970s and 1980s, together with the resumption of diplomatic relations between the two 'sisters in socialism' in 1991, has seen relations mushroom. This is especially so in the three above-mentioned provinces, where border crossings, literal and symbolic, legal and illegal, regulated and irregular, have become even more of a daily routine.

Within China, too, the increased priority accorded to Southeast Asia has led to a process of revalorization of China's southern borderlands. Seen until relatively recently as lagging behind, or backward (*luo hou*, 落后), with insinuations of danger, remoteness and of primitive peoples, the central government re-nominated Yunnan province, for example, as a bridgehead (*qiaotoubao*, 桥头堡) to Southeast Asia, of great strategic significance (Sigley, 2014). In fact Yunnan, which together with its two neighbouring provinces of Guizhou and Guangxi borders Viet Nam, was only brought under

China's dynastic system after the Mongol conquest during the Yuan dynasty (1271–1368), and subsequent Ming dynasty (Crossley et al., 2006). At the time, local minorities were regarded by Emperor Jiajing (1521–1566/67) as 'wily and deceitful, barbarous, rebellious and perverse', 'without human morality' and no better 'than the birds and the beasts' (Eimer, 2014: 189). (Equally, Vietnamese borderlands minorities in Viet Nam's Northern Mountain Region are also widely believed to be 'backward by lowlands Vietnamese'; Tran, 2003.) Only in 1899 was the former Dai kingdom of Sipsongpanna[2] formally incorporated into the Qing dynasty, while the Dai king continued to rule over the autonomous region of Banna until 1953, when he was compelled to abdicate by the Chinese Communist Party (CCP).

THE SIX PILLARS OF SINO-ASEAN REGIONALISM

In this section I fill in the details of the six pillars of Sino-ASEAN relations: economics, knowledge mobility, historical background, Chinese regional diaspora, territorial disputes and regional perceptions of Chinese minorities.

Economic Relations

The intricate and long-standing nature of relations between China and its ASEAN neighbours notwithstanding, China's dramatic economic rise over the past three decades, as well as growing China–ASEAN industrial and commercial complementarity, has helped to stimulate deeper relations, including in higher education (Welch, 2011b; Jarvis and Welch, 2011). But it is not merely China's stellar gross domestic product (GDP) growth since reform and opening was instituted in the late 1970s that was responsible (State Council, 2015a): it was also China's increasing regional engagement and support for its ASEAN neighbours (Xinhua, 2011). In the wake of the regional currency crisis of the late 1990s, for example, China's support to its neighbours was widely appreciated, as were repeated affirmations of 'China's peaceful rise', and its endorsement of the Treaty of Amity and Co-operation with ASEAN, and Joint Declaration on Strategic Partnership for Peace and Prosperity, in 2003 (Vaughan and Morrison, 2006; Whitney and Shambaugh, 2008; Cheow, 2004). Further Chinese support in the aftermath of the terrible regional tsunami of 2004, and soft loans to ASEAN member states, as well as substantial funding for key development projects, further helped to cement regional relations (Hirono, 2010; Laksmana, 2011; *China Daily*, 2014b).

More recently, the inception of the China–ASEAN Free Trade Area (CAFTA) in early 2010 has provided numerous opportunities for ASEAN member states, in both goods and services. The latter have been boosted by the spectacular growth of the Chinese middle class in recent years, now estimated to total around 160 million (Kharas, 2011; Goodman, 2008). An example is the steep rise in Chinese outbound tourism: four of the top ten destinations for Chinese tourists in 2011 were ASEAN member states. Inbound tourism from ASEAN is also growing, with 4.98 million visits in 2008 (Tong and Chong, 2010: 7). With China's more than 115 million outbound visits in 2014, and an expanding middle class in Singapore, Indonesia, Thailand and Malaysia, regional tourism is set only to expand, notwithstanding some of the issues sketched below (*China Daily*, 2012a, 2014a; State Council, 2015b).

This growth in tourism is boosting demand for associated services, such as specific forms of higher education and Chinese language in the region. ASEAN is now a sizeable priority within China's higher education policy, which also includes projection of its soft power within the region via around 30 Confucius Institutes (Yang, 2012). While the persistent influence of nationalism in regional service sector trade was seen in the establishment of the first Confucius Institute in Viet Nam, at Ha Noi University in late 2013 (*Hanban News*, 2013), over some local resistance, at much the same time overall ASEAN–China trade overtook that with Japan in 2011, rising 24 per cent annually to become third-largest, after the European Union (EU) and United States of America (USA) (*China Daily*, 2012a; see Figure 8.1).

Likewise, massive Chinese investment in Indonesia's resources

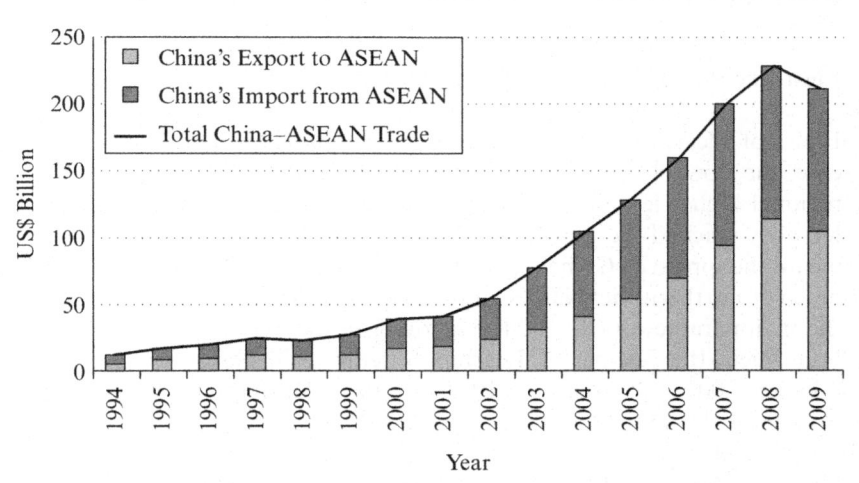

Source: Tong and Chong (2010: 4).

Figure 8.1 China–ASEAN total trade, 1994–2009

sector proceeded, despite a history of ambivalence which meant that, somewhat like Viet Nam, formal diplomatic ties were not resumed until 1990 (Laksmana, 2011). Responding to this growth, Zhang Wei, Vice-Chairman of the China Council for the Promotion of International Trade, recently argued that in light of faster growth in trade with ASEAN than with the EU or the USA (of which the latter, in particular, is still beset by economic headwinds), ASEAN will surpass the other two in the next few years: 'Thanks to zero tariffs, preferential trade policies, and geographic advantages . . . ASEAN will become China's No 1 trading partner by 2015' (*China Daily*, 2012b, 2013). His predictions were borne out: in 2013, bilateral trade reached US$444 billion, and if China joins the recently announced ASEAN Framework for Regional Comprehensive Economic Partnership (RCEP), as some indications suggest it might, the trend would only be further reinforced (*China Daily*, 2014c; *Star Malaysia*, 2012; Wu and Mealy, 2012; Williams, 2012).

Equally, however, increased regional dependence on China presents something of a risk. The East Asia Forum data shows potentially too many China eggs in ASEAN's basket, contributing as much as 80 per cent of developing East Asia's GDP (Rahardja and World Bank, 2012). It is no surprise, therefore, that the current slowdown in China is directly affecting ASEAN economies. A rebalance towards service sector trade and higher-value production could potentially mitigate such effects.

Epistemic Routes

Flows of ideas, however, are just as important as trade in goods. In this case, the flow of ideas is also long-standing, and has helped to reshape regional higher learning. When China was first unified, (c.220 BCE), its territory reached the Red River Delta (current Viet Nam). *Inter alia*, this meant the spread of Chinese poetry, astronomy, medicine and arithmetic in much of northern Viet Nam. Confucian philosophy (of education) became the major framework for higher learning in the region, as any visitor to Van Mieu, the Temple of Learning/Literature in Ha Noi can confirm (Gelber, 2007: 52; Welch, 2010a: 197–199). During the Tang dynasty (618–907), the famed *Four Books* and *Five Classics* became the centrepieces of the temple curriculum in what is now Viet Nam. Scholars travelled in both directions, some more as teachers, others more as learners. The enduring influence, especially in areas such as moral education, meant that Confucius became revered in Viet Nam as 'the teacher of Ten Thousand Sovereigns'. Indeed, 'examinations based on Confucianism, as applied in

China, were organized ... for more than eight centuries (from 1075 to 1919) in Viet Nam' (Yang, 1993: 6).

Beyond the philosophy of Confucianism, religion formed a further epistemic bridge. Buddhists in China and current Southeast Asia were in contact from the sixth century CE. Islamic scholars in what is now China and ASEAN were also in contact; Islamic higher learning centres in current Southeast Asia were long connected to China (Chang, 1988; Gelber, 2007; Welch, 2012a, 2012b). The Silk Road and maritime Silk Road represented other regional tributaries contributing to intellectual concourse between Muslims (Heidhues, 2001).

Long-standing Regional Relations

Clearly, then, regionalism was well entrenched in both trade and intellectual commerce for at least a millennium, if not longer. Intra-regional trade began around the third century BCE, grew in the Three Kingdoms period, and again in the Tang dynasty (618–906), although only significantly much later (Wang, 2000). Historical accounts record trade between China and current-day Viet Nam, Cambodia, Java and Sumatra during the first millennium BCE, Chinese voyages of exploration to Southeast Asia in the third century, significant contact between Buddhists in China and their counterparts in Southeast Asia during the fifth and sixth centuries, and later concourse among Muslim communities in China and what is now Indonesia (Chang, 1988; Gelber, 2007; Welch, 2012a, 2012b). In the Yuan dynasty (1279–1368), the expansionist Kublai Khan sought to extend China's territory and influence to the region, notably Java. But relations were not just one-way. Trade and exploration occurred in both directions, including by ancestors of today's Malays and Indonesians who were active regional seafarers more than 2000 years ago.

In the late thirteenth and fourteenth centuries CE, Chinese traders, including non-Han Muslims, settled in current Viet Nam, Cambodia, around the Gulf of Thailand, and in parts of current Malaysia, Java and Sumatra. The final decades of a weakened Ming dynasty in the early seventeenth century saw more explorations by Chinese traders, although this was paralleled by massacres of Chinese settlers in Manila and Batavia (the former name for Jakarta; Reid, 2008).

But the exploits of Admiral Zheng He, who led seven voyages to the region between 1405 and 1433, taking Chinese products to some neighbours whilst bringing back other articles, remains the most outstanding example, although many details remain a mystery (for a map of his voyages, see *The Economist*, 2006; *National Geographic*, 2005). A Muslim, Zheng would have felt comfortable among the Muslim cultures of what are today Malaysia and Indonesia, but the significance of his voyages was both larger and more enduring, according to the historian Richard von Glahn: 'Zheng He reshaped Asia. Maritime history in the fifteenth century is essentially the Zheng He story, and the effects of Zheng He's voyages' (Gunde, 2004; see also *The Economist*, 2006).

Regional Diaspora

Zheng He's voyages and active regional trade by Chinese merchants, principally Fujienese and Hokkienese, laid the foundations for a contemporary regional diaspora now estimated to total between 16 and 20 million (Chang, 2008; Welch, 2012a). While the disproportionate weight exercised in several regional economies by ethnic Chinese minorities (Yeung, 1999) is relatively common, there are very differing proportions of Chinese within ASEAN member states, from as little as 1.5 per cent in Viet Nam (see Table 8.1) to around 60 per cent in Singapore. Research from elsewhere suggests that Chinese identity among the worldwide diaspora of perhaps 35 million or more (some estimate as high as 50 million) remains strong, at least among the current generation, and that increasingly highly educated overseas Chinese communities (*huaqiao*) retain a keen interest in China's development and largely wish to contribute (Yang and Welch, 2010; Welch and Zhang, 2008; Da and Welch, 2016; Welch and Hao, 2012). Across ASEAN, however, it is not merely proportions of ethnic Chinese which differ significantly within national populations.

Of all Southeast ASEAN states, Viet Nam, with perhaps the most minuscule proportion of ethnic Chinese, has perhaps the most troubled relationship. According to a respected local economist, there is cultural resistance to learning Mandarin (which at least in part explains the local resistance to the establishment of Viet Nam's first Confucius Institute, alluded to above). Another index is evident in local nomenclature: 'All the streets in Viet Nam are named according to generals and emperors that have been fighting against the Chinese invasion for 2000 years' (Pak, 2012).

Territorial Disputes

An increasingly troublesome feature afflicting regional relations is the spread of territorial disputes between China and several of its ASEAN neighbours (Bowring, 2012a; Severino, 2012; Li, 2012). China borders Viet Nam, Myanmar (Burma), and Laos to its south, whilst also sharing sea borders with many Southeast Asian countries. China's maritime disputes with the Philippines and Viet Nam in the South

Table 8.1 The Dragon, the Tiger Cub

Country	Population, 2011 (millions)	% Chinese	GDP per capita, 2011 (PPP, US$)	Development status. HDI rating, 2011	FDI to China, 2008 (US$ million)	FDI from China, 2008 (US$ million)	GDP growth, 2011 (%)
China	1346	100*	8400	Developing. 687	–	–	9.24
Viet Nam	87.9	1.5	3300	Developing. 593	2	120	5.89

Notes:
PPP = purchasing power parity; HDI = Human Development Index; FDI = foreign direct investment.
* Approximately 8.5 per cent of the population are from China's 55 designated minorities.

Sources: 'Country comparison: GDP per capita (PPP)', (n.d.), by CIA. Retrieved 13 September 2012, from https://www.cia.gov/library/publications/the-world-factbook/rankorder/2004rank.html; '2011 World Population Data Sheet', (2011), by PRB. Retrieved 13 September 2012, from www.prb.org/pdf11/2011population-data-sheet_eng.pdf; East Asia Institute (2010); Congressional Research Service (2012).

173

China Sea in 2011 were followed in 2012 by another confrontation with the Philippines, and a Vietnamese law asserting sovereignty over the *Hoang Sa* (Paracel Islands, known in Chinese as *Xisha*), and *Quan dao Truong Sa* (the Spratly Islands, known in Chinese as *Nansha*) provoking sharp Chinese criticism (Bowring, 2012b; Torode, 2012; Xinhua, 2012; China Defense Mashup, 2012; *South China Morning Post*, 2015c). The Philippines again protested, in early 2015, at Chinese maritime activity around the Fiery Cross Reef (*SCMP*, 2015b), while Viet Nam, Malaysia and the Philippines are currently all scrambling to boost their defence capabilities and ties (*Diplomat*, 2015a, 2015b; *South China Morning Post*, 2015b).

Clearly, then, despite enhanced regional economic integration, and a perception by several ASEAN states that China's rise may offset their dependence on the US, China's assertiveness in the region has given rise to some reserve and hedging on the part of its ASEAN neighbours (Osborne, 2006; Wang, 2005; Whitney and Shambaugh, 2008; Taylor, 2012). This certainly includes Viet Nam, which is engaging in some strategic rebalancing. This includes reaching out to its neighbours (*South China Morning Post*, 2015a) whilst also being courted by India, Japan and others. Most recently, China has reasserted its determination to pursue peaceful neighbourly negotiations, announcing in November 2014 at the Central Work Conference on Foreign Relations that it 'ranked relations with its neighbours higher in priority than relations with the United States and other great powers' (*Straits Times*, 2015). While, as seen above not resiling from robust assertion of its territorial claims, it is also now emphasizing 'win–win' diplomacy, further trade and cooperation, and open discussions on a code of conduct, 'when the time is ripe' (Sutter and Huang, 2012; see also Prantl, 2012).

Anti-Chinese Sentiments

The numerous territorial disputes are arguably fuelling long-standing regional concerns about the disproportionate influence of Chinese minorities on national economies. These occasionally erupt into violence against local Chinese groups, as seen most recently in Viet Nam (Reuters, 2014). Bloody examples of recent decades include the murder of many members of the *Partai Komunis Indonesia* (PKI) in Indonesia in 1965, numbers of whom were killed simply due to their Chinese origin (Farram, 2010: 392; Suryadinata, 2003; Wang, 2005; Pramudatama, 2012). Indonesia–China relations, only reinstituted in 1990, have long been affected by a common sentiment that saw ethnic-Chinese Indonesians as 'Other' (Laksmana, 2011). Anti-Chinese riots broke out in 1998, in Jakarta, Medan and other cities in Indonesia, while bilateral relations – frozen in 1967 – did not fully recover until around 1999 (Conboy, 2002).

In Malaysia, too, bloody riots between Chinese Malaysians and ethnic Malays (known as *Bumiputras*), in 1969. Preferential policies for ethnic Malays, including educational quotas, were meant to redress the comparatively weak position of *Bumiputras* in Malaysian society and its economy, but in practice continue to discriminate against ethnic Chinese. Viet Nam, at war with China as recently as 1979, saw bloody anti-Chinese demonstrations in 2011 and 2012, and again in 2014 in response to rising maritime tensions between the two (Nguyen, 2012).

(IR)REGULAR REGIONALISM IN THE SOUTHERN BORDERLANDS

The six pillars sketched above challenge the conventional wisdom; one that views Sino-ASEAN relations through the prism of economics. History, culture, ethnicity, security allegiances, nationalism and domestic political agendas, including those of the great powers, all help to shape both the quantity and quality of regionalism.

This is no less so on the periphery. Sino-ASEAN regionalism is by no means uniform, and as argued above, the borderlands represent a test case of the limits of regionalism. The liminal quality of borderlands regions continues to resist, and at times defy, the regulatory architecture of both state and regional authority (Eimer, 2014; Chan, 2013).

This is clearly the case in China's southern borderlands of Guangxi, Guizhou and Yunnan, where much of the cross-border flows (trafficking of young women as wives or prostitutes, selling babies, drug smuggling, gambling, jade smuggling, smuggling of vehicles, illegal logging, corrupt mining), while routine, are irregular and illegal (*New York Times*, 2015; *International New York Times*, 2015; Eimer, 2014: 186ff, 200, 225–231; Chan, 2013: 89–105, 108–115; *China Daily*, 2014; Evans et al., 2000). In a context where 'borderlanders . . . cross state boundaries daily and conduct everyday cross-cultural interactions' (Chan, 2013: xi), it is also necessary for the social researcher to enter into the same world; to suspend conventional perceptions of borders, and to themselves become something of a border-crosser, engaged in transgressive and disruptive modes of thinking.

The porous nature of the border in this region has long been underpinned by the common ethnicity of minorities on both sides, such as the Dai, for whom ethnicity trumps nationality. Even today, while most Dai inhabit China's Yunnan province, there are significant numbers in

Myanmar (c. 200 000), Laos (119 000), Thailand (78 000) and Viet Nam (3700). It is thus no surprise that, for many Dai in Banna:

> Their language, cultures, traditions and religions overrule the frontiers which were imposed on Southeast Asia in the near past. The individual minorities feel a far greater sense of kinship with their cousins across the borders than they do with the Han ... nationality is far less important than ethnicity, and the fact that they are technically Chinese is almost an irrelevance. (Eimer, 2014: 163, see also pp. 175ff, 188–89; Barrett, 2012: 183–191)

Simple geography is also significant. The fact that Yunnan alone, for example, has a border with Southeast Asia of some 4000 kilometres makes it hard to regulate or police. And it is not just the Dai people whose reach extends across borders. There are estimated to be around 400 000 Wa people in Yunnan alone, with strong connections across porous borders to Wa state in Myanmar (whose United Wa State Army is perhaps 20 000 strong, and responsible for, *inter alia*, substantial opium cultivation and trans-border drug trade). But Beijing's view that the local minorities inhabiting its southern borderlands are no threat to its rule, unlike more troublesome borderland regions such as Tibet or Xinjiang, for example, also contributes to relatively fewer resources being devoted to regulating cross-border flows. Indeed, some have characterized Han views of its southern border minorities, such as the purportedly hospitable and charming Dai, as a form of orientalism, with which locals are at least superficially complicit whilst lamenting in private the loss of their language and culture: 'None of the schools teach Dai now', and, 'You have to become a monk to learn how to read and write it' (Eimer, 2014: 175, 181):

> It is as if an unseen veil segregates them from the Chinese. Behind it, they preserve the most valuable aspects of their identity – language, culture and a religion that transcends borders – which would likely antagonize the CCP if put on show. (Eimer, 2014: 174)

Geography is also complicit in blurring borders: parts of China's southern border cut across rainforests, or comprise rivers, meaning that in some parts, 'it is possible to drift across frontiers without knowing you have done so' (Eimer, 2014: 164). Sometimes such border crossings involve (variable) payments; sometimes none. Observes Chan: 'there were only two policeman in the border crossing district. We paid them some money and carried goods to the other side. We helped them make a living' (Chan, 2013: 95). Clearly, in such borderlands, the Emperor is indeed far away.

CHINA, VIET NAM AND HIGHER EDUCATION

How do these intertwined elements play themselves out, in current China–ASEAN relations, especially in higher education? The sketch of the six pillars above highlights *inter alia* the evident substantial diversity within ASEAN. But this means that some selection on my part is necessary. Given the proximity and borderlands focus, Viet Nam is selected for analysis. Following a sketch of similarities and differences in the two systems, China's borderland regions' higher education relations with Viet Nam is taken as a test case.

With a population of around 90 million, Viet Nam is still classed as a developing country with significant economic growth rates and a substantial, if less well developed, higher education system than either China or several other ASEAN member states. As sketched above, it has a particularly complex history of China relations, on the one hand having fought a war as late as 1979, whilst on the other hand often following China's example in terms of policies and programmes, including in education. This includes a planned major increase in private higher education to the year 2020, as part of the higher education reform agenda (Welch, 2010a). Although ethnic Chinese make up no more than 1.5 per cent of the overall population, their influence on the economy significantly outweighs this modest proportion.

Neither the fact that Viet Nam is a sister in socialism to China, nor the disparity in size and economic weight between the two, has diminished the vigorous expression of nationalist sentiments that, as seen above, erupted again in the form of deadly anti-Chinese riots as recently as 2014. Viet Nam, as its history suggests, has a long history of insisting on its independence (as French, Chinese and US and Allied military forces can attest). *Doi Moi*, the process of reform and 'reconstruction' instituted in 1986, is the most obvious example of Viet Nam instituting reforms broadly mirroring that of China, if somewhat later. Another example consists of Viet Nam's accession to World Trade Organization (WTO) membership, six years after China. Bilateral trade and investment has increased significantly, and was given further impetus by the inception of the China–ASEAN Free Trade Agreement (CAFTA) of 2010, but still constitutes a small proportion of the total inflow of foreign direct investment (FDI) to both China and Viet Nam. As a result of some key major projects, China's FDI to Viet Nam is said to have leaped from US$371 million in 2012 to US$2.3 billion in 2013, according to Viet Nam's Ministry of Planning and Investment (MPI) figures (Xinhuanet, 2014). While bilateral trade and investment still strongly favour China, each is likely to have been affected by the recent territorial disputes, while China's outbound tourism to Viet Nam fell by almost 30 per cent annually, to 135 000 in August 2014 (*Wall Street Journal*, 2014).

REGIONAL TRADE AND RELATIONS IN HIGHER EDUCATION

While precise data are hard to come by, it is clear that rising service sector trade between China and ASEAN has been evident for some time, and that this certainly includes higher education (UNCTAD, 2004; Welch, 2011b; CRI, 2009). Overall, recent FDI flows to service sector industries in ASEAN accounted for around half of total ASEAN FDI in 2008 (ASEAN, 2009: 12–13).

While recent estimates have set the figure for worldwide trade in education services at around US$2.2 trillion, growth has been faster in developing-country contexts where the service sector occupies a lower proportion of total GDP, and growth in the service sector is seen as an economic goal. Growth has been particularly vigorous in developing Asia (Ng and Tan, 2010; ADB, 2012). The move to enshrine education as part of service sector trade under the General Agreement on Trade in Services (GATS), while criticized by educationists for listing education as a tradable commodity, is also enabling the more precise tracking of transnational forms of educational delivery of services (Welch, 2011b).

A recent Asian Development Bank study underlined that earnings from trade in higher education services still favoured the wealthier, English-language systems, but also revealed that significant (and much faster) growth was evident in Asia. While earnings from trade in higher education services still favoured traditional exporters such as the USA, the United Kingdom (UK) and Australia, newer Asian competitors such as Singapore, Malaysia and China were making substantial inroads (ADB, 2012: 37–38; Welch, 2011a). China alone has more than 300 000 international students enrolled in its higher education system, of which in 2011, 13 549 stemmed from Viet Nam (a rise from 7310 in 2006) (WENR, 2014; Welch, 2010a, 2010b). By contrast, Viet Nam, with few international students enrolled but at least 50 000 of its own enrolled overseas, is a net importer of higher education services, including from China (Welch, 2010a).

One consequence of the China–ASEAN Ministers of Education 'Double 100 000 Plan', adopted as part of the Guiyang Declaration in August 2010 (that set a target of 100 000 Chinese and ASEAN students enrolled in each other's universities by 2020), is a substantial boost in cross-border flows of students in both directions, although the imbalance indicated above, in China's favour, is likely to persist. China is also generous with scholarships to students from ASEAN, including Viet Nam. The plan is to raise the number of scholarships to ASEAN students to 10 000 by 2020.

CROSSING BORDERS IN HIGHER EDUCATION

In analyses of Asian higher education, hierarchy and stratification are often found to be critical to understanding. The above analysis, however, modifies this key point significantly. While no Chinese university from the three borderlands areas of Yunnan, Guizhou and Guangxi Zhuang Autonomous Region[3] are among the ranks of 985 universities (China's top tier) or are listed in the Academic Ranking of World Universities (ARWU), they are of critical importance to sustaining Sino-Vietnamese relations in higher education. The same is of course true in some of China's other border regions, where universities also considered of modest status in national and world terms are of crucial importance in sustaining cross-border regional relations (Welch and Yang, 2011).

But hierarchy and status still differentiate the two systems. Major differences in both scale and, particularly, quality are evident. According to the Shanghai Jiaotong's robust ARWU, China now has 32 higher education institutions (HEIs) listed among the top 500 worldwide (Yang and Welch, 2012). Like much of Southeast Asia, Viet Nam is yet to have any of its HEIs listed, although its plans to create 'model universities' using loans from the World Bank and the Asian Development Bank, and the expertise and resources of selected foreign partners, are explicitly aimed to lift quality and act as a benchmark for domestic HEIs. Of regional framework agreements and consortia in higher education, it is notable that no Vietnamese university is yet a member of the Association of Pacific Rim Universities (APRU) network, or of UNIVERSITAS 21, although they do include Fudan University and Shanghai Jiaotong University, both from China (APRU, n.d.; AUN, n.d.). Notably, however, Viet Nam National University, Ha Noi, and Vietnam National University – Ho Chi Minh City (VNU-HCM), are both members of the ASEAN+3 network that includes, of five People's Republic of China (PRC) universities, three key HEIs from the three above-mentioned border provinces: Guangxi University, Guizhou University and Yunnan University (AUN, n.d.).

From the Vietnamese perspective, its relatively less-developed higher education system and levels of infrastructure leaves it less well positioned to leverage cross-border collaboration, in two senses. Firstly, most obviously China's size and weight, as well as a more developed higher education system, leaves it in the driver's seat, to some extent. Although, as indicated, Viet Nam's history is one of stubborn independence, China also needs

Viet Nam. Secondly, relative even to some of its more developed fellow ASEAN member states, Viet Nam's developing economic status and less-developed higher education system also confer fewer advantages. A further inhibitor consists of intermittently difficult relations with its large and troublesome neighbour (although recent steps have been taken by both sides to quieten the tensions that threatened to endanger bilateral relations).

Viet Nam's long, intermittently troubled history of China relations includes key elements that have shaped its higher learning institutions and ideologies; notably the major and enduring influence of Confucianism (Welch, 2010). Viet Nam's peripheral status within the global knowledge network also translates into generally dependent relations with Chinese higher education (Welch, 2010a, 2010b). As seen above, many more Vietnamese students study at Chinese universities than the reverse, a situation that is broadly paralleled by scholarships (Xinhua, 2013). This, however, does not do justice to the much closer relations between borderland institutions, the so-called 'quiet achievers' in China's *Guangxi Zhuang Autonomous Region* (GZAR) and Yunnan (Yang, 2012). Training of Vietnamese civil servants and teachers is offered by both Yunnan and Guangxi, where each had enrolled several thousand students in their regional HEIs by around 2008, with several thousand students from Guangxi studying in ASEAN countries, including Viet Nam, which hosted the largest number. In Yunnan, links are equally diverse and dense, including '3+1' joint degree programmes with ASEAN countries (three years in the home country, one year in the partner country) and joint degree programmes with Viet Nam. Hundreds of Chinese language teachers have been trained at Yunnan University and Yunnan Normal University to work in ASEAN countries (Yang, 2012). Table 8.2 summarizes the relations across the bilateral relations in higher education, according to the four GATS modes, albeit not indicative of scale (WTO, n.d.).

At one of the key borderland universities listed above, research conducted in 2014 highlighted that educational cooperation, while mutual, was not equal, consisting largely of recruitment of ASEAN scholars. Research cooperation was envisaged, however. As one interviewee put it, 'we would like to accommodate researchers from ASEAN countries to do their research here, in our university. Meanwhile, we plan to send out our researchers to the ASEAN countries' (I1, 2014). Interviewees confirmed that almost 90 per cent of international students were from ASEAN, with a significant proportion from Viet Nam: 'In recent years, a large number of Vietnamese students come to study at our business school, majoring in international trade, business administration and accounting' (I1, 2014; see also I4).

Flows in the reverse direction were more modest, and largely restricted to

Table 8.2 Summary, China–Viet Nam cross-border educational services

State	Mode I	Mode II	Mode III	Mode IV
Viet Nam		VNU language courses for Chinese students Chinese students at Vietnamese universities		*Chinese consultants training Vietnamese*
China		*Vietnamese students at Chinese universities Training of Vietnamese civil servants and teachers*		

Note: Italics indicate Chinese exports; non-italics indicate Chinese imports.

Source: Modified from Welch (2011b).

certain areas: 'in terms of student exchange, our students go to Vietnam . . . primarily for language study' (I1, 2014), although another interviewee pointed to cooperation with Viet Nam in areas of mutual concern, such as environmental studies. On the whole, China's more developed higher education system meant that cooperation, while mutually valued, was not equal: 'this is one-way cooperation, which means we help those ASEAN countries to train their talents in the field' (I1, 2014). 'In terms of theory, we're relatively more advanced than Laos and Vietnam' (I5, 2014). Singapore, however, it was acknowledged, was 'more advanced' (I6).

Here, too, hierarchy played a role, with one interviewee admitting that: 'Few students from more developed members like Singapore, Malaysia and Philippine come to our institution for study. We don't have even a single student from Philippine, Malaysia or Singapore.' Moreover, it was acknowledged that, of the ASEAN students in China, borderland universities were not necessarily their first choice: 'Even if they come to China for study; most of them will go to Beijing rather than Guangxi' (I1, 2014). The profoundly stratified nature of Chinese higher education was similarly seen as an obstacle for borderland universities by I4: 'What they know are only Peking University or Tsinghua'.

Another respondent argued that it was the lack of research strength which constituted a barrier to more effective cross-border cooperation: 'the main obstacle could be the weakness in research capacity of "Borderlands" University. The university provides substantial support to ASEAN research. But we need to attract more talents to improve the research capacity' (I3, 2014). For one interviewee, from a business school, the borderland university occupied an interstitial position in its regional relations, with Viet Nam being placed in a particular light: 'for our university, if we go to Singapore or Malaysia, we learn from them, and if we go to Laos and Vietnam, they learn from us' (I5, 2014). For another interviewee from the same school, however, the problem of hierarchy was a larger one: 'We don't really know ASEAN countries, and we understand them in our respective way. And in developing the cooperation with ASEAN, we should follow the rule of "trade" rather than "aid", regarding them as equal economic players. But we treat them as inferior to us' (I6, 2014).

Other interviewees, however, argued that China's borderland HEIs had specific advantages, including the regional proximity that enabled them to function as a bridge:

> First, the geographical advantage: [borderland university] is proximate to ASEAN countries. Second, the geographical advantage will bring policy learning. Since we are close to ASEAN countries in terms of geography, the university may pay more attention to cooperation with ASEAN countries and develop particular policies to boost the cooperation. With these policies, investment of financial and human resources will be realistic. Second, because of the close relationship we have developed with enterprises and local government, we could operate employment-oriented continuing education programmes. Like those 1+1 or 2+1 programmes run in universities in the UK, we could develop these kinds of programmes and our students could have internship in appointed companies or industries. These programmes with internship opportunities will be more attractive to students. (I2, 2014; see also I5)

Another interviewee also listed transport linkages as a regional advantage for borderland institutions, while the same interviewee pointed to the success of colleagues in securing a substantial research grant to work on aspects of regional relations. Indeed an index of the rising importance attached to ASEAN within China is that both central and regional governments are providing substantial support for such projects. Ethnicity was seen as a further advantage, with a specialist in minority research pointing to cross-border links: 'Among the minorities in the Northern part, there are many descendants of Chinese *Chuang*. I have been to the villages in Northern Vietnam; people there are very hospitable to the Chinese *Chuang*' (I4, 2014).

Territorial tensions in the relationship between China and its neighbours were acknowledged, but 'economic cooperation is used as a means to conciliate those conflicts' (I1, 2014) Higher education was seen as a means to assist in such conciliation: 'China has to do more work in promoting Chinese culture in our ASEAN members' (I1, 2014). At least one interviewee alluded to possible resistance on the part of some Vietnamese students, indicating that unwillingness to integrate with local people was common and that some of these students 'will disseminate their negative attitudes towards China' (I4, 2014) when they return home. A possible solution was offered by a respondent from the Business School, who argued that both secondary and primary education sectors should also be opened up to ASEAN students: 'If these international students come to China for primary education and stay here till graduate from universities, they will know China better and become the real agent of China when they go back to their home countries' (IL6). Better communication was seen as a solution to differences between systems: 'I think we don't know each other adequately. A regular communication mechanism has not yet been established' (I6).

Ideological affinities provided another axis of cross-border cooperation, with one interviewee underlining the significance of ideology in recruitment: 'the majority of international students come from Socialist countries such as Vietnam and Laos' (I6, 2014). But research collaboration was also affected, with another interviewee pointing to a bilateral 'Borderlands' programme on Marxism in Viet Nam and China that was being conducted with selected Vietnamese universities.

An index of change, noted by one interviewee, linked the greater status accorded current Vietnamese students, to Chinese efforts to enhance its regional influence: 'Before, in the 1990s, universities in China didn't want Vietnamese students since usually they were poor and couldn't bring financial benefits to our universities. But now things changed. They are welcomed now because we want to boost the influence of China in those countries' (I4, 2014).

IRREGULAR AND REGULATORY REGIONALISM

How far does the above sketch of borderland relations in higher education illuminate debates on regionalism? Given the somewhat peripheral, if changing, status of China's southern borderlands, and of Viet Nam, in the global knowledge network, the range and depth of regional relations in higher education are impressive (Yang, 2012). While more research is needed into borderland regional relations in general, there is clearly considerable potential for extending their range and depth. Notwithstanding the substantial obstacles articulated above, common interests and joint practical priorities are able to proceed beneath great power politics, and regional territorial disputes.

What the analysis also problematizes, however, is the character and limits of regionalism. Several analysts have contrasted the more embryonic, emergent quality of ASEAN regionalism with the more established regional architecture of the EU, including in higher education

(Robertson, 2008; Jayasuriya, 2003, 2010). More than one author has pointed to the substantial gap between lofty ASEAN rhetoric and declarations, and the more limited range of actual accomplishments (Welch, 2012a). Jayasuriya's critique of the triumphalism of ASEAN regionalism pointed to its focus on 'formal regional "institutions" . . . to the detriment of the understanding of the domestic political mainsprings of regional governance' (Jayasuriya, 2003: 199). This, he has argued, limits the capacity of regulatory regionalism. Other analysts have pointed to nationalist resistance among several ASEAN member states as a further brake on progress (Pesek, 2012).

If this is the case for ASEAN, what of the case for China–ASEAN regionalism, which despite growing and thickening links, including in higher education, many would not acknowledge to be a region? And how much more so does this apply in the peripheries and borderlands characterized by 'floating populations', mobility and connectivity (Carney, 2009), in a 'cartography of connections' (Larsen and Beech, 2014: 207) that also embraces in this instance, historical and contemporary, legal and illegal, fluxes and flows of ideas, people, timber, drugs and gems? In a context where significant progress has been made on the ground by the 'quiet achievers' (Yang, 2012) against a wider background of largely irregular flows of people, goods and services (Evans et al., 2000), might this not be better characterized as irregular regionalism (Scott, 2009)?

It is argued here that there is great potential for deeper and wider relations in regional higher education and that such a development could also help break down barriers of understanding, and contribute to deepening regionalism. Extending existing 'borderlands' research collaboration on common priorities such as the environment, and marine research, as well as deepening people-to-people exchanges (Sutter and Huang, 2012), including more Vietnamese students studying in Chinese 'borderlands' universities, and more Chinese students enrolled in Vietnamese universities, could significantly strengthen the bonds of regionalism whilst at the same time helping to break free of the prism of economics through which China–ASEAN regionalism is still conventionally viewed.

NOTES

1. The corollary expression '*Ban Jun Ru Ban Hu*' can be translated as 'To be close to the Emperor is to be close to the Tiger'.
2. The Chinese term '*Xishuangbanna*' reflects the Dai name, meaning 12 rice fields, or 12 pieces of land. It stems from Ming dynasty times.
3. The first two are provinces, the third is designated an Autonomous Region, a status like other border regions of China, such as the Xinjiang Uyghur Autonomous Region.

REFERENCES

ASEAN (2009), ASEAN Investment Report 2009. Accessed 13 September 2012 at http://www.aseansec.org/documents/AIR2009.pdf

ASEAN Universities Network (AUN) (n.d.), ASEAN + 3 UNet Member Universities. Accessed 5 January 2015 at http://www.aunsec.org/membership.php

Asia Pacific Research Universities (APRU) (n.d.), Member universities. Accessed 5 January 2015 at http://apru.org/members/member-universities

Asian Development Bank (ADB) (2010), Viet Nam. Preparing the Higher Education Sector Development Project (HESDP). Accessed 13 September 2012 at http://www2.adb.org/documents/reports/consultant/vie/42079/42079-01-vietacr-01.pdf

Asian Development Bank (ADB) (2012), Counting the cost. Financing higher education for inclusive growth in Asia. Accessed 13 September 2012 at http://www.adb.org/sites/default/files/pub/2012/counting-cost.pdf.

Barrett, T. (2012), *The Chinese Diaspora in South-East Asia. The Overseas Chinese in Indo-China*. London: I.B. Tauris.

Bowring, P. (2012a), China failing geography, history. *Australian*, 8 June. Accessed 13 September 2012 at http://theaustralian.newspaperdirect.com/epaper/viewer.aspx.

Bowring, P. (2012b), Island mentality ignores history. *South China Morning Post*, 22 April. Accessed 13 September 2012 at http://www.scmp.com/article/998912/island-mentality-ignores-history.

Carney, T. (2009), Negotiating policy in an age of globalization: exploring policyscapes in Demark, Nepal and China. *Comparative Education Review*, **53**, 63–88.

Chan, W-C. (2013), *Vietnamese–Chinese Relations at the Borderlands*. London, Routledge.

Chang, S.-D. (2008), The distribution and occupations of overseas Chinese. In Reid, A. (ed.), *The Chinese Diaspora in the Pacific*. Aldershot: Ashgate, pp. 33–51.

Chang, Y. (1988), The Ming empire: patron of Islam in China and Southeast and West Asia. *Journal of the Malaysian Branch of the Royal Asiatic Society*, **61**(2), 1–44.

Cheow, E.T.C. (2004), China's rising soft power in Southeast Asia. *PacNet*, 3 May, 19a.

China Daily (2012a), ASEAN China to become top trading partners. *China Daily*, 20 April. Accessed 13 September 2012 at http://www.chinadaily.com.cn/cndy/2012-04/20/content_15094898.htm.

China Daily (2012b), More travellers from mainland going overseas. 13 April.

China Daily (2013), China–ASEAN trade to bloom on new target. 10 October.

China Daily (2014a), Guangxi ready to crackdown on drugs. 3 November.

China Daily (2014b), Outbound tourism flies high with 100m visits. Asia Weekly, 12–18 December.

China Daily (2014c), Forging ahead with shared vision. Asia Weekly, 12–18 December.

China Defense Mashup (2012), China gets tough as Viet Nam claims disputed islands. Accessed 13 September 2012 at http://www.china-defense-mashup.com/china-gets-tough-as-Viet Nam-claims-disputed-islands.html.

China Radio International (CRI) (2009), Singapore's NTU sets up center for Chinese officials. Accessed 13 September 2012 at http://english.cri.cn/6909/2009/12/14/1461s535442.htm.
Conboy, K. (2002), Troubled courtship: military ties between China and Indonesia. *China Brief*, **2**(20). Accessed 13 September 2012 at http://www.jamestown.org/programs/chinabrief/single/?tx_ttnews%5Btt_news%5D=3527%26tx_ttnews%5BbackPid%5D=192%26no_cache=1.
Crossley, P, Siu, H. and Sutton, D. (eds) (2006), *Empire at the Margins. Culture, Ethnicity and Frontier in Early Modern China*. Oakland, CA: University of California Press.
Da, W-W. and Welch, A. (2016), Educative and child-rearing practices among recent Chinese migrants in Australia: continuity and change. In Chou, C. (ed.), *Chinese Educational Models in a Global Age. Transforming Practice into Theory*. London: Palgrave Macmillan. pp. 231–248
Diplomat (2015a), Philippines blasts China on South China Sea reclamation work. http://thediplomat.com/2015/01/philippines-blasts-china-on-south-china-sea-reclamation-work/.
Diplomat (2015b), The Philippines, Malaysia and Viet Nam race to South China Sea defense modernization. http://thediplomat.com/2015/01/the-philippines-malaysia-and-Viet Nam-race-to-south-china-sea-defense-modernization/.
The Economist (2006), China beat Columbus to it, perhaps. http://www.economist.com/node/5381851.
Eimer, D. (2014), *The Emperor Far Away: Travels at the Edge of China*. London: Bloomsbury.
Evans, G., Hutton, C. and Eng, K-K (eds) (2000), *Where China Meets Southeast Asia: Social and Cultural Change in the Borderlands*. London: Palgrave.
Farram, S. (2010), The PKI in West Timor and Nusa Tenggara Timur: 1965 and beyond. *Bijdragen tot de Taal-, Land-en Volkenkunde*, **166**(4), 381–403.
Gelber, H.G. (2007), *The Dragon and the Foreign Devils: China and the World 1100BC to the Present*. London: Bloomsbury Books.
Goodman, D. (ed.) (2008), *The New Rich in China Future Rulers, Present Lives*. London: Routledge.
Gunde, R. (2004), Zheng He's voyages of discovery. Accessed 16 September 2012 at http://www.international.ucla.edu/article.asp?parentid=10387.
Hanban News (2013), Chinese Premier Li Keqiang attends the signing ceremony of the Confucius Institute at Ha Noi University, Viet Nam. http://english.hanban.org/article/2013-10/18/content_512308.htm.
Heidhues, M.S. (2001), *South East Asia: A Concise History*. New York: Thames & Hudson.
Hirono, M. (2010), How to play a 'responsible great power' role: China's post-tsunami assistance to Aceh. Accessed 16 September 2012 at http://www.eastasiaforum.org/2010/06/26/how-to-play-a-responsible-great-power-role-chinas-post-tsunami-assistance-to-aceh/.
International New York Times (2015), In China, few real victories in 'People's War' on Drugs. 26 January.
Jarvis, D. and Welch, A. (2011), Introduction. In Jarvis, D. and Welch, A. (eds), *ASEAN Industries and the Challenge from China*. London: Palgrave Macmillan, pp. 1–19.
Jayasuriya, K. (2003), Introduction: governing the Asia Pacific, beyond the 'new regionalism'. *Third World Quarterly*, **24**(2), 199–215.

Jayasuriya, K. (2010), Learning by the market: regulatory regionalism, Bologna, and accountability communities. *Globalisation, Societies and Education*, **8**(1), 7–22.
Kharas, H. (2011), Can the Asian middle class come of age? East Asia Forum. http://www.eastasiaforum.org/2011/06/12/can-the-asian-middle-class-come-of-age/.
Laksmana, E.A. (2011), Variations on a theme: dimensions of ambivalence in Indonesia China relations. *Harvard Asia Quarterly*, **13**(1), 24–31.
Larsen, M. and Beech, J. (2014), Spatial theorising in comparative and international education research. *Comparative Education Review*, **58**(2), 191–214.
Li, M.J. (2012), China's non-confrontational assertiveness in the South China Sea. Accessed 16 September 2012 at http://www.eastasiaforum.org/2012/06/14/china-s-non-confrontational-assertiveness-in-the-south-china-sea/.
National Geographic (2005), China's Great Armada. http://ngm.nationalgeographic.com/ngm/0507/feature2/map.html.
New York Times (2015), The plunder of Myanmar. http://www.nytimes.com/2015/01/24/opinion/the-plunder-of-myanmar.html?_r=1.
Ng, P.T. and Tan, C. (2010), The Singapore global schoolhouse: an analysis of the development of the tertiary education landscape in Singapore. *International Journal of Educational Management*, **24**(3), 178–188.
Nguyen, H. (2012), Internet stirs activism in Viet Nam. Accessed 13 September 2012 at http://yaleglobal.yale.edu/content/internet-stirs-activism-Viet Nam.
Osborne, M. (2006), *The Paramount Power: China and the Countries of Southeast Asia*. Sydney: Lowy Institute for International Policy.
Pak, J. (2012), Is English or Mandarin the language of the future? Accessed 16 September 2012 at http://www.bbc.co.uk/news/magazine-17105569.
Pesek, W. (2012), Millions stagnate in poverty as Indonesia indulges in economic nationalism. Accessed 13 September 2012 at http://www.smh.com.au/business/millions-stagnate-in-poverty-as-indonesia-indulges-in-economic-nationalism-20120622-20tgm.html.
Pramudatama, R. (2012), May tragedy remembered. *Jakarta Post*, 13 May. Accessed 16 September 2012 at http://www.thejakartapost.com/news/2012/05/13/may-tragedy-remembered.html.
Prantl, J. (2012), Five principles for a new security order in the Asia Pacific. Accessed 18 June 2012 at http://www.eastasiaforum.org/index.php?s=%2C+Five+principles+for+a+new+security+order+in+the+Asia+Pacific.
Rahardja, S. and World Bank (2012), What China's economic prospects mean for Indonesia. Accessed 13 September 2012 at http://www.eastasiaforum.org/2012/08/09/what-china-s-economic-prospects-mean-for-indonesia/.
Reid, A. (2008), Introduction. In Reid, A. (ed.), *The Chinese Diaspora in the Pacific*. Aldershot: Ashgate, pp. xv–xxviii.
Reuters (2014), Viet Nam stops anti-China protests after riots, China evacuates workers. http://www.reuters.com/article/2014/05/18/us-china-Viet Nam-idUSBREA4H00C20140518.
Robertson, S. (2008), Europe/Asia regionalism, higher education and the production of world order. *Policy Futures in Education*, **6**(6), 718–728.
Scott, J. (2009), *The Art of Not Being Governed. An Anarchist History of Uplands Southeast Asia*. New Haven, CT: Yale University Press.
Severino, R. (2012), A code of conduct for the South China Sea? *PacNet*, 17 August, 45A.
Sigley, G. (2014), Yunnan: China's bridgehead to Southeast Asia and beyond.

Diplomat. http://thediplomat.com/2014/04/yunnan-chinas-bridgehead-to-southeast-asia-and-beyond/.
South China Morning Post (2015a), Can Viet Nam have its cake and eat it? January 17.
South China Morning Post (2015b), Asia on alert. January 17.
South China Morning Post (2015c), China widens works in disputed waters: Manila. January 22.
Star Malaysia (2012), Singapore to give full license to 2 Chinese banks. 7 July. Accessed 13 September 2012 at http://in.reuters.com/article/2012/07/06/singapore-china-banks-idINL3E8I624T20120706.
State Council (2015a), China's GDP growth in past 20 years. http://english.gov.cn/policies/infographics/2015/01/20/content_281475042218063.htm.
State Council (2015b), Chinese outbound travellers in 2014. http://english.gov.cn/policies/infographics/2014/12/16/content_281475024688112.htm.
Straits Times (2015), Repairing China's image of 'regional bully' a priority for Xi. 7 January.
Suryadinata, L. (2003), Patterns of political participation in four ASEAN states: a comparative study. In Wang, L.-C. and Wang, G. (eds), *The Chinese Diaspora: Selected Essays*, Vol. 1. Singapore: Eastern Universities Press, pp. 64–83.
Sutter, R. and Huang C.-H. (2012), China muscles opponents on the South China Sea. *Comparative Connections.* Accessed 13 September 2012 at http://csis.org/files/ publication/1202qchina_seasia.pdf.
Taylor, B. (2012), Storm in a teacup over South China Sea. *Australian*, 11 May. Accessed 13 September 2012 at http://www.theaustralian.com.au/opinion/world-commentary/storm-in-teacup-over-south-china-sea/story-e6frg6ux-1226352425072.
Tong, S.Y. and Chong, C.S.K. (2010), China–ASEAN free trade area in 2010: a regional perspective. EAI Background Brief No. 519, Singapore: East Asia Institute, National University of Singapore.
Torode, G. (2012), Rocky patch. *South China Morning Post*, 19 April. Accessed 19 April 2012 at http://www.scmp.com/article/971158/rocky-patch.
Tran, D. (2003), Culture environment and farming systems in Vietnam's northern mountain region. *Southeast Asia Studies*, **41**(2), 180–205.
UNCTAD (2004), *World Investment Report, 2004: The Shift Towards Services.* New York, USA and Geneva, Switzerland: UN.
Vaughan, B. and Morrison, W.M. (2006), China–Southeast Asia relations: trends, issues and implications for the United States. Report No. RL32688. Washington, DC: Congressional Research Service.
Wall Street Journal (2014), Oil rig standoff with China won't hurt FDI Viet Nam says. http://www.wsj.com/articles/oil-rig-standoff-with-china-wont-hurt-fdi-Vietnam-says-1410254314.
Wang, G. (2000), *The Chinese Overseas: From Earthbound China to the Quest for Autonomy*. Cambridge, MA: Harvard University Press.
Wang, G. (2005), China and Southeast Asia: the context of a new beginning. In Shambaugh, D. (ed.), *Power Shift: China and Asia's New Dynamics*. Berkeley, CA: University of California Press, pp. 187–204.
Welch, A. (2010a), Internationalisation of Vietnamese higher education: retrospect and prospect. In Harman, G., Hayden, M. and Nghi, P.T. (eds), *Reforming Higher Education in Viet Nam: Challenges and Priorities*. Dordrecht: Springer, pp. 197–214.

Welch, A. (2010b), Viet Nam, Malaysia and the Global Knowledge System. In Portnoy, L., Bagley, S. and Rust, V. (eds), *Higher Education and International Competitiveness.* Chicago, IL: Chicago University Press, pp. 143–160.

Welch, A. (2011a), *Higher Education in Southeast Asia: Blurring Borders, Changing Balance.* Abingdon: Routledge.

Welch, A. (2011b), The dragon, the tiger cubs and higher education: competitive and cooperative China–ASEAN relations the GATS era. In Jarvis, D. and Welch, A. (eds), *ASEAN Industries and the Challenge from China.* London: Palgrave Macmillan, pp. 39–122.

Welch, A. (2012a), Regionalism and the Limits of Regionalism in Indonesian Higher Education. In Hawkins, J. and Neubauer, D. (eds), *Regionalism in East Asian Higher Education.* London: Palgrave Macmillan, pp. 24–42.

Welch, A. (2012b), Contributing to the Southeast Asian knowledge economy? Australian offshore campuses in Malaysia and Viet Nam. In Nelson, A.R. and Wei, I.P. (eds), *The Global University: Past, Present and Future Perspectives.* London: Palgrave Macmillan, pp. 45–73.

Welch, A. and Hao, J. (2012), Returnees and diaspora: twin sources of innovation in Chinese Higher Education. *Frontiers of Education in China*, **8**(2), 214–238.

Welch, A. and Yang, R. (2011), A Pearl on the Silk Road? Internationalizing a Regional Chinese University. In Palmer, J., Roberts, A., Ha Cho, Y. and Ching, G. (eds), *The Internationalization of East Asian Higher Education. Globalization's Impact.* New York: Palgrave Macmillan, pp. 63–89.

Welch, A. and Zhang, Z. (2008), The Chinese knowledge diaspora: communication networks among overseas Chinese intellectuals. In Epstein, D., Boden, R., Deem, R. and Wright, S. (eds), *Geographies of Knowledge, Geometries of Power: Framing the Future of Education,* London: Routledge, pp. 338–354.

Whitney, C.B. and Shambaugh, D. (2008), *Soft Power in Asia. Results of a 2008 Multinational Survey of Public Opinion.* Chicago, IL: Chicago Council on Global Affairs and East Asia Institute.

Williams, B.R. (2012), Trans-Pacific Partnership (TPP) countries: comparative trade and economic analysis. Accessed 13 September 2012 at http://fpc.state.gov/documents/organization/193710.pdf.

World Education News and Reviews (WENR) (2014), Higher education in Viet Nam. May. http://wenr.wes.org/2014/05/higher-education-in-Viet Nam/.

World Trade Organization (WTO) (n.d.), The General Agreement on Trade in Services (GATS): objectives, coverage and disciplines. http://www.wto.org/english/tratop_e/serv_e/gatsqa_e.htm.

Wu, D. and Mealy, M. (2012), Explaining 'competing' visions: ASEAN-RCEP, TPP, FTAAP. *PacNet*, 26 June, 40.

Xinhua (2011), China ASEAN cooperation: 1991–2011. Accessed 20 September 2012 at http://news.xinhuanet.com/english2010/china/2011-11/15/c_131248640_17.htm.

Xinhua (2012), China–ASEAN education collaboration on fast track. Accessed 20 September 2012 at http://news.xinhuanet.com/english2010/indepth/2011--08/18/c_131058805.htm.

Xinhua (2013), Viet Nam to send 3000 teachers abroad for higher education in 2014–2015. December 19.

Xinhuanet (2014), Interview: more Chinese investment boosts China–Viet Nam trade ties. http://news.xinhuanet.com/english/indepth/2014-01/16/c_133050466.htm.

Yang, H.-Y. (1993), Confucius. *Prospects. The Quarterly Review of Comparative Education*, **23**(1–2), 211–219.

Yang, R. (2012), Internationalisation, regionalization, and soft power: China's relations with ASEAN member countries in higher education. *Frontiers of Education in China*, **7**(4).

Yang, R. and Welch, A. (2010), Globalisation, transnational academic mobility and the Chinese knowledge diaspora: an Australian case study. *Discourse. Australian Journal of Educational Studies*, **31**(5), 593–607.

Yang, R. and Welch, A. (2012), A world class university for China? The case of Tsinghua. *Higher Education*, **63**(5), 645–666.

Yeung, H.W.C. (1999), The internationalisation of ethnic Chinese business firms from South East Asia: strategies, processes and competitive advantage. *International Journal of Urban and Rural Research*, **23**(1), 103–127.

Yudhoyono, S. (2014), Special Address at the Opening Ceremony of the 6th World Chinese Economic Forum. Chonging, China, December.

9. Good friends and faceless partners: educational cooperation for community building in the Barents Region

Marit Sundet

INTRODUCTION

Can educational cooperation between higher educational institutions (HEIs) in Russia and Norway contribute to developing a sense of community in the Barents Region? This question stems from political intentions to strengthen the social, cultural and economic relations between the countries. In speeches, treaties and statements (e.g., Putin, 2010; White Paper, 2011–2012), institutions throughout the region are encouraged to work together to develop joint academic programmes and research projects with the idea of raising the level of regional expertise and producing new and sorely needed knowledge across a wide range of fields. The Barents Region is a 21-year-old macro-political construction; a formalized multilateral collaboration between a number of countries within a geographically limited area. Aside from strong commercial, environmental and resource-related interests, there is also a so-called 'people-to-people cooperation' among the leading objectives for development of the region. The idea is that such projects may build bridges across international borders and create a close and beneficial coexistence. Various types of educational collaborations are involved in this particular category of objectives.

In attempting to provide an answer to this question on whether bilateral educational cooperation contributes to the development of a regional community, I begin by presenting an empirical example that will be described in greater detail later on in the chapter. I will then briefly point to several perspectives on the factors that encourage organizations to incorporate institutional changes such as those that have been initiated by countries in the Barents Region. Thereafter, I will elaborate on what characterizes the actual cooperation referred to in my example. The idea is to explore how the involved HEIs' motivation to participate is associated with the political expectations that these types of people-to-people projects will result in closer and improved relations between people in the region.

EDUCATIONAL COOPERATION

The educational cooperation used as an example here is comprised of one Norwegian and seven Russian institutions of higher education. Geographically, these institutions are spread over a large area (1 755 800 sq. km) known as the Barents Region. This collaboration began on a small scale, at the time of the new millennium. At the outset, one enthusiastic academic at the Norwegian HEI primarily drove the project. The establishment process, in and of itself, was quite typical for how a strategically gifted individual may take advantage of new negotiating terms that arise as a result of changes in an organization's institutionalized surroundings. Among the changes involved, there were two factors in particular that should be highlighted. One factor was the awakening of possibilities after the Cold War, born of a close political cooperation to face unresolved issues and challenges encompassing a range of fields. The other major factor was the realization of large and ample opportunities to harness natural resources and develop business in the northern regions. The oil industry, fisheries, mining and other businesses based on natural resources, however, are connected to environmental considerations and sustainability. Exploitation of natural resources and environmental challenges are, therefore, central issues in the political cooperation. Additionally, both Russia and Norway have strategic geopolitical and defence interests in the region. The development of the bilateral relationship, therefore, has the function of preserving the peace as well.

From the Norwegian perspective, Russia comprises a cornerstone of the northern political arena (White Paper, 2011–2012: 11), while the northern regions are simultaneously described as Norway's most important strategic area in foreign politics. From the Russian side, Foreign Minister Sergei Lavrov spoke at a 2008 meeting in Kirkenes about the Barents Cooperation as an example of Russia's desire to work together with its neighbouring countries. In a speech in Moscow on the Barents Cooperation, President Putin emphasized the significance that the Russians place on such work by pointing out, among other things, that 'preserving the Arctic as a zone of peace and cooperation is of the utmost importance for Russia' (Putin, 2010).[1]

As a foundation for the educational collaboration, two areas of prioritization are often referred to. One is the development of knowledge in a range of different fields that primarily include the natural science disciplines. The other is the so-called 'people-to-people cooperation' involving approximately the same number of fields, where education is brought into focus as a particularly critical area of collaboration. With cooperation in the areas of research and education as a priority, the Norwegian side has invested a considerable amount of financial support, primarily toward the natural sciences here as well. Additionally, they have provided clear expectations in the form of politically formulated goals for all the relevant institutions including treaties, White Papers and speeches. These types of political expectations have had a clear influence on the adaptations made by HEIs in the Barents Region; a subject that will be addressed in more detail below.

The other institutionalized innovation that is important to highlight is the net-based University of the Arctic, which was established in 1997 by the Arctic Council and, therefore, is primarily a circumpolar collaboration between eight member countries. It was through University of the Arctic that the Norwegian catalyst discovered how he would connect his own HEI to Russian educational institutions. Over time, he succeeded in establishing what, today, is a relatively well-functioning educational cooperation between eight HEIs in the Barents Region. The academic programmes, which all lead to a BCS degree (Bachelor of Circumpolar Studies), have experienced consistent annual growth and, in 2012, the total number of Russian students registered was well over 300. The total number of Norwegian students tied to the BCS programmes, however, is far more modest.

As shown in the map in Figure 9.1, there are large geographical distances between the cooperating HEIs in this network. Although some of the Russian HEIs are located in the same city, there are nonetheless considerable differences between them in relation to size (from 1600 to 20 000 students), academic profile, financial foundation, management principles and strategies for internationalization. To explain these differences in greater detail would encompass a broad introduction into a complicated Russian educational system and the comprehensive reforms it is currently undergoing, a topic that would require a chapter of its own. The Norwegian HEI, University of Nordland*, is the institution that enrols the most Russian students in Norway each year, of which 75 per cent apply for the BCS programme.

In practice, the BCS cooperation is run by one coordinator at each of the Russian HEIs, and two from the Norwegian HEI. I hold the position of leader for the network while also occupying a leading role at the University of the Arctic. Aside from the regular and relatively frequent contact we have via the Internet, there is a formal annual meeting involving

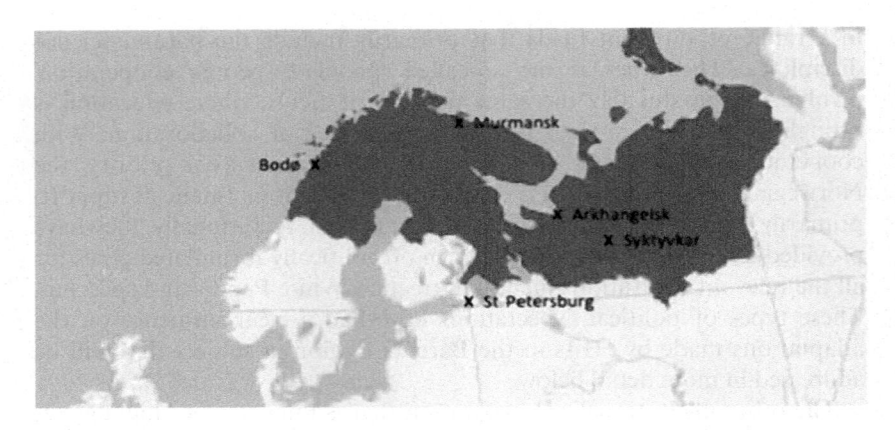

Note: Bodø (1 HEI): University of Nordland. Murmansk (3 HEIs): International Institute of Business Education, Murmansk State Humanities University, Murmansk State Technical University. Arkhangelsk (1 HEI): The Northern (Arctic) Federal University. Syktyvkar (2 HEIs): Syktyvkar State University, Komi Republican Academy of State Service and Administration. St Petersburg (1 HEI): State Polar Academy.

Figure 9.1   Location of HEIs participating in educational cooperation

orientation and policy formation, where the hosting responsibilities rotate amongst the HEIs. Since each coordinator often has also at least one assistant join the meeting, there are usually 18 to 20 people present each time. The work of this network is explained in more detail elsewhere (Sundet, 2015).

In order to approach the question of whether this educational cooperation contributes in some way to building a sense of community from a people-to-people perspective, I refer to data that have been collected through a larger research project on institutional collaboration and student exchange between Norway and Russia. Because the educational cooperation referred to also exists in competitive versions tied to other HEIs in Russia and Norway,[2] these are also included in the research project's database.

In terms of data for this chapter, I draw upon a series of sources. Ten interviews with different HEIs were carried out: three in Murmansk, one in Arkhangelsk, two in Syktyvkar and one in St Petersburg. The three Norwegian institutions included in the data collection are located in each of the three northernmost counties of Norway. Many of the informants are also involved in a number of similar educational cooperation. Seventeen interviews were carried out at Russian HEIs, including four rectors, four vice-rectors and nine BCS coordinators. In addition to these

31 interviews, I draw upon detailed information that I have recorded on the educational cooperation over time, specifically a multitude of conversations with colleagues and key persons at the various HEIs involved in my role as academic director. Having held this position for many years, observations and impressions throughout my tenure form some of the empirical foundation.

REGIONAL ISOMORPHISM OF THE EDUCATIONAL COOPERATION

The basis of current institutional theory is that organizations operating within the same organizational field are characterized by a structural convergence over time. In the context of this chapter, the organizational field consists of HEIs and is both international and complex. In principle, it should not be limited to the Barents Region. The concept refers to the idea that organizations operating within the same functional areas will eventually come to resemble one another; not just in the form of organizational structures and formal procedures but also in the way that they influence each other's norms and perceptions of reality. The organizational field is institutionalized by creating mutual norms, as well as through understandings of problems and perceptions of their own and others' roles through interactive social processes.

This isomorphism – that the organizations adapt to one another and their surroundings through processes that mutually shape and coordinate them – may easily be seen by the educational cooperation as creating a direct and almost exclusive context of speeches, treaties and measures that provide meaning and guidelines for the cooperation in the Barents Region. It is, therefore, important to differentiate between that which is specifically regional and that which is typical for the international development within the organizational field of which the HEIs are a part.

The following explanation uses DiMaggio and Powell's (1983) three mechanisms of isomorphic change as a guide. The first of these mechanisms is 'coercive isomorphism', describing when an organization is pressured into implementing certain solutions or taking on specific duties through a form of persuasion or invitations from the surrounding environment. The methods used in formulating speeches and treaties express clearly, if not quite specifically, what the authorities in both countries expected of their educational institutions in the Barents Region. For the HEIs involved in the educational cooperation, this undoubtedly feels as much like genuine pressure as it does as generous invitations, thus making it seem somewhat mandatory to comply. Additionally, political and economic adaptations are made that, collectively, represent not only stimuli and tempting possibilities, but also a clear imperative for the HEIs to act.

The second isomorphic mechanism is defined as 'mimetic processes' and points to how the organization imitates its surroundings. In the context of this chapter, this refers to other HEIs globally as well as in the Barents Region. Educational and research collaboration across borders is a strong and growing international trend, of which BCS is only a small part. In order to demonstrate that a HEI is both contemporary and 'fashionable', it will adopt successful solutions and new ways of acting from the international environment. Such adaptations have a legitimizing effect because they give testament to an institution's ability to keep up with the trends, and follow in the footsteps of recognized and popular HEIs out in the world, eventually allowing it to be compared to the same institutions it regards so highly.

The third isomorphic mechanism is referred to as 'normative pressures', and is particularly connected to how professional norms and academic standards influence the shaping of the HEIs' strategies to a great degree. The more the individual HEI is involved in the international network, the more it will come to resemble the institutions it cooperates with over time.

Viewed from the perspective of the three isomorphic mechanisms, it is reasonable to conclude that the educational cooperation surrounding the BCS programme is driven by a coherent Russian and Norwegian political will expressed through the desire for a multifunctional Barents Region. It is naturally far from a coincidence that this collaboration has been established at a time when internationalization is one of the core concepts among the leadership at HEIs the world over. It is a necessary prerequisite to waking the interest of those very institutions. Furthermore, it is positive, useful and educational in that it provides free access to experience, solutions and strategies. The Barents Cooperation opens an arena for the HEIs in the region to more easily take part in the internationalization process, identify themselves as internationalists, and comply with professional standards and norms and academic habitus. The isomorphism, in itself, will lead to a structural convergence, thereby suggesting that the educational cooperation comprises a central people-to-people project and an important element in the building of community in the Barents Region.

In reaching such a conclusion, the educational cooperation is viewed as a social and cultural construction in line with the way most buildings are perceived and assessed according to the part that sticks up out of the ground, and less seldom according to the foundations. Therefore, I would like to invite the reader on a tour beneath the surface to delve more deeply into this educational cooperation and look more closely at the seams. In the study of institutions, it is not an unusual phenomenon to overlook the fact that there are people inside, and that it is the people – not the institutions – who interact with one another.

INSTITUTIONALIZATION: ACTION AND MOTIVE

In many ways, the educational cooperation in the Barents Region may seem like a cumulative process with regionalizing effects. It increases in scope as new relations are established across borders and, eventually, the participants in the network get better acquainted with each other's institutions. This can initially seem like a good foundation for a growing community and, in fact, it is well on the way to being realized. The question is, however: where does the focus of the researcher lie and what may be accomplished, when all is said and done, to hold this most fragile community together? Let me begin with a comparison.

For many years as part of a long life together, an older couple went to monthly concerts at the local symphony hall. Without exception, they dressed up, left early and sat in their regular seats in the half-full concert hall. In her later years, the wife told her husband that these musical experiences had been life-sustaining for her, while at the same time she had basically hated all the small-talk and cultural snobbery that went on during the pauses and in the foyer bar afterwards. The husband had to admit that it was precisely the social aspects of the whole thing – the chit-chat, discussion and laughter – that had got him to join her for the concerts at all. He had never really liked the music.

In our context, this story can serve as a basis for the question on what institutionalization is all about. Does it have to do with the monthly ritual of getting dressed up, going to a concert and drinking a glass of wine, only to return home again afterwards? Or, on the contrary, is it the desire to go, along with the experience of being there, that are the institutionalized characteristics of this couple's monthly routine? The first motivation is of an external nature and points merely to action. The second is of a value-based nature and refers to an inner drive that gets two people to establish a set routine. The third possibility that could emerge from this story is connected to the couple's individual abilities and characteristics: that her ear for classical music and his musicality for small-talk do not necessarily mirror their normative interests and devotions. A fourth element that should be addressed is the strategic side of the situation: she lets him mingle with other people during the interval and at the bar afterwards so that he will be motivated to join her for the concert. He joins her for the concert because it gives him the opportunity to meet other people. A fifth aspect of this example is that two people carry out a set ritual together that, on the outside, may appear to mean the same for both of them, while each of their value-based reasons and particular affinities to act are quite different. Awareness of this parallelism, like the knowledge that small children play together without really playing with each other, is often lacking in studies on institutionalization. It is these five aspects – the external, the value-based, the distinct, the strategic and the parallel – that I will apply when discussing the regionalizing significance of the educational cooperation.

THE EXTERNAL ASPECT

The collaboration between the Norwegian and Russian HEIs produces exam results and candidates who move on to further studies or work. The BCS courses receive positive evaluations, and satisfied students take hold of their diplomas while expressing gratitude for a wonderful educational experience and talented teachers. The network of key individuals who organize and drive these studies work well together; something that, in practice, constitutes the most important prerequisite for the cooperation and its yield of candidates (Sundet, 2015). In this field, it may metaphorically be regarded as the womb in a long-term pregnancy called internationalization. The Russian HEIs can point to the fact that a large number of their students receive international education and can decorate themselves with academic grades according to the criteria of the Bologna Process. On the other hand, the Norwegian HEIs can point to the fact that they educate a considerable number of foreign students. To a certain degree, the educational cooperation has also resulted in Russian researchers being included in projects initiated by Norwegian members of the BCS network, financed by the Research Council of Norway. In other words, when viewed from the outside, this collaboration seems to symbolize a process of advancement in which interaction between important players and integration of central fields may be interpreted as providing influential effects in a regionalizing process in the Barents Region.

THE VALUE-BASED ASPECT

Once the BCS network began to take shape, and the members became better acquainted, each individual's value-based and normative understandings became more evident and, as often happens when relations become closer, the members began to show more clearly who they are and what their opinions and viewpoints represent. In an educational cooperation, however, the individuals' norms and values are subordinate to formalized principles, statutes and guidelines for how the collaboration should function. Legitimization of decisions in individual cases is thus achieved by referencing the formal framework for the network, while individual opinions on the same cases may be quite divergent and are only confidentially expressed one-on-one. In some cases where reason and values have not corresponded with the applicable decisions and principles, we have attempted to establish a practice of compliance with what certain individuals consider desirable and necessary rather than following what is prescribed in formalized guidelines.

In many ways, the work within the network appears to be in line with Berreman's (1962) concept of 'back stage and front stage'; that is, with one arena that is hidden from outsiders and another that is open to review by the public. From this perspective, the participants in the network have the ability to discuss amongst themselves to achieve what is both appropriate and correct. Through the working process, values and norms are defined, as Selznick (1957) describes, when institutionalization occurs by enshrining key values in an organization, which are shared and defended by its members over time. It then follows that these values and norms develop a regulatory function for what is desirable and viable within the network. At the same time, they comprise the abstract contracts and loosely defined references that bind the participants together, create a sense of belonging, and give meaning and identity to the individuals as well as the duties for which they are responsible (Sundet, 2015).

On the other hand, many of the external conditions for action are also of a value-based character and primarily reflect political prioritizations that have been made within the framework of cultural, social and economic prerequisites. Where the educational collaboration is concerned, this applies to prioritizations that reflect how the 'powers that be' in the various countries assess the importance of and desire for this type of bilateral development work. The educational level in Russia is considerably higher than that in Norway.[3]

When compared with the Russian efforts to support domestic education, the international educational collaboration has not been as highly esteemed. However, the educational authorities have recently set a long line of new objectives for this field in relation to, for example, improved language training, increased number of foreign stipends and more joint academic programmes at a higher level with foreign HEIs. At this point in time, though, many of these measures are indefinitely postponed (Kolle, 2014). Our informants refer to the fact that their HEIs do not have specific budgets for internationalization work, and that the lack of resources should be seen as an indication of how critically the authorities evaluate bilateral cooperation. The informants additionally feel that low salaries among academic staff do not help to encourage extra efforts in areas that fall outside of the core duties. Furthermore, they claim that only a few of the teachers and researchers who use their time on internationalization have idealist or altruistic motives: first and foremost, they have individual objectives and are more concerned with their own careers than they are with supporting a self-sacrificing, 'inter-people' initiative. At the Norwegian HEI involved in this unique cooperation as well, internationalization does not hold any particular value beyond the recognition gained from having numerous foreign HEIs as collaborative partners, large numbers of foreign students, and a multitude of academic articles published in international books and journals. The last benefit, incidentally, does not even involve a need for the researcher to leave their office. The staff connected to BCS is small and, on top of a heavy teaching load, daily communication with Russian colleagues in the network and a considerable number of travel days, they face strict demands for scientific output. When it comes to resources, the staff's salary and a modest sum for running costs comprise the budgeting categories for the educational cooperation. Earnings and finances are the everyday concepts and values, while internationalization is more often only addressed with a few eloquent words at a gala event.

THE DISTINCT ASPECT

In this context, the distinct aspect is not tied to individual persons but to properties of political, social, economic and cultural circumstances, and to characteristics of the individual institutions involved in the collaboration. In all of these areas, the differences between countries can be relatively large. Within the network, it is essential that these differences are not placed in a qualitative parameter but are rather briefly and positively considered as necessary givens. In certain limited fields, hope, aspirations and the occasional concrete suggestion may arise to change the circumstances of a HEI and, as a rule, these have to do with problematic bottlenecks and obstacles to administrative processes.

When the informants are asked about the structural characteristics that they feel are of particular significance to the educational cooperation, they point almost exclusively to factors that make difficult or hinder optimal participation from the Russian side. When they argue that the BCS cooperation functions quite well, it is because the programme recruits a large number of Russian students to the Norwegian HEI. The other side of the coin is that only a modest number of Norwegian youth choose to study at the Russian HEIs. There are many reasons for this, the most important of which is that the Russian educational institutions have a severe lack of courses available in English in addition to the fact that they have yet to implement the Bologna Process grade structure and European Credit Transfer System (ECTS) system. According to federal legislation, this requires all students, including foreigners, to take exams in certain mandatory courses connected to the Russian programme. Another major point that the informants bring up is the Russian HEIs' lack of autonomy when it comes to shaping and changing their programmes of study. Most academic programmes are planned and developed outside the universities and come as mandates from the Department of Education and Research. Therefore, staff at the universities have little or no opportunity to develop their own programmes. This involves a lack of ability for the individual HEIs to offer flexible and proactive adaptation to innovations and trends in the international education market.

Several of the informants claim that foreign students and their special needs for academic adaptation receive too little attention in Russia. This is also explained by structural characteristics of the Russian system that may additionally rationalize the lack of engagement in international work among academic staff at the HEIs. It has already been mentioned that low salaries and absence of budgetary resources for such work sway academic interest in other directions. Moreover, informants point to the small number of Russian researchers who speak English as a considerable obstacle that continues to stand in the way of participation in international programmes. Last but not least, our informants believe that Russian HEIs lack knowledge and perspectives on international educational and research collaboration. They have little or no experience with this type of bilateral or multilateral work process, and the threshold for taking the initiative oneself or accepting foreign invitations to collaborate on such work is relatively high.

The opposite holds true for the Norwegian HEIs. In the past few years, interest in international educational and research collaboration has risen considerably, and most of these institutions have agreements with cooperating partners worldwide. The numbers of those agreements often more accurately reflect their symbolic significance than the practical significance of the cooperation. In other words, many of the intended agreements with foreign universities do not go beyond the intentional stage and are more often employed as pontifical attributions at the involved HEIs than as a foundation for concrete joint projects.

We could, therefore, ask why the BCS cooperation is not only operative but also productive and successful. On the Russian side of the equation, we have HEIs with generally little experience, relatively limited competence and few incentives to engage in international teamwork. On the Norwegian side, we have HEIs that seem to have somewhat broader competence and more resources in the field. At the same time, they have numerous other cooperating partners in Western countries that they more closely and structurally relate to in various areas, which would suggest that they are more compatible to collaborate with. It is thus reasonable to assume that the answers for why the BCS programme functions so well should be viewed in the context of the unique circumstances that exist within the Russian–Norwegian educational cooperation.

Among such unique circumstances are the various incentives that have been developed through the macro-political collaboration between Russia and Norway; something I will elaborate on below. As with most forms of institutional bilateral connections, the motivation to participate in the BCS cooperation does not primarily stem from altruistic and compassionate feelings for others, but rather from an assessment of the advantages and possibilities that may be derived from such transactions. The Barents Cooperation and northern region politics have been criticized for being primarily concerned with cooperating on environmental issues, exploitation of natural resources and traditional trade. The critics also point to a lack of knowledge, and the absence of viewpoints on other possible areas of collaboration that could generate comparable benefits within the region (Young and Einarsson, 2004; Bærenholdt, 2007). It was obvious that education was considered a possible field of cooperation from the start. It was unclear, however, exactly which aspects of education the collaboration would focus on. What eventually became evident was that the mutual benefits of an educational cooperation could not simply be adopted. On the contrary, it needed to be developed from the perspective of the one fundamental question for all HEIs involved: not surprisingly, 'What's in it for me?' The answer to this question gives an indication of what constitutes the fundamental driving force of the cooperation.

For the couple who had very different reasons for their monthly visits to the symphony hall – hers being the musical experience, his being the social experience – it does not have to do with the unique aspects of the concerts, meaning the music in itself and the social aspects of being there. First and foremost, it has to do with characteristics of these two people and how they each strategically choose to suffer through the other's favourite part of the evening in order to get to the part they themselves love. Without bringing too much of the suffering and sacrificial aspects of this example into the reasoning process, it would nonetheless be naive to tone down or underestimate the strategic factors related to the justification for the collaboration between the Russian and Norwegian HEIs. The excitement of success has a tendency to place an attractive veil over the critical eye.

THE STRATEGIC ASPECT

The requirement to earn money is decisive in whether the study programmes at Norwegian HEIs are successful and viable or whether they need to be reshaped or discontinued. At the Norwegian HEI involved in the educational cooperation discussed here, the BCS programme has a high reputation, primarily due to the fact that it generates income. The fact that the programme contributes symbolic capital, in the form of active participation in international education, and is the underlying cause of large externally financed research projects at the institution, is simply seen as a fringe benefit. Here as well, it seems that core activities are limited to the traditional academic disciplines and established professional studies, while studies that are driven in cooperation with foreign institutions are more easily considered as temporary applications.

This short-term perspective stems from an uncertainty tied to several factors surrounding the BCS programme. One such factor is the debate that is currently simmering in Norway on the adoption of study programme fees for foreign students; something that, if accepted, will eliminate the decisive advantage the Norwegian HEIs have in the competition for Russian students. Another factor is that running the programme requires an enormous amount of work in the form of administration, daily Internet communication, and a large number of travel days to exchange necessary information and maintain contact with the network. On top of teaching and research duties, this constitutes a workload that limits the recruitment of academic staff and essentially deters colleagues from getting involved. A third factor is connected to unforeseen changes at the cooperating HEIs that, in turn, change the prerequisites and level of access for students. A fourth and very contemporary factor is international disquiet and crises like the one currently unfolding between Western countries and Russia, in which mutual political and economic sanctions are an important part of the dialogue. Among the responses to the fact that Norway has joined the European Union (EU) sanctioning measures, there is naturally a fear of decreased efforts in the Barents Cooperation, which would have serious consequences for the BCS programme. So far, however, there is little indication that Russia will not hold true to its statements on the significance of the positive development in this region.

Investing heavily in this educational cooperation could, therefore, fall under the African saying that goes something like this: 'Only idiots measure the depth of the river with both legs'. The Norwegian HEI prefers to follow the advice of its own proverb to 'strike while the iron is hot'; that is, as long as the possibility of a profitable collaboration exists, it is only natural to invest. On the other hand, it would be irresponsible to invest more than an unpredictable future dictates. Taken to the extreme, the practical importance of 'profitable' means that prioritization should fall in the order of financial earnings, potential research projects and symbolic capital above cultural interaction and mutual learning. What the politicians and public speakers express through the open microphone is not in line with what is actually prioritized when it comes down to it. This point, although perhaps taken to an extreme, can also be verified.

From a Russian perspective, it is interesting to enter into collaboration with Norwegian HEIs due to the cost-free element of the study programme and the fact that only part of the programme needs to be completed on campus in Norway. According to my informants, this is a major reason behind the stream of Russian students coming to Norwegian HEIs. Another and important argument offered by the informants is that the educational cooperation puts pressure on the forward movement to implement the Bologna Process since it constitutes the reference point for the BCS grading structure. Equally beneficial, the cooperation also provides a form of training in how Russian HEIs should academically and administratively apply these principles. Studies show that Russia participates half-heartedly in the Bologna Process, among other things, because the educational and research budgets are characterized by the challenging times Russia faces economically (Kolle, 2014). The informants feel that the cooperation with Norwegian institutions has a positive effect on the implementation process, and that it is strategically critical since it strengthens the positions and possibilities of participating Russian HEIs both nationally and internationally.

This goal-oriented adaptation to a regional education market is stimulated through incentive systems. Some of these are of a financial nature, while others reflect political intentions toward bilateral cooperation that encourage HEIs in both countries to come together on student exchange, development of educational programmes and shaping of joint research projects. As previously mentioned, when it comes to financial stimuli, those on the Norwegian side are already connected to the financial model for the running of educational institutions, which has two relevant characteristics in this context. One is that education is also free for foreign students. The other is that close to a quarter of the individual HEIs' budgets are determined according to the number of exams successfully taken each year. This means that it is extremely advantageous for the HEIs to import students and, additionally, to support them in ways that result in the highest number of students passing their exams.

Similar to what occurs in Norway, the Russian financial stimulation of international educational cooperation is directed toward students coming to Russia. In fact, financial support in Russia is primarily used to subsidize foreign students (up to 15 000) and to provide housing for them in addition to stipends that are in line with those of Russian students (Kolle, 2014). Aside from the fact that the Russian HEIs have another type of financing than in Norway, and that the number of BCS students in Russia is low, the financial aspects of the collaboration are not of particular significance to the Russian institutions. On the contrary, according to the informants, the most important factor for them is to comply with political expectations to strengthen the competitive edge that Russian higher education has in relation to other countries. They also need to position themselves individually in relation to the national competition for students and tactically relate to constant structural changes within the sector.

The understanding that internationalization is a transformation of higher education (Trondal et al., 2001) characterizes the thinking of both countries' educational institutions. Standing on the outside is like taking a seat in the audience instead of playing an active role in the play; and the processes of change and learning with cumulative and competence-building effects increases the lead the participants have on the audience. In the BCS cooperation, financial incentives are far more important for the Norwegians than for the Russians, while the political expectations for what should be accomplished are most critical for all of the HEIs, primarily due to the existential implications. When instincts for self-preservation take hold, these expectations could almost be seen as the institutions' political imperatives. In other words, the BCS educational cooperation should be viewed, first and foremost, as one of many steps in the strategic adjustments of all HEIs involved.

THE PARALLEL ASPECT

The couple at the concert, while sharing a mutual interest, had very divergent motives for it. They did not share in each other's experience other than that of sitting next to each other while they were at the concert. There is a similarity that may be transferred to the cooperating HEIs involved in this study, in that they interact with each other while having relatively different motivations for the cooperation. The natural argument to that idea would be that it is the results that count; in this case, that the education of students through the BCS programme has created a competence that may optimally benefit the entire Barents Region community. The fact that the cooperative partners' motives are different should hold little significance as long as the candidates complete their education and the assessments of both the students and the programme of study are positive. However, my line of questioning is of another nature in that I am asking whether the educational cooperation, in and of itself, contributes to the building of community in the Barents Region. My observations, together with impressions from the informants, provide the basis for interpreting the interaction between the involved HEIs as a parallelism; that is, a set of simultaneous actions that have intentional consequences in which the benefits for each HEI are far more important than the interaction with other HEIs, and where the interaction, therefore, is primarily a means to an end rather than being the goal itself.

There is, however, the glue that holds the HEIs together; a common link and a critical prerequisite to the successful operation of the educational cooperation – namely, the network of coordinators. In addition to their academic and administrative positions, they have taken on the role of intermediary, interpreter and negotiator. Furthermore, they serve as tailors when the programme of study needs to be adapted to the HEIs' individual shapes and sizes, shoehorns to help it glide more easily into the standard models, and fire extinguishers when internal sparks result in small fires at the participating HEIs. The network is characterized by an inner solidarity that is of both a mechanical and an organic nature (Durkheim, 1893 [1997]). It is mechanical in that the participants should resolve the same issues and work together to lift each other up. On the other hand, it is organic in that one party has abilities and resources, needs and contributions that another party does not. The criteria for dependence are many, and the possibility for success lies in highlighting the mutual benefits of this joint dependence. The individuals in the network meet regularly in the flesh, follow up both small and large issues, and keep in close contact no matter what.

Agreements are entered into, contracts are written, principal questions are discussed and plans are made for the future. It is within this network that the real internationalization takes place; where the metamorphosis from vague intentions to practical implementation demands that each participant be active yet pragmatic, engaged yet realistic, short-sighted yet patient, stubborn yet understanding, goal-oriented yet willing to learn and, most of all, convinced that the network is a workshop for the shaping of ideas on how conflict-ridden and occasionally irresolvable problems should be managed (Sundet, 2015). In this context, internationalization often means uniting those who are incompatible, which happens in a practical way through this network. On the institutional level, there is often a lack of understanding, knowledge and interest for such network processes. Thus, the HEIs can easily be equated with cruise ship passengers or hotel guests in that progress, maintenance, safety on board, facilitation, serving and all other services happen through the network. At the same time, the HEI representatives find themselves at parties with one another having to position themselves in the same arena without doing much more than giving each other a bit of attention, exchanging a few polite comments if necessary, and showing a modicum of appropriately managed behaviour while still maintaining some distance.

CONCLUDING REMARKS

It is precisely when the focus is shifted from the individual to the institutional level that the difference between good friends and faceless partners becomes evident. The HEIs represent the formal and impersonal aspects of the cooperative, while the network embodies the informal and personal aspects. As I have shown, the external picture of the HEIs' activities is that the BCS programme is a successful joint project where the educational cooperation functions well. The political values that refer to the people-to-people dimension of the Barents Cooperation treaties, however, are not the primary motivating force for the HEIs to enter into this mutual educational project. On the contrary, it is the unique characteristics of the HEIs and the institutional environments of both countries that make the BCS programme interesting and that make the educational collaboration a relatively limited but nonetheless strategic area of focus for each HEI. Therefore, the question of whether the educational cooperation contributes to the building of community in the Barents Region should be answered with a 'yes' – on condition that we distinguish between the faceless and impersonal partnership between the HEIs, and the collegial and far more close and personal relations between the individuals involved in the social collaborative processes from which the concrete results of BCS emerge.

To a certain degree, it will always be this way as long as institutions are made up of people. After all, when visiting an institution, we sit down with the people, not the organization. Furthermore, without the HEIs, these collaborating individuals would only be seen as private persons with little to represent, little reason to meet and little to offer one other besides themselves. On the other hand, when we talk about establishing a regional community, it is on the individual level that relations grow and ties are developed. However, as long as the work of the BCS network is only loosely tied to the individual HEIs, where it is seen as an unpredictable, volatile and temporary cooperative project with only a marginal connection to the core operation of the HEI, these educational institutions will not be able to develop closer ties.

Based on this simple reasoning, I would like to close by presenting three central points. First of all, while politics seems to be a parade of abstract symbols, it appears mostly as a sequence of pictures in the head, placed there by debate experts and different types of media (Edelman, 1964). In the politically rhetorical creation of symbols that occurs through the interstate dialogues on educational cooperation in the Barents Region, this people-to-people dimension is not given any specific content other than the idea that it will eventually lead to positive relations on a meso-level, meaning between institutions.

This chapter shows that this requires a connection of cultural translators, social designers and talented practitioners from the HEIs involved. Symbols and politics should be interpreted and placed into local institutional contexts in ways that are acceptable and meaningful for the individual HEIs as well as for the collective of HEIs that participate. This refers to those who are delegated to the network who, when they meet, have the mission of sending white smoke up the chimney before they go home again. Without a well-functioning network, cooperation is not established and, therefore, no sense of community is achieved.

Secondly, the biggest challenge for the participants in the network seems to be that the educational cooperation does not quite get under the skin and into the heart of the HEIs, or to the core, as Selznick (1957) defines the organization's central values. This has many reasons and the explanations vary from one HEI to another, as I have shown. Even though the shaping of the academic programmes is made compatible through the network processes, they are primarily applied only superficially to the institutions' other activities. With few exceptions, internationalization is on the lips of the leadership, but there still seems to be quite a gap between idle talk and practical action. Internationalization cannot be bought over the counter; on the contrary, it has to do with a learning process that each individual HEI has to go through on its own, and a need to prioritize by setting aside sufficient time and resources. This chapter reveals that there are significant differences in this area between institutional and individual levels, in particular among those individuals who engage in internationalization through active participation in the educational network. It also reveals that individual knowledge in this field is rarely institutionalized, which incidentally does not apply specifically to this context but is a general characteristic of learning within organizations.

Thirdly, if a HEI pulls out of the cooperation, it will naturally pull out its delegation as well. The work of the network constitutes a critical element of the building of international bridges, which contributes in a practical way to creating a regional understanding. This further contributes to construction in the Barents Region; construction that will vanish if the educational cooperation disappears, because the educational cooperation would cease to exist if the HEIs no longer see the value in maintaining it. It is sustained primarily because the HEIs want to build a region, but above all because this collaboration is currently in their own interests.

One could conclude that, while the HEIs integrate to a certain degree, it is the network that drives such integration. In other words, to the degree that the educational cooperation contributes to developing a sense of community in the Barents Region, this does not occur on an institutional level, but first and foremost through fragile networks.

NOTES

* From 1 January 2016, the University of Nordland was renamed as Nord University due to the merger with the University College in Nesna and the University College in Nord Trøndelag.
1. Other than northwest Russia and northern Norway, northern Sweden and northern Finland are also included in the Barents Region. The Barents Cooperation was formally established at the signing of the Kirkenes Declaration in 1993. In addition to the four countries in the Barents Region, Denmark, Iceland and the European Union also took part in the signing of the Kirkenes Declaration. Representatives from the countries that signed the Kirkenes Declaration are all members of the Barents Euro-Arctic Council (BEAC) which meets every other year at the foreign minister level in the country that has responsibility for chairmanship for the given period. Chairmanship rotates between the four Barents countries. The goal is to promote economic and social development in the Barents Region, thereby contributing to a peaceful development in the northernmost part of Europe. Canada, France, Germany, Italy, Japan, the Netherlands, Poland, the United Kingdom and the United States of America all have observer status at BEAC meetings. For further information on the Barents Cooperation, see Blakkisrud and Hønneland (2006), Hønneland (2007), Pursiainen (2001), Staalesen (2010) and (former Norwegian foreign minister) Støre (2010a, 2010b), among others.
2. Title of the research project: 'Higher Education in the High North: Regional Restructuring through Educational Exchange and Student Mobility'. The project is financed by the Research Council of Norway. For further information on the project, see https://www.forskningsradet.no/prosjektbanken_beta/#/project/220702.
3. In 2011, 53 per cent of the Russian population in the age group of 25 to 64 years had completed an education beyond upper secondary school, while Norway lies closer to the average of 32 per cent for Organisation for Economic Co-operation and Development (OECD) countries (OECD, 2014).

REFERENCES

Bærenholdt, J.O. (2007), *Coping with Distances. Producing Nordic Atlantic Societies*, Oxford: Berghahn Books.
Berreman, G. (1962), *Behind Many Masks: Ethnography and Impression Management in a Himalayan Village*, Society for Applied Anthropology, Monograph no. 4, Washington, DC: American Anthropological Association.
Blakkisrud, H. and Hønneland, G. (eds) (2006), *Tackling Space: Federal Politics and the Russian North*, Lanham, MD: University Press of America.

DiMaggio, P.J. and Powell, W.W. (1983), 'The Iron Cage Revisited: Institutional Isomorphism and Collective Rationality in Organizational Fields', *American Sociological Review*, **48**, 147–160.

Durkheim, E. (1893 [1997]), *The Division of Labour in Society*, New York: Free Press.

Edelman, M. (1964), *The Symbolic Uses of Politics*, Chicago, IL: University of Illinois Press.

Hønneland, G. (2007), 'Norway and Russia in the Barents Sea: Cooperation and Conflict in Fisheries Management', *Russian Analytical Digest*, 20: 9–11.

Kolle, H. (2014), *Samarbeid med Russland i høgare utdanning: Føresetnader, utfordringar og moglegheiter* (Cooperation with Russia in higher education: preconditions, challenges and opportunities), Rapportserie No 04, Oslo: SIU (Norwegian Centre for International Cooperation in Education).

OECD (2014), 'OECD Economic Survey: Russian Federation', accessed July 2014 at http://www.oecdbetterlifeindex.org/countries/russian-federation/.

Pursiainen, C. (2001), 'Soft Security Problems in Northwest Russia and their Implications for the Outside World: A Framework for Analysis and Action', Helsinki UPI Working Papers No.31.

Putin, V. (2010), 'Speech and Closing Remarks to Arctic Forum in Moscow', http://icr.arcticportal.org/index.php?option=com_contentandview=articleandid=1746:full-text-of-putins-speech-a-closingremarks-.

Selznick, P. (1957), *Leadership in Administration*, New York: Harper & Row Publishers.

Staalesen, A. (2010), 'New Times for Barents Cooperation', in Atle Staalesen (ed.), *Talking Barents: People, Borders and Regional Cooperation*, Kirkenes: Norwegian Barents Secretariat, pp. 9–24.

Støre, J.G. (2010a), '"Most is North" The High North and the Way Ahead – an International Perspective', Lecture at the University of Tromsø, 29 April, http://www.regjeringen.no/en/dep/ud/Whats-new/Speeches-andarticles/ speeches_foreign/2010/Most-is-north.html?id=602113.

Støre, J.G. (2010b), 'Norway and Russia. Taking Northern Knowledge to the Next Level', Northern Arctic Federal University (NArFU), Arkhangelsk, 17 September, http://www.regjeringen.no/en/dep/ud/Whats-new/Speeches-and articles/speeches_foreign/2010/northern_knowledge_next_level.html?id=614593.

Sundet, M. (2015), 'The Ties That Bind – the Roles and Mundane Practices of Networks in Constructing Educational Internationalization in the High North', *Globalisation, Societies and Education*, DOI: 10.1080/14767724.2015.1095074.

Trondal, J., Stensaker, B., Gornitzka, A. and Maassen, P. (2001), *Internasjonalisering av høyere utdanning. Trender og utfordringer* (Internationalisation of higher education. Trends and challenges), Skriftserie nr. 28, Oslo: NIFU (Nordic Institute for Studies in Innovation, Research and Education).

White Paper (2011–2012), *Report no. 7 to the Storting. The High North*, Oslo: Ministry of Foreign Affairs.

Young, O.R. and Einarsson, N. (2004), 'Introduction: Human Development in the Arctic', in N. Einarsson, J.N. Larsen, A. Nilsson and O.R. Young (eds), *Arctic Human Development Report*, Akureyri: Stefansson Arctic Institute, pp. 15–41.

10. Transregionalism and the Caribbean higher educational space
Tavis D. Jules

INTRODUCTION

This chapter sets out to survey the origins and consequences of the shift of a regional governance mechanism from an 'immature' to a 'mature' form of regionalism, and reflect on its influence on the coordination of activities of higher education across the Caribbean Community (CARICOM)[1] leading to what can be referred to as 'transregionalism'.[2] The central argument in this chapter is that: (1) the absence of supra-nationality within CARICOM's governance structure led to what is referred to as a form of 'immature regionalism', where decisions made at the regional level were not necessarily implemented at the member state level; and that (2) what is referred to as 'mature regionalism' has emerged as a governance mechanism aimed at ensuring that regional decisions are implemented at the national level. In essence, the criterion of the 'maturity' of the regionalism is the degree to which policy decisions agreed upon at by Heads of Government, the highest decision making body, or by other institutions of CARICOM will be operationalized into the domestic laws of member states across the region.

As a result, rather than such collective decisions having to be approved separately by all members, they will 'have the force of law throughout the region'. It seems clear that the model for 'mature' regionalism is the EU, where Community rules cannot be overturned or ignored at the member state level. As the Lewis Report, 'Managing Mature Regionalism', put it:

> Consistent with proposals to improve the effectiveness of Caribbean integration institutions based on relevant EU [European Union] experiences, it is proposed that the system of Community Law already recognised in the provisions of the Revised Treaty of Chaguaramas, should be amplified to cater for the continuous creation of Community Law through the organs and institutions of the Caribbean Community. This should be achieved through the instrumentality of collaboration between the Conference of the Heads of Government and Ministerial Councils (including the Legal Affairs Committee) on the one hand and the Commission on the other. (Lewis, 2006: 6)

Following from this, in this chapter I argue that the Caribbean higher educational space (CHES) can be seen as a form of transregionalism, which will be taken as representing a particular way of conceptualizing the different forms of coordination of regional governance mechanisms or its 'metagovernance' (Jessop, 2000, 2004). Here I make a distinction between governance mechanisms, the coordinating of complex organizations, and system and governance activities – that is the funding, provision, ownership and regulation of education (Dale, 2005). In this context, transregionalism represents the shared 'space between and across regions in which its constituent parts (individuals, communities and organizations) operate [sic]' (Dent, 2003: 224). Metagovernance is seen, not as mode of governance, but rather a way of explicating the forming of self-organization that is reshaping the framework within which collaboration and social learning are developed and coordinated (Jessop, 2004).

In the Caribbean context, metagovernance is a functional concept to explain the 'coordination of relations of complex interdependence' (Jessop, 2004: 62) within shared spaces between and across the Caribbean region. Metagovernance is particularly applicable to CARICOM since it respects the principles of sovereignty (which speaks to its intergovernmentalist nature) and 'collibration' (which includes modes of cooperation and is a feature of its neofunctionalism character), both of which are core defining features of the conceptual pillars of Caribbean integration. In other words, the focus here is on the modes of coordination of independent activities across different territorial scales (above and below the national level) and the functional domains of governance.

This chapter is developed as follows. First, I review the origins of mature regionalism through an account of the changing nature and expectations around the role of higher education across the different waves of Caribbean regionalism (old regionalism, open regionalism and mature regionalism). Second, I use the concepts of strategic coordination and metagovernance (also known as meta-steering); that is, the 'use of higher-order mechanisms to collibrate different modes of governance (markets, states and other forms of imperative coordination, networks)' (Jessop, 2000: 345) to describe how different modes of non-economic or functional spaces (education, health, transportation, and telecommunications) of Caribbean integration are coordinated across functional and territorial divides by the process of functional cooperation.[3] Here, mature regionalism is seen as an example of a higher-order mechanism of governance and it is suggested that transregionalism – the use of horizontal models of governance – represents a particular conceptual approach to study how governance mechanisms steer different modes of coordination. Implicit in this framework is that tertiary educational institutions are now an integral part of the political project of regionalism in the Caribbean Single Market. Third, I consider three broad scenarios that are changing Caribbean integration in an era that has come to symbolize the retreat, by nation-states, towards regional trading agreements (RTAs) as the pausing of globalization occurs, or what has been called the 'gated global' (*The Economist*, 2013). Finally, I explain the role of institutions in regionalism and function of regionalization in steering the higher education agenda. This is done by suggesting that the CHES, a pluri-scalar borderless educational space, is being transformed to conform with the expectations of mature regionalism as educational governance activities have been moved out of the national realm into the regional jurisdiction. Although state sovereignty is preserved in theory, in practice governance activities are coordinated regionally. I conclude the chapter by suggesting future discussions around the maturing of regionalism within the context of the free movement regime.

ORIGINS AND SHIFTING GEOMETRY

It was the Grand Anse Declaration (CARICOM, 1989) that laid the foundation of the regional integration process. In Article 45 of the Revised Treaty of Chaguaramas it is stipulated that 'Member States commit themselves to the goal of the free movement of their nationals within the Community' (CARICOM, 2001: 27). Here I briefly describe how the CHES is being shaped by strategies aimed at developing forms of coordination that are in turn challenging the hold of nationalist tendencies in governing activity.

Within the new geometries that functional spaces now occupy within the Caribbean, 'new scales emerge and/or existing scales gain in institutional thickness, new mechanisms to link or coordinate them also tend to emerge. This in turn often prompts efforts to coordinate these new coordination mechanisms' (Jessop, 2000: 342). As globalization reorders and protectionism rises, within education 'different actors look[ing] for the best means of inserting themselves into the spatial, scalar and temporal divisions of labour' (Jessop, 2000: 342) giving rise to different institutional dynamics, and governance and regulatory mechanisms across different scalar levels.

Although a few institutions of higher education were founded in the 1800s in places such as Belize and Jamaica, the turn of the century saw an influx of educational opportunities within CARICOM due to investment in education. The regional university, the University of the West Indies (UWI; formerly the University College of the West Indies), was established in 1948 with its first campus in Jamaica (Mona) and other campuses in Trinidad (St Augustine) in 1960, Barbados (Cave Hill) in 1963, and the Open Campus in 2008, under Article 22 of the Revised Treaty of Chaguaramas. The UWI is designated as an Associate Institution of CARICOM that 'enjoys important functional relationships which contribute to the achievement of the objectives of the Community . . . and such other entities as may be designated by the Conference' (CARICOM, 2001: 15).

The Caribbean Examination Council (CXC), established in 1972, is also recognized as an Institution of CARICOM under Article 21 of the Revised Treaty. At the beginning of the new millennium, CXC was tasked with administering the Caribbean Vocational Qualification (CVQ). The CVQ assesses the competency of occupational standards created by the practitioners, field experts, and employers. Further, the standards allow for the portability of national credentials across nations based on the tiered levels of certification mastery. As formal institutions of CARICOM, the UWI and CXC are functional entities with responsibilities for creating policies and performing functions in relation to cooperation, and hence are responsible for the metagovernance of what can be described as mature regionalism. However, in an era defined by the ability of Caribbean nationals with the necessary qualification to move under the auspices of the new skills regime, the landscape of higher education now consists of close to 100 accredited private and public, two-year and four-year, and specialty institutions which now operate regionally.

As the charter of regionalism has changed, so too has its nodal scale, thus engendering the relativization of scale across different regionalisms where old scales are reordered or broken down and new ones emerge through different mechanism of governance, giving rise to mature regionalism. One outcome is that new institutions are developed and are envisioned to work alongside old institutions. In 1967, Sir Philip Sherlock, the second Vice-Chancellor of the UWI, believed that 'educational cooperation' was the instrument to be used to foster regional awareness (Parkins, 2007). The notion of regional cooperation was widely accepted in the region, and the Association of Caribbean Universities and Research Institutes (UNICA) was founded in 1967 to foster cooperation among the Higher Education Centres in the Caribbean Region.

UNICA was unique in that it encompassed all nations touched by the Caribbean Sea, regardless of cultural and national differences. Prior to the establishment of UNICA, only a select number of individuals were able to create connections with their counterparts in other nations. The association helped to redefine relationships between nations, and offered more intentional opportunities to network across borders, in turn creating opportunities for institutions to have an impact on the economic, social and cultural development of nations of the Caribbean.

New challenges have arisen as UNICA and education provision in the Caribbean have grown. Most notably, the globalization of higher education and the increase in institutional partnerships has caused UNICA to question the quality assurance mechanisms adopted by the different members of the region (Parkins, 2007). Indeed, UNICA views quality assurance and certification as playing an essential role in regulating educational institutions and in ensuring they are meeting the standards as well as protecting the cultural mores and values of the region.

The Second Special Meeting of the Standing Committee of Ministers Responsible for Education (SCME) (1997) had both a cultural and institutional mandate and vision. Culturally, it aimed to facilitate the 'Vision of the ideal Caribbean person' (CARICOM, 1997) or the 'neo-Caribbean citizen' (Jules, 2014). This individual is expected to: demonstrate that they are psychologically secure; value differences based on gender, ethnicity, religion and other forms of diversity as sources of strength and richness; be environmentally astute; be responsible and accountable to family and community; have a strong work ethic; be ingenious and entrepreneurial; have a conversant respect for the cultural heritage; exhibit multiple literacies, independent and critical thinking to the application of science and technology to problem-solving; and embrace the differences and similarities between females and males (CARICOM, 1997).

Institutionally, it established a Regional Accreditation Mechanism (RAM). The RAM was tasked with the execution of the policy, as detailed in the Revised Treaty of Chaguaramas. It was to allow for different categories of skilled nationals to move between CARICOM nations, as well as being closely linked to qualifications issued by National Accreditation Bodies (NABs). Thus, 'RAM has promoted quality assurance and program harmonization at the tertiary level, as well as established common standards and measures for accreditation and the mutual recognition of qualifications' (Jules, 2008: 290). Regional accreditation is seen as an essential part of the CARICOM Single Market and Economy (CSME) in order to ensure the facilitation of the regional skills regime through the recognition of credentials issued by higher education institutions in the region.

In line with the mandates of the RAM, ten of the 15 CARICOM states have NABs, councils or presiding ministries of education, with the micro states outsourcing accreditation to the United States and European nations. Hall and Cameron (2007) found that most of the English-speaking Caribbean nations had gained their independence by 1987, and also had established national colleges in order to develop their human capital. In a rush to gain credibility, institutions acted upon various measures to develop their programmes. Regional governments were frustrated with the diverging structures, and in 1988 they demanded that CARICOM nations develop a cohesive mechanism for equivalences, articulation, and accreditation. Additionally, educational leaders saw an opportunity to collaborate to address the growth of the educational landscape.

The 1990s was a period of higher education reform across the region. In response to the growing scrutiny that universities and colleges were facing, the UWI sought to create a network between Caribbean institutions (Nettleford, 2000). A collection of university and college officials, comprised of vice-chancellors, presidents, principals and chief executive officers, were assembled to establish the Association of Caribbean Tertiary Institutions (ACTI) in 1990 and was to become a formal network of higher education institutions (Nettleford, 2000; Hall and Cameron, 2007). Through two subcommittees, the ACTI was tasked with reviewing and creating mechanisms to ensure the equivalence, articulation and accreditation of an increasing number of programmes across higher education institutions.

HORIZONTAL GOVERNANCE AND TRANSREGIONALISM

In this section I discuss the rise of mature regionalism as a governance mechanism that steers different modes of coordination within integrative projects, or what has been identified as metagovernance. Until recently, several authors (see McBrian, 2001; Nicholls et al., 2001; Payne and Gamble, 1996; Girvan, 2001, 2011) have noted that Caribbean regionalism has suffered from an implementation deficit. As such, the existing literature does not provide an adequate understanding for the study of a complex regime (or transregional regimes, as discussed below) which is amalgamated under a singular legal instrument that is regional in scope and embedded in the 'suitable structures of regional governance to manage an integrated economic space' (Lewis, 2006: 1), or what has been called 'mature regionalism' under the Rose Hall Declaration on Regional Governance and Integrated Development (CARICOM, 2003).

Mature regionalism can be seen as a machinery of governance or a horizontal mode of governance in that it preserves the basic character of CARICOM as a community of sovereign states. Furthermore, it focuses on deepening Caribbean economic relationships through structural changes (decision-making, management, implementation and enforceability), as opposed to widening Caribbean economic integration through 'open regionalism' through liberalizing economic integration whilst integrating the World Trade Organization regime rules into the Revised Treaty of Chaguaramas (Girvan, 2006; Jules, 2014; Odle, 2006; Pollard, 2012).

In doing so, mature regionalism, with its implicit expectations around steering, is now a metagovernance mechanism since it states that 'critical policy decisions of the Community taken by Heads of Government, or by other Organs of the Community, will have the force of law throughout the Region as a result of the operation of domestic legislation' (CARICOM, 2003: 1). Thus, it is expected that mature regionalism will still have a core functional element.

Within the framework of Caribbean regionalism, the move towards mature regionalism represents the rise of strategic coordination, which is a spatio-temporal horizon of metagovernance or meta-steering,[4] and represents what Jessop (2000: 333) calls 'the strategic dimension of co-evolution of specific social forces' that gives rise to national policy spaces experiencing a 'geometry of insertion', where ideas and practices that were developed externally could be inserted in another place. The challenge with studying the shifting 'geometries of higher education space' (Robertson, 2010) in the Caribbean is that the existing literature does not lend itself to the easy use of such concepts, because Caribbean regionalism is now intertwined with 'hemispherical regionalisms' (a generic term used to describe political and economic relations of regional blocs within the Western hemisphere). At the same time, the relationships between the different regional projects is unclear since both forms of regionalism are viewed as the 'path-shaping efforts of economic, political and other social forces to influence, steer or govern the nature and direction of their co-evolution' (Jessop, 2000: 333).

Within this context, state-led economic projects across different territorial scales in the 15 frontier markets of CARICOM were a response to Friedmanesque monetarism policies advanced through political projects known as 'Thatcherism' in the United Kingdom, and 'Reaganonomics' in the United States. These projects both promoted and reinforced globalization as a process and in turn gave birth to distinctive regional governance projects at new scales now dominated by a multiplicity of actors, institutions and reforms. We see here the movement from interregionalism, premised upon dialogues between representatives across different regions, and 'regulatory regionalism' (Jayasuriya and Robertson, 2010), where common standards are endorsed by national bureaucracies and adopted towards what I identify as 'transregionalism'. Transregionalism refers to the use of horizontal models of governance through 'external governance' as an 'attempt to bind neighboring countries into common policy frameworks [which] has been interpreted as an answer to this changed geopolitical landscape' (Lavenex and Wichmann, 2009: 84).

Transregionalism builds upon concepts of networked governance (see Lavenex, 2008; Lavenex and Wichmann, 2009) by singling out a 'set of formal and informal institutions that cut across and connect different geographical regions ... through a combination of regional, inter-regional and bilateral norms and forums' (Betts, 2011: 25). Where Jayasuriya (2003) speaks of 'embedded mercantilism' to characterize the export-orientated industrialization strategy of Southeast Asia, CARICOM's strategy of open regionalism in the form of production integration, and the governance mechanism of mature regionalism, can be seen as a new form of transregionalism in that these two regional projects are concurrently regulating educational governance activities. In essence, transregionalism provides a different articulation in identifying the 'relativization of scale' (Jessop, 2000) at the regional level since it draws attention to a 'more structural, institutionalist view on the expansion of the boundaries of regional integration and the continuities and disruptions between internal policies and their external dimension' (Lavenex, 2008: 939).

TRANSREGIONALISM AND HIGHER EDUCATION

Here, I follow Gibson's (2002: 2) logic that transregionalism 'is a structural attempt to combine a range of states within a coherent unified framework', particularly in this instance of region-to-region relations.[5] CARICOM is a 'trans-regional regime' (Jules, 2008, 2013) in that it supports, legitimizes and institutionalizes international and regional patterns of supremacy, accumulation and exploitation by stipulating a set of implicit and explicit beliefs, standards, rules and procedures around which member states' expectations converge in education (Jules, 2012). Moreover, within the transregional space that CARICOM occupies and where governance instruments associated with mature regionalism exist, they are based on the establishment of frameworks (reducing transactional costs) and coordination of actors' expectations (improving quality and quantity of information available to states) as issues arise within any given policy space.

As a transregional regime, the regional space that higher education inhabits in the Caribbean is now defined by the functional or non-economic aspects of regionalism that are based on strategic coordination of metagovernance in order to engender a Caribbean region without barriers. This transregional space is a product of the post-Cold War period that has been shaped by the twin forces of the collapse of ideological pluralism (competing modules to engender national development) and the restructuring of regional projects from a common market based on free trade (old regionalism) towards trade liberalization and expanding membership. This has created the development of linkages with third states (open regionalism) under the Grand Anse Declaration (CARICOM, 1989) and now movement towards deeper regionalism through the Caribbean Single Market and Economy (mature regionalism).

The previous arguments of transregionalism can now be applied to the CSM that came into being in 2006, with 13 of CARICOM's now 15 member states actively participating in its regime instruments, namely the movement of goods regime, skills regime, services regime, capital regime, and the 'right to establish' regime – that is, CARICOM citizens may establish companies and business enterprises in any CARICOM nation and be treated as a local national. The CSM exhibits open regionalism by removing fiscal, legal, physical, technical and administrative barriers across CARICOM countries to allow for different regimes to function in a single large market and economic space. The different regimes of the CSM constitute a 'multinational integration framework' (Greene, 2005) that is 'multi-functional' (Girvan, 2005) by combining three distinct elements of transnational integration: (1) the retention of the common market that pools resources together in specific areas; (2) functional integration so that state sovereignty is non-negotiable with the possibility of federalist integration; and (3) supranationality in the form of shared sovereignty in the future. Even though the core components of the CSM are economic in scope, it has regional mechanisms and supporting institutions (such as the Caribbean Court of Justice and Regional Accreditation Mechanisms) as well as engaging national regulatory agencies (for example NABs and regional and national standard-setting bodies)[6] have been created to support it and designed to govern the coordination of 'functional space' within CARICOM.

Coupled with this, Caribbean integration now functions in spaces where CARICOM's members share membership in a multiplicity of regional blocs (discussed in the next section). Thus, Caribbean tertiary educational space is now a construct of 'regional political projects' (Jayasuriya, 2003) that are governed by the functional mechanisms of capital reproduction, regulation and regionalization (functional processes) in the interest of promoting regionalism (economic outcome) across different scales. In theory, the supporting institutions of the CSM are given legal jurisdiction under the Revised Treaty of Chaguaramas (CARICOM, 2001) and are now responsible for the educational governance activities and regulatory mechanism.

The movement towards transregionalism and transregional governance has resulted in forms of metagovernance where the Caribbean states still have a dominant role in educational governance (implementation), although the traditional educational governance activities (funding, provision, ownership and regulation) have now become regional in nature and scope. However, the mechanisms of educational governance have changed, and the educational outputs are wider and no longer national state-driven and -directed (these outputs are now just state-coordinated). Once the bastion of human resource development, the university and its institutions are now 'self-determining, self-regulatory and self-directed' (Nettleford, 2000) producers and suppliers of services that are customer-driven, reviewer-ranked, and which no longer attend to national aspirations.

THE CHANGING POLITICS AND GEOMETRY OF CARICOM REGIONALISM

Historically, the Latin America and the Caribbean (LAC) region has used integrative political projects in the form of 'old regionalism' or 'closed regionalism' which is inwards-looking and is intended to spur economic development. Old regionalism promoted the manufacturing sector through import-substituting industrialization (ISI) – focusing on self-sufficiency and movement away from external dependency – whilst closing trade to those member states who were not part of the bloc. First and foremost, CARICOM has been designed to combine 'elements of "intergovernmentalism"', (which recognizes the continuing importance of individual Member States in determining the path of the integration process), and elements of "neo-functionalism", (which is premised on the principle of shared sovereignty or the collective exercise of such sovereignty in specified areas)' (CARICOM, 2006: 14).

This combination of intergovernmentalism and neofunctionalism that now drives CARICOM's political project – and which differs from the European Union's idea of supranationalism – is based on the principles of proportionality and subsidiarity. On the one hand, proportionality means that the 'institutional arrangements devised for Community action shall not exceed what is necessary to achieve' (Lewis, 2006: 5) the actions specified in the Revised Treaty. On the other hand, subsidiarity, which forms the basic character of CARICOM as a community of sovereign states, 'asserts that regional action would not be pursued in cases where action by individual Member States is sufficient to achieve the specific goals of the Community' (ibid.).

Given the limitations of supra-nationalism as it currently exists within CARICOM and the resolution by CARICOM states that they are first and foremost sovereign states, metagovernance becomes relevant for explaining thinking behind the new governance mechanisms, since 'metagovernance instances can be established to coordinate the myriad subordinate forms of governance – this would re-introduce the principle of sovereignty or hierarchy that growing social complexity and globalization now rule out' (Jessop, 2004: 65).

The simultaneous rise of regional and hemispherical integrative projects are clearly reshaping regionalisms in Latin America and the Caribbean (LAC). When coupled with the retreat towards RTAs as a consequence of the changing nature of both globalizing and regionalizing processes, it could be argued that this is giving way to 'gated global' (*The Economist*, 2013). Each of these dynamics is elaborated below.

In terms of the rise of regional integrative projects, today in LAC they range from customs unions that organize trade (for example, the Andean Community of Nations, CAN, formerly the Andean Pact; the Caribbean Free Trade Agreement, CARIFTA, now the Caribbean Community, CARICOM; the Latin American Integration Association, ALADI, formerly the Latin American Free Trade Association, ALALC; and the Southern Common Market, MERCOSUR), to complex currency and monetary unions (for example, the Caribbean Single Market of 2006; and the Eastern Caribbean Currency Union of the Organization of Eastern Caribbean States). The ways of conceptualizing regional political projects in the small (and micro) states and small island developing states (SIDS) of the Caribbean must take into account the 'existential threats' (Girvan, 2010) that challenge their economic vulnerability, food security and ecological fragility. CARICOM's integration project is facing its most demanding exogenous and endogenous pressures from competing hemispherical projects and regionalisms. Regional projects in LAC were never viewed as complementary systems – given their history and cultural outlooks – and thus there was never a push towards coordinating or standardizing these systems. As discussed below, this becomes more complex when one considers that several of the 15 members of CARICOM are also members of other sub-regional groupings or hemispherical groupings.

With the revision by CARICOM countries to the Original Treaty in 2001, provisions were made for the principle of 'open regionalism' or 'new regionalism' that calls for the removal of protectionism in the form of trade barriers that inhibit intraregional trade. However, the Caribbean model of new regionalism is now giving rise to transregionalism since it allow states to become part of several regional agreements at once, subsequently fostering 'the emergence of a multi-level decision-making structure: sub-state entities, states, regional forums, macro-regions and trans-regional spaces' (I Vidal, 2008: 43). In CARICOM, open regionalism (in the form of production integration: 'organisation of integrated regional industrial complexes from raw materials to finished Products', Girvan, 2006: 8) as an economic process is concerned with widening the economic arrangements through the CARICOM Single Market and Economy to allow for the creation and embedding of different regimes (movement of skills, labour, capital services and the right to establishment).

However, it was not until 2010 that regional leaders took notice of the perceived new threats to integration projects when Guyana and Suriname joined the Union of South American Nations (UNASUR), which combined two existing customs unions, the Southern Common Market (MERCOSUR) and the Andean Community of Nations (CAN). In 2011, 13 CARICOM states[7] were part of the contingent of 33 countries that signed the Declaration of Caracas, creating the Community of Latin American and Caribbean States (CELAC) that is now focused on deeper integration. In 2012 Haiti, Suriname and Saint Lucia[8] acceded to the Bolivarian Alliance for the Peoples of Our America (ALBA) (see Muhr, Chapter 12 in this volume), of which CARICOM members Antigua and Barbuda, Dominica and Saint Vincent and the Grenadines[9] were already members.

Additionally, CARICOM members belong to other regional zones aimed at promoting economic cooperation; namely the 25-member grouping of the Association of Caribbean States and the 28-country Sistema Económico Latin-American y del Caribe (SELA, the Latin American and the Caribbean Economic System). The emergence of transregionalism, where countries are members of the same regional blocs within the same geopolitical and geohemispherical spaces, raises questions about the 'compatibility or incompatibility of different governance regimes and their implications for the overall unity' (Jessop, 2004).

It is thus now possible to see regional and hemispherical projects or regionalism across different spaces and scales, and a retreat towards RTAs in light of the slowing of globalization and economic liberalization, as related to what has been called the rise of 'gated globalization' (*The Economist*, 2013). This implies the need for new ways to theorize the study of regional levels. Within this 'gated global' we are also seeing the 'gated regional', which is even less bureaucratic than the previous era and whose defining feature is openness at the regional level in the form of protectionism against non-regional members. In fact, an era of open regionalism now exists side-by-side with the mature regionalism that has been built as a governance mechanism to facilitate the implementation of CSM-related instruments.

In the post-2008 financial crisis era, the new orthodoxy of state capitalism has tended to lead to a retreat to hidden protections that regional trading agreements can offer countries. Whilst historically RTAs have been seen as offering an alternative to globalization by conferring full entry into the global knowledge economy, today RTAs facilitate the expansion of education into a tradable commodity whilst at the same time protecting and promoting national interests (Jules, 2014). Such a retreat towards RTAs has significant consequences for Caribbean integration, since these institutions fund a significant part of specialized projects that reinforce the core tendencies of regionalism.

CONCLUDING THOUGHTS

Transregionalism is one outcome of the rescaling of higher education governance and its changing geometry. As a result, the CHES now promotes its own governance mechanisms in the form of educational cooperation whilst at the same time being subjected to external regulation to ensure programmes are competitive. The changing nature of regionalism in the Caribbean, with the proliferation of new political projects regionally and hemispherically, means that higher education regulations now have to be standardized, coordinated and regionalized. Both endogenous and endogenous forces are penetrating tertiary education in the Caribbean in relation to the nature, scope, function, space and governance of the sector. Caribbean higher education now exists in a spatio-temporal horizon of metagovernance that is driven by functional cooperation and governed by mature regionalism. Here, mature regionalism can be seen as a new form of metagovernance, which is the collibration of different governance mechanisms, on the one hand, and the governance of the different relationship among these different modes of coordination (Jessop, 2000) on the other. Mature regionalism, therefore, has given birth to a new set of institutions that are now responsible for the coordination of higher education activities.

For CARICOM, the new merging landscape of regional and hemispherical projects is a minefield that is likely to have a substantive impact upon intra-state relations and the overall governance of tertiary education. Jayasuriya and Robertson (2010) suggest that regulatory regionalism is distinctive in that it does not impose a regulatory template but fosters relationships and connections that transform the geographical scales that it occupies, accommodates diverse patterns of national governance, and functions as a set of metaconstitutional standards. This chapter has attempted to focus on the soft forms of the governance processes and mechanism of political projects of regulatory regionalism. In the Caribbean, the ideas of coordination, collaboration and commonality that can be seen as the outcome of regulatory regionalism have always existed, however, their degree and intensity has varied since the establishment of CARICOM.

In fact, the ways in which higher education is governed and regulated across different scales has not changed. It is the intensity of the processes that continues the metamorphosis of the region from immature to mature as new demands are placed upon the regulatory system. While the mechanisms (cooperation and collaboration) of regionalization have remained consistent, regionalism has been morphing, expanding and contracting across the Caribbean. In fact, a distinctive feature of regionalism in the Caribbean today is that several countries are members of different regional blocs, but they suffer from 'political resistance [due to] national circumstances and interests, absence of supranationality in governance and administrative and institutional deficiencies at the national level' (Bishop et al., 2011: 20). Given that memberships are intertwined across different regional blocs, it is particularly difficult to speak of Caribbean or Latin American integration, but instead it makes more sense to talk of a 'pan-regional' or 'pan-hemispherical' integration mélange that combines the political, social, economic and ideological aspirations of these countries in a shifting set of social and spatial relations.

NOTES

1. CARICOM's current members are Antigua and Barbuda, Barbados, Belize, Dominica, Grenada, Guyana, Haiti, Jamaica, Montserrat, Saint Kitts and Nevis, Saint Lucia, Saint Vincent and the Grenadines, Suriname, and Trinidad and Tobago. However, the Bahamas and Haiti are not members of the Caribbean Single Market and Economy.
2. My use of 'transregional' in this chapter has also been described as 'interregionalism' when contextualizing the process of the Asia–Europe Meeting (see Aggarwal and Fogarty, 2004; Dent, 2003; Kim, 2003; Song, 2007).
3. Functional cooperation is one of the four pillars (the others being economic integration, foreign policy coordination and, added in 2007, security) of Caribbean integration as enshrined in the Revised Treaty of Chaguaramas.
4. Jessop (2003) reformulated his conceptualizations of meta-steering as metagovernance.
5. Historically transregionalism would be applied to EU–Latin America and Caribbean (EU–LAC) summit relations, but in the changing landscape of Caribbean and Latin American relations transregionalism can now be expanded to account not only for North–South relations but also South–South relations. Also, since 1981, CARICOM has been engaged in transregionalism relations, when the Organization of Eastern Caribbean States (OECS), as a sub-regional entity within CARICOM, was created and all of the OECS states acceded to CARICOM. Today, the seven full members (Antigua and Barbuda, Dominica, Grenada, Montserrat, Saint Kitts and Nevis, Saint Lucia, and Saint Vincent and the Grenadines) are still members of CARICOM, while Anguilla (a full member of CARICOM) and the British Virgin Islands are associate members of the OECS.
6. Examples of such regional bodies are such as the Caribbean Regional Organization on Standards and Quality (CROSQ) that was established under Article 67 of the Revised Treaty of Chaguaramas (CARICOM, 2001).
7. Members of CELAC: Antigua and Barbuda, Bahamas, Barbados, Belize, Dominica, Grenada, Guyana, Jamaica, Saint Lucia, Saint Kitts and Nevis, Saint Vincent and the Grenadines, Suriname, and Trinidad and Tobago.
8. Haiti, Suriname and Saint Lucia were admitted to ALBA in 2012.

9. Dominica joined in 2008, and Antigua and Barbuda, and Saint Vincent and the Grenadines, joined in 2009.

REFERENCES

Aggarwal, V. and E.A. Fogarty (2004), Between Regionalism and Globalization: European Union Interregional Trade Strategies. In V. Aggarwal and E.A. Fogarty (eds), *EU Trade Strategies: Between Regionalism and Globalism*. London, UK and New York, USA: Palgrave, pp. 1–40.

Betts, Alexander (2011), The Global Governance of Migration and the Role of Transregionalism. In Rahel Kunz, Sandra Lavenex and Marion Panizzon (eds), *Multilayered Migration Governance: The Promise of Partnership*. New York: Routledge, pp. 23–45.

Bishop, M., N. Girvan, T. Shaw, S. Mike, R. Kirton, M. Scobie, D. Mohammed and M. Anatol (2011), Caribbean Regional Integration. A Report by the UWI Institute of International Relations. http://cms2.caricom.org/documents/9774-iir regionalintegrationreportfinal.pdf (accessed 25 April 2016).

CARICOM (1989), Grand Anse Declaration and Work Programme for the Advancement of the Integration Movement, July 1989. Grand Anse, Granada.

CARICOM (1997), Creative and Productive Citizens for the Twenty-first Century. Paper presented at the Eighteenth Meeting of the Conference of Heads of Government of the Caribbean Community, Montego Bay, Jamaica. http://www.caricom.org/jsp/communications/meetings_statements/citizens_21_century.jsp?me nu=communications.

CARICOM (2001), *Revised Treaty of Chaguaramas*. http://www.sice.oas.org/trade/caricom/caricind.asp.

CARICOM (2003), *The Rose Hall Declaration on Regional Governance and Integrated Development*. Georgetown: CARICOM. http://www.caricom.org/jsp/communications/meetings_statements/rose_hall_declaration.jsp?menu=com munications.

CARICOM (2006), *Report of the Technical Working Group on the Governance of the Caribbean Community*. Republic of Trinidad and Tobago: CARICOM. http://archive.caricom.org/jsp/community/twg_governance_report.pdf.

Dale, R. (2005), Globalisation, Knowledge Economy and Comparative Education. *Comparative Education*, 41(2), 117–149.

Dent, C.M. (2003), From Inter-regionalism to Transregionalism? Future Challenges for ASEM. *Asia Europe Journal*, 1(2), 223–235.

The Economist (2013), Gated Globe. 12 October. http://www.economist.com/news/special-report/21587384-forward-march-globalisation-has-paused-financial-cris is-giving-way (accessed 25 April 2016).

Girvan, N. (2001), Reinterpreting the Caribbean. In F. Lindahl and B. Meeks (eds), *New Caribbean Thought*. Kingston: University of the West of Indies Press. http://www.normangirvan.info/wp-content/uploads/2007/09/reinterpreting-the-caribbean-2001.pdf (accessed 25 April 2016).

Girvan, N. (2005), Whither CSME? *Journal of Caribbean International Relations*, 1(April), 13–32.

Girvan, N. (2006), Production Integration: A Critical Perspective. In K. Hall and D. Benn (eds), *Production Integration in CARICOM; From Theory to*

Action. Kingston: Ian Randle Publications, pp. 8–29. http://www.normangirvan.info/wp-con tent/uploads/2007/09/production-integration-a-critical-perspective-jan-06.pdf.

Girvan, N. (2010), Are Caribbean Countries Facing Existential Threats? http://www.normangirvan.info/wp-content/uploads/2010/11/existential-threats.pdf (accessed 25 April 2016).

Girvan, N. (2011), Is ALBA a New Model of Integration? Reflections on the CARICOM Experience. *International Journal of Cuban Studies*, 3(2–3),157–180.

Greene, E. (2005), Free Movement of Persons: The Vision and the Reality. CARICOM Directors of Government Information Services, 16–17 March.

Hall, K. and R. Cameron (eds) (2007), *Higher Education Caribbean Perspective*. Kingston: Ian Randle.

I Vidal, L.L. (2008), The Theoretical Contribution of the Study of Regionalism and Interregionalism in the ASEM Process. In L.H. Yeo and L.L. I Vidal (eds), *Regionalism and Interregionalism in the ASEM Context – Current Dynamics and Theoretical Approaches*. Barcelona: CIDOB, pp. 31–70.

Jayasuriya, K. (2003), Introduction: Governing the Asia Pacific – Beyond the 'New Regionalism'. *Third World Quarterly*, 24(2), 199–215.

Jayasuriya, K. and S.L. Robertson (2010), Regulatory Regionalism and the Governance of Higher Education. *Globalisation, Societies and Education*, 8(1), 1–6.

Jessop, B. (2000), The Crisis of the National Spatio-Temporal Fix and the Tendential Ecological Dominance of Globalizing Capitalism. *International Journal of Urban and Regional Research*, 24(2), 323–360.

Jessop, B. (2003), Governance and Metagovernance: On Reflexivity, Requisite Variety, and Requisite Irony. In H.P. Bang (ed.), *Governance, as Social and Political Communication*. Manchester: Manchester University Press, pp. 142–172.

Jessop, B. (2004), Multi-level Governance and Multi-level Metagovernance Changes in the European Union as Integral Moments in the Transformation and Reorientation of Contemporary Statehood. In I. Bache and M. Flinders (eds), *Multi-Level Governance*. Oxford: Oxford University Press, pp. 49–74.

Jules, T.D. (2008), Re/thinking Harmonization in the Commonwealth Caribbean. Audiences, Actors, Interests, and Educational Policy Formation. Doctoral thesis, Teachers' College Columbia, New York.

Jules, T.D. (2012), Re-reading the Anamorphosis of Educational Fragility, Vulnerability, and Strength in Small States. *Current Issues in Comparative and International Education*, 1(15), 5–13.

Jules, T.D. (2013), Ideological Pluralism and Revisionism in Small (and Micro) States: The Erection of the Caribbean Education Policy Space. *Globalisation, Societies and Education*, 11(2), 37–41.

Jules, T.D. (2014), Trans-regional Regimes and Globalization in Education: Constructing the Neo-Caribbean Citizen. In I. Silova and D. Hobson (eds), *Globalizing Minds: Rhetoric and Realities in International Schools*. Chapel Hill, NC: Information Age, pp. 249–275.

Kim, J. (2003), Sub-regionalism, Regionalism, Trans-regionalism: Implications for Economic Integration and International Trade Policies. *Asia Europe Journal*, 1(2), 183–196.

Lavenex, S. (2008), A Governance Perspective on the European Neighbourhood

Policy: Integration Beyond Conditionality? *Journal of European Public Policy*, **15**(6), 938–955.
Lavenex, S. and N. Wichmann (2009), The External Governance of EU Internal Security. *Journal of European Integration*, **31**(1), 83–102.
Lewis, V.A. (2006), Managing Mature Regionalism: Regional Governance in the Caribbean Community. Report of the Technical Group on Governance Appointed by CARICOM Heads of Government. October. CARICOM.
McBrian, H. (2001), Open Regionalism: CARICOM Integration and Trade Links. In V. Bulmer-Thomas (ed.), *Regional Integration in Latin America and the Caribbean: The Political Economy of Open Regionalism*. London: ILAS London, pp. 275–294.
Nettleford, R. (2000), Contrasting Problems Facing Universities in the Developed and Developing Worlds: The Same Difference. In Glenford D. Howe (ed.), *Higher Education in the Caribbean: Past, Present, and Future Directions*. Kingston: University of the West Indies Press, pp. 24–44.
Nicholls, S., P. Samuel, P. Colthrust and E. Boodoo (2001), Open Regionalism and Institutional Developments among the Smaller Integration Schism of CARICOM, the Andean Community and the Central America Common Market. In V. Bulmer-Thomas (ed.), *Regional Integration in Latin America and the Caribbean: The Political Economy of Open Regionalism*, London: ILAS, pp. 141–164.
Odle, M. (2006), Production Integration in the CSME: A Business Perspective. In D. Benn and K.O. Hall (eds), *Production Integration in CARICOM: From Theory to Action*, Kingston: Ian Randle Publications, pp. 30–55.
Parkins, L. (2007), Building Bridges of Collaboration in Higher Education: The UNICA Situation. In Kenneth O. Hall and Rose Marie Cameron (eds), *Higher Education: Caribbean Perspectives*. Kingston: Ian Randle Publishers, pp. 166–173.
Payne, A. and A. Gamble (1996), Introduction: The Political Economy of Regionalism and World Order. In A. Gamble and A. Payne (eds), *Regionalism and World Order*, London, UK and New York, USA: Palgrave, pp. 1–20.
Pollard, D.D. (2012), Interrelationships between Community and National Competition Rules. In K. Hall and M. Chuck-A-Sang (eds), *Managing Mature Regionalism*. Bloomington, NY: Trafford Publishing, pp. 78–197.
Robertson, S. (2010), The EU, 'Regulatory State Regionalism' and New Modes of Higher Education Governance. *Globalisation, Societies and Education*, **8**(1), 23–37.
Second Special Meeting SCME (1997), Report of the Second Special Meeting of the Standing Committee of Ministers Responsible for Education (REP.97/2/69 SCME [Spec.]). May. Bridgetown, Barbados: CARICOM.
Song, W. (2007), Regionalisation, Inter-regional Cooperation and Global Governance. *Asia Europe Journal*, **5**(1), 67–82.

11. MERCOSUR, regulatory regionalism and contesting projects of higher education governance

Daniela Perrotta

INTRODUCTION

Higher education (HE) governance is far from being exclusively shaped by national policy-making frameworks. In fact, the territorial politics of the (sub-)nationally located state are being challenged by a complex set of regulations and norms established in the international and supra-regional arenas. At the same time, these regulations and norms generate ideas and discourses of HE governance that also stimulate practices within HE institutions (HEIs). Yet the tendency is to continue to study the higher education sector as if its governance arrangements are entirely located at the (sub-)national scales.

To overcome this implicit methodological nationalism, avenues for research have been opened by the study of how regional integration schemes are transforming the scales for policy delivery (Jayasuriya and Robertson, 2010). Many regional integration agreements (RIAs) – including those in Latin America (see Muhr, Chapter 12 in this volume) and the Caribbean regionalism (see Jules, Chapter 10 in this volume) – have settled norms for the HE sector and most of the regional policies are bypassing the territoriality of politics of the state. Here the concept of 'regulatory regionalism' (Jayasuriya and Robertson, 2010; see also the Introduction to this volume) is particularly fruitful to assess these thickening configurations of norms, regulations and policies, which are crafting HE governance across the globe.

In the case of Latin America and Caribbean (LAC) regionalism, the peculiar features of the RIAs are rooted in their institutional hybridity as well as their inherent tensions regarding scope, depth and vision for regionalism. There are at least three contesting and/or overlapping projects of regionalism present in the LAC regional map. Firstly, a project of hegemonic regionalism rooted in the new regionalism schemes launched during the 1990s that considered trade liberalization as an end in itself, and that the region consisted in an instrument to foster competitiveness. The paradigmatic cases are the asymmetrical free trade agreements (FTAs) signed by Chile, Colombia and Peru, the North American Free Trade Agreement (NAFTA) and the recently created Pacific Alliance. Secondly, a post-hegemonic scheme erected after several political, social and economic crises in several countries led to the emergence of renewed political forces that reclaimed welfarist projects domestically and regionally, based upon the principles of cooperation and solidarity. These 'regional structures [are] characterized by hybrid practices as a result of a partial displacement of dominant forms of US [United States]-led neoliberal governance in the acknowledgement of other political forms of organization and economic management of regional (common) goods' (Riggirozzi and Tussie, 2012: 11–12), with the Union of South American Nations (UNASUR) a typical case. And thirdly, a counter-hegemonic scheme was posed by Venezuela alongside the Bolivarian Alliance for the Peoples of Our America – Peoples' Trade Agreement (ALBA-TCP). As Muhr (2011) indicates, it is the case of a geopolitical and geostrategic project ruled by principles radically different from those of the new regionalism schemes, such as solidarity, cooperation, complementarity, reciprocity and sustainability (Muhr, 2011: 105).

The Southern Common Market (MERCOSUR)[1] represents a post-hegemonic case, after the political and economic turmoil of the beginning of the millennium – alongside the emergence of New Leftist governments – the integration project shifted towards the inclusion of social policies, citizenship rights and other mechanisms to reduce asymmetries, and the development of a productive model of regional integration. However, MERCOSUR holds a 'birthmark': it was created under the new regionalism bias and its institutional framework reflects the emphasis on trade liberalization, whilst at the same time it built upon the rapprochement of Argentinean and Brazilian relations during the mid-1980s, which was based upon a developmental model rooted in industrial and scientific and technological complementarities.

As we will see, MERCOSUR's regional regulations, norms and policies are bypassing domestic policy processes in agendas of integration (HE agenda), mainly supported by transnational (and trans-oceanic) epistemic communities and/or advocacy networks, in order to prompt domestic change (policy change, institutional change) so as to support these groups' interests. Consequently, the concept of 'regulatory regionalism' (Hameiri and Jayasuriya, 2011; Jayasuriya and Robertson, 2010) is fruitful to assess MERCOSUR's regionalism in HE, the implications of regional policies on domestic arenas, and the emergence of contesting projects for HE regionalism. 'Regulatory regionalism' stresses how national agencies are crafting a softer means of governance as a result of the connections and exchanges they are developing with their foreign counterparts. As a result, regulatory regionalism does not necessarily lead to uniform and homogeneous regulatory standards; on the contrary, it is a useful tool to assess the way in which regulatory regional projects occur in layers, even overlapping ones. This approach enables us to analyse contesting situations that transform the territorial space within the state by means of the incorporation of regional agendas within the domestic institutions. Additionally, Hameiri and Jayasuriya (2011) define 'regulatory regionalism' as also involving the institutional spaces of regional regulations within national policy and political institutions. Thus, the focus of inquiry is no longer on the creation of supranational rules and institutions; instead, attention is paid to the political process of region-building, which is simultaneously national and regional.

This point of view allows us to overcome the traditional division (quasi-antagonistic) between nation-states and supra-national regional institutions that is posed by both neofunctionalist and intergovernmentalist literatures (Perrotta, 2013a). Moreover, it allows us to move away from narrow studies that are focused mainly on the commercial aspects of integration and to proceed with the study of social policies at the regional level. According to Phillips (2001), emerging forms of regional regulation, rely more on the active participation of national agencies in regulatory practices rather than on formal treaties or international organizations.

In this chapter I will argue that the development of MERCOSUR's regulations for higher education has shaped at least three contesting projects of governance. Firstly, a project embedded in MERCOSUR's 'birthmark' between a developmental model of regional integration and the emergence of a new regionalism typical scheme. This project aimed at strengthening the goal of the common market. A second project is rooted on the need to support local HEIs in a highly competitive regional and global market by the creation of a quality certificate of the region. I call it MERCOSUR's 'brandmark' to distinguish the particular case of regulatory regionalism. Finally, a third project is deeply connected with the European Union (EU) as a case of regulatory state regionalism (Robertson, 2009a) that is diffusing to the South American region, especially in the policy area of academic mobility. The three projects are present currently and bring together several groups of actors with competing interests and values about HE governance and MERCOSUR. These ongoing projects and processes are challenging MERCOSUR's regulatory regionalism. In order to reveal their dynamics, this chapter examines MERCOSUR's regional policies for higher education over the period 1991–2014 that are subject to three domains: (1) accreditation and quality assurance of undergraduate university degrees; (2) academic mobility; and (3) inter-institutional cooperation.

MERCOSUR'S REGULATORY REGIONALISM AND HE GOVERNANCE

Throughout its more than 20 years of development, the MERCOSUR Education Sector (SEM) has consolidated a solid institutional framework so as to fulfil the goals of educational integration. It could be pointed out that SEM's functioning recognizes at least three phases (Perrotta, 2011, 2013b). The first (1991–2001) aimed at building its institutional structure, establishing bonds of trust among the governments' officials through the exchange of information about the characteristics of national educational systems and creating common indicators to obtain comparable information. During the second phase (2001–2008), the first regional programmes started to be implemented. The greatest political achievements were the establishment of protocols for the recognition of qualifications (for academic purposes) and the implementation of the first regional policy: the experimental mechanism for the accreditation of undergraduate university degrees in MERCOSUR, Bolivia and Chile (Mecanismo Experimental de Acreditación de Carreras de Grado Universitario, MEXA).

Within the period, other policies were designed and implemented (for example, secondary education). It is also possible to point to a process of strengthening of policies as the experimental Academic Quality Assurance (AQA) policy turned into a permanent system (the accreditation system of undergraduate university degrees for the regional recognition of their academic quality in MERCOSUR and associated states: Acreditación Regional de Carreras Universitarias del Sur, ARCU-SUR) and a regional fund started to be negotiated (the MERCOSUR Educational Fund, FEM). The third period began in 2011 as a result of the modification of the institutional structure and the implementation of regional policies in various areas of action (elementary and secondary education, special programmes regarding human rights, a Youth Parliament and so on), and a new area for policy delivery was created: teacher training.

An interesting feature to note about SEM's functioning is the fact that both member states and associated states participate in this regional arena and implement regional policy initiatives. The first two countries that joined the intra-zone trade area were Chile and Bolivia; alongside MERCOSUR's development, Colombia, Ecuador, Peru and Venezuela joined the free trade area and therefore could start participating in SEM's negotiations. However, as these countries – according to their status – are not forced to implement MERCOSUR's initiatives regarding HE unless they have signed up to it in a commitment, the implementation paths have been different in each case. Currently, all of them belong to SEM and actively participate and implement policies.

However, two cases must be highlighted: first, the change of status of Venezuela after completion of the adhesion process in 2012; second, the impasse in Paraguay's participation as a result of the *coup d'état* (2012) when MERCOSUR prohibited its political participation. The combination of the two situations generated some turmoil within SEM as Venezuela needed to absorb many regional norms and regulations while contacts with the Paraguayan delegation were stopped. Since the return of democracy in Paraguay, relations have been reconstructed. The Venezuelan addition to MERCOSUR as a full member, however, generates important questions about how the RIA is going to process it: Venezuela's education projects under the regional scheme (prompted within the ALBA-TCP) are quite different from those of MERCOSUR. This situation questions whether SEM would undergo a new stage in its development.

Within the institutional structure, the decision-making body is the Meeting of Ministers of Education (RME), followed by the Regional Coordinating Committee (CCR), composed by officials from the ministries. The CCR, in turn, is assisted by Regional Commissions for Coordination (CRCs) of four areas: Basic Education (CRC-BE), Higher Education (CRC-HE), Teacher Training (CRC-TT)[2] and Technological Education (CRC-TE). Finally, there are thematic advisory commissions and temporary bodies.

The regional agencies for the delivery of HE policies are: CRC-HE, the Meeting of National Accreditation Agencies (RANA), MERCOSUR's Mobility Programme Ad Hoc Commission (CAhPMM), the Working Group on Postgraduate Programmes (GTPG), the Working Group on Recognition of Degrees (GTR), the Management Group of 'MARCA' and the MERCOSUR Centre for Studies and Research in Higher Education (NUCLEO).

These bodies are intergovernmental, which also means that frequently delegates are also in charge of negotiations in other forums, such as UNASUR and the Community of Latin American and Caribbean States (CELAC), as well as the Organization of American States (OAS), the Organization of Ibero-American States (OEI), the United Nations Educational, Scientific and Cultural Organization (UNESCO), and so on. Participation of non-governmental actors has been low or non-existent (the only university that composes the national delegation of its country is the University of the Republic, Uruguay). It must be noticed that SEM is subordinated to the Common Market Council (CMC, the top decision-making body of MERCOSUR). This situation suggests that non-trade agendas have a peripheral position within the policy-making arrangements of the RIA. Such a situation presents both functional and democratic deficits (Caetano et al., 2009). Despite the deficits detected, several regional policies have been put in force. The fact that SEM started operations in 1991, which led to a self-enforcement process, and its typical organization of the work by Operational Plans, explains the success in policy delivery.

The axes for policy delivery in HE within SEM are: recognition and accreditation, mobility, and inter-institutional cooperation. The three dimensions were not planned to be consecutive, but in practice SEM's initiatives followed that order by an incremental and gradual implementation path that started with the experimental AQA mechanism, then 'spilled over' to the first mobility programme (of accredited degrees) and finally fostered inter-institutional cooperation activities. These last are the most recent policies and reflect the broadening of the HE regional agenda, as it is given in the current Operational Plan (2011–2015).

The first regional policy was the implementation in 2002 of the experimental mechanism for the accreditation of undergraduate university degrees in MERCOSUR, Bolivia and Chile (MEXA). The degree courses of undergraduate programmes that were subject to the AQA under MEXA were medicine, engineering and agronomy. After the implementation of this pilot instrument, by the year 2006, 55 undergraduate degrees and diplomas obtained MERCOSUR's quality stamp: medicine, 8; engineering, 28; and agronomy, 19. Argentina accredited 14 diplomas; Bolivia, 9; Brazil, 12; Chile, 5; Uruguay, 8; and Paraguay, 7 (see Figure 11.1).

Two policies resulted from MEXA. The first was an accreditation system of undergraduate university degrees for the regional recognition of their academic quality in MERCOSUR and associated states (ARCU-SUR),

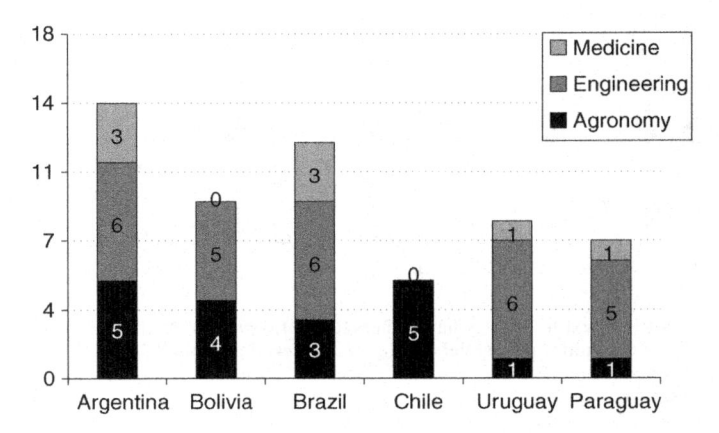

Figure 11.1 Results of MEXA, 2002–2006

signed in 2008, as an international treaty amongst parties (DEC CMC N° 17/08). ARCU-SUR also broadened participation to many of the associated states and incorporated new disciplines: veterinary, architecture, nursing and dentistry. By the first semester of 2012, the results of ARCU-SUR showed that 109 degrees obtained MERCOSUR's quality stamp: Argentina, 36; Bolivia, 10; Chile, 5; Colombia, 10; Uruguay, 14; Paraguay, 23; Venezuela, 11; and Brazil, 0. During the first semester of 2012, 137 undergraduate courses were implementing the procedure: Argentina, 18; Paraguay, 4; Uruguay, 2; and Brazil, 113. As can be seen, Brazil only started to implement ARCU-SUR in 2012 to fulfil its regional commitments. This situation generated tensions with the rest of the members, and mainly with Argentina, one of the main promoters of the regional AQA policy. Figure 11.2 illustrates this situation.

The first programme for the mobility of undergraduate students was launched as a consequence of the AQA regional policy: the regional academic mobility programme for the courses authorized by MEXA (known as MARCA). It was designed in 2005 and launched in 2006, and 57 students participated. It should be pointed out that when MEXA

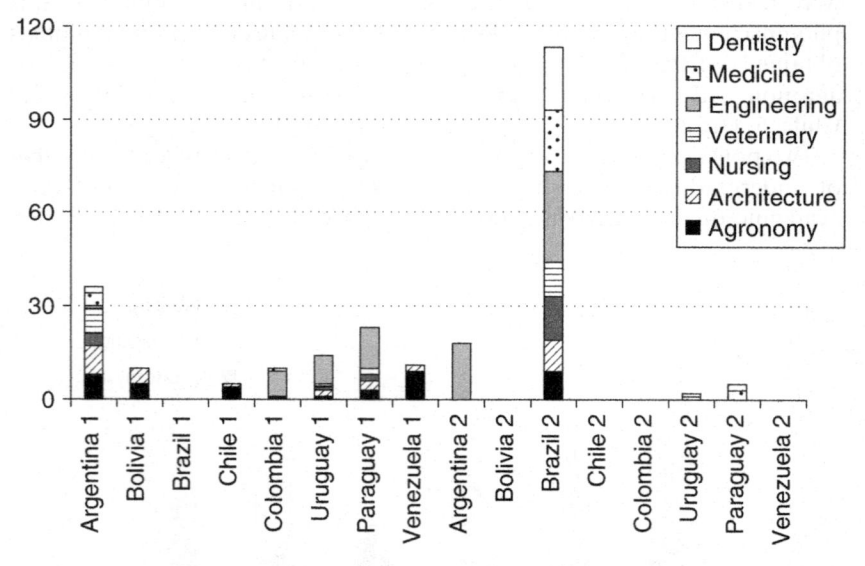

Note: Number 1 next to country name refers to *AQA completed* by the 1st semester 2012; number 2 next to country name refers to *AQA in process* during the 1st semester 2012.

Source: Author.

Figure 11.2   Results of ARCU-SUR, 2008–2012

became ARCU-SUR, the regional mobility programme for students of accredited degrees continued under a new denomination: the regional academic mobility programme for accredited courses under the accreditation system of university degrees in MERCOSUR and associated states.

The mobility experience entails spending a semester at a university in a country other than the country of origin. The first mobility experience was in agronomy courses that had been accredited by MEXA. MARCA for agronomy was a pilot, and the number of students to be mobilized was five for each of the first 17 MEXA-accredited degrees: 85 students were to be mobilized, that is, 25 (28 per cent) Argentina; 15 (18 per cent) Bolivia and Brazil, respectively; 20 (23 per cent) Chile; 5 (6 per cent) Paraguay and Uruguay, respectively; but only 57 students actually took part. This problem has not yet been overcome. From its inception in 2006 up to 2010, 985 places have been available. However, the number of students actually mobilized is much lower: 580 in total. The EU has been close to the implementation of the mobility policy, providing funds and (related to this) demanding regulations that had not yet been elaborated within MERCOSUR: for instance, free visas for students who mobilize through MARCA.

The latest available data of mobility flows (2014) show a moment of impasse in the regional integration process. The number of places agreed is 444 but these do not include all the participating countries (see Figure 11.3). The allocation of flows is as follows: Argentina, 38.5 per cent; Brazil, 37.4 per cent; Bolivia, 18.2 per cent; Uruguay, 4.1 per cent; and Chile, 1.8 per cent. Indeed, there are no flows to Paraguay or Venezuela. This situation is explained by Venezuela trying to absorb these regional policies after its inclusion, and whilst Paraguay is being reincorporated after it had been banned from political participation within MERCOSUR's bodies following the *coup d'état* that dismissed former President Lugo.

All in all, from 2002 to 2008, regional policies were related to quality assurance. From then on, SEM would start regulating other areas. Some of the initiatives were built upon pre-existing bilateral cooperation programmes between Argentina and Brazil; others were stimulated by the availability of funds, especially from the EU.

The first initiative was a set of actions targeted to the postgraduate level; the 2011–2015 Plan settled a 'Comprehensive System for Quality Promotion of Postgraduate Programmes within MERCOSUR' organized by a working group according to three lines of action: (1) a programme of joint research projects; (2) a partnership programme to strengthen postgraduate courses; and (3) a training programme for human resources. The first line of action is aimed at strengthening cooperation in Doctoral

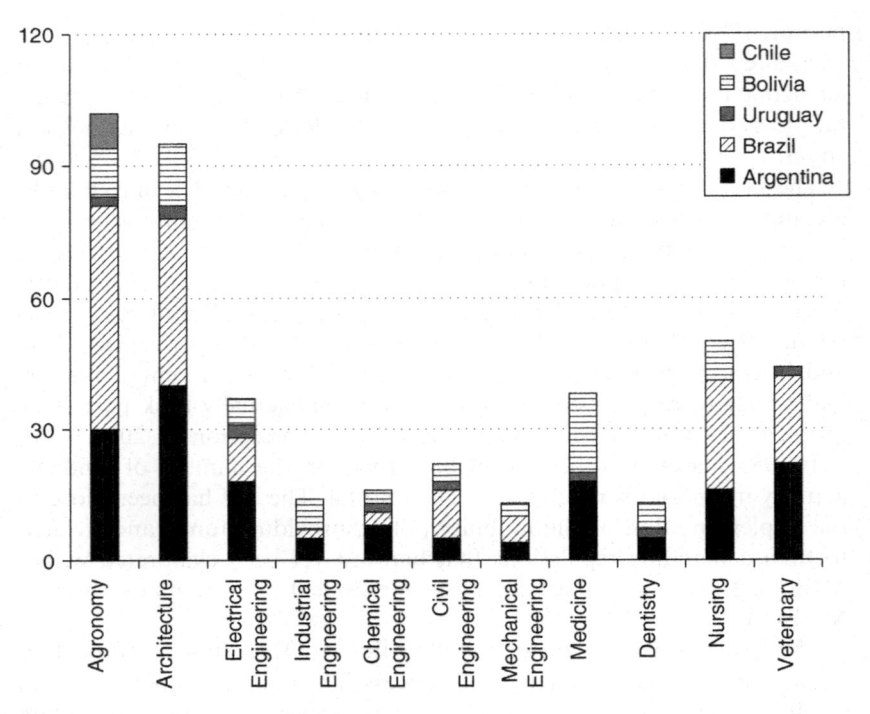

Figure 11.3   MARCA mobility flow, 2014

programmes of excellence in HE institutions from MERCOSUR member states (Argentina, Brazil, Chile, Paraguay, Uruguay and Venezuela); it would last two years and could be extended (two more years). The aim was to stimulate the exchange of teachers and researchers. The second line of action, based on the principle of solidarity, seeks a particular partnership from the association of a graduate programme of excellence with one that is less developed in order to strengthen it. Thus, it is aimed at trying to reduce asymmetries between higher education systems in the region. Participating countries and duration are similar to the aforementioned. The third line of action is the awarding of scholarships for Doctoral university professors in the institutions of the region. It is worth noting that this type of regional cooperation was set up from bilateral cooperation programmes (Argentina and Brazil); in other words, it is an experience of regionalizing bilateral cooperation actions.

The second initiative, MARCA for Professors, was built upon the experience of MARCA for students. The goal is to strengthen institutional cooperation and the training of professors. The universities that have degrees accredited by ARCU-SUR are to establish cooperation projects, and the exchange of faculty is among these projects. As an example, in the Argentine case, four institutions in the country coordinated networks with other institutions in the areas of architecture, chemical engineering, agronomy and electronic engineering.[3]

The third initiative, the MERCOSUR Mobility Programme (PMM) project, is co-funded by the EU. It was under negotiation from 2005, but only implemented in 2010. The project targets the four initial member states and has a double aim: (1) to create a sense of belonging and regional identity; and (2) to achieve a common educational space (the Regional Space for Higher Education, RSHE).[4] The PMM was implemented by the formation of academic networks, the launch of a pilot programme for student mobility of unaccredited degrees, and the establishment of campaigns designed to inform HEI.

Additionally, other exchange programmes include university partnership programmes for the mobility of MERCOSUR undergraduate professors in all areas of knowledge so as to stimulate the approximation of the curriculum frameworks and foster mutual recognition of degree structures and the exchange programme of Portuguese and Spanish teachers so as to foster bilingualism.

The fourth initiative was in the area of inter-institutional cooperation, where the NUCLEO was created in 2011.[5] Three purposes guide its actions: to promote knowledge production about HE and RIAs; to encourage research about the contributions of HE to MERCOSUR; and to propose initiatives and actions that will strengthen the formulation of public policy and guide decision-making. These goals relate to the systematization and analysis of information of the HE systems and to the need to foster communication vehicles among stakeholders. The first action was the implementation of a digital journal; then came the organization of several seminars; and later on, the NUCLEO started subsidizing research networks. All in all, MERCOSUR Educativo has succeeded in nurturing the political agenda for HE over time, especially during the last decade.

REGULATORY REGIONALISM AND CONTESTING PROJECTS FOR HE GOVERNANCE

As mentioned, MERCOSUR's decision-making bodies are purely intergovernmental, which means that national delegates from member and associated states compose the regional bodies. Additionally, the participation of non-governmental actors within SEM's agencies has been nil, except for the case of the University of the Republic (Uruguay). In other words, the negotiation of regional policies has been purely intergovernmental.

However, despite these institutional features, MERCOSUR's norms, policies and regulations for HE have been set in motion, and in many cases have bypassed domestic policy processes and introduced policy change at the national level. These regional initiatives have been fostered by transnational (or trans-oceanic) epistemic communities and/or advocacy networks to prompt domestic policy changes that support interest groups with a stake in the outcome.

As a result, MERCOSUR's regulatory regionalism has consequences regarding HE governance, which does not strictly lead to the convergence of standards. On the contrary, as regulatory regionalism is a contested process transforming the territorial space of the state, it is not surprising that several regulatory projects for HE are present at both the regional and the national scale, sometimes moving on parallel tracks, sometimes overlapping, but most of them challenging the territorial politics of the state. All in all, the analysis of MERCOSUR's regional policies for HE during the last two decades provides us with an in-depth understanding about these phenomena. At least three projects of HE governance can be pinpointed within MERCOSUR's regulatory regionalism.

Project 1: MERCOSUR's Birthmark Tension: Development versus Competitiveness

The first regional policy for HE, set in force in 2002, focused in the area of AQA: the MEXA Memorandum was signed by the four initial member states together with Chile and Bolivia. However, the 2002 version of MEXA was built upon a previous Memorandum signed in 1998: 'Memorandum of Understanding about the implementation of an experimental mechanism for the accreditation of undergraduate degrees so as to recognize university diplomas within MERCOSUR's countries' ('Memorandum 1998'). This agreement was signed as a result of a request posed by the executive body of MERCOSUR (Grupo Mercado Común, GMC) in 1996 in an effort to prompt free mobility of professionals within the region. By then the demand for labour mobility in professional disciplines (law, accountancy and civil engineering) was linked to the creation of a mechanism to recognize university diplomas.

As a result of the request, SEM began to build an initiative to cope with GMC interest to expedite cross-border professional mobility. However, not all the national delegations participated actively in the first steps of the creation of this mechanism, especially Argentina, as it was undergoing its own policy reforms in the field of HE. One of the main elements was establishing a national system of evaluation and accreditation of universities.

Memorandum 1998 established that the diplomas to be accredited would be in agronomy, medicine, and engineering, and three advisory commissions of experts were settled: three experts per country (one from the professional association, one from public universities, one from private universities) were chosen (36 experts in total) to define the evaluation criteria from a regional approach. The coordination of the work within SEM was subject to the Working Group of Specialists in Evaluation and Accreditation (GTAE). As a result of the work, the regional criteria of quality for the three disciplines were agreed which led to the creation of instruments and procedures of evaluation. By the year 2000 (while a pre-test was conducted), the national AQA agency of Argentina (National Commission of University Evaluation and Accreditation, CONEAU) had begun to participate regularly at the regional level as the agency had completed its first domestic accreditation process (in medicine). Since then CONEAU has led the process.

Despite progress being made, a new Memorandum was signed in 2002, which changed the initial provisions. Firstly, one of the controversial elements of Memorandum 1998 was that it stated that the dictum of the experts (after the evaluation procedure) would have a mandatory character if the decision was reached unanimously. This situation would potentially have created a supra-national agency, above national AQA agencies, which was not viable (and still is not). Secondly, another problematic issue was the fact that recognition of diplomas does not necessarily encompass cross-border mobility of labour in order to work in another country. This relates to the fact that in most of the countries, the exercise of professions is regulated by permissions obtained by different types of mechanisms settled by associations. Thirdly, alongside the neoliberal reform of HE which established renewed control mechanisms over institutions, the strong tradition of autonomy of public universities would be undermined by regional regulations. As a result, public universities also opposed the mechanism. The creation of a comprehensive regional accrediting body would largely reduce the sovereignty of states, the prerogatives of professional associations and the autonomy of universities. The result was as expected: Memorandum 2002 made sufficient changes so as to overcome opposition and install a different project.

All in all, the first project of HE governance recalls the initial goal of MERCOSUR: to create a common market involving the free movement of labour. This project is influenced by a developmental model of pursuing regional integration that is rooted in previous experience within the region (related to the 1960s Latin American Association of Free Trade, and the integration process between Argentina and Brazil of the mid-1980s) and with some influence of how the European experience was perceived back then (as a successful process).

The actors in this project are national delegates involved in the creation of the common market (a developmental group) which echoed the group of delegates interested in the free trade zone (who wanted to advance the trade of services as it began to be incorporated at the multilateral level). Of course the two groups have divergent interests regarding the regional integration scheme: the first group pursued a developmental model, and the second a 'new regionalism' scheme. The role assigned to HE was also different. For the first group, HE was a cornerstone for strengthening the common market and deepening the integration process; for the second group, HE was perceived as a tradable service. For both groups, MERCOSUR should advance the liberalization of the areas that were most needed at the level of the regional market to ensure competitiveness: medicine, agronomy and engineering.

As a result of pressures from interest groups and organized actors, Memorandum 2002 was passed and everything relating to labour mobility regarding services was derived to the GMC. It should be highlighted that the vision that prevailed was a more pragmatic one, as recognition of diplomas shifted towards recognition of quality of the undergraduate programmes, and also reflecting the fact that the most advanced national frameworks for AQA influenced the regional negotiation agenda.

However, in the last several years negotiations regarding recognition of university diplomas have been reinitiated; in particular, the current Operational Plan mentions the need to advance in this area, and it has created a working group within SEM to deal with the issue. It is still a problematic agenda, however, as professional associations need to be involved in the process.[6]

Project 2: MERCOSUR's Brandmark for Quality Assurance of Selected University Diplomas

In 2002, MEXA was passed, incorporating MERCOSUR's associated states (Chile and Bolivia). The original goal of recognition of degrees for enhancing the labour market shifted towards the objective of assessing regional quality standards as a stepping-stone for recognition of diplomas. There was a need to assure academic quality and not to interfere with the regulation of the professions. Thus, freedom of movement of professionals was set aside: the Ouro Preto Protocol had consolidated the customs union and the 'quasi-automatic' recognition of diplomas implied in Memorandum 1998 undermined sectoral interests. Consequently,

MERCOSUR reproduced domestic differentiation between recognition of degrees and permits for professional practice. SEM is in charge of recognition of degrees, while professional practice – and therefore labour mobility – is under the Group of Trade of Services (within the GMC).

Memorandum 2002 established that RANA would coordinate the process, and that domestic implementation would be done by either national AQA agencies or by an ad hoc commission for those cases for which there was not yet such a body. The mechanism could be synthesized in the following steps: the call for accreditation; the elaboration of self-evaluation reports by the selected HEIs; the visit of experts to the HEIs and elaboration of the evaluation reports; the possibility to answer some points of the evaluation report; the decision of a dictum; and the publicity of results. It must be highlighted that the mechanism was implemented in all the countries at the same time as in each of the three disciplines, and the evaluation reports were discussed within regional meetings of experts supported by RANA bureaucrats. As a result, the gathering of the experts promoted a socialization process that led to the formation of an embryonic regional identity among governmental officials and experts.

However, the creation of MERCOSUR's 'quality stamp' ('brandmark') reflects how several interests merged and crafted a particular way of pursuing regional AQA, its drivers and results. Firstly, the decision to proceed to the accreditation of the quality of professional diplomas relates to the fact that the productive model of MERCOSUR and its parties was to be reinforced: to stimulate intra-regional labour mobility, especially in those areas that are crucial in terms of the economic structures of the countries, on one side, and the particular needs posed by an underdevelopment context – such as a demand for health assistance – on the other. It must also be borne in mind that one of the most salient characteristics of most HE systems is the influence of the professional model of the university; MERCOSUR reinforces that trend.

Secondly, the mechanism was based on a particular logic: a club logic. As the original goal had shifted towards a more practical – and competitive – one of improving the recognition of undergraduate degrees within the region so as to strengthen a regional HE market and enhance HEIs on the global market, quotas per country were established. There are two reasons that explain why not all HEIs could apply for the regional AQA procedure. On the one hand, as with the functioning of a club – in this case, a group of HEIs that share certain characteristics and whose organization gives them benefits – there are conditions for membership: only the most prestigious universities could obtain MERCOSUR's quality stamp and therefore fulfil the goal of enhancing top HEIs in order to compete in the global market. On the other hand, the establishment of quotas also worked as an instrument to deter a massive participation from Brazilian HEIs: the idea was to prevent Brazil from obtaining all the benefits of the quality stamp for itself, and leveraging the distribution of benefits per country. Therefore, the distribution of quotas to the parties relates to the competitive bias of MERCOSUR.

However, the 'club logic' of functioning had a positive consequence in terms of regional cooperation, because a club is also based upon the principle of solidarity. The value of MERCOSUR's quality stamp relates to the fact that all the parties complied with the procedures, especially during the experimental mechanism, because all the undergraduate degrees under assessment were subject to a regional discussion and the dictum was decided within that common space. As a result, the more-developed members (in terms of technical expertise, material resources and institutional capacities) ended up contributing support to the less-developed ones in order to implement the procedures. Such contributions resulted in transferring know-how, financing activities and organizing the regional meetings in strategic locations.

Thirdly, the EU acted as a case of regulatory state regionalism (Robertson, 2009b) with the normative power to influence other regions – in this case MERCOSUR – in the world. In fact the first ideas regarding the design of the mechanisms recalls the initial steps of the European Higher Education Area, and the creation of the Bologna Process. Indeed, during the negotiations to create the mechanism, the EU tried to promote a system of credit transfers. But MERCOSUR's position was not in favour of such homogenization and settled, instead a mechanism based upon quality assurance and the respect of both national and institutional particularities. Memorandum 2002 and MEXA reflect an autonomous path in the pursuit of regionalization of HE.

Meanwhile, an epistemic community regarding AQA became more visible as the experimental mechanism was being implemented, crystallizing in the creation of the Ibero-American Network for Quality Accreditation in Higher Education (RIACES). The existence of this epistemic community collaborated in the dissemination of the AQA procedures, which were applied following the specificities of each state. At the same time, this process fed back to the regional policy. This epistemic community included amongst its members the presence of European scholars and practitioners in the field, and was supported by UNESCO's International Institute for Higher Education in Latin America and the Caribbean (IESALC) and its bi-regional experiences. The socialization process that was generated as a result of the intensity of contacts within the regional framework also favoured the creation of this epistemic community, which then resulted in joint academic productions between officials of different countries (see Robledo and Caillón, 2009).

In 2008, MEXA became a permanent system with the signature of the ARCU-SUR treaty. It locked in the focus of the regional policy on quality assurance and left aside the original goals of recognition of degrees and mobility of workers. There were three major changes in the move from MEXA to ARCU-SUR. Firstly, convergence of policies proved to be crucial for AQA agencies in order not to duplicate efforts. The underlying motto is that, as the AQA process is expensive and demands an important technical effort, the coordination of calendars makes it more efficient. Therefore, currently, regional schedules match national accreditation calendars. Secondly, the need for time convergence has negatively affected the AQA regional policy. This has led to the mechanization of the implementation, leaving aside the important effect in terms of region-building at the regional gathering of experts (decisions about accreditation are reached at the national level). Thirdly, the policy has been broadened as a result of new members participating: Colombia, Ecuador and Venezuela. Yet the enlargement of the mechanism poses new challenges. For instance, Argentina's position could be challenged by the Colombian delegation as it is a country that has been implementing AQA policies for a long time but it has a more privatized HE system. The implementation of the regional AQA policy triggered policy diffusion processes at the domestic level, encompassing the peculiarities of each country.[7] The following is a summary of findings regarding domestic change.

Argentina was the only one of the four member states that already had an explicit AQA regulation: CONEAU was created in 1996 (HE Law N° 24.521). At the time of implementation of MEXA (2002), Argentina had already settled the AQA process and as a result CONEAU influenced the process of establishing mechanisms and instruments for the AQA regional policy. The typical features of the domestic AQA policy were transferred to the AQA regional policy model. The Argentinean delegation became a crucial policy transfer actor as CONEAU officials started transferring expertise to the other members (and continue to do so, as more associated states are participating in ARCU-SUR), offering courses, technical support, and so on. As a result, there is harmony between domestic and regional regulations; such harmonization implied neither policy nor institutional changes. On the contrary, the AQA regional policy, according to CONEAU officials, is considered to be less exhaustive than the national policy (the quality standards diverge).

In the case of Brazil, at the time of the regional negotiations there were no specific AQA regulations, and nor did a national agency exist. Instead, there was strict regulation regarding the evaluation of the HE system:

institutions, courses, scholars and students. It is a comprehensive model of control that began in the 1980s and which continues today, reinforced through the HE evaluation system (National System of Higher Education Assessment, SINAES). This regulatory framework was adapted to cope with the provisions established in the regional mechanism without creating major institutional innovations.[8] During the experimental phase, Brazil contributed to the implementation of the AQA policy by providing technical and financial support to the process. Brazil indeed became its paymaster by means of its material and financial resources for the mechanism to be fulfilled. The position changed after the signature of the ARCU-SUR treaty because domestic implementation of AQA policy stopped after 2012. This situation caused some misunderstandings and mistrust between the national delegations. Indeed it can be argued that Brazil did not have to undergo major changes to cope with regional AQA policy and depended instead on the national structure and regulation. It was not a priority policy issue, unlike unilateral HE internationalization policies, which have been strengthened, though there is a process of coordination with Argentina (the leading voice in AQA).

The major impact of AQA regional policy in terms of domestic change is observed in the case of Paraguay. The Memorandum indicated that the process was to be organized by national agencies of accreditation and that these countries which did not have such a body should proceed to create it. Paraguay had no AQA regulation, so an HE law was set in force which created a national agency for the evaluation and accreditation of HE (National Agency for Assessment and Accreditation of Higher Education, ANEAES). Consequently, the process of domestic change could be partly explained by the policy diffusion process from the regional level, and the socialization of actors within this arena. Firstly, domestic political actors used the 'regional obligation' to install the discourse of AQA policy and the need to improve the HE regulatory framework. Secondly, the characteristics of MEXA shaped the configuration of the national AQA policy. If we take into consideration that the regional AQA policy was built upon the Argentinean AQA policy, can the policy diffusion process be seen as top-down (from MERCOSUR to Paraguay)? Or, was the policy diffusion process a more horizontal one (from Argentina to Paraguay)? CONEAU had an important role during the implementation of the regional AQA policy by training the national delegations of other countries, especially Paraguay, Uruguay and Bolivia. Therefore, Argentina was able to impose the domestic AQA model in the regional negotiation and to legitimate such a position from a discourse of being the only country with the expertise to do so. Meanwhile, an epistemic community regarding AQA became more visible and collaborated in the dissemination of the AQA procedures. All in all, in Paraguay the diffusion process led to the convergence of policies that led to a harmonization of procedures.

The case of Uruguay is quite unique and relates to its university tradition. As a result of the regional AQA policy, the current situation can be characterized as one of peaceful coexistence between the regional policy, on one side, and the segmentation and differentiation of national policies alongside the self-regulation of the University of the Republic (UdelaR), on the other. To comprehend such complexity, it must be pointed out that the National Constitution states that UdelaR is regulated by its own local laws. As a consequence, the national Ministry of Education has no binding power over UdelaR. Thus, UdelaR has composed the national delegation of SEM. Uruguay set in force an ad hoc commission that included the presence of three actors (government, UdelaR, private institutions). Several projects to create an Agency for the Promotion and Quality Assurance of Tertiary Education (APACET) had been discussed, but none of them could be adopted (and would not be adopted in the medium term). The discourse about the need to adjust to the regional requirement was prompted by the government and the private sector but it did not lead to domestic change as the position of UdelaR is stronger. However, in this scenario, the AQA regional policy was implemented in Uruguayan public and private HEIs. The interesting results are, firstly, that UdelaR submitted to the AQA policy of MERCOSUR even though it rejected doing so at the national level. Therefore, UdelaR considers that MERCOSUR's 'stamp' is valuable and should not be ignored. Secondly, it was the first time that the three actors had sat together at the same negotiation table to discuss HE public policies. As a consequence, the domestic regulatory framework remains the same whilst also coexisting with the regional policy requirements.

All in all, the results of the AQA regional stamp show an autonomous way of pursuing the regionalization of HE that strengthened the position of some (top) universities within a regional and global HE market, even though amongst the unintended consequences it also fosters a cooperative bias. This model, the MERCOSUR 'brandmark', was stimulated by the role of national AQA agencies, specially the Argentinean one, the requirement to leverage the presence of all parties (so that national interests were not undermined), and the need to set a gradual and autonomic model than could deter the pressures exerted by the EU.

Project 3: The Bolognization of MERCOSUR

In order to unpack the project that relates more to the EU as a normative power, the policy area to analyse is academic mobility. However, recent actions undertaken by SEM regarding AQA policy are challenging the so-called 'autonomous path'.

Mobility policies have been fertile soil for the influence of the EU for two reasons:[9] on the one hand, the EU is broadly perceived by SEM's bureaucrats as a model of successful regional integration that has resulted both from socialization processes, including assiduous contacts amongst actors which have led to changes in their identities (especially during the negotiations of the framework agreement and when implementing joint initiatives), and from persuasion. On the other hand, the EU became a paymaster of MERCOSUR's mobility programmes, which means alongside the bi-regional agreement, the EU has been able to impose rewards and costs, including conditionality, technical capacity-building and financial assistance. The bi-regional agreement had a chapter regarding HE, and MERCOSUR parties have applied to the Framework Programmes for Research and Technological Development. As a result of the funding obtained, the EU could impose methodologies and procedures; for example, the need for free visas for exchange students within the region was a condition set by the EU. Technical capacity was also involved in building actions involving bi-regional relations, in turn prompting emulation and mimetic processes. Currently, the EU is financing two relevant programmes within SEM: the PMM and the SEM Support Programme (PASEM).

Regarding this policy issue, many actors are interested in advancing this project. Firstly, there are those governmental authorities seeking to provide a sustainable framework for their goals vis-à-vis bottlenecks generated by the lack of continuous funding. Secondly, HEIs are motivated to strengthen ties with the EU so as to foster linkages with European institutions, reproducing a traditional – and highly asymmetric – practice of international cooperation. This complex net of material resources and highly valued reputation from the EU is attractive to both actors, and generates a newer version of an older path which now focuses on fostering bonds among LAC institutions and even the Global South based upon horizontal cooperation and mutual recognition. More recently the EU has retuned its actions within the region and is now adopting a more trenchant approach. However, as problems regarding recognition of studies undertaken abroad (within the region) hinder advancements in mobility, accreditation policy is in focus again.

In the case of AQA, MERCOSUR has managed to shape its own model of regional policy, even though it is possible to detect some emulation mechanisms during the negotiation of the policy. The latter refers to the fact that the EU tried to influence 'good practices' that were being developed at home; that is to say, in order to fulfil the goal of free labour (professionals) mobility, the first step was to have recognition of diplomas as well as agreements of mutual recognition between professional associations.[10] In order to do so, 'best practice' was the proposal to establish a harmonized degree structure and apply the system of credit transfers and a regional (that is, international) AQA agency. However, the path chosen by SEM neither undertook the structural reform of the degrees nor advanced the creation of an international agency.

Nevertheless, renewed discourses about the need to learn from Bologna and the accreditation process are present in SEM's bodies. During the creation of MEXA and its transformation into ARCU-SUR, RANA officials could mediate and manage the influence of the EU (that was backed up by offers of huge amounts of funding); currently RANA has hired a consultant to analyse the AQA procedure that has in turn installed the 'Bologna Yes' debate again. In order to understand this situation, it must be noted, firstly, that national delegates of member states have changed, especially in countries that lead the process (Argentina is the paradigmatic example), and these changed bureaucratic interests are more likely to accept the Bologna package. Secondly, the associated states that are currently participating in the regional agenda have highly privatized HE systems (Peru, Colombia, Chile) and also have signed FTAs with many developed countries, including the US and the EU. Such 'Open Method of Coordination (OMC) Plus' agreements include provisions for the liberalization of HE services. As a result, the MERCOSUR 'brandmark' regarding AQA policy is being challenged by the strong influence of how national and regional actors perceive the EU. This situation, and the peculiarities highlighted in the mobility of policy, are leading to what might be described as the Bolognization of MERCOSUR.

CHALLENGES TO REGULATORY REGIONALISM PROMPTED BY MERCOSUR

The landscape of LAC regionalism – and in particular, South America – challenges many of the projects that result from MERCOSUR's regulatory regionalism. The way these tensions are channelled has led to the reconfiguration of actors and interests and may well introduce changes to MERCOSUR's regulatory net.

To begin with, the ALBA-TCP, as Muhr (2011) pinpoints, is a counter-hegemonic regional project and that characterization is important in order to comprehend that in the field of education it has set up the ALBA Education Grand National Programme. Two main policies have been implemented: the University Network for the Peoples of ALBA

(UNIALBA) and the Experimental National University of the Peoples of the South (UNISUR) (Muhr, 2010). Both initiatives have created undergraduate and graduate programmes in medicine, education and the geopolitics of fuel. UNIALBA is organized with a nodal structure for the exchange and mobility of students, professors and officials. UNISUR relies on Venezuela's structure for HE. The underlying principles are solidarity, complementarity, defence, and respect for sovereignty and free self-determination of peoples.

UNASUR, despite its dynamism regarding health policies, has not advanced much in the field of education. A South American Council of Education created in 2013 from the previous Council of Education, Culture, Science, Technology and Innovation (2010) has only pointed out that actions to converge with MERCOSUR are to be fulfilled. The policy area that is targeted is quality assurance, and the need to converge relates to the fact that UNASUR parties are almost the same as MERCOSUR's composition if we consider both member and associated states, except for Guyana and Suriname.

In the case of CELAC, HE initiatives are bound to the bi-regional forum: in 2013 the first Academic Summit EU–CELAC was pursued in Santiago de Chile so as to reinforce the Euro-Latin American space. The Declaration of Santiago on University Cooperation in HE, Science, Technology and Innovation and Proposals to Chief of State and Government of EU–CELAC Summit highlights issues such as social inclusion, quality education, accreditation and degree recognition, professional permits for work, development of basic and applied research, linkages with the environment and university–private sector partnerships. These topics are also present in other bi-regional agreements involving the EU. However, one novelty of the current state of negotiations is that the LAC region has created a network: the Association of Rectors of LAC Universities (ACRULAC) which is currently formulating an Action Plan to present to CELAC authorities.

Finally, the Pacific Alliance is implementing the policy coordination of national actions in the mobility of students, professors and researchers. In fact, a Platform of Mobility has established a scholarship programme between Mexico, Colombia, Chile and Peru. Since its creation in 2013, 444 exchanges have been granted: 29 per cent Mexico, 35 per cent Chile, 18 per cent Colombia, and 18 per cent Peru; 87 per cent of the grants were for undergraduate students and 13 per cent were for Doctoral and research exchanges. All in all, the Alliance's strategy is to make visible unilateral actions within the regional framework; which is different from building a regional policy.

As is clear from this complex map, by unpacking regionalist projects we can see a scenario of tensions and reactions to MERCOSUR's regulatory regionalism; the ALBA-TCP is the most radical case, and it is not fully complementary to other cases. It is interesting to highlight that MERCOSUR member states have settled national policies that are related to the Venezuelan case and therefore could be a starting point for deepening ALBA education actions. However, there is a disconnection between advancement in terms of accession to rights and inclusion of national policies for HE at the domestic level (MERCOSUR member states), and the agenda for the delivery of regional policies in MERCOSUR mainly focused on mobility and AQA.

UNASUR represents an overlapping case: the regional agenda is trying to cope with MERCOSUR's policies. This situation does not yet pose risks to Project 2 discussed above, as conflicts are being negotiated through MERCOSUR where currently five members have a definitive voice. However, within UNASUR, Argentina loses its capacity to influence other actors and to lead the project, unlike in the case of MERCOSUR, where Argentina is a key promoter of policy delivery.

CELAC and the Alliance challenge MERCOSUR's trends (discussed in Project 2) as they are reinforcing Project 3, which in turn is tightly connected to the EU's overall influence on the region. In the case of CELAC this is more direct: the LAC forum is concentrating on the negotiations with the EU so as to create an HE space between the two regions. The creation of ACRULAC allows us to assess how interested HEIs are in advancing relations with the EU. The Alliance is pursuing a model that relates to the strengthening of HEIs in the world market.

CONCLUSION

In this chapter I have sought to assess how MERCOSUR reconfigures HE governance and, in doing so, bypasses the territorial policy of the state. In fact, national agencies are crafting this net of regulations that affects HE institutions and actors as the result of the development of transnational functions. In order to grasp these phenomena, I largely drew on regulatory regionalism as an approach to understanding region-building.

The process of unpacking MERCOSUR's regulatory regionalism shed light on three contesting projects of HE governance. Each project pursues divergent goals in regionalisms and the regionalization of HE, some complementary and others competing and conflicting. The configuration of actors also varies amongst projects, whilst it must be emphasized that most of them are governmental bureaucracies with little or no influence of other actors. In a scenario that allows the participation of other actors (such as ACRULAC), we might raise questions about both continuities and changes in the three projects. The fact that a broad epistemic community, both global and regional, is still present relates to the strengthening of some trajectories of action.

However, one of the major issues has to do with how the projects are also challenged by recent changes in the LAC landscape of regionalism, especially by the renewed relations of the region with the EU. This situation is highly problematic for MERCOSUR (unlike other RIAs) because its main project (the MERCOSUR 'brandmark') rejects, at least partially, the perception that the EU is a role model to imitate. Discordant voices with the EU process are being left aside too often at present, which represents a potential drawback to the creation of an autonomous path to regionalizing AQA policies. This scenario leads to the uneven development of the HE sector within the region, and may be placed under even greater pressure if MERCOSUR decides to follow the Pacific Alliance path in regionalizing HE.

NOTES

1. It was created in 1991 by the Asunción Treaty between Argentina, Brazil, Paraguay and Uruguay. The first addition as a member state is Venezuela, since 2012.
2. The area of teacher training is the newest (it dates from 2011). The work within this area is supported by the SEM Support Programme (PASEM), which was created as a result of bi-regional cooperation (MERCOSUR–EU); that is, it is funded by the EU. While its creation was under negotiation, doubts were raised about whether it should be 'a sector' itself or under the CRC-HE instead (as teacher training in Brazil is performed in the university sector). In the end it was created as a separate sector.
3. Data obtained from Ministry of Education of Argentina, http://portales.educacion.gov.ar/spu/cooperacion-internacional/cooperacion_multilateral/mercosur-educativo/ (accessed 11 September 2014).
4. The initiative to create an RSHE was first placed in the regional negotiation arena at the XXXII RME (June 2007). Later on, the 'Conceptual Document about the RSHE' was approved during the XXXIV RME (December 2008).
5. Linked to the genesis of the creation of the NUCLEO, two processes are highlighted: first, the creation of a MERCOSUR Center for Training and Research in Meteorology, proposal approved at the XXIX RME; second, the proposal to create a MERCOSUR Institute of Advanced Studies (IMEA) followed by the discussion to create a University of MERCOSUR. The latest initiative never materialized because in the same year (2007) Brazil unilaterally began the implementation of the IMEA in Foz-do-Iguacu (as a result of an agreement between the Federal University of Parana and Itaipu Binational). This situation led to discontent among the partners. Nevertheless, Brazil created the Federal University of Latin American Integration (Universidade Federal da Integração Latino-Americana, UNILA). It was endorsed by law in 2010.
6. It must be noted that there are at least two ways to fulfil the goal of professional mobility: (a) centralized regulation (vertical approach); and (b) mutual recognition of regulatory frameworks (horizontal approach). The former requires a harmonization process where new standards are agreed and national standards are to be changed in order to fulfil the centralized premise. This process of harmonization relates to

regulatory convergence as the goal is to assure the equivalence of technical standards, professional qualification and licensing requirements. This is the case with the EU. The latter approach is based upon the idea of acceptance among jurisdictions that their professional regulatory system meets certain standards. As a result, it is built around the cooperation between professional bodies and/or governments (Sá and Gaviria, 2011: 309–310).
7. In order to comprehend the main characteristics of the AQA regional policy, the varied ways in which the policy attempts to tackle structural and regulatory asymmetries between HE systems should be acknowledged; the different academic cultures and university traditions of each country; and the divergent capacities of the governmental agencies (financial resources, human resources, power resources). These elements provide us with an understanding of the process of domestic change (Perrotta, 2013c).
8. However, since 2012, a project to create a national AQA agency is being discussed at the parliamentary level.
9. Recall Börzel and Risse's (2009, 2011) arguments about the mechanisms of direct influence exerted by the EU on other countries: (a) physical or legal coercion; (b) manipulating utility calculations by offering incentives (positive or negative); (c) socialization; (d) persuasion.
10. It must be mentioned that in 1995 the bi-regional framework agreement was signed and the EU was advocating for its own regional integration model within a context of competence with the US, which had initiated negotiations for the creation of a Free Trade Area of the Americas (FTAA). In the case of cooperation activities regarding universities, see Perrotta (2008).

REFERENCES

Börzel, T. and Risse, T. (2009), Diffusing (Inter-) Regionalism. The EU as a Model of Regional Integration. Working Paper, KFG The Transformative Power of Europe, 26. www.transformeurope.eu.
Börzel, T. and Risse, T. (2011), From Europeanisation to Diffusion: Introduction. *West European Politics*, **35**(1), 1–19.
Caetano, G., Vazquez, M. and Ventura, D. (2009), Reforma institucional del MERCOSUR: análisis de un reto. In G. Caetano (ed.), *La reforma institucional del MERCOSUR. Del diagnóstico a las propuestas*, Montevideo: Trilce, pp. 21–77.
Hameiri, S. and Jayasuriya, K. (2011), Regulatory Regionalism and the Dynamics of Territorial Politics: The Case of the Asia-Pacific Region. *Political Studies*, **59**, 20–37.
Jayasuriya, K. and Robertson, S.L. (2010), Regulatory Regionalism and the Governance of Higher Education. *Globalisation, Societies and Education*, **8**(1), 1–6.
Muhr, T. (2010), Counter-Hegemonic Regionalism and Higher Education for All: Venezuela and the ALBA. *Globalisation, Societies and Education*, **8**(1), 39–57.
Muhr, T. (2011), Conceptualising the ALBA-TCP: Third Generation Regionalism and Political Economy. *International Journal of Cuban Studies*, **3**(2–3), 98–115.
Perrotta, D. (2008), La cooperación en MERCOSUR: el caso de las universidades. *Temas*, **54**, 67–76.
Perrotta, D. (2011), Integración, Estado y mercado en la política regional de la educación del MERCOSUR. *Puente @ Europa*, **9**(2), 44–57.
Perrotta, D. (2013a), La integración regional como objeto de estudio. De las

teorías tradicionales a los enfoques actuales. In Elsa Llenderrozas (ed.), *Teoría de Relaciones Internacionales*, Buenos Aires: Editorial de la Universidad de Buenos Aires (EUDEBA), pp. 197–252.

Perrotta, D. (2013b), La vieja nueva agenda de la educación en el MERCOSUR. *Densidades*, **13**, 43–76.

Perrotta, D. (2013c), MERCOSUR Brand: Regionalism and Higher Education. Paper presented at Regionalism, Norm Diffusion and Social Policy: Dealing with Old and New Crises in Europe and Latin America, Frei Universitat Berlin.

Phillips, N. (2001), Regionalist Governance in the New Political Economy of Development: 'Relaunching' the Mercosur. *Third World Quarterly*, **22**(4), 565–583.

Riggirozzi, P. and Tussie, D. (2012), The Rise of Post-Hegemonic Regionalism in Latin America. In P. Riggirozzi and D. Tussie (eds), *The Rise of Post-Hegemonic Regionalism: The Case of Latin America*, Vol. 4, Dordrecht: Springer, pp. 1–16.

Robertson, S. (2009a), The EU, 'Regulatory State Regionalism' and New Modes of Higher Education Governance. Paper presented at the panel 'Constituting the Knowledge Economy: Governing the New Regional Spaces of Higher Education' de la Conferencia de la International Studies Association realizada en New York, New York. http://www.bris.ac.uk/education/people/academicStaff/edslr/publications/slr30.

Robertson, S. (2009b), The EU, 'Regulatory State Regionalism' and New Modes of Higher Education Governance. Paper presented at the conference on Constituting the Knowledge Economy: Governing the New Regional Spaces of Higher Education, New York. http://www.bris.ac.uk/education/people/academicStaff/edslr/publications/slr30.

Robledo, R. and Caillón, A. (2009), Procesos regionales en educación superior. El mecanismo de acreditación de carreras universitarias en el MERCOSUR. Reconocimiento regional de los títulos y de la calidad de la formación. *Educación Superior y Sociedad*, **14**(1), 73–97.

Sá, C. and Gaviria, P. (2011), How Do Professional Mutual Recognition Agreements Affect Higher Education? Examining Regional Policy in North America. *Higher Education Policy*, **24**, 307–330.

12. South–South development cooperation and the socio-spatial reconfiguration of Latin America–Caribbean regionalisms: university education in the Brazil–Venezuela 'Special Border Regime'

Thomas Muhr*

INTRODUCTION

This chapter approaches the changing geometries of Latin America–Caribbean regionalisms through the lens of South–South cooperation and the role of university education in the construction of a Brazil–Venezuela cross-border sub-region termed 'Special Border Regime'. Within the general reintensification of South–South cooperation in the geographical area, I concentrate on the Brazil–Venezuela official development cooperation between 2003 and 2015 and the transformation of the Southern Common Market (MERCOSUR) in relation to the Bolivarian Alliance for the Peoples of Our America – Peoples' Trade Agreement (ALBA-TCP), to argue that a South–South cooperation counter-space is being produced in which university education is sought to be re-established as a fundamental right and state responsibility.

With the conclusion of the Venezuelan government's 12-month *pro tempore* presidency of the MERCOSUR in July 2014, a Joint Declaration for the 'promotion of the establishment of a Complementary Economic Zone' was issued among the member states of MERCOSUR, the ALBA-TCP, Petrocaribe and the Caribbean Community (CARICOM). Governed by the South–South cooperation principles of complementarity, solidarity and cooperation, established as such by the Group of 77 Charter of Algiers of 1967, this zone avowedly seeks the promotion of 'inter-dependent' and 'integral' development, 'fair trade' and 'productive integration', to reduce 'economic asymmetries', 'poverty' and 'social exclusion' (MERCOSUR, 2014a, 2014b). As the outcome of ten consecutive summits in the respective regional fora between February 2012 and July 2014, this announcement accentuates the profound reconfiguration of the geometries of Latin America–Caribbean regionalisms since the turn of the millennium, manifest in the emergence of a third generation of de-colonialist and counter-imperialist regionalisms: the ALBA-TCP/ Petroamérica (Petroandina, Petrocaribe, Petrosur),[1] the Union of South American Nations (UNASUR), the Community of Latin American and Caribbean States (CELAC), and the transforming MERCOSUR and CARICOM, from second to third generation regionalisms. By drawing on Söderbaum and van Langenhove (2006), I have conceptualized the first generation of Latin America–Caribbean regionalisms as state-led, inward-oriented, modernization-driven, related to the import substitution industrialization development model; the second generation as outward-oriented (so-called 'open') regionalisms within global processes of neoliberalization; and the third generation as post-neoliberal counter-hegemonic projects constructed jointly by states and social forces, drawing from neostructuralist and socialist theory within a South–South cooperation rationale (Muhr, 2011b; also, Ojeda, 2010).[2] The notion of generations (rather than waves or phases) underscores that patterns of regionalisms with different empirical qualities can coexist and overlap and that regionalisms may evolve from previous generations through processes of transformation linked to distinct political economic (that is, ideological) projects.

Frequently described as separate, incompatible and/or competing projects,[3] the analytical lens of South–South cooperation in conjunction with a socio-spatial methodology, however, reveals the commonalities, interrelatedness and convergence of these third generation regionalisms. As I discuss in greater detail elsewhere, South–South cooperation as an idea, social practice and multidimensional set of processes has in Latin America–Caribbean been reinvigorated in its 'Cold War' spirit (see Sá e Silva, 2009) by the governments of Cuba (with the launch of the Integral Health Programme for Central America and the Caribbean in 1998 and the creation of the Latin American School of Medicine, ELAM, in 1999), Venezuela (from 1999, with the presidency of Hugo Rafael Chávez Frías) and Brazil (from 2003, with the presidency of Luis Inácio Lula da Silva): as more horizontal (egalitarian and just, at times – but not necessarily – altruistic) diplomatic, trade, aid and investment relations and exchanges of mutual benefit and for national and collective self-reliance, self-determination and independence, to liberate the (semi-)periphery from the exploitative unequal terms of trade with the core while strengthening its political autonomy within the (neo)colonial and imperialist global system, historically associated with the United Nations New International

Economic Order (Muhr, 2016). In contrast to North–South official development assistance, South–South cooperation seeks a more integral and holistic approach to development across such areas as agriculture, culture, economy, education, energy, environment, finance, food, health, infrastructure, knowledge, law, military, production and the humanitarian (Lengyel and Malacalza, 2011; Mawdsley, 2012).

This chapter approaches these changing geometries of Latin America–Caribbean regionalisms through the role of university education[4] in the construction of the Southern Venezuela–Northern Brazil Special Border Regime. Central to the analysis is the transformation of MERCOSUR since 2003, which has received little attention in especially the Anglophone literature that tends to take MERCOSUR as a static project. While elsewhere I have analysed the socio-spatial intertwinednesss of the ALBA-TCP and UNASUR (Muhr, 2008, 2011a), throughout this chapter I use the case of Brazil–Venezuela South–South cooperation to illuminate the socio-spatial convergence of the 'new' MERCOSUR and the ALBA-TCP, as has become explicit in the imminent creation of the Complementary Economic Zone. These socio-spatial reconfigurations of Latin America–Caribbean regionalisms produce a South–South cooperation 'counter-space' (Lefebvre, 1991) in which, *inter alia*, university education is becoming re-established as a fundamental right and state responsibility.[5]

METHODOLOGICAL NOTES

Regions are here understood as socially constructed rather than geographically designated 'self-evident blocks of terrestrial space' (Agnew, 2013: 12), and the concept of 'region' denominates an inter- or supra-national unit, while a 'sub-region' is produced through interlinkages and interdependencies across state borders involving sub-national units of governance (Fawn, 2009: 11). A relational rather than absolute methodology thus theorizes space as produced through interrelations and interactions, that is, through strategic alliances or competition and conflict among different classes, class fractions or groups representative of classes at and across different spatial scales within the national territories (state and society) as well as inter- and transnationally (regionally and globally) in the 'struggle for (and in) space' (Lefebvre, 1991: 56). Since social relations of solidarity and reciprocity, together with redistribution, are distinctly different to capitalist exchange (Polanyi, 2001 [1944]; Gibson-Graham, 2006: Chapter 3), the shared social practices, relations and processes of South–South cooperation produce what Henri Lefebvre calls a 'counter-space'. Moreover, as '*[s]ocial spaces interpenetrate one another and/or superimpose themselves upon one another'* (Lefebvre, 1991: 86, italics original), a socio-spatial analysis captures the co-existence of different development projects (capitalist and the emerging socialist) within and across Latin American–Caribbean territories in the present conjuncture. The multidimensionality of South–South cooperation, however, requires going beyond the political economic associated with class (the forces and relations of production) in an analysis of counter-spatiality to simultaneously consider natural, social, political, economic, gender, environmental and cultural relations, flows and connectivities (Massey, 1994: 4; Harvey, 1996: Chapter 4). Finally, a socio-spatial analysis means neither to repudiate the state nor to discard national territorial space and state power over that space, which is of primary relevance for instance with respect to national legislation and intergovernmental cooperation through which processes and projects as analysed in this chapter can either be supported or contested (e.g., Agnew, 1994; Brenner and Elden, 2009; Moisio and Paasi, 2013; Paasi, 2012; Varró and Langendijk, 2013).

PRODUCING A SOUTH–SOUTH COOPERATION COUNTER-SPACE: BRAZIL–VENEZUELA OFFICIAL COOPERATION IN THE CONTEXT OF THE ALBA-TCP AND MERCOSUR[6]

Created by Cuban and Venezuelan presidents Castro and Chávez in 2004, the ALBA-TCP constitutes the first formalization of South–South cooperation at the regional scale in the twenty-first century. Throughout the 2000s, the South–South discourse and practices of solidarity, complementarity, cooperation and reciprocity, which govern the ALBA-TCP, became inter- and transnationalized as well as institutionalized through the Venezuelan government's leadership, however, in dialectical relation with politically like-minded social and political forces at different scales (Muhr, 2010b: Table 1). In the course of this, cooperation among Brazilian and Venezuelan state and non-state actors started with the Recife Accord (Acta de Recife) of 25 April 2003, became consolidated as a 'strategic alliance' from 2005 (e.g., Bolivarian Republic of Venezuela and Federative Republic of Brazil, 2005), and intensified from September 2007 (Lula da Silva's second term in office) with the institution of quarterly presidential meetings.[7] Accordingly, while between 2003 and 2007 Brazil–Venezuela intergovernmental cooperation was principally framed by the (then predominantly neoliberal) rationales of MERCOSUR, the Andean Community, the Initiative for the Integration of Regional Infrastructure in South America (IIRSA) and the Inter-American Development Bank, by

2008 a discursive shift had occurred as the principles of solidarity, complementarity, cooperation and reciprocity became internalized in the bilateral cooperation discourse.[8]

Concomitantly, after entering into crisis in the late 1990s, the revitalization of MERCOSUR from 2003 on has involved a reconstruction of the originally neoliberal initiative by the 'new left' governments of Argentina and Brazil (both entering office in 2003) and Uruguay (from 2005), in relation to the adhesion of the Bolivarian Republic of Venezuela as a full member in 2006 (MERCOSUR, 2006a), with the explicit objective of 'reconstructing' the neoliberal project (RBV, 2007: 48), and the Plurinational State of Bolivia in 2012 (in the process of ratification by the member states at the time of writing in 2015) (MERCOSUR, 2012c). Despite full ratification in 2012 only, from 2006 on Venezuela transcended the mere status of associate member and started participating in such meetings as the 32nd Meeting of the Education Ministers, in which the accreditation of careers and the mutual recognition of titles were discussed (MERCOSUR, 2007). In this process of transformation, the objective of 'overcoming neoliberalism' (MERCOSUR, 2006b: Point 3) became associated with the multidimensional, integral development approach of South–South cooperation as the principles of solidarity, complementarity (related to the creation of productive synergies) and cooperation (with respect to production, technology and knowledge transfer) were adopted (e.g., MERCOSUR, 2005a, 2006a, 2006b, 2012a, 2012b, 2012d).

This is important, as historically MERCOSUR, as a second generation regionalism little more than a customs union and export platform, had been dominated by the interests of transnational capitalist class fractions: in the 1990s, MERCOSUR was a highly uneven project with activities concentrated in 20 per cent of its territorial space and 14 of its approximately 500 major cities, predominantly in the coastal (or nearby) areas of southern Brazil, southern Paraguay, Uruguay and north-central Argentina; 60–80 per cent of the intra-regional trade occurred within industrial chains controlled by capitalist multi- or transnational corporations (Britto García, 2009: 125). The 'paradigm shift' in MERCOSUR (Briceño Ruiz, 2012), associated with neostructuralist theory that remobilizes the state as an actor in development planning, financing and coordination for repayment of the 'social debt' (e.g., Federative Republic of Brazil, 2007a; MINCI, 2004; Sunkel, 1993), has been summed up thus:

> Mercosur stopped being just a free trade agreement ... the new governments aimed to find a new way to respond to the realities of the global economy in which the social and productive dimensions complement trade ... the new social institutions designed in the 2000s aimed to transform the regional bloc

into a space in which to coordinate social policies and promote a social and compassionate economy. (Briceño Ruiz, 2012: 175)

The idea of 'solidarity economy' (MERCOSUR, 2006b: Point 12) became consolidated in the Strategic Plan for Social Action (MERCOSUR, 2012a: 63), which frames the Social and Solidarity Economy for Regional Integration programme financed through the MERCOSUR Structural Convergence Fund (Fondo para la Convergencia Estructural del MERCOSUR, FOCEM). Operational since 2006, and although still small in scale, by the end of 2012 FOCEM had approved funding for more than 40 projects in housing, transport, energy, productive integration (chains and networks), biosecurity, capacity-building, sanitation and education (MERCOSUR, 2012b). As in the ALBA-TCP, micro, small and medium-sized community-based enterprises and co-operatives are particularly promoted. Thus the Social and Solidarity Economy for Regional Integration programme seeks to counter the uneven development produced by capitalist surplus extraction through public policies regarding human rights, healthcare, education, culture (indigenous peoples), production and socio-labour (informal labour) (MERCOSUR, 2012a: 45–68; Ferraro, 2013), to 'contribute to the reduction of the severe social, economic, productive and commercial asymmetries, contain the rural exodus (of especially young people), [and] restrain contraband and labour exploitation' in the historically marginalized border zones.[9] The Southern Venezuela–Northern Brazil border zone is a declared priority area (Federative Republic of Brazil, 2007a: 15; 2007b: 37; Presidência da República, 2003: 7–8; 2007; RBV, 2001: 93; 2007).

The consecutive MERCOSUR Education Sector (Sector Educativo del MERCOSUR, SEM) Plans echo these shifts: although the 2000 Plan's third Strategic Objective refers to 'solidarity cooperation' (MERCOSUR, 2000: 4), this principle became specified and consolidated only in the subsequent two Plans, in which solidarity connotes 'support . . . to those countries that under certain particular conditions cannot entirely or only partially comply with a project or other activity of interest to them' (MERCOSUR, 2005b: 13; 2011: 11), and cooperation refers to the existing intra-Mercosur asymmetries and differences (MERCOSUR, 2005b: 13; 2011: 11).

Although the strategic objectives have not essentially changed over time, the Plans have become increasingly framed by the crisis of global capitalism and Latin America–Caribbean independence (MERCOSUR, 2011), calling for 'profound structural change' (MERCOSUR, 2005b: 5). While the construction of a MERCOSUR 'education space' (MERCOSUR, 2011: 4) assumes a strategic role in regional integration in all three Plans, the purpose of education for 'competitiveness' (MERCOSUR, 2000: 2) has been removed from the 2005 and 2011 Plans. Similarly, neoliberal 'human resources' formation (MERCOSUR, 2000: 4) has become superseded by 'human development' (MERCOSUR, 2005b: 10, 2011: 13). This is implicitly related to the critical question of what education for what development: while the 2000 Plan follows the hegemonic 'education for all' agenda by narrowly focusing on formal education and restricting the right to education to 'basic education' (primary and medium) (MERCOSUR, 2000: 4), the subsequent Plans consider modalities such as adult and non-formal education (MERCOSUR, 2005b: 11) while reclaiming education as a 'human right and public and social good' (MERCOSUR, 2011: 4), *inter alia* through a 'democratization' of higher education at the undergraduate level, particularly to strengthen local and regional productive networks (MERCOSUR, 2011: 46). As in Venezuela and the ALBA-TCP education space, this integral approach to education, which links education to local socio-productive development whilst promoting education at all levels and modalities equally (Muhr, 2010a), is materializing in MERCOSUR through such strategies as the planned implementation of literacy and post-literacy campaigns and the creation of a MERCOSUR distance education university. Although private sector actors per se are not excluded (MERCOSUR, 2011: 67), a redefinition of the role of education in development can be discerned: from an education space originally created within the neoliberal rationale (Gomes et al., 2014: 164–165), towards education for the construction of a productive solidarity economy.

Analogously, the Brazilian and Venezuelan governments inherently reject the reductionist global consensus of primary education for all by adopting an integral, systemic vision in which education and development are dialectically interrelated, while countering the fragmentation of education by, firstly, considering all the different modes as intrinsically connected and reciprocally reinforcing (formal and non-formal, literacy, youth, special needs, vocational, technical and adult education); and secondly, by widening access to all levels of education, from nursery and infant to postgraduate (Federative Republic of Brazil, 2007b; Muhr, 2008, 2011a). Subsequently, as in the ALBA-TCP, 'public education accessible for all sectors of the population' is reclaimed as a 'fundamental human right'; the 'universalization of higher education' is considered essential for promoting the 'self-determination of the peoples', 'shared development' and the 'union of the peoples of the South'; and 'solidarian cooperation and complementarity' among the higher education systems includes academic mobility, joint study centres, courses and research programmes in the mutual interest, and the creation of academic, publishing and dissemination networks, for generating 'human talent' (rather than 'human capital') (Bolivarian Republic of Venezuela and Federative Republic of Brazil, 2008a, 2008b, 2008c).

This discursive shift is matched by increased tertiary gross enrolment: in Brazil, from 17 per cent in 2003 to 29 per cent in 2013 (INEP, 2013), and in Venezuela from 28 per cent in 2000 to 79 per cent in 2008 (UNESCO, 2010) and 82 per cent in 2014 (MPPEU, 2015: 11). While in both countries public universities (federal, state, municipal) are free of charge, and neither government has outlawed private education, the strategies adopted, however, differ substantially. In Venezuela, state expansion through the municipalization of university education has since 2003 involved the creation of the Bolivarian University of Venezuela (UBV) and several non-formal missions, above all Misión Sucre and Misión Alma Mater, the latter of which has meant the transformation of 29 state-financed university institutes and colleges into national experimental universities, as well as the creation of more than 30 new universities and education institutes. More than 1300 university centres, so-called *aldeas* ('university villages'), were operating in educational institutions, prisons, military garrisons and libraries in all 335 municipalities in 2013 (MPPEU 2014a: 2305–2306), as part of the effort of transforming the uneven development geographies. Thus, the share of private sector gross enrolment, which rose from 27 per cent in 1989 to 44 per cent in 1998 (when Chávez was first elected), was reduced to 28 per cent in 2008 and is stated at 23 per cent in 2012 (as compared to 65 per cent public and 12 per cent autonomous) (Muhr, 2011a, Table 5.5; MPPEU, 2012). In Brazil, in contrast, massifying tertiary education has been achieved through increased privatization and commodification. There, private sector gross enrolment was at an already high 60 per cent in 1995 and 70 per cent in 2002 (when Lula da Silva was first elected), rose to 75 per cent in 2008 (Gomes et al., 2014: Table 9.3), and minimally decreased to 74 per cent in 2011 (calculation based on INEP, 2014). Nonetheless, as has been argued, the Lula da Silva government's effort of reversing the neoliberal trend has involved strengthening the state sector through recomposing and increasing the public sector budget, and the creation of 14 new state universities alongside more than 50 campuses linked to existing federal universities and 78 new federal professional and technical colleges (Gomes et al., 2014: 175–177).

In addition, private sector regulation has been reinforced within the University for All Programme (Programa Universidade para Todos), and anti-elitist policies have involved the introduction of a quota system to reduce race-class (as interrelated and mutually reinforcing dimensions of) discrimination in access to public universities, while students in order to be eligible for state funding to attend private universities have to come from low-income households and public secondary schools (private school students are excluded from such studentships) (Federative Republic of Brazil, 2007b: 27–30; Gomes et al., 2014: 177; McCowan, 2007; Santos, 2014). While it is easy to dismiss these efforts as potentially ineffective and not far-reaching enough, they nonetheless point to a reclaiming of university education as a state responsibility. The obvious limitations may be explained by the constraints imposed by the overt class struggle in the Brazilian state apparatus since Lula da Silva entering office, manifest for example in Lula da Silva supporting the Venezuelan adhesion to MERCOSUR throughout 2006–2009, blocked however during this period by the Federal Senate despite ratification in the Chamber of Deputies.[10]

While it is certainly the case that the liberalization, privatization and commodification of higher education are 'deeply embedded in the institutional structures' within the Brazilian territory (Gomes et al., 2014: 177), a study of the university education and development transformations in MERCOSUR and Latin America–Caribbean generally requires transcending a Brazil-centrism and viewing national and regional education policies as dialectically produced within the larger reconfigurations of the geometries of regionalisms in the geographical area. In this respect, public university education has not only been strengthened in Venezuela, but in the ALBA-TCP education space generally, manifest in: the creation of the University Network for the Peoples of ALBA (UNIALBA); the progressive recognition of university degrees within the ALBA-TCP education space; an ALBA-TCP scholarship programme from which more than 4000 students from 48 Latin America–Caribbean, African, Asian and Middle Eastern countries have benefited (in 36 Venezuelan universities); the 'Salvador Allende' Latin American School of Medicine (Venezuela) with 2348 students from 42 countries in 2013; the Latin American School of Medicine (ELAM) in Cuba, from which close to 21000 students from 123 countries had graduated in Integral Community Medicine by 2013; and the Latin American Agroecological Institute "Paulo Freire" (IALA), established in Venezuela between the Bolivarian Republic of Venezuela, the Brazilian Landless Movement (MST), and Vía Campesina (Muhr, 2010a; MPPEU, 2014b; ALBA-TCP, 2014). While other examples could be added, it is also noteworthy that gross enrolment in the public sector still appears to dominate in such MERCOSUR members as Argentina and Uruguay, stated at 73 per cent (Argentina, in 2008) and 89 per cent (Uruguay, in 2007) (UNESCO, 2011). The following case study of the construction of the Brazil–Venezuela Special Border Regime exemplifies the ongoing democratization of university education through a state-driven policy of deconcentration from the urban centres (in which the extractive private providers are concentrated) to the entire territories, whilst illuminating the socio-spatial convergence of Latin American–Caribbean regionalisms.

A SPECIAL BORDER REGIME: CREATING CROSS-BORDER SYNERGIES IN UNIVERSITY EDUCATION AND DEVELOPMENT

Historically, the Brazil–Venezuela border area has been an underdeveloped and remote zone, socio-economically characterized by illegal mining and the associated problems, especially contraband, drug trafficking, environmental contamination, (child) prostitution and violation of indigenous rights. With the objective of providing a development alternative while claiming state sovereignty over that area, the cross-border project has been integral to the intergovernmental agenda since the 2003 Recife Accord, and materialized in 2010 with the establishment of the Special Border Regime between the border towns Pacaraima (Municipality of Pacaraima, Roraima state, Brazil) and Santa Elena de Uairén (Municipality of Gran Sabana, Bolívar state, Venezuela) (Bolivarian Republic of Venezuela and Federative Republic of Brazil, 2010a, 2010b). Spatially, however, the sub-region extends to Ciudad Bolívar and Puerto Ordaz in the Venezuelan state of Bolívar and to Boa Vista and Manaus in the Brazilian states of Roraima and Amazonas, respectively. This transnational scale in the South–South counter-space is materially produced through infrastructure projects (a fibre optic connection provided by the Venezuelan state company CANTV; Venezuelan electricity supply to Northern Brazil; road, rail, river and air connections) and trade, financial (mutual opening of state banks on both sides of the border), military, industrial (exchange of knowledge, experience and technology in support of small entrepreneurship and biodiversity), security (training of members of Bolívar state police forces in Roraima) and education relations. Concrete projects include 'endogenous development nuclei', 'binational nuclei of self-sustained development', 'urban endogenous development poles' and 'local production networks', a 'Development Motor District', as well as through imageries such as the 'Amazonas–Orinoquia Axis', the 'Puerto Ordaz–Manaus Axis', 'Linked Border Localities', and a cross-border 'development pole' named the 'International Socialist Commune "Pablo Freire"',[11] governed by 'the principles of complementarity, cooperation and solidarity' (Bolivarian Mayoralty of Gran Sabana, 2010: 156, 159). Although many of especially the socio-productive development projects are at the planning stage and/or under construction only, existing initiatives include a binationally managed agricultural research centre; an International Centre for the Attention of Migrant Women (maltreatment, trafficking) operating in both Pacaraima and Santa Elena de Uairén; efforts to legalize dual nationality; a Local Border Card (Cédula Vecinal Fronteriza) that permits the tax-free cross-border flow of subsistence goods purchased for personal consumption in either of the border towns; a cross-border public transport system; and free-of-charge health and education services mutually accessible on either side of the border. In 2012, school children were crossing the border on a daily basis within the MERCOSUR Twin Border Schools programme.[12]

Since 2004, a university *aldea* has been operating inside the barracks of the Bolivarian Armed Forces near Santa Elena de Uairén (Aldea Universitaria Gran Sabana Fuerte Roraima), which is the largest of several *aldeas* in the municipality of Gran Sabana (Venezuela). The unusual location is explained by the fact that both Santa Elena de Uairén and Pacaraima are territorially demarcated by national parks and indigenous lands, which legally impedes the construction of new buildings, leaving the garrison as the only option. While this contributes to overcoming the separation of the military and the community, the land issue restricts not only the expansion of university activities but border zone development generally. The space constraints, however, have also generated a 'model of university integration', as one interviewee termed it, as six Venezuelan public universities complement each other in the process of municipalization: Misión Sucre, through which UBV programmes are delivered, the National Experimental Polytechnic University of the Armed Forces (Universidad Nacional Experimental Politécnica de la Fuerza Armada Nacional, UNEFA), National Experimental University of Guayana (Universidad Nacional Experimental de Guayana, UNEG), Experimental Pedagogical University Liberator (Universidad Pedagógica Experimental Libertador, UPEL), National Open University (Universidad Nacional Abierta, UNA) and the National Experimental University Simón Rodríguez (Universidad Nacional Experimental Simón Rodríguez, UNESR). With each of these universities offering its own areas of expertise, synergies are generated within the shared vision of forming professionals committed to the community. This is practised, for example, by UNEG providing academic support to development policy-making through workshops. In mid-2012, the *aldea* had about 800 students attending morning, afternoon, evening and weekend classes and, located close to the airport, university education is also provided by air to remote indigenous communities.

Both formal and informal relations have been established between these universities and their public counterparts in Brazil: within an interstate framework (that is, the federal states of Bolívar in Venezuela and Amazonas and Roraima in Brazil) cooperation agreements exist between

UNEG and the Federal University of Amazonas (Universidade Federal do Amazonas, UFAM), the Federal University of Roraima (Universidade Federal de Roraima, UFFR), and Roraima State University (Universidade Estadual de Roraima, UERR); and between UBV Bolívar and the UFAM. Student exchange and academic mobility (visiting professors) is taking place in both directions, in accordance with the principle of complementarity, thus generating transnational synergies: Brazilian students from as far away as Manaus and Boa Vista are attracted by courses that are either not offered in their immediate environments or are subject to access restrictions, such as medicine. According to one interviewee, most of the students of the National Programme of Integral Community Medicine are Brazilian, come to live in Santa Elena de Uairén and Pacaraima, and some stay on after graduation. Venezuelan students may study tourism in the Pacaraima branch of Roraima State University, and the Tourism Department of Boa Vista facilitates placements and internships. Academic mobility includes UNEG staff working in the Pacaraima branch of Roraima State University, joint workshops (knowledge and experience exchange on an annual basis) and language courses. In 2012, there were also students from such countries as Ecuador and Peru studying in this cross-border zone.

CONCLUSIONS

In this chapter I have advocated a socio-spatial approach for the study of the transforming geometries of Latin America–Caribbean regionalisms. The Special Border Regime, as a case study of the socio-spatial convergence of Brazil and Venezuela, and the ALBA-TCP and MERCOSUR, illustrates that these national and regional projects cannot be territorially demarcated from one another as they have become intertwined through the shared social practices, relations and processes (flows and connectivities) of South–South cooperation. Even though South–South cooperation is not a socialist project per se, it nonetheless produces a counter-space within which a socialist project (a socialist space governed by non-capitalist social relations) can evolve, and has been evolving in the form of the ALBA-TCP: while the prevailing historical structure (global capitalism) is not necessarily directly challenged, even in part reproduced through, for instance, direct investment and surplus value extraction, it is simultaneously resisted as an alternative configuration of forces – a rival structure or counter-spatiality – is being produced (see Cox, 1981). A socio-spatial analysis allows us to 'see' not only the intricate intertwinedness, interrelatedness, interdependence and co-constitutive production of the ALBA-TCP and MERCOSUR, but also the simultaneous transformation of other generations of regionalisms through a politics of place, space and scale involving state (potentially 'state-in-revolution') and 'organised society' actors (Muhr, 2008, 2013b). While these processes have been ongoing for more than a decade, the imminent formation of the Complementary Economic Zone among ALBA-TCP/Petrocaribe, CARICOM and MERCOSUR underscores the arguments developed.

The holistic and integral vision of education generally, and the role of university education in the construction of the Special Border Regime in particular, are exemplary of a Latin American–Caribbean counter-hegemonic conception of what university education should look like, and what purpose it should serve. I here suggest that the ongoing transformations present a counter-movement to the oft-stated 'Europeanization of Mercosur' (Azevedo, 2014). After all, policies of mutual recognition of titles and academic mobility do not necessarily imply borrowing from the colonial-imperialist project, but may be necessary in any integration project irrespective of its ideological base; for 'regional citizenship', in this case defined by 'solidarity' for the 'reduction of asymmetries'. Therefore, rather than the 'mandate for higher education' in Latin America–Caribbean being 'regional and global competitiveness' (Gomes et al, 2014: 179), these policies contribute to emancipation, liberation and transformation through South–South cooperation at regional and global scales. This is reiterated in joint statements, such as that of the chancellors of the MERCOSUR member states on the (postponed) MERCOSUR–European Union negotiations, in which the MERCOSUR governments demand the recognition of the 'development differences' among the two parties and 'the right to apply policies that preserve the socially inclusive development models' (MERCOSUR, 2013). This includes, with the increasing convergence of the ALBA-TCP and MERCOSUR education spaces, and despite limitations, the state-driven democratization of university education: its de-privatization and decommodification, and its re-establishment as a fundamental right.

NOTES

* I would like to thank the UK Society for Latin American Studies (SLAS) for support in the form of a postdoctoral travel grant for research in the Brazil–Venezuela border region in 2012.
1. ALBA-TCP and Petroamérica have been theorized as one political project (Muhr 2008, 2011a), which is manifest in shared institutions (e.g., ALBA Bank, ALBA Caribe Fund). They are therefore referred to as ALBA-TCP/Petroamérica and ALBA-TCP/Petrocaribe.

2. I use 'counter-hegemonic' in the Gramscian sense, in contrast to (neo)realist narratives of supposedly 'post-hegemonic' regionalisms. Also, I use 'post-neoliberal' as a historical, periodizing term rather than as a (usually weakly defined, if at all) ideological concept (see Lazarus, 2011: 6), referring to the abandonment of neoliberalism as the dominant 'development' paradigm in Latin America–Caribbean.
3. In Muhr (2013a) I provide a critique of that literature.
4. I follow the Venezuelan government in using 'university' rather than 'higher' education (in Castilian, '*superior*'), as the latter suggests a hierarchization that is incompatible with an integral approach to education that views all levels and modalities of education as complementary and equally important to individual and collective development. Throughout the text, 'university education' is used interchangeably with 'tertiary education'.
5. The arguments presented draw from content and discourse analysis of more than 600 official documents from 2000–2015, including 81 cooperation documents signed among Brazilian and Venezuelan state and non-state actors between 2003 and 2013, municipal, national and regional development plans, and 17 months of ethnographic fieldwork in the emerging South–South cooperation space since 2005, one month of which was in the emerging Special Border Regime in 2012 involving participant observation and 13 semi-structured and open-ended interviews with officials at different levels of the policy-making processes, academics at the Bolivarian University of Venezuela (UBV) Ciudad Bolívar, as well as local-scale actors in distinct cooperation and integration initiatives on both sides of the Brazil–Venezuela border.
6. MERCOSUR was founded in 1991 by the neoliberal governments of the Argentine Republic, Federative Republic of Brazil, Oriental Republic of Uruguay and the Republic of Paraguay. As is detailed below in the text, the Bolivarian Republic of Venezuela and Plurinational State of Bolivia joined as full members in 2006 and 2012, respectively. Associate members are the Republic of Chile, Republic of Colombia, Republic of Ecuador, Republic of Peru, Co-operative Republic of Guyana and Republic of Suriname, the latter two in process of adhesion as full members in 2015. The ALBA-TCP has in 2014 as full members Antigua and Barbuda, Bolivarian Republic of Venezuela, Commonwealth of Dominica, Plurinational State of Bolivia, Republic of Cuba, Republic of Ecuador, Republic of Nicaragua, Saint Vincent and the Grenadines, and Saint Lucia. The 19-member Petrocaribe (created in 2005) can be analysed as a sub-regional integration strategy within the ALBA-TCP (Muhr, 2008, 2011b).
7. According to my own count, in the years 2003–2006 approximately 30 cooperation declarations, conventions, memoranda, agreements, letters of understanding, letters of intent and statutes were signed between the Brazilian and Venezuelan governments and state institutions (banks, companies, foundations, ministries, research institutes, universities, Venezuelan missions), as well as sub-national state and non-state actors and social forces; this increased to (at least) 159 documents between 2007 and the first half of 2013.
8. In a joint Chávez–Lula da Silva press statement of September 2004, three months before the formalization of ALBA, Chávez proposes to use the bilateral strategic alliance to 'promote a solidarity economy' (Bolivarian Republic of Venezuela and Federative Republic of Brazil, 2004: Point 18). The accompanying Business Manifesto sets as its targets 'true measures of cooperation, complementation and social inclusion, taking into account the asymmetries among the economies of both countries' (Entrepreneurs of the Bolivarian Republic of Venezuela and Federative Republic of Brazil, 2004). Reference to the ALBA-TCP norms was made as early as in 2005 (see Corporación Venezolana de Guayana and Companhia Vale do Rio Doce, 2005). A hybrid discourse during that period simultaneously promotes South–South cooperation while emphasizing the 'fundamental' role of neoliberal projects in Latin America–Caribbean integration, especially the Community of South American Nations (which became reconstituted as UNASUR in 2008) (Bolivarian Republic of Venezuela and Federative Republic of Brazil, 2005). The stated discursive shift coincides with Chávez's and Lula da Silva's institution of quarterly meetings, as from then on the discourse became

framed by the South–South cooperation principles and ALBA-TCP concepts associated with the construction of socialism, such as 'integral development' and '*el buen vivir*' (the good living) through a 'communal', 'solidarian' or 'social economy'; concepts that have also become internalized in the MERCOSUR discourse.
9. See http://ismercosur.org/proyectos/economia-social-y-solidaria/ (accessed 2 June 2014).
10. This relates to general criticisms of the Lula da Silva government not having implemented a 'real' development alternative. However, besides the still prevailing extreme heterogeneity within the government (now also Dilma Rousseff's) and the Workers' Party within the coalition governments since 2003, until 2005 the government was constrained by an International Monetary Fund (IMF) agreement signed by the preceding Cardoso administration shortly before exiting. This is underscored by the fact that key development plans were only published towards the end of Lula de Silva's first term, such as the National Policy for Regional Development and the Plan for the Development of Education (Federative Republic of Brazil, 2007a, 2007b), suggesting that the first administrative period principally served the mere conception of alternatives to neoliberalism. After payment of the multilateral debts and cancellation of the IMF agreement, 'alliances with regional and international powers that could counter imperial power' were viewed as conducive to implementing 'structural reforms' and a 'new development path' in the domestic sphere (Mineiro, 2014).
11. The *Commune* is the central organizational unit of state–society restructuring in Venezuela.
12. Schools have become transnationally twinned in the Brazil–Argentine border zone since 2005, the Brazil–Paraguay and Brazil–Uruguay borders since 2008, and the Brazil–Venezuela border zone since 2009. The original mission of providing bilingual and intercultural education, however, has been extended with the MERCOSUR 2011 Education Plan, aiming for these twin schools to become organically embedded within the wider, integral processes of cross-border economic and productive, social and infrastructural integration (Bolivarian Republic of Venezuela and Federative Republic of Brazil, 2009; MERCOSUR, 2005b; 2011: 16, 31–32).

REFERENCES

Agnew, J.A. (1994), 'The territorial trap: the geographical assumptions of international relations theory', *Review of International Political Economy*, **1**(1), 53–80.
Agnew, J.A. (2013), 'Arguing with regions', *Regional Studies*, **47**(1), 6–17.
ALBA-TCP (2014), ALBA-PTA Management Report 2004–2014, '10 Years Consolidating Solidarity and Integration among the Peoples of Our America', Executive Secretariat, del ALBA, http://alba-tcp.org/public/documents/decimo/English/Management_report.pdf.
Azevedo, M.L.N. de (2014), 'The Bologna Process and higher education in Mercosur: regionalization or Europeanization', *International Journal of Lifelong Education*, **33**(3), 411–427.
Bolivarian Mayoralty of Gran Sabana (2010), *Plan Estratégico de Desarrollo Municipio*, Gran Sabana, Santa Elena de Uairén, June.
Bolivarian Republic of Venezuela/Federative Republic of Brazil (2004), *Declaración de Prensa Conjunta en Ocasión del Encuentro de los Presidentes de la República Federativa del Brasil, Luiz Inácio da Silva, y de la República Bolivariana de Venezuela, Hugo Rafael Chávez Frías*, Manaus, 15 September.
Bolivarian Republic of Venezuela and Federative Republic of Brazil (2005),

Comunicado Conjunto: Alianza Estratégica Venezuela–Brasil, Caracas, 14 February.
Bolivarian Republic of Venezuela and Federative Republic of Brazil (2008a), *Comunicado Conjunto*, Recife, 26 March.
Bolivarian Republic of Venezuela and Federative Republic of Brazil (2008b), *Memorando de Entendimiento entre el Ministerio del Poder Popular para la Educación Superior de la República Bolivariana de Venezuela (MPPES) y el Ministerio de Educación de la República Federativa de Brasil*, Recife, 26 March.
Bolivarian Republic of Venezuela and Federative Republic of Brazil (2008c), *Entendimiento entre el Ministerio del Poder Popular para la Educación Superior de la República Bolivariana de Venezuela (MPPES) y la Fundación de Perfeccionamiento de Personal de Nivel Superior de la República Federativa de Brasil* (CAPES), Recife, 26 March.
Bolivarian Republic of Venezuela and Federative Republic of Brazil (2009), *Comunicado Conjunto de los Presidentes Hugo Chávez Frías y Luiz Inácio Lula da Silva, en Ocasión del Encuentro Presidencial Realizado en el Proyect Agrario Socialista Plancie de Maracaibo*, Maracaibo, 16 January.
Bolivarian Republic of Venezuela and Federative Republic of Brazil (2010a), *Acuerdo entre el Gobierno de la República Bolivariana de Venezuela y el Gobierno de la República Federativa del Brasil sobre Localidades Fronterizas Vinculadas*, Brasilia, 28 April.
Bolivarian Republic of Venezuela and Federative Republic of Brazil (2010b), *Acuerdo entre el Gobierno de la República Bolivariana de Venezuela y el Gobierno de la República Federativa del Brasil para el Establecimiento de un Régimen Especial Fronterizo*, Caracas, 6 August.
Brenner, N. and Elden, S. (2009), 'Henri Lefebvre on state, space, territory', *International Political Sociology*, **3**(4), 353–377.
Briceño Ruiz, J. (2012), 'New left governments, civil society and constructing a social dimension in Mercosur', in B. Cannon and P. Kirby (eds), *Civil Society and the State in Left-led Latin America*, London: Routledge, pp. 173–186.
Britto García, L. (2009), *América Nuestra. Integración y Revolución (vol. II)*, Caracas: Fondo Cultural del ALBA.
Corporación Venezolana de Guayana and Companhia Vale do Rio Doce (2005), *Memorando de Entendimiento entre la Corporación Venezolana de Guayana y Companhia Vale do Rio Doce*, Caracas, 14 February.
Cox, R.W. (1981), 'Social forces, states and world orders: beyond international relations theory', *Millennium: Journal of International Studies*, **10**(2), 126–155.
Entrepreneurs of the Bolivarian Republic of Venezuela and Federative Republic of Brazil (2004), *Manifiesto Empresarial de Manaus*, Manaus, 15 September.
Fawn, R. (2009), "Regions" and their study: where from, what for and where to?', *Review of International Studies*, **35**(S1), 5–34.
Federative Republic of Brazil (2007a), *Política Nacional de Desenvolvimento Regional (Sumário Executivo)*, Brasilia: Ministério da Integração Nacional.
Federative Republic of Brazil (2007b), *The Plan for the Development of Education. Reasons, Principles and Programs*, Brasilia: Ministerio da Edução.
Ferraro, D. (2013), *Políticas e iniciativas en MERCOSUR en el ámbito de la integración fronteriza, SP/XXIV-RDCIALC/Di No. 14-13*, Caracas: SELA.
Gibson-Graham, J.K. (2006) *A Postcapitalist Politics*, Minneapolis, MN: University of Minnesota Press.
Gomes, A.M., Robertson, S.L. and Dale, R. (2014), 'Globalizing and regionalizing

higher education in Latin America', in D. Araya and P. Marber (eds), *Higher Education in the Global Age. Policy, Practice and Promise in Emerging Societies*, London: Routledge, pp. 160–183.
Harvey, D. (1996), *Justice, Nature and the Geography of Difference*, Oxford: Blackwell.
Instituto Nacional de Estudos e Pesquisas (INEP) (2013), 'Censo da educação superior 2013', accessed 8 September 2015 at http://download.inep.gov.br/educacao_superior/censo_superior/apresentacao/2014/coletiva_censo_superior_2013.pdf.
Instituto Nacional de Estudos e Pesquisas (INEP) (2014), 'Sinopses Educação Superior', accessed 12 October 2014 at http://portal.inep.gov.br/superior-censosuperior-sinopse.
Lazarus, N. (2011), 'What postcolonial theory doesn't say', *Race and Class*, 53(1), 3–27.
Lefebvre, H. (1991), *The Production of Space*, transl. by D. Nicholson-Smith, Oxford: Blackwell.
Lengyel, M. and Malacalza, B. (2011), 'What do we talk when we talk about South–South cooperation? The construction of a concept from empirical basis', paper presented at the IPSA–ECPR Joint Conference, São Paulo, 16–19 February, http://www.ctc-health.org.cn/file/2012060833.pdf.
Massey, D. (1994), *Space, Place, and Gender*, Minneapolis, MN: University of Minnesota Press.
Mawdsley, E. (2012), *From Recipients to Donors: Emerging Powers and the Changing Development Landscape*, London: Zed Books.
McCowan, T. (2007), 'Expansion without equity: an analysis of current policy on access to higher education in Brazil', *Higher Education*, 53(5), 579–598.
MERCOSUR (2000), *Plan Estratégico 2001–2005*, http://www.sic.inep.gov.br/es-ES/documentos-categoria/finish/7-planos-planes/411-plano-2001-2005.html.
MERCOSUR (2005a), *Iniciativa de Asunción sobre Lucha contra la Pobreza Extrema*, Asunción, 20 June.
MERCOSUR (2005b), *Plan del Sector Educativo del MERCOSUR 2006–2010*, http://www.sic.inep.gov.br/es-ES/documentos-categoria/finish/7-planos-planes/412-plano-2006-2010.html.
MERCOSUR (2006a), *Protocolo de Adhesión de la República Bolivariana de Venezuela al MERCOSUR*, Caracas, 4 July.
MERCOSUR (2006b), *Declaración Final*, Brasilia, 14 December.
MERCOSUR (2007), *XXXII Reunión de Ministros de Educación de los Países del MERCOSUR*, MERCOSUR/XXXII RME/ACTA No. 01/07, 1 June.
MERCOSUR (2011), *Plan de Acción del Sector Educativo del MERCOSUR 2011–2015*, http://www.sic.inep.gov.br/es-ES/component/jdownloads/finish/7/414.html.
MERCOSUR (2012a), *Plan Estratégico de Acción Social*, Asunción: Instituto Social del MERCOSUR.
MERCOSUR (2012b), *Comunicado Conjunto de los Presidentes de los Estados Partes del MERCOSUR*, Mendoza, 29 June.
MERCOSUR (2012c), *Protocolo de Adhesión del Estado Plurinacional de Bolivia al MERCOSUR*, Brasilia, 7 December.
MERCOSUR (2012d), *Comunicado Conjunto de los Presidentes de los Estados Partes del MERCOSUR*, Brasilia, 7 December.
MERCOSUR (2013), *Comunicado Conjunto de los Cancilleres de los Estados Partes*

del MERCOSUR sobre el Estado Actual de Negociación MERCOSUR – Unión Europea, Caracas, 31 October.
MERCOSUR (2014a), *Declaración Conjunta de los Estados Partes del Mercado Común del Sur (MERCOSUR) para Promover el Establecimiento de una Zona Económica Complementaria entre los Estados Partes del Mercado Común del Sur (MERCOSUR), los Países Miembros de la Alianza Bolivariana para los Pueblos de Nuestra América (ALBA-TCP), los Países Miembros de PETROCARIBE y los Miembros de la Comunidad del Caribe (CARICOM)*, Caracas, 29 July.
MERCOSUR (2014b), *Informe de la Presidencia Pro Témpore Venezolana del MERCOSUR (PPTVEN), July 2013–July 2014, Acta No. 01/14, XLVI Ordinary Meeting of the Council of the Common Market*, Caracas, 28 July.
Mineiro, A. (2014), 'Brazil: from cursed legacy to compromised hope?', TNI Working Paper, July.
Ministerio de Comunicación e Información (MINCI) (2004), *Desarrollo Endógeno. Desde Adentro, Desde la Venezuela Profunda*, Caracas: MINCI.
Ministerio del Poder Popular para la Educación Universitaria (MPPEU) (2012), *Logros de la Educación Universitaria 2012*, Caracas: MPPEU.
Ministerio del Poder Popular para la Educación Universitaria (MPPEU) (2014a), *Memoria 2013*, Caracas: MPPEU.
Ministerio del Poder Popular para la Educación Universitaria (MPPEU) (2014b), *Resolución No. 0023, Gaceta Oficial de la República Bolivariana de Venezuela*, No. 40.350, 6 February.
Ministerio del Poder Popular para la Educación Universitaria (MPPEU) (2015), *Memoria y Cuenta*, Caracas: MPPEU.
Moisio, S. and Paasi, A. (2013), 'Beyond state-centricity: geopolitics of changing state spaces', *Geopolitics*, **18**(2), 255–266.
Muhr, T. (2008), 'Venezuela: Global Counter-Hegemony, Geographies of Regional Development, and Higher Education For All', PhD thesis, University of Bristol, https://www.academia.edu/3343656/Venezuela_Global_Counter-Hegemony_ Geographies_of_Regional_Development_and_Higher_Education_For_All._ University_of_Bristol_2008_.
Muhr, T. (2010a), 'Counter-hegemonic regionalism and higher education for all: Venezuela and the ALBA', *Globalisation, Societies and Education*, **8**(1), 39–57.
Muhr, T. (2010b), 'TINA go home! ALBA and re-theorizing resistance to global capitalism', *Cosmos and History: The Journal of Natural and Social Philosophy*, **6**(2), 27–54.
Muhr, T. (2011a), *Venezuela and the ALBA: Counter-Hegemony, Geographies of Integration and Development, and Higher Education For All*, Saarbrücken: VDM/ Akademikerverlag.
Muhr, T. (2011b), 'Conceptualising the ALBA-TCP: third generation regionalism and political economy', *International Journal of Cuban Studies*, **3**(2–3), 98–115.
Muhr, T. (2013a), 'Rivalry or cooperation? The ALBA-TCP, UNASUR, and Brazil-Venezuela sub-regionalism', paper presented at the ISA CISS with UNU-CRIS, Bruges, Belgium, 19 June, https://www.academia.edu/5000852/ Rivalry_or_Cooperation_The_ALBA-TCP_UNASUR_and_Brazil-Venezuela_ Sub-Regionalism_ISA_CISS_with_UNU-CRIS_Conference_Bruges_Belgium_ 19_June_2013.
Muhr, T. (2013b), 'Counter-globalization and a revolutionary politics of place, space and scale: the transnational construction of the ALBA-TCP in Nicaragua, El Salvador and the USA', in T. Muhr (ed.), *Counter-Globalization and Socialism*

in the 21st Century: the Bolivarian Alliance for the Peoples of Our America, London: Routledge, pp. 46–62.
Muhr, T. (2016), 'Beyond "BRICS": ten theses on South–South cooperation in the 21st century', *Third World Quarterly*, **37**(4), 630–648.
Ojeda, T. (2010), 'La cooperación Sur–Sur y la regionalización en América Latina: el despertar de un gigante dormido', *Relaciones Internacionales*, **15**(October), 91–111.
Paasi, A. (2012), 'Commentary. Border studies reanimated: going beyond the territorial/relational divide', *Environment and Planning A*, **44**(10), 2303–2309.
Polanyi, K. (2001 [1944]), *The Great Transformation*, Boston, MA: Beacon Press.
Presidência da República (2003), *Decree No. 4.793*, 23 July.
Presidência da República (2007), *Decree No. 6.047*, 22 February.
República Bolivariana de Venezuela (RBV) (2001), *Líneas Generales del Plan de Desarrollo Económico y Social de la Nación 2001–2007*, Caracas: RBV.
República Bolivariana de Venezuela (RBV) (2007), *Líneas Generales del Plan de Desarrollo Económico y Social de la Nación 2007–2013*, Caracas: RBV.
Sá e Silva, M.M. (2009), 'South–South cooperation: past and present. Conceptualization and practice', in L. Chisholm and G. Steiner-Khamsi (eds), *South–South Cooperation in Education and Development*, New York: Teachers College Press, pp. 39–59.
Santos, S.A. dos (2014), 'Affirmative action and political dispute in today's Brazilian academe', *Latin American Perspectives*, **41**(5), 141–156.
Söderbaum, F. and van Langenhove, L. (2006), 'Introduction', in F. Söderbaum and L. van Langenhove (eds), *The EU as a Global Player: The Politics of Interregionalism*, London: Routledge, pp. 1–14.
Sunkel, O. (ed.) (1993), *Development from Within*, London: Lynne Rienner.
UNESCO (2010), *Global Education Digest 2010*, Montreal: UNESCO Institute for Statistics.
UNESCO (2011), *Global Education Digest 2011*, Montreal: UNESCO Institute for Statistics.
Varró, K. and Langendijk, A. (2013), 'Conceptualizing the region – in what sense relational?', *Regional Studies*, **47**(1), 18–28.

13. Higher education and new regionalism in Latin America: the UNILA project
Paulino Motter and Luis Armando Gandin

INTRODUCTION

In this chapter we analyse the project of the Federal University of Latin American Integration (UNILA), created in 2010, from the initiative led by President Lula (2003–2010). Its *sui generis* character, which distinguishes it from other Brazilian federal public universities (generally named after the host state, for example the Federal University of Rio de Janeiro, Federal University of Rio Grande do Sul, Federal University of Paraná, and so on), sets out its institutional mission: to contribute to the advancement of Latin American integration. Fully funded by the Brazilian government, UNILA is part of the network of federal public universities, established and maintained by the central government. What sets it apart is its transnational mission, and claims to it being the first Brazilian bilingual (Portuguese and Spanish) university. A further innovation is its openness to teachers, researchers and students from all of the countries of Latin America and the Caribbean.

With this appeal, UNILA has attracted a great deal of interest in the Latin American academic community since its beginning. Inspired by the utopia of an integrated and united Latin America in its diversity and plurality, the establishment of UNILA took place in the wake of the recent efforts of Brazil, the region's largest country and the only one colonized by Portugal, to reconcile with its neighbours in Spanish America after remaining apart throughout its history. In a regional context marked by broad political, economic and social change, Brazil took on a greater role by prioritizing the strengthening of the Southern Common Market (MERCOSUR) and regional integration in its foreign policy, and as a key strategy of integration into the global economy.[1] UNILA can therefore be seen as an initiative driven by these two strategic aims of the Brazilian state.

Historically, the genesis of Latin American universities is closely associated with the process of state formation and the construction of national identity. The commitment of the public university to the national Brazilian project is one of the principles of its legitimacy. In South America, Brazil's universities were developed much later than those of its neighbours. Its first higher education institutions appeared only after the arrival of the Portuguese Royal Family in 1808, and the concept of a university took shape even later, at the beginning of the twentieth century. Therefore, from a historical perspective, how can we understand the Brazilian state's undertaking of UNILA? Does its concept represent a departure from the historical nexus between the nation-state project and the university? How can one overcome the inherent contradictions arising from a university entirely funded by the Brazilian state, whose interests as an emerging regional power could undermine the university's autonomy, which is an indispensable requisite for UNILA to carry out its specific institutional mission?

These are some of the questions at the heart of the debates promoted by the commission set up by the Ministry of Education in 2008; to formulate the project of a university devoted to Latin American integration (IMEA, 2009a). The international call for insights and reflections on the proposal made by the commission that same year brought a wealth of opinions and ideas on the challenge of setting up a 'university with no flag and national borders' (IMEA, 2009b). The challenge of designing a public university along these lines suggests that the Brazilian state envisions regional integration as a long-term strategic goal. Thus, the regional vocation ascribed to UNILA reaffirms the paramount importance that Brazil has given to the integration of Latin America as a condition to fulfil its ambitions as a regional leader and a 'global player'.

Not surprisingly, one of the first challenges that UNILA has had to face in order to achieve recognition and legitimacy in the Latin American academic community is that of eliminating any doubt as to whether its establishment would be part of the intention of Brazil to exercise regional hegemony. The size of the Brazilian economy and the increasing presence of Brazilian private investment in the countries of the region have raised suspicion among its neighbours that Brazil is carrying out a kind of sub-imperialism, reproducing the relations of domination and dependence which have historically linked Latin America to the core countries, especially the United States.

CONCEPTUALIZING REGIONALISMS: OLD AND NEW

The study of regionalism began, for the most part, with a European-centred vision. The case of the European Union is one that inspired the first studies (Breslin et al., 2002b). The new regionalism approach is much more global in its scope and more pluralistic and is also much more directed to the outside than to the inside (Söderbaum, 2003). In addition, what characterizes 'new' regionalisms (as opposed to the 'old' ones), besides the obvious exponential increase in regional agreements, is the fact that the state is not the only actor pursuing the integration agenda. As Breslin et al. (2002a: 17) put it: 'an understanding that state actors are but one set of key agents among potentially many is at the heart of newer approaches'.

Even though we understand the importance of not exaggerating the role of the state, we side with those who, in the study of new regionalisms, take the middle road between a state-centric perspective, on the one hand, and one that does not see any role for national states in these new arrangements, on the other. It is important to point out that the UNILA initiative shows us that both the state and institutions that are relatively autonomous (universities and research institutions) have played a critical role in these forms of new regionalism. The empirical data show in the case that we are considering here it would be a mistake to either over- or underestimate the role of these macro and micro actors in the constitution of a potential new regional arrangement in Latin American higher education.

Yet another crucial cautionary note should be stressed when we talk about regionalisms in different guises. The discourse of new regionalism has been currently populated by a strictly economic and hegemonic approach. Several supra-state global institutions, such as the World Bank, the World Trade Organization (WTO), and the International Monetary Fund (IMF) – the so-called international financial institutions or IFIs – use this discourse to tackle the problem of economic competitiveness and productivity. Being aware of this use, we want to defend the idea that there is another possible way of talking about new regionalisms. Hettne (2003) defines this alternative as the 'new regionalism approach' (NRA) and explains the competing approaches in a passage that defines precisely the major difference between them:

> Whereas for the IFIs, regionalism was a phenomenon that could be analysed through standard economic theory, the NRA contained an interdisciplinary framework. Whereas the IFIs conceived the new regionalism as a trade promotion policy, building on regional arrangements rather than a multilateral framework, for the NRA regionalism was a comprehensive multidimensional programme, including economic, security, environmental and many other issues. Whereas the normative point of view of the IFIs was that regionalism, at best, could be a second-best contribution to the task of increasing the amount of world trade and global welfare, and at worst a threat against the multilateral order, the NRA held that regionalism could contribute to the solving of many

problems, from security to environment, that were not efficiently tackled on the national level and to which there were no market solutions. Whereas the new regionalism according to the IFIs was 'new' only in the sense that it represented a revival of protectionism or neo-mercantilism, the NRA saw the current wave of regionalism as qualitatively new, in the sense that it could only be understood in relation to the transformation of the world economy. (Hettne, 2003: 24–25)

This critical approach to deal with new regionalisms offers a valuable model to analyse the case of UNILA, since it takes into consideration not only an economic view of the relationships between regional actors, but also the cultural, political and social dimensions. Yet a further advantage of the idea of 'new regionalisms' is the fact that it avoids a simplistic notion of globalization and localization. Last but not least, this more critical approach takes into consideration an understanding of contemporary regionalism both from an endogenous perspective, according to which regionalization is shaped from within the region by a large number of different actors, and an exogenous perspective, according to which regionalization and globalization are intertwined articulations involving contradictory as well as complementary global transformations (Hettne, 2003: 26).

The concept of globalization is crucial here though one that has to be used with caution. Rather than assuming a more liberal (or neoliberal) discourse of globalization as the natural form of market expansion, a critical approach to globalization and new regionalisms (one that we incorporate in this chapter) emphasizes the cultural and political and not only the economic in these relations amongst various regional and global actors. In dealing with such a multitude of actors and interactions, this approach rejects a homogenous or top-down concept of globalization and regionalization. As Hettne says: 'regional multilateralism or, in short, multi-regionalism, rejects cultural hegemony and accepts "the desirability of a world order reconstructed to accommodate intercivilizational identities and aspirations" (Falk, 2000: 157)' (Hettne, 2003: 37).

This is crucial to understanding UNILA's approach to dealing with regional integration, not as a way of reaching a 'one-size-fits-all' solution to the problems of the South American countries, but as a means of building and sharing new knowledges and epistemologies. Indeed, universities are crucial for alternative regional integration, and for Boaventura Sousa Santos (2006), this could be addressed at the university level by, amongst many other things, rethinking what 'extension' (or service) means in higher education. He argues that extension activities should be 'designed to address the problems of social exclusion and discrimination in such a way as to give voice to the excluded and discriminated social groups' (ibid.: 86). Not only do the communities have a lot to gain by learning through the university, but universities also need to learn how to listen to these communities and to open up their doors to this alternative form of knowledge. Universities can be a locale where a multiplicity of knowledges dialogue with each other, and can therefore act as enablers for real and authentic democratic integration.

What we have been discussing until now is sufficient to conclude that although universities are key institutions in establishing the indispensable connections to promoting regional dialogue and integration, not all universities will be able to provide the critical approaches required for a counter-hegemonic new regionalism which will include both the new extension approach and the cultivation of an 'ecology of knowledges' from across the Latin American region. This is perhaps the greatest challenge and possibility for UNILA. In Latin America, where there are active social movements that push the limits of common sense on social issues, there is a need to incorporate, without taming or sanitizing them, the kinds of questions being proposed by these emerging actors. This is where UNILA will face challenges in its vocation as a site for diversity, and for critical approaches with a regional scope. Imagining a new regional space, one that establishes the possibility of new political and epistemological alliances, is what is at the heart of UNILA.

A DEMOCRATIC LATIN AMERICA: CHALLENGES, EMERGENCIES AND POSSIBILITIES

As mentioned, UNILA came into life in a regional context of rapid political, economic and social transformations. The re-democratization movement that has taken place in the last two decades, reshaping Latin America's political landscape and bringing about the emergence of reformist and left-leaning governments in almost every country, has turned the region into a space of new participatory possibilities which, in the last few years, have been undercut by seeming intractable social and economic problems. With few exceptions, the so-called progressive governments in the region have not yet delivered on their promises of stable democracy, social inclusion and economic prosperity. On the contrary, economic uncertainties, political instability, inequality, social exclusion and violence continue to be fixtures of most Latin America's countries. But the democratic effervescence that accompanied the arrival of left-wing parties in power in the region has also unleashed an unprecedented process of political activism, social mobilization and participation. It remains to be seen whether this ideological shift toward the left, which followed the neoliberal wave in the 1990s, is losing its strength and beginning a slow movement backwards, motivated by growing popular frustration in the face of the difficulty of the progressive governments in the region fulfilling their promises of change.[2]

The democratic experiments under way in Latin America have brought with them, as one of the main political novelties, the emergence of a new regionalism, which attempts to promote regional integration in opposition to the hegemony exerted by the United States throughout much of the twentieth century. The defeat of the Free Trade Area of the Americas (FTAA/ALCA), an agreement proposed by the United States and formalized at the Summit of the Americas that was held in Miami in 1994, opened up an opportunity for the strengthening and enlargement of MERCOSUR, and the launching of various concurring initiatives for regional integration. The oldest is the Andean Community of Nations; followed by the Bolivarian Alliance for the Peoples of Our America (ALBA), led by the late Venezuelan leader, Hugo Chávez; the Union of the South American Nations (UNASUR); and the most recent and most inclusive of all, the Community of Latin American and Caribbean States, whose establishment was announced at the Summit of the Unity of Latin America and the Caribbean, held in Cancún, Mexico, in 2010.

The defeat of the FTAA led the United States (US) to review its strategy for the region. The new challenge was in bilateral free trade agreements. This 'one by one' strategy paid off and the US has already signed bilateral free trade agreements with Chile, Peru and Colombia, with which it also maintains a military cooperation agreement. One of the clauses of MERCOSUR prevents members from signing bilateral free trade agreements. Negotiations with the European Union have been going on for more than a decade without a final agreement being reached and this has increased domestic opposition to MERCOSUR in Brazil, particularly from the business sector.

The chief challenge for the advance of the process of regional integration is that of overcoming asymmetries. Brazil accounts for almost half of the economy of South America, and its exports also account for more than 40 per cent of the commercial flow in the region. Therefore, as Lima and Coutinho rightly point out, Brazil's economic weight results in the country becoming accountable for 'the main responsibility in terms of regional institutions, with the risk that they do not develop fully or that those that already exist do not consolidate' (Lima and Coutinho, 2005: 9). They go on to assert that 'the legitimacy of a cooperative Brazilian leadership depends on the level of generosity which Brazil, as the strongest country, is ready to show'.

There are clear signs that, under the leadership of progressive governments, this new Latin American regionalism may advance towards a solidarity-based community. The establishment of a MERCOSUR Structural Convergence Fund (FOCEM) and UNILA itself are projects which clearly point towards a form of integration based on cooperation and solidarity.

BUILDING A LATIN AMERICAN HIGHER EDUCATION AREA: TOWARDS REGIONAL INTEGRATION

In the last two decades, the commitment of universities to the process of regional integration has flourished in Latin America. Although the global phenomenon of the internationalization of higher education is not entirely new in the region, given that its leading academic institutions have been historically prone to emulate university models imported from the developed countries, the recent network-building efforts between Latin America universities can be seen as a potent endogenous driving force toward regional integration. Various initiatives made by governments, international organizations and universities themselves have stimulated the enlargement and strengthening of transnational university cooperation, academic mobility, and the mutual recognition of degrees and diplomas. In Latin America there is thus a strong tendency toward the regionalization of higher education, which points to the same goals as the Bologna Process in the European context.

We shall now briefly describe and contextualize some of these concurring initiatives aimed at creating an integrated Latin America higher education space, which will in turn help us to understand the UNILA project. The first project to merit attention is the MERCOSUR Education Sector (SEM), which brings together and coordinates educational policies of the member countries and the formation of common policies. Set up with a policy plan signed by the ministers of education of the member countries in 1991, SEM is still a forum for interaction between the governmental players, but it has little capacity to formulate and implement regional educational policies. This demonstrates the low level of institutionalization that has been achieved by MERCOSUR. This fact does not reduce its importance as an emerging supra-national example of the interlinking and coordination of educational policies. It is also interesting to note that the scope and effectiveness of the SEM resolutions have been greater in the area of higher education. This can partially be attributed to the fact that the national university policies and systems are more centralized than the national systems of basic education.

The best results which have been reached in the last two decades have depended upon the harmonization of the higher education legislations of each country, aiming at agreements which recognize university degrees and diplomas, on the one hand, and academic exchange within MERCOSUR, on the other. The MERCOSUR Educational Sector Plan stresses that the strategic priorities for the area of higher education are the strengthening of academic exchange programmes, the possibility of mutual recognition of degrees and diplomas, and the adoption of a system that will accredit professions within MERCOSUR (see also Perrotta, Chapter 11 in this volume). This process will not take place without tensions and problems, as the national states will find it difficult to give up the sovereignty of legislating on the organization of higher education, and ceding professional regulation to a supra-national body. It is interesting to note that the UNILA project was born from the failure of the proposal to set up the University of MERCOSUR, a 2006 Brazilian government project, which was readily supported by Argentina, but not by its smaller partners, Paraguay and Uruguay, who were suspicious of committing to co-fund such a transnational university enterprise.

Another important regional higher education project also introduced in 1991 a few months before the establishment of SEM, is the Association of the Montevideo Universities Group (AUGM).[3] This association, initially made up of eight public universities in the four member countries of MERCOSUR, has gained new members and today includes 30 universities from six countries, including Chile and Bolivia, who have joined MERCOSUR as associate countries. The AUGM has remained tied to the following aims, which are defined in its Act of Foundation:

> to contribute to the processes of regional and sub-regional integration; to strengthen its ability to qualify personnel, to develop research and increase transfer [of knowledge and technology]; to carry out continuing education in order to aid the development of the people of the sub-region; to consolidate a critical mass of information in strategic areas; to strengthen the management structures of member universities; to intensify the interaction between the university and society as a whole. (Schwab and Wainer, 2007)

The Montevideo Group is a pioneering experiment of network-building in the MERCOSUR area. One of its principal mottos has been the strong defence of the public university, under considerable attack during the neoliberal surge and the fiscal crisis which swept through the countries of the region in the 1990s. In contrast to the official agenda of SEM – dictated by the ministers of education and therefore directly influenced by the reigning political climate – in its initial years, the Montevideo Group took on a counter-hegemonic role of resistance to neoliberal reforms which the governments of the region, following the Washington Consensus, tried to impose in response to the economic slump and the crisis of the state. The ideological shift that has taken place in South America in the last decade has opened out the discussion on regional integration, and has pressed the Montevideo Group to move from contesting the hegemonic globalization process, to challenging and envisioning alternative models of regionalization and integration.

The discussions on the university crisis and the redefinition of its role in the so-called 'knowledge society', with all the contradictions this concept suggests, came together in the Declaration of the Regional Conference on Higher Education in Latin America and the Caribbean (IESALC-UNESCO, 2008) that launched the third and broadest attempt to create a regional space for higher education. Organized by the United Nations Educational, Scientific and Cultural Organization (UNESCO) International Institute for Higher Education in Latin America and the Caribbean (UNESCO-IESALC), this conference, held in Cartagena, Colombia, in 2008, made a bold statement against the incorporation of education as a commercial service within the framework of the WTO, and reasserted a shared regional vision of higher education as a 'social public good, a universal human right, and a responsibility of the State' (IESALC-UNESCO, 2008). Before the UNESCO World Conference on Higher Education, held in Paris in 2009, the Regional Conference mapped out the challenges and opportunities faced by higher education in the region in the light of regional integration and of changes in the global context.

It is fair to say that the values and principles embraced in the CRES Declaration of 2008, and the guidelines and recommendations to governments and higher education institutions in the CRES 2008 Action Plan, unite the programmes of SEM and the Montevideo Group, and reflect the ideological leaning of the past decade. The political importance of the two documents comes from the fact that the main actors in the area of higher education reached a consensus around a common agenda to strengthen regional integration and the internationalization of higher education, in addition to criticizing and condemning the commercialization and privatization of education as a menace to social cohesion and the surpassing of regional inequalities. 'Under no circumstances can education be guided by regulations and institutions intended for commerce, nor by the logic of the market. The move from that which is national and regional toward that which is global (a global public good) has as a consequence the strengthening of existing hegemonies' (CRES, 2008: 3).

It is therefore clear that CRES 2008 supports a regional integration strategy that recognizes universities as a fundamental actor:

The history and progress through cooperation has turned our higher education institutions into actors that have a vocation for regional integration ... [T]hey are the appropriate protagonists to meaningfully connect local and regional cultural identities, and to work actively to overcome the strong asymmetries prevailing in the region and the world in the face of the global phenomenon of the internationalization of higher education. (ibid.: 7)

In order to ensure effective regional integration, the CRES 2008 Declaration calls for the creation of a Latin American and Caribbean Research and Higher Education Area (ENLACES in Spanish). Finally CRES 2008 recommends an increase in cooperation between Latin America and the Caribbean and other parts of the world, particularly South–South cooperation, and within this framework, also with African countries. The CRES 2008 Declaration and the Action Plan have an ambitious strategy for the regional integration of education in Latin America. And it is in this context that the UNILA project, which will now be examined, can be seen as an innovative proposal for a transnational, or regional, initiative in higher education in Latin America.

UNILA: THE CHALLENGE OF DESIGNING A TRANSNATIONAL PUBLIC UNIVERSITY

UNILA is a public, free-tuition university funded exclusively by the Brazilian government. Its specific institutional aim is to 'qualify human resources who will help Latin American integration, regional development and cultural, scientific and educational exchange in Latin America, especially in the Common Market of the South – MERCOSUR'. The federal law which created UNILA – Law no. 12 189, of 12 January 2010 – established two conditions which had to be fulfilled by the new university: (i) UNILA would carry out its mission in border regions, especially in terms of academic exchange, cooperation and solidarity with the member countries of the MERCOSUR and other Latin American countries; and (ii) the courses given at UNILA would preferably be in areas of mutual interest of countries in Latin America, especially the member countries of MERCOSUR, with an emphasis on themes involving exploitation of natural resources and cross-frontier biodiversity, regional social and linguistic studies, international relations, and the other areas considered strategic for regional development and integration (Law 12 189/10).

What differentiates and distinguishes UNILA from other Brazilian public universities is its regional focus and international scope; these are features which make it stand out as the first higher education institution set up and maintained by the Brazilian state to act in a space which sits above and beyond its own territory. When the project was publicly announced in December 2007, the Ministry of Education set an ambitious goal, proposing that in five years UNILA should have 10000 students and 500 professors. Half of the faculty and students should come from Brazil and half from other Latin American countries. As the Brazilian National Congress took two years to pass the federal law authorizing and enabling the Ministry of Education to establish UNILA, the new university effectively began its life in the first semester of 2010 and admitted its first undergraduate students in the second semester of that same year. Within this time framework, by 2015 UNILA aimed to be fully implemented. However, by the time the 2014 academic year was approaching its end, current figures for enrolment and faculty fell short of the goals. Presently, UNILA offers 17 undergraduate programmes and only one graduate program, with an approximate enrolment of 1400 students coming from 11 countries. Meanwhile, the university has already hired around 250 professors and 460 technical staff. The slow pace of enrolment points to the challenge UNILA faces to attract and retain students from other Latin American countries.

UNILA was conceived from its inception as a bilingual university, with Portuguese and Spanish as its official languages to be used interchangeably: in the selection processes to contract teaching staff; the admission of students; and, in teaching, academic work and evaluation. This does not mean that it conceives of Latin America as a bilingual region. Fortunately, UNILA has not forgotten Latin American cultural ethnic and linguistic diversity, and indeed a number of the most innovative undergraduate and postgraduate programmes being developed cover the fields of Latin American languages, culture, literature and identity. For instance, there is an intercultural teacher-training course for indigenous Guarani teachers.

The main innovations which have been promised by UNILA are in its potential regional links with already existing university networks, its political and educational conception, the format and content of its courses, an 'ecology of knowledge' approach, a genuinely Latin American commitment, and the opportunity to establish a clear and strong regional link between universities, social actors and public policy. All of these possibilities can only be put into practice if the aims and the intentions that have been announced are carried out effectively in the consolidation and implementation of the project. The three key ideas which provide the cement for the UNILA project are: (1) sincere and mutually respectful national and transnational interaction; (2) a commitment to sustainable economic development, linking it to social justice and environmental balance; and (3) the reciprocal sharing of scientific and technological resources and knowledge with university teachers and students throughout Latin America (IMEA, 2009a: 16).

The UNILA project incorporates the following ethical and political values: the freedom to teach and research in an inter- and transdisciplinary culture, today considered necessary to seek solutions to the challenges of the problems of Latin America; the strengthening of cultural relations and the valuing of the culture and memory of Latin America; promoting exchange and cooperation while respecting cultural, religious and national identities; the consolidation and strengthening of democracy in the region; and greater reciprocal knowledge between Latin America countries to help regional integration.

The strict adherence of UNILA to these core values, whether in inter-university relations and with governmental and social actors in the regional context, or in its teaching, research and extra-curricular programmes, will determine how successful and coherent the project will be. The first undergraduate programmes clearly show that UNILA intends to follow the principles of the original conception of its project, adopting an inter- and transdisciplinary approach to seeking solutions for emerging Latin American problems. This focus is similar to the vision which was repeatedly put forward by the former Brazilian Minister of Education, Fernando Haddad, for whom the vision and vocation of UNILA should be to 'think of concrete solutions to our common problems'. Thus, as a research university, UNILA should be most concerned with cross-border problems and cooperate in the formulation of solutions for supra-national problems. Its research programmes should have a close link with regional policies and the development of public policies.

INNOVATION AS A DISCURSIVE TOOL: WHAT IS REALLY NEW ABOUT UNILA?

From the first papers on the project released by the Ministry of Education in late 2007, UNILA has adopted an unabashed discourse of innovation, professing the ideals of the University Reform of Córdoba[4] and finding inspiration in so-called paradigmatic Brazilian universities, among which the University of Brasília (UnB) and the State University of Campinas (UNICAMP), both created in the 1960s, are always referred to.[5] Its formulators set out to: 'from the beginning think of the conception of UNILA with innovative ambition and foresight' (IMEA, 2009a). However, the task would prove far more challenging and, to some extent, more frustrating than had been anticipated. As would be evident in the first years of the new institution, the generous idea of designing an academic organization, an educational project, and in proposed undergraduate courses which were radically different from existing models in other Brazilian universities, came up against legal obstacles, the status quo of regulated professions and, especially, an academic culture averse to change and innovation.

The first factor to inhibit the range of the movement towards innovation at UNILA, especially with regard to its organizational and academic structure, is the fact it belongs to the federal system of higher education, and is therefore subject to the same legal framework governing other public institutions. The limitations inherent in this highly regulated and centralized system that grants limited autonomy to federal state universities are well known, especially in the financial and administrative areas. This regulatory inflexibility has already proven fatal to the realization of some of the most innovative aspects of the UNILA project, such as the 'equal participation of teachers and students from Brazil and other Latin American countries' (IMEA, 2009a). In fact, although the law that created the UNILA permits, and indeed encourages, the recruitment of teachers from various countries of the region, this legal statute has had little effect as it clashes with the general norms of the Brazilian legislation that prevent contracting non-Brazilians.[6] As a result, to date UNILA has an extremely small number of non-Brazilian teachers on its staff, thereby compromising its bilingual character and threatening its transnational vocation.[7]

The difficulties encountered by UNILA to recruit and retain students from other Latin American countries may also be attributed, in large part, to legal, administrative and financial constraints arising from its subordination to the federal system of higher education.[8] From the early admissions process, it became evident that in order to attract foreign students with the desired profile for UNILA, it would be necessary to set up, apart from free education, a policy to assist students in a number of ways in order to meet their housing, food, transportation, health and living needs. In the first two years of operation, due to the relatively small number of students and a generous budget for student welfare, it was possible to extend these benefits to Brazilian and foreign students alike. From 2012 onward, UNILA has had to live with the harsh reality encountered by other public universities; that is, limited resources for student welfare.[9] Thus, it has become increasingly difficult to attract a large number of students from other countries, and indeed this is one of the most serious threats to the project of creating a Latin American university.

Exogenous and structural barriers to the full development of the innovative project promised by UNILA are more easily seen and pointed out. However, it is more subtle and difficult to elucidate the endogenous contradictions and resistances that have emerged during the implementation process of the new university. Two main factors have contributed to this: on the one hand, the contradictions and failures of the execution of the project; on the other, the prevalence of an academic culture that is recalcitrant in embracing change. UNILA has not remained immune to these factors. If initially the originality of the proposal served to attract great interest from the academic community, the policy of recruitment and the retention of teachers and administrative aides, through public competition, as Brazilian federal law requires, has not guaranteed the selection of staff committed to building an innovative and differentiated university project.

In spite of all these constraints and challenges, UNILA has sought to live up to its promises of innovation and novelty. Great collective effort has been undertaken in the formulation of a proposed academic architecture, coherent and convergent with two fundamental principles in its political-pedagogical project: (1) the adoption of an inter- and transdisciplinary approach to the curriculum in response to the contemporary trend of the disciplinary organization of knowledge and its consequent 'compartmentalization', reflected in the departmentalized structures of universities; and (2) the valuing of intercultural dialogue by recognizing the cultural diversity of Latin America and its acceptance as one of the ethical pillars of the UNILA curriculum. The challenge of giving 'historical concreteness' to this utopia still has a long way to go. The president of the implementation committee, Hélgio Trindade, warned of the likely gap between the idealized proposal and 'the reality that has emerged from the dialectic of various [adverse] circumstances' (IMEA, 2009a).

In fact, giving concrete shape to the original conception of the UNILA project has proven to be a great challenge. The organizational structure and academic architecture would only be established in 2013 with the development and adoption of the Statutes and General Regulations of the university, a task that involved, in a participatory manner, the three segments of the emerging university community: faculty, technical staff and students. What stood out as the main innovation of the academic organization of UNILA was the creation of four Latin American institutes based upon broad areas of knowledge: (1) arts, culture and history; (2) economics, society and politics; (3) life sciences and nature; and (4) technology, infrastructure and territory. To these institutes are linked interdisciplinary centres. Each institute has a superior deliberative council whose function is to oversee the activities of teaching, research and extension. The three segments of the academic community have equal representation on these councils, as well as on the other governance organs of UNILA. For example, on the University Council, the highest body of the institution, each category has the right to appoint eight representatives elected by their peers.

This is the aspect that has been the most controversial during the drafting of the statute, creating clashes between the three categories: faculty, technical staff and students. Parity in the academic governing bodies was adopted by Brazilian public universities in the context of democratic transition in the 1980s. This model of university governance has been challenged and revised in several public universities in the past two decades in order to give greater weight to the teaching staff. For UNILA, with its unique characteristics, its implementation poses an even greater challenge. The experience, still in development, has generated large-scale internal mobilization, but its results have not yet been evaluated. UNILA adopted a model of participatory democratic governance based on the coexistence of parity between the three areas at all organizational levels. For an institution embedded in the Latin American context, marked by successive ruptures and outbreaks of authoritarianism, the emphasis in the UNILA statutes and regulations on the participation and democratic deliberation of its members assumes the character of a bold political statement in defence of democracy.

FINAL REMARKS

What lessons can be learned from the first five years (2010–2015) of this promising university project? First of all, the planning of UNILA clearly underestimated the challenges of creating a transnational and multicultural higher education setting. Existing regional power relations, economic asymmetries, political imbalances and cultural oppression tend to be reproduced even within a transnational and diverse university community which embraces, as its core values, integration through cooperation and solidarity. Second, the premise that the local community would enthusiastically embrace and support the establishment of a new public university with the singularity granted to UNILA, has so far proven to be naïve. Any effective university–community integration over the longer term will only be achieved through permanent dialogue, commitment, mutual understanding and, above all, collaborative work, to solve real problems. Fortunately, this is already taking place through many extension initiatives and community-based research endeavours.

It will be interesting to follow UNILA in the coming years, to see whether and how it will be able to navigate the contradictions of being both an institution with relatively high autonomy, and at the same time an institution constrained by the same set of rules governing faced by all of the other public federal universities. The development of the UNILA project provides both a challenge and a chance to create a public university with a special institutional mission which could break with the traditional paradigm which links and subordinates the university to the formation of the nation-state and the affirmation of national identity. The conception of UNILA also provides a unique opportunity to establish a university committed to a new epistemology of knowledge through an approach based upon social importance and relevance that speaks directly to the 2008 CRES Declaration.

Different to the dogmatic positivist conceptions of science, which saw empiricism and rationalism as the quintessence of scientific method, UNILA could, and should, be both open and receptive to a diversity of knowledges, thereby surpassing the dichotomy between scientific knowledge and the university, on one hand, and non-scientific knowledge from outside the university, on the other. This new paradigm has the potential to be imbued with those intercultural and ethical values, and the need to surpass disciplinary borders when tackling problems so as to enable it to engage with pressing local, national and global challenges. This is particularly because of the emphasis that the UNILA project gives to inter- and transdisciplinary areas, although in truth it is much easier to support these ideas than actually make them an effective component of the curriculum and teaching practice. Nevertheless, UNILA is an attempt to seek democratic solutions to the dilemmas and challenges of Latin America, and a means to discover sustainable forms of social and economic development that might prefigure new solutions to the challenges of social inequality and poverty.

NOTES

1. Created in 1991 through the Treaty of Asunción, the Southern Common Market (MERCOSUR) was originally designed as a free trade agreement, formed by Argentina, Brazil, Paraguay and Uruguay. In 2012 Venezuela joined the group as a full member. Chile, Bolivia, Colombia, Ecuador and Peru take part as associate members.
2. President Dilma Rousseff's narrow victory for a second term in the 2014 presidential election, after a bitter and hard-fought campaign, points to the erosion of the PT's support among key constituencies and the risk of political backlash in the coming years.
3. For an overview on this university network, see its official site: http://grupomontevideo.org/sitio/.
4. This movement, led by students, broke out in 1918 at the Universidad de Córdoba, Argentina, spreading rapidly to other universities in Argentina and Latin America. Its main aims were to modernize and democratize the university. The resulting reform strengthened university autonomy, academic freedom, university extension and student activism.
5. Created by reformist educators, UnB by Darcy Ribeiro and Anísio Teixeira, and UNICAMP by Zeferino Vaz, both would become the benchmark for other public universities. 'Only an entirely planned new university, structured on flexible bases, can open up prospects for the speedy renewal of our higher education', stated the general plan for the implementation of UnB in 1962.
6. Constitutional Amendment No. 11 of 30 April 1996, allows for the hiring of teachers, technicians and foreign scientists by Brazilian universities, 'according to the law'. However, Brazilian law is still fairly restrictive, making access difficult for non-Brazilians to faculty positions at public universities.

7. Less than 5 per cent of the approximately 250 teachers at UNILA are from other countries. Although open to non-Brazilians, public competitions for faculty positions are not attracting huge demand from non-Brazilians. Among the few non-Brazilians who have been contracted, most have lived in Brazil and, to some extent, integrated into Brazilian culture.
8. The budget of the federal universities is set by the central government. Resources are allocated for specific purposes, leaving little or no autonomy for universities to define their own priorities.
9. In 2010 the federal government introduced the National Student Assistance Programme (PNAES), as part of efforts to democratize access and ensure that young people from low-income families did not drop out of public universities. Since then, coverage for student welfare has been expanded. But while there has been a significant increase in resources, they are still far from meeting the demands of federal universities.

REFERENCES

Breslin, S., Higgott, R. and Rosamund, B. (2002a), 'Regions in comparative perspective', in S. Breslin, C.W. Hughes, N. Phillips and B. Rosamund (eds), *New Regionalisms in the Global Political Economy*, New York: Routledge, pp. 1–19.
Breslin, S., Hughes, C.W., Phillips, N. and Rosamund, B. (eds) (2002b), *New Regionalisms in the Global Political Economy*, New York: Routledge.
Falk, Richard (2000), *Human Rights Horizons: The Pursuit of Justice in a Globalizing World*, New York, USA and London, UK: Routledge.
Hettne, B. (2003), 'The New Regionalism revisited', in F. Söderbaum and T. Shaw (eds), *Theories of New Regionalism: A Palgrave Reader*, New York: Palgrave, pp. 22–42.
IESALC-UNESCO (2008), 'Declaration of the Regional Conference on Higher Education in Latin America and the Caribbean – CRES 2008', available at http://www.iau-hesd.net/sites/default/files/documents/2008_-_declaration_of_th e_regional_conference_on_higher_education_in_latin_americe_and_the_carabe an_fr.pdf.
Instituto Mercosul de Estdusos Avançados (IMEA) (2009a), 'AUNILA em Construção: um projeto universitário para a América latina', Foz do Iguaçu: IMEA.
Instituto Mercosul de Estdusos Avançados (IMEA) (2009b), 'UNILA: consulta internacional: contribuições à concepção, organização e proposta políticopedagógica da UNILA', Foz do Iguaçu: IMEA.
Lima, M. and Coutinho, V.M. (2005), 'Globalização, Regionalização e América do Sul', Análise de Conjuntura OPSA, n. 6, maio de 2005.
Santos, B. de S-S. (2006), 'The university in the twenty-first century: toward a democratic and emancipatory university reform', in R. Rhoads and C.A. Torres (eds), *The University, State, and Market: The Political Economy of Globalization in the Americas*, Stanford, CA: Stanford University Press, pp. 60–100.
Schwab, S. and Wainer, J. (2007), *Asociación de Universidades Grupo Montevideo: 15 años de historia*, Montevideo: Asociación de Universidades Grupo Montevideo.
Söderbaum, F. (2003), 'Introduction: theories of New Regionalism', in F. Söderbaum and T.M. Shaw (eds), *Theories of New Regionalism: A Palgrave Reader*, New York: Palgrave, pp. 1–21.

14. Regionalization, higher education and the Gulf Cooperation Council
Tahani Aljafari

INTRODUCTION

Changes in the higher education landscape that now constitute the Gulf Cooperation Council countries the United Arab Emirates (UAE), Bahrain, Oman, Qatar, Kuwait and Saudi Arabia, together with the growth of the Gulf Cooperation Council (GCC) since its establishment in the early 1980s, provide an important vantage point through which to study the ongoing spatial dynamics of constructing regions more generally, and the Gulf region in particular.

Responding to both national and global pressures, higher education providers in the region are being challenged to provide more opportunities for accessible, better-quality education and training for its citizens, as well as becoming a locus of attraction for globally talented students and researchers. At the heart of this pressure is the attempt by the countries of the region to move away from being dependent upon resource extraction, to a new model of development: that of knowledge-based economies as a basis for ongoing national and regional economic survival.

The GCC was launched with the signing of a charter on 25 May 1981. Although originally conceived of as a means of strengthening the defence of the Arab Gulf region, the charter called for the coordination and integration in all fields, the harmonization of regulations across the GCC, the establishment of a free trade area and creation of a common external tariff, the coordination of economic development within the GCC, and the strengthening of ties among citizens of the member states. The preamble to the statute establishing the emergent GCC stressed the links between the six countries, their special relationship and common features, similar systems based upon the Islamic faith, common historical, social and cultural patterns and a common destiny and unity of purpose also assisted this cooperation. Religion, Arabic language and family ties similarly strengthened the special relationship between the member states and facilitated communication and networking between them.

Yet political analysts have disagreed over the main reasons for the formation of this regional project. Suggested purposes have ranged from geographical locations (Zahlan, 1998) and security purposes to shared economic interests (Hanieh, 2010). The security argument is supported by many incidents of uprisings. For instance, the six states witnessed the growth of left-wing and Arab-nationalist movements from the 1950s to the 1970s, presenting them with numerous external and internal threats. Later, the 1979 Iranian Revolution and the subsequent Iran–Iraq War pushed the Gulf states to make common cause to protect their teetering monarchies. In addition, the Arab states have suffered from internal uprisings and armed attacks by underground organizations, such as in Oman with the Dhofar rebellion, in Saudi Arabia (1979), Bahrain (1981) and Kuwait (1983). All these factors confirmed the belief of the six GCC member countries that if they did not hang together, they would hang separately. Consequently, the GCC member states embarked on a unification process, making it a particularly interesting case of a region.

Yet regardless of what scholars refer to as the main reasons behind the formation of the GCC, the GCC countries have nevertheless committed themselves to a constitutionalized association ostensibly to nurture shared economic interests: 'The evidence for GCC would appear to be more clearly that the association was conceived to be, and was intended to develop, as an association for purposes of securing shared economic advantages for its Members States and societies' (Al-Khalifa, 2007: 86).

Whilst progress has been slow in comparison to the speed of economic integration in regions like Europe, and more latterly regions such as the Association of Southeast Asian Nations (ASEAN) and the Southern Common Market (MERCOSUR), Low and Salazar (2010: vii) argue that by the beginning of the twenty-first century the GCC has been making some headway towards greater economic integration:

> After starting with the limited goal of establishing a free trade area (FTA), the GCC moved towards a unified bloc, including a customs union established in 2003, and a common market established in 2008. It is now aiming for monetary union; a project that was supposed to happen by 2010 then postponed. These targets and time frames have been supported by the region's steady economic expansion, driven by high oil prices and a booming commercial sector.

As in other developing countries, policy-makers within the GCC region have looked to universities to take a leading part in this challenge, through inviting in universities from other parts of the world to generate increased capability and establishing world-class universities as a proxy of global competitiveness. The implication here is that these higher stocks of advanced knowledge and skill will increase individual and national capability. Investing in region-building is also seen as a means to managing growing global competition. It is within this context that researchers have also begun to focus on the 'rise of the region' which has increasing become a focal scale for economic activity associated with the increasing importance of knowledge (Hardill et al., 2006).

The question to be explored in this chapter is: what kind of region is the GCC, and what role does higher education play in this? How might we understand and explain the nature and consequences of the recent developments in the Gulf Cooperation Council countries and emerging region of the GCC over the past decade? Drawing upon empirical work (interviews, document analysis) conducted over the period 2009–2011 as part of a wider Doctoral study on higher education (HE) and the GCC, I explore the ways in which the GCC countries have put into place a number of strategic internationalization activities in higher education in order to foster the countries' movement from an oil-based economy to a knowledge-based economy. However, as will be shown, HE initiatives tend to remain firmly located in national territorial spaces rather than those initiatives having a regional character. These national initiatives have been given high priority and are underpinned by massive resources. In my conclusions I explore some reasons for this rather symbolic approach to regionalism, arguing that whilst we can see the GCC as a 'regional arena', for the moment as a response to political and global circumstances, very little is institutionalized and embedded at the regional scale. This is largely the result of historic tensions and competition between the GCC countries.

THE POLITICAL ECONOMY OF THE GULF STATES

Before discussing the actual position of GCC countries among the energy-producing countries, it is important to present some politico-economic facts about these states. These six countries of the Arabian Peninsula are a group of family-based fiefdoms, which have over a long period of time evolved into independent states. Most importantly, GCC countries can be characterized by rentierism. As Kamrava et al. put it:

> these states have little in common in terms of history, make-up, and ideological dispositions and legitimacy. But they do have in common rentier political economies, albeit to varying degrees [and] the emerging rentier dynamics were superimposed on evolving institutional arrangements as state-building processes were already underway ... [whilst] state leaders across the GCC have framed globalization in terms consistent with evolving notions of nationalism. More specifically, they have presented global economic engagement as an integral aspect of the national project. (Kamrava et al., 2011: 5)

The classic formulation of Gulf Arab 'rentierism' has been set out by Luciani (1995: 12), who defines it as:

> A state that economically supports society and is the main source of private revenues through government expenditure, while in turn supported by revenue accruing from abroad, does not need to respond to society. On the contrary, a state that is supported by society, through taxes levied in one form or another, will in the final analysis be obliged to respond to social pressure.

GCC countries fall into the first category. These countries, except Bahrain, enjoy an extremely high level of public and private sector wealth from their oil and, increasingly, gas revenues. For GCC countries, oil revenues are assumed to be the prize (as a scarce commodity, source of profits or element of control vis-à-vis other powers). For the rest of the world, the region is most typically understood as the location of the world's key oil- and gas-producing states. In other words, at least from the outside, this oil-based natural wealth reduces the region to being analytically treated as a giant oil-field rather than a region with its own history, struggles and social relations (Hanieh, 2010).

These unusual political economies have as a result detached the oil monarchies from their local socio-economic realm by virtue of rent. The ruling elites have acquired relative autonomy from society, and this gives them the ability to pursue national goals without accountability. With a firm desire to maintain their privileges and position of power over the longer term, the ruling elites have subdued all sorts of political activism. They have been helped by a high level of wealth and high standards of living which have, in turn, historically served to suppress widespread demand for change.

In this context, the elites are very small in size and the hierarchies between the king, princes and commoners are very strict. Clienteles are local and do not represent broader social groups. Moreover, the oil monarchies have lacked an administrative tradition so that societal checks on bureaucracy which might be present elsewhere are not present in this context. Combined with family politics, this meant that the unprecedented growth of bureaucracy in the 1950s was not accompanied by much rationalization. Although some new agencies helped to increase the provision of public services, the sudden availability of resources also led to uncontrolled, Byzantine, expansion based on patronage.

However, more than this, as Partrick put it:

> a narrow conception of the nation predominates in Gulf Arab countries in which sub-state tribal and sectarian fealties are strong, and loyalties to a larger national entity beyond the state are lacking . . . [and] a growing set of Khaleeji institutions through the mechanisms of the GCC itself were a reflection of a

top-down construct that had not fundamentally altered an essentially realist, state-orientated way of managing their individual affairs. (Partrick, 2012: 47, 60)

One major consequence of this is pointed out by Kamrava et al., who argue that:

> state leaders across the GCC have framed globalization in terms consistent with evolving notions of nationalism . . . while rentierism has enabled the state to funnel oil and gas revenues into society and secure a measure of political acquiescence, it has also made the state dependent on maintaining its patronage position for fear of adverse consequences. (Kamrava et al., 2011: 1, 12)

This emphasis on nationalism and competition points to potentially fissiparous tendencies in the regional organization.

HIGHER EDUCATION AND THE GULF STATES

From the early 1980s, GCC countries used their revenue to build the infrastructure of their countries, providing vital services to their nations, including higher education. Years later the GCC countries were committed to improve their higher education and training sectors in order to move beyond being rentier states and to diversify their economy. The challenge of the rapidly changing world has promoted GCC governments to consider how well their existing HE institutions are preparing the citizens of tomorrow to respond effectively to the opportunities provided by globalization, and helping the countries to move from an oil economy to a knowledge economy.

The six GCC countries recognize that this would not happen without the cooperation between multiple actors and agencies including the higher education and business sectors, which was seen as something to which traditional universities in the GCC region seemed incapable of contributing. For the GCC region, it was a transformative moment when the leaders adopted the discourses of internationalization and neoliberalism in order to foster change and development in the region. Eventually, the economic and political pressures have resulted in profound changes in higher education development. However, this was not a straightforward issue.

The international pressures on GCC countries increased after the event of 9/11 when international experts analysed the situation and advised them to focus internally and to modify their education systems. In December 2001, the Supreme Council (SC) of the GCC introduced 11 indicators to investigate and trace the developments and achievements of GCC national universities. It was found that although GCC countries made recognizable efforts in the HE sector, these were not enough to meet the local demands and compete internationally.

Senior individuals, ministers and experts looked at the gap between universities' output and saw the need of each state to expand its economy by investing in knowledge widely. Generally, this gap was shaped by a government's decision to focus on the arts, the humanities and religious studies in order to perpetuate traditional culture. However, the knowledge economy demands more technical and managerial skills in order to achieve a higher level of capacity to enable a country to find itself a place in the world's new economic system.

GCC countries begun following international organizations such as the United Nations and implemented their recommendations at all levels of education. The GCC advisory board's initiatives and recommendations for actions are built on a multidimensional analysis of the region, bearing in mind that higher education, as in other countries throughout the world, faces many challenges. These main challenges are political, economic, socio-cultural and technological, and they are profoundly affecting the security and the well-being of the Gulf societies. The region is experiencing major changes in patterns of behaviour, habits, values, attitudes and concepts. The situation calls for real and effective actions to face these challenges.

In the mid-2000s McGlennon (2006) pointed out that GCC countries' investment in research and development (R&D) remained at developing-world levels. Despite their improved competitiveness in the Arab World Competitive Report (AWCR) in the higher education and training (HE&T) category, and although the region scored better than North Africa and Levant, the GCC countries were still lagging behind the Organisation for Economic Co-operation and Development (OECD) countries. They needed to have an advanced economy by developing cutting-edge products or services and/or use unique processes. It is a complex process that starts with investing in HE&T, because innovation involves complex products and production processes require a skilled workforce. The HE&T category is significant because countries cannot move up the development ladder without investing in this vital sector.

The problem was put in a nutshell in the 2010 Arab World Competitive Report's recommendation: going forward, the report suggested, GCC countries will need to continue to diversify their economies away from the hydrocarbon sector. This move will require an appropriately educated labour force, sophisticated businesses, and sufficient innovative capacity to achieve the levels of productivity necessary to sustain the high wages prevalent in the sub-region. Although the sub-region is home to sophisticated, globally operating businesses, their low innovative capacity could restrain diversification efforts if not addressed (Hanouz and Khatib, 2010: 8).

In contrast to the harsh criticism the GCC higher education sector received from international organizations, Davidson and Mackenzie Smith (2008) presented a positive overview. They acknowledged the recent rapid expansion of HE in the GCC region and reported that in two generations the region had changed from having the smallest higher education population in the Middle East to producing a new generation whose achievements are close to the standards set by the OECD. The strong economic position for GCC countries enabled them to provide new developments in higher education, such as a variety of new universities and programmes, including an international scholarship programme, private universities, virtual learning and borderless campuses (Wilkins, 2011).

Openness and international integration were required in order to modernize. One notable instance of this occurred when the World Trade Organization's General Agreement on Trade in Services (GATS) started to create an impact on higher education in GCC countries (Donn and Al-Manthri, 2010). Robertson et al. (2002) point out that the General Agreement on Trade in Services negotiations, along with a proliferation of bilateral agreements, have promoted higher education as an important area for international competitiveness via regional and global trade. Accordingly, higher education institutes have started to be linked with external interests and spaces including those that are regionally and globally anchored.

In fact, GCC countries started to implement different approaches of internationalization with a high degree of priority and resources. Over recent years, higher education in the GCC region has been undergoing extensive development as the result of a dynamic and complex internationalization policy resulting from globalization (Donn and Al-Manthri, 2010). This has given rise to new initiatives, which are innovative and unique models of higher education in the GCC region and will be the focus of the section on 'New National Developments', below.

THE GULF COOPERATION COUNCIL: IN WHAT SENSE A REGION?

Given the focus of this book – regionalisms – the important question regarding the Gulf states and the GCC, is: in what sense is it a region? Or, put another way, what kind of regional frontiers or horizons are advanced, or not, and why?

Seen from the vantage point of 2016, it can be argued that the GCC has not developed any significant or indeed notable steps towards the stage of integration. GCC member states are still negotiating regional projects without leaving their comfort zone, the cooperation stage or soft regionalism. The GCC's reactions to the global economic and political changes suggest that even without integration initiatives, the GCC is made up of different actors and formations derived from markets, private investment, the policies and decisions of companies or organizations, as well as state-led initiatives. These practices could be interpreted as a regionness that has different level of integrations. Arguably, the level of GCC regionness has not progressed from mere regional space to a deeper institutionalized polity with a permanent structure of decision-making and stronger capability as a global actor. However, Riggirozzi (2012) argues that there is a type of regionness that challenges the 'old' versus 'new' regionalism. Based on this debate, the configuration of the GCC regional project departs from the usual approach to regional integration to focus on the creation of new spaces for (regional) consensus-building, resource-sharing, autonomous development and power decentralization. Hence, the distinction between 'regions as actors' and 'region as arenas' is crucial to understanding the divergent outcomes in terms of region-building or regionness, with the GCC firmly in the latter camp.

What the above suggests is that we understand the GCC as a regional space for action driven by new consensuses over practices and cooperation in politico-institutional socio-economic and cultural arenas (Riggirozzi, 2012: 427). Dynamics in these arenas are driven by different actors, projects of integration, linkages mechanisms, institutional structures and distributive consequences, which is in contrast with the notion of regionalism as a coherent model, and regionness as a cohesive (acting) subject or actorness (Schmitt-Egner, 2002: 192–195).

HIGHER EDUCATION AND THE GCC

The GCC considers the HE sector a key element in the sustainable development of GCC countries. Although HE authorities in the GCC have been involved in HE development since the mid-1980s, this involvement has largely been a shift towards cooperation and coordination guided by the GCC countries' perception of shared interests and concerns, albeit alongside national interests. However, the strength of the commitment to the regional project can be questioned: the lack of a regional constitution and regional governance structure tends to result in a great deal of 'shop talk' and not many achievements. One well-placed interviewee also claimed that the GCC had missed many opportunities to promote cooperation between member states.

In the late 1970s, the GCC decided to build an HE institute, specifically, a Gulf university. With this in mind, the General Convention of Arab Education for the GCC was held in Bahrain where it was decided to establish the Arabian Gulf University (AGU) in the Kingdom of Bahrain. At that time, HE institutes did not exist in the capital cities of GCC countries. The SC realized the importance of university and higher-level education in GCC society. The AGU came about as a result of cooperation between GCC countries to satisfy their need for specialists and experts in various occupational fields.

Although the AGU did not develop any sort of regional significance in terms of collaboration with the research staff or students of other countries' universities, it has accomplished international collaboration[1] efforts, with the United Nations University and the Paris Chamber of Commerce. The only collaborative efforts among GCC countries are that Saudi Arabia offered the infrastructure and the rest of the GCC countries supplied the AGU with the required academic and administrative staff. The dean must be from one of the GCC countries, and the position is renewed every four years. Although the GCC has endeavoured to make the vision of the AGU a reality, the AGU has not reflected the imagined level of cooperation that leaders of the GCC wanted, largely due to barriers that the GCC countries face.

It seems that in the case of the GCC, opportunities and barriers are two faces of the same coin, and the actual situation appears vague and uncertain. Before discussing the kinds of strategic change needed, it is essential to find out what prevents HE sector entities from working together as a region. One interviewee was particularly critical of the GCC: he referred to the lack of cooperation at a micro level as being largely due to the fact that the member states of the GCC do not want to delegate any sort of state authority to other actors, and in this case upward to the GCC. As a result the GCC has no unitarian market or single currency, and no GCC citizenship or equality for work and residency between citizens of member states.

By 2012, it had been more than five years since GCC experts introduced the strategic action plan to enhance the regional project. Up to now, very little has happened. One of my interviews from the Department of Education in the General Secretariat of the GCC suggests a set of changes that would include HE, that might boost GCC activity:

> I feel HE institutions in GCC countries should look into the following possible changes or future policies: 1. Reduce the differences between private and public providers of HE in every state. 2. Adopt local education mobility

policies (for students, staff, researchers and administrators) in order to reduce various gaps in management, quality and institutions' structures. 3. Investigate possible similarity in skills required for graduates to obtain various university degrees, whether academic or professional skills. 4. Professional regional meetings in various disciplines should be held at HE institutions in GCC countries. 5. Introduce common councils, committees and centres specializing in different aspects of HE, such as quality, enrolment, international ranking, research priority, and so on.

Abouammoh, a key figure who has worked with the GCC HE authorities, conducted an evaluation of the GCC's achievements. He argued that in general, progress of the GCC states towards a more homogenous regional system is very slow (Abouammoh, 2009). And though a committee of ministers of HE is one of several GCC committees that meet regularly and discuss issues of concern, and although also at the end of every meeting a set of general recommendations is presented, it seems that there is a lack of power to make the recommendations work. The HE local authority in each state has more power than the HE regional committee.

Surprisingly, the GCC HE committee has shifted from discussing regionalism to inter-regionalism. According to Abouammoh (2009: 13–15), there have been many efforts to encourage further European Union (EU)–GCC cooperation with programmes such as the Erasmus Mundus programme, Tempus and the Jean Monnet Programme in cooperation with non-EU higher education institutions. At the university level, GCC states host many branches of European universities or European university campuses. Yet it is clear that whilst it is possible to identify a common geography in these collaborations, in truth these are largely nation-to-nation or institution-to-nation negotiations rather than region-to-region. Indeed the GCC countries have carried out individual collaboration schemes with international partners all over the world, including the United States, Canada, Australia, the United Kingdom, and some of the East Asian countries.

Does this mean that the region is simply symbolic? Or does it serve a purpose? Could it be that choosing to move from regionalism to inter-regionalism implies that the GCC HE committee has concluded that the regional project will never be accomplished, or is being practical and responding to the processes of globalization? Söderbaum et al. (2005: 377) argue that inter-regionalism creates and legitimizes regional actors. According to them: 'As regions consolidate and become stronger, they are also likely to turn outward. Hence, it is to be expected that they will find it attractive to relate to other regions, because this will be both "effective" and at the same time increase the legitimacy of their actorness as regions.'

The EU is considered the most significant actor. It would appear that the GCC is aware of the position of the EU, and its shift towards inter-regionalism is meant to intensify the geopolitical significance of the GCC as a region. The GCC authorities seem to be keen to find a solution to any obstacle that reduces the chance of cooperation with the EU.

Yet a regional process is dependent on each Gulf state committing some effort toward that project. However, each state has developed the kind of policy that can work in its own context, including the HE innovations that I highlight below, without considering any coordinated effort with other GCC countries. Further, most private HE institutions in the UAE are intended for expatriates, while in other GCC countries they are there to fill the increasing enrolment capacity of national students in HE. Consequently, the differences in the nature of support and the multilateral vision of HE authorities create a non-homogeneous environment for competition and cooperation.

NEW NATIONAL DEVELOPMENTS IN THE REGION

In this section I highlight novel developments in the Gulf region, show how different they are, and explore why. Three Gulf state initiatives are examined: Education City Qatar (ECQ), inaugurated in 2003 with four US universities; Dubai International Academic City (DIAC) in 2007; and King Abdullah University of Science and Technology (KAUST), launched in 2009.

ECQ, DIAC and KAUST have become significant landmarks in the academic field in the GCC region. The emergence of these three new developments has been encouraged by the desire of the leaders of GCC countries to develop their higher education sectors. These were a response to the GCC (2008) document on higher education, entitled: 'Highlights: the process of the development of the HE sector in the States of the Cooperation Council (the decisions and the achievements)'. This document encouraged the six GCC countries to go international and create a difference in the higher education sector by: (1) establishing international collaborations with world-class research centres and universities; (2) introducing neoliberalism into the higher education sector through the permission for business to fund and support research; and (3) developing private higher education institutes and universities which are autonomously managed.

Two crucial features are to be noted about the new higher education developments within the GCC region. The first is that they are being uniquely shaped by national rather than regional politics. The second is that they are distinctly different from the organizational forms that

Table 14.1 Main characteristics of the three projects

	Model	Ownership	Governance	Funding
ECQ	Educational city which hosts satellite campuses, 8 branches of elite international universities and colleges, and one national institute	Qatar Foundation for Education, Science and Community Development (QF) is an independent, government-funded, non-profit, chartered organization	Joint Advisory Board Members (JABM); consists of members from the universities' board of trustees and QF members	QF (State of Qatar)
DIAC	Dedicated free zone for higher education, 24 international universities and colleges and 3 national universities	TECOM Investments, a subsidiary of Dubai Holding (for-profit, government-owned company)	Dubai Technology and Media Free Zone Authority (DTMFZA) and universities' board of trustees	TECOM (Emirate of Dubai)
KAUST	International graduate-level research university with global collaborations and research alliances	Private non-profit university	Independent board of trustees	Private ownership

have classically underpinned, and shaped, higher education as a sector, and universities as institutions, by emulating the ways that countries like Singapore and Malaysia invited in departments from world-leading universities.

Table 14.1 shows the main features of ECQ, DIAC and KAUST in terms of model, ownership, governance and funding strategy. These three new higher education spaces have also been developed very differently. Decentralization is an apparent strategy, either from the local authority or from the federation, as in the case of Dubai, whilst Qatar established the Qatar Foundation for Education, Science and Community Development (QF) as a private non-profit organization to help institutionalize and operationalize the project. Dubai reorganized and rearranged a previous initiative and then institutionalized it within its main authority and premises; its operationalization has been borrowed totally from the business sector as the partnership model.

In contrast, KAUST was a completely new development, a challenge that required unconditional political and economic support. Though the 'contents' were different, in each case, it was the the leaders' vision which provided the guidance for an imagined economy ('Khaleeji Capital'[2]) to be discursively constituted and materially reproduced in the GCC region. By highlighting the mechanisms of the new developments within GCC region higher education, one can imagine these new developments as possible new actors, which through their agency may transform and reconstruct the landscape of higher education.

In a visit to the three developments, I met with senior leaders at QF (ECQ), DIAC and KAUST. The main purpose of my interviews, was to find out how far these new developments saw regionalism as a priority. In ECQ, regionalism was described by senior officials as significant for wealth accumulation in the GCC region to ensure the sustainability of national projects, which in turn was linked to the development of the GCC workforce. My interviewees showed an awareness of the GCC region as a political project in which the six countries share one geopolitical space and have similar concerns.

Interviewees at KAUST stressed that the size and capacity of ECQ meant that it is capable of catering not only for Qatari students but also for students from across the GCC region. In the summer of 2010 the research journal of QF announced a regional research collaboration between QF and KAUST. Saudi Arabia is regarded as a major political body within the GCC region and the whole world, and it considers that the region's mission and research collaboration agenda are part of its own legacy for the region, as the country with the largest economy within the GCC region.

DIAC provided a mixed picture. According to my interviewees, it is a project that is considered a leading space for higher education capacity, but also one that is sceptical about regional integration due to the region's performance in research and development. It was pointed out that regional collaboration should come from the highest authority in each country and not just an organizational policy. However, as indicated in its mission, DIAC aims to cater for the needs of GCC region nationals who have very limited opportunities within their own countries. The General Director of DIAC explained that the variety of available institutions and programmes makes DIAC different from both ECQ and KAUST, which are built on collaborations with prestigious international research institutes and target elite students only.

CONCLUSIONS

Two main conclusions may be drawn about the nature and consequences of HE regionalism in the GCC. The first is that the reactions of the GCC countries to the global economic and political changes suggest that even without integration initiatives, the GCC region is constructed out of different actors and interests derived from markets, private investment, the policies and decisions of companies or organizations, as well as state-led initiatives. These practices could be interpreted as a regionness that has different levels of integration. Arguably, the GCC regionness has not progressed from mere regional space to a deeper institutionalized polity with a permanent structure of decision-making and a stronger acting capability as a global actor: region as actor. However, Riggirozzi (2012) argues that there is a type of regionness that challenges 'old' versus 'new' regionalism, and on this basis I have argued that we can in fact understand the GCC as a regional arena for action driven by new consensuses over practices and cooperation in politico-institutional, socio-economic and cultural arenas (Riggirozzi, 2012: 427). Dynamics in these arenas are driven by different actors, projects of integration, linkages mechanisms, institutional structures and distributive consequences, which is in contrast with the notion of regionalism as a coherent model, and regionness as a cohesive (acting) subject or actorness (Schmitt-Egner, 2002: 192–195). A key political economic dynamic is that of 'rentierism' and what Hanieh (2010) calls 'Khaleeji Capital' which gives particular shape and form to the region as an arena, an area, and its decoupling of the national from the regional in very important ways. Higher education is often mobilized to manage advancing the idea of a region in and for itself, but to a large extent this fails.

For the second conclusion, I draw on the work of Mazawi (2012: 70), the leading scholar in this area. He makes five main points. First, that regional education agencies do not enjoy a binding role at this time, and a concerted and proactive regional policy on HE remains largely lacking. Second, that existing policies and agreements are only loosely coupled with GCC regional dynamics and labour market flows, as well as with other higher education systems across the Arab region. Third, that the lack of a regional policy, precisely under conditions of spiralling investment in 'national' schemes through the private (international) sector, may prove to exacerbate regional implosion carried under the weight of generalized competition in the field of HE. Contemplating a GCC academic region requires what Mazawi has called a holistic approach that considers higher education in relation to political, economic and cultural dynamics. He also argues that policies should be sensitive to intra- and inter-regional spatial dynamism in negotiating contradictions, and the ever-changing demands placed on higher education. Fourth, a viable notion of a GCC academic region would need to clarify the role that multilateral agreements can play in promoting regional pools of opportunity for students and faculty. Finally, the states of the GCC would need to consider the effects of uncoordinated intra-regional expansion when developing 'magnet' higher education opportunities which would ultimately deepen the dependency of all GCC states on outside providers.

All in all, and by way of a final conclusion, the GCC provides a fascinating case of a region, but not in conventional theoretical terms. This suggests that in theorizing regions, we need to be more attentive to the way in which regional processes are mediated by different cultural, historical and political arrangements which shape the nature, forms and outcomes of the region as an arena of contestation. In the case of the GCC, its largely symbolic form draws attention to the continuing dominance of national competitive state projects.

NOTES

1. http://www.agu.edu.bh/english/university/uni_cooperation.aspx.
2. 'The circuits of capital are increasingly cast at the pan-Gulf scale, and a capitalist class – described as *khaleeji-capital* – is emerging around the accumulation-opportunities presented within the new regional space. The formation of *khaleeji*-capital represents the development of a class increasingly aligned with the interests of imperialism and has important ramifications for understanding the region's political economy' (Hanieh, 2010: 35).

REFERENCES

Abouammoh, A. (2009), *The Role of Education: Trends of Reforms and EU-GCC Understanding*, Riyad: Centre for Higher Education Research and Studies.

Al Khalifa, R.I.D. (2008), 'The Gulf Cooperation Council: Regional, Institutional and Legal Development', PhD, University of Exeter, Ethos database.

Davidson, Christopher and Mackenzie Smith, Peter (eds) (2008), *Higher Education in the Gulf States: Shaping Economies, Politics, and Culture*, London: Saqi.

Donn, Gari and Al-Manthri, Yayha (2010), *Globalisation and Higher Education in the Arab Gulf States*, Oxford: Symposium.

GCC (2008), 'Highlights of the Processes and Developments of the Higher Education in the Gulf Cooperation Council, Decisions and Achievements', Riyadh: The General Secretary of the Gulf Cooperation Council, accessed at http://sites.gcc-sg.org/DLibrary/index.php?action=ShowOneandandBID=32.

Hanieh, A. (2010), 'Khaleeji-Capital: Class-Formation and Regional Integration in the Middle-East Gulf', *Historical Materialism*, **18**(2), 35–76.

Hanouz, M.D. and Khatib, S. (2010), *The Arab World Competitiveness Review 2010*, Geneva: World Economic Forum.

Hardill, Irene, Benneworth Paul, Baker, Mark and Budd, Leslie (eds) (2006), *The Rise of the English Regions?*, London: Routledge.

Kamrava, M. et al. (2011), 'The Political Economy of the Gulf Summary Report', Washington, DC: Center for International and Regional Studies, Georgetown University.

Low, L. and Salazar, L. (2011), 'Gulf Cooperation Council – the Rising Power and Lessons for ASEAN', *Institute of Southeast Asian Studies*, **12**, 3–53.

Luciani, Giacomo (1995), 'Resources, Revenues, and Authoritarianism in the Arab World: Beyond the Rentier State?', in Rex Brynen, Bahgat Korany and Paul Noble (eds), *Political Liberalization and Democratization in the Arab World: Theoretical Perspectives*, Boulder, CO: Lynne Rienner, pp. 211–227.

Mazawi, A. (2012), 'Policy, Politics of Higher Education in the Gulf Cooperation Council Member States: Intersections of Globality, Regionalism and Locality', in C. Davidson and P. McKenzie Smith (eds), *Higher Education in the Gulf States*, London: Saqi Books, pp. 59–72.

McGlennon, D. (2006), 'Building Research Capacity in the Gulf Cooperation Council Countries: Strategy, Funding and Engagement', *Second International Colloquium on Research and Higher Education Policy*, Vol. 29, November.

Partrick, N. (2012), 'Nation in Gulf States', in D. Held and K. Ulrichsen (eds), *Transformations of the Gulf: Politics, Economics and the Global Order*, London: Routledge, pp. 47–65.

Riggirozzi, P. (2012), 'Region, Regionness and Regionalism in Latin America: Towards a New Synthesis', *New Political Economy*, **17**(4), 421–443.

Schmitt-Egner, P. (2002), 'The Concept of "Region": Theoretical and Methodological Notes on its Reconstruction', *Journal of European Integration*, **24**(3), 179–200.

Söderbaum, Fredrik, StÅlgren, Patrik and Van Langenhove, Luk (2005), 'The EU as a Global Actor and the Dynamics of Interregionalism: a Comparative Analysis', *Journal of European Integration*, **27**(3), 365–380.

Wilkins, Stephen (2011), 'Who Benefits from Foreign Universities in the Arab Gulf States?', *Australian Universities' Review*, **53**(1), 73–83.

Zahlan, R.S. (1998), *The Making of the Modern Gulf States: Kuwait, Bahrain, Qatar, the United Arab Emirates and Oman*, Boston, MA: Unwin Hyman.

Index

9/11 149, 317

Abouammoh, Abdulrahman 298
Academic Cooperation Association
  (ACA) 69, 83
Academic Credit Transfer Framework
  for Asia (ACTFA) 109, 118, 136
Accrediting Agency of Chartered
  Colleges and Universities
  (AACCUP) 119
Acharya, Amitav 126, 148, 156, 160
Association of African Universities
  (AAU) 94–95
Accreditation Committee of
  Cambodia (ACC) 119
Adelman, Cliff 39
African and Madagascan Council for
  Higher Education (CAMES) 95
African, Caribbean and Pacific Group
  of States (ACP) 89
African Higher Education Area
  (AHEA) 94
African Higher Education
  Harmonisation Strategy 95
African Union (AU) 89, 94
  Commission (AUC) 94
Agnew, John 255, 256
Allègre, Claude 2, 33, 34, 91
Andean Community of Nations
  (CAN) 221–222, 256, 277
Arab Gulf Region 313
Arab World Competitive Report 294
Arabian Gulf University (AGU) 297
Arctic 192–194, 209
Argentina 11, 233–236, 238–239, 240,
  243–244, 247, 249–250, 257, 261,
  279, 287
Asia Europe Meeting (ASEM) 3, 5,
  143–165
  Credit Transfer System (ACTS)
    117–118, 120, 133, 141, 154

  Education Area 18
  Meeting of Ministers for Education
    (ASEM ME) 152, 154
Asia Pacific Economic Cooperation
  (APEC) 1–2, 5–6, 40, 128, 137,
  141, 149
Asia Pacific Research Universities
  (APRU) 179
Asian Development Bank (ADB) 8,
  133, 178
Assessment of Higher Education
  Learning Outcomes (AHELO)
  97–98
Association for the Development of
  Education in Africa (ADEA) 95
Association of Caribbean States 222
Association of Caribbean Tertiary
  Institutions (ACTI) 216
Association of Rectors of LAC
  Universities (ACRULAC) 248,
  250
Association of Caribbean Universities
  and Research Institutes (UNICA)
  214
Association of Southeast Asian
  Nations (ASEAN) 124–165
  Comprehensive Investment
    Agreement (ACIA) 126
  Credit Transfer System (ACTS)
    117–118, 120, 133, 141
  Economic Community (AEC) 109,
    126, 130
  Free Trade Area (AFTA) 6, 126, 128
  Framework Agreement on Services
    (AFAS) 126, 128, 134, 136
  International Mobility for Students
    Programme (AIMS) 109,
    113–114, 137, 138
  Investment Area (AIA) 126
  Ministers of Education Meetings
    (ASED) 147

Political-Security Community
(APSC) 109
Qualifications Reference Framework
(AQRF) 115–116, 134
Quality Assurance Network
(AQAN) 111, 118, 135
Socio-Cultural Community (ASCC)
109, 126, 130
University Network (AUN) 18, 108,
110, 117–118, 121, 124, 127,
131, 133–141, 179
Association of the Montevideo
Universities Group (AUGM) 279
Australia 2, 4, 18, 35, 38, 39, 40, 58, 87,
108, 131, 134, 137, 138, 140, 147,
162, 178, 298

Bahrain 289–290, 292, 297
Barents Region 3, 36, 19, 191–210
Barroso, José 38
Bilingual 237, 267, 272, 282, 284
Bishop, Julie 39
Bolivia 231, 233–236, 238, 240, 244,
257, 266, 279, 287
Bolivarian Alliance for the Peoples of
Our America (ALBA) 3, 11–12,
26, 222, 225, 247, 249
   Peoples' Trade Agreement (Tratado
   de Comercio de los Pueblos or
   TCP) (ALBA-TCP) 20, 229,
   232, 247, 249, 253–256, 258,
   259, 261, 264–265, 266
Bologna
   Declaration 34, 53–54, 60–61, 70,
   74
   Follow-Up-Group (BFUG) 34–36,
   55–56, 60, 62, 77, 86, 147, 153,
   159
   Activity Groups 35
   Ministerial Meetings 34–35, 54, 57,
   89
     Bergen (2005) 87, 90
     Berlin (2003) 153
     Bologna (1999) 34, 53–54, 60–61,
     70, 74
     Bucharest (2012) 88
     Budapest/Vienna (2010) 88
     Leuven/Louvain-la-Neueve (2009)
     35, 37, 88–89
     London (2007) 37

Prague (2001) 54, 70, 86–87
Yerevan (2015) 88
Process *xiv*, 2, 11, 16–17, 24–48,
49–84, 134, 143, 147, 153, 156,
158–159, 162, 198
External Dimension
Policy Forum 35, 37, 57, 58, 85, 88,
92, 93
Borderlands 18, 19, 166–190
Brazil 11, 19, 20, 35, 38, 228–288
Brisbane Communiqué 134, 138
Breslin, Shaun 4, 144–145, 274

Cambodia 104, 108, 119–120, 127, 130,
139, 171
Canada 35, 88, 209, 298
Capitalism 1, 26–27, 44, 222, 258, 264
Caribbean 5, 12, 19–20, 89, 95,
211–227, 228, 232, 242, 253–271,
272, 277, 280, 281
Caribbean Community (CARICOM)
12, 211–227, 254, 265
Caribbean Examination Council
(CXC) 214
Caribbean Free Trade Agreement
(CARIFTA) 221
Caribbean Single Market 213, 219,
221, 224
Caribbean Vocational Qualification
(CVQ) 214
Castro, Fidel 256
Chávez, Hugo 11, 254, 256, 260, 266,
277
Chile 88,
China 5, 18, 32, 35, 38, 40, 73, 83, 104,
108, 125–126, 141, 147, 155, 161,
166–190
China–ASEAN Free Trade Area
(CAFTA) 168, 177
Circumpolar Studies 19, 193
Cold War 8, 14, 51, 103, 125–126, 192,
218, 254
Commodification 260–261, 265,
Community of Latin American and
Caribbean States (CELAC) 5, 222,
225, 232, 248, 249, 254
Convention for the Recognition of
Higher Education Qualifications
34
Confucianism 18, 170–171, 180

Index

Confucius Institute 169, 172
Convention for the Recognition of Higher Education Qualifications 34
Corbett, Anne *xiv*, 3, 28, 53, 56, 58, 68
Council of Europe (CoE) 3, 6, 25, 35, 37, 51, 53–57, 62, 87
Critical Realism 18, 145
Curricula 1, 11, 20, 28, 39, 54, 71, 76, 81, 95–97, 112, 119–120, 159, 170, 237, 283, 285, 287
Cyprus 155

Dale, Roger 1–48, 65–84, 92, 156, 161, 212
Delors, Jacque 28
Denmark 162, 209
Dent, Christopher 4–5, 149
Diaspora 18, 166, 168, 172
Directorate General of Education and Culture (DGEAC) 69, 70–71, 73, 77
Dubai 299–300
Dubai International Academic City (DIAC) 299–301

Economy
  Global Knowledge-based 15, 27, 29, 30, 32–34, 38, 39, 41, 44, 59, 110, 120, 128, 140, 156, 161, 223, 257, 272, 275, 291, 293, 294
  Regional 4, 10, 18, 20, 26, 33, 44, 106, 115, 167, 175, 177, 215, 219, 222, 224, 258, 259, 266, 267, 273, 277, 293, 294, 301, 303
Ecuador 231, 243, 264, 266, 287
Education City Qatar (ECQ) 299–301
Education, Audiovisual and Culture Executive Agency (EACEA) 75, 79
EDULINK 95
East African Community (EAC) 96
Erasmus 14, 65–66, 68–69, 70, 153
Erasmus Mundus (EM) 14, 16–17, 28, 38, 65–84, 149, 298
  Alumni Association (EMA) 76, 80
  Master Course (EMMC) 80, 83
Europe 49–64, 65–84, 85–102, 125, 127, 143–165, 209, 273, 278, 290
  Borders 27, 88, 92, 148
  Normative Power Post-war 27, 30, 39, 85, 92, 99, 150, 196, 198, 245
  7–8, 28, 37
European
  Centre for Higher Education (Centre Européen pour l' Enseignement Supérieur, UNESCO) (CEPES) 56–57
  Credit Transfer System (ECTS) 60, 90–93, 95, 96, 133, 154, 201
  Commission (EC) *xiv*, 2, 5, 17, 24, 28, 30–35, 37–38, 40–42, 54, 55–58, 61–62, 65–69, 71, 73, 75, 78, 81, 85, 93, 99, 147, 149, 152–153, 156, 159, 161, 162
  Council 30, 31, 33–34, 59
  Cultural Convention 35, 55, 56, 59, 87
  Economic Area (EEA) 75
  Higher Education Area (EHEA) 24, 26, 34–37, 41, 43, 49–64, 76–86, 87–94, 107, 121, 147, 150, 162
  Qualifications Register 39
  Research Area (ERA) 16, 24, 26, 30, 33, 40–41, 43–44, 74
  Union (EU) 1, 2, 5, 9, 10, 13, 14, 16, 17, 24–48, 49, 51, 53, 56, 57, 58, 59, 65–83, 88–89, 91, 94–95, 99, 133, 138, 149, 150, 151, 153, 156, 161, 162, 170, 183, 203, 211, 224, 230, 235, 237, 242, 245, 246–251, 298–299
  Universities 16, 24, 61, 72, 79, 88, 298
  University Association (EUA) 70, 77, 90, 153, 162
Europeanization 24, 80, 265

Federal University of Latin American Integration (UNILA) 11, 20, 250, 272–288
Federal University of Amazonas (Universidade Federal do Amazonas) (UFAM) 264
Finland 209
France 2, 28, 76, 83, 91, 96, 149, 155, 161, 209

Free Trade Agreements (FTA) 1, 5, 6, 126, 128, 168, 177, 221, 229, 247, 277, 290
Freire, Pablo 261–262

General Agreement on Trade in Services (GATS) 128, 178, 180, 295
General Agreement on Tariff and Trade (GATT) 6, 128
German Academic Exchange Service (Deutscher Akademischer Austauschdienst) (DAAD) 83, 96, 118, 137, 153, 155
Germany 3, 28–29, 76, 138, 140, 149, 154, 162, 209
Gulf Cooperation Council (GCC) 289–304
Gulf States 290, 295
Guyana 222, 224–225, 248, 266

Haas, Ernst 9
Haiti 222, 224–225
Hettne, Bjorn 4, 7–11, 25, 49–52, 107, 274, 275
Higgott, Richard 4, 144–145

Ibero-American Network for Quality Accreditation in Higher Education (RIACES) 242
Iceland 209
Imperialism 273
India 5, 32, 38, 73, 83, 125–126, 161–162
Indonesia 103, 108–109, 114, 119–120, 126, 130, 134, 138–139, 141, 155, 169, 171–172, 174–175
Intergovernmentalism 220
International Association of Universities (IAU) 87
International Institute for Higher Education in Latin America and the Caribbean (UNESCO) (IESALC) 242, 280
International Institute for Educational Planning (UNESCO) (IIEP) 85
International Monetary Fund (IMF) 267, 274
Inter-American Development Bank 256

Inter-University Council for East Africa (IUCEA) 96
Inter-regionalism xiv, 2–3, 5, 17, 52, 298–299
Investment 81, 107, 110–111, 126, 128, 156, 169, 177, 182, 213, 254, 273, 294, 296, 300, 302
  Foreign Direct 169, 173, 177, 264
Iran 290

Jamaica 213, 224–225
Jayasuriya, Kanishka 12, 13, 26, 184, 217, 218, 219, 223, 228, 229, 230
Jean Monnet Programme 298

Katzenstein, Peter 148, 160
Keynesianism 8, 29
King Abdullah University of Science and Technology (KAUST) 299, 300, 301
Knowledge 20, 61, 74, 105, 109, 132, 143, 157, 180, 183, 191–3, 201–202, 206, 208, 237, 255, 257, 262, 264, 275–276, 279–280, 282, 285, 287, 290–291, 294
  Based Economy 3, 15, 21, 26–27, 29, 30, 32, 33–34, 52, 58, 110, 120, 128, 140, 156, 159, 223, 289, 293
  Based Society 110, 131, 280
  Enterprise 31, 109, 110, 182, 219, 258, 279
  Mobility 18, 147, 166–168, 180, 183, 257, 283
  R&D 31, 43, 294
Kok, Wim 32, 38
Kok Review 32
Korea 104, 108, 141, 147, 155, 161, Kuwait 289–290

Laos 172, 176, 181–183
Latin America and the Caribbean (LAC) 5, 20, 220–221, 228, 242, 272–277, 280–281
Latin American and the Caribbean Economic System (Sistema Económico Latin-American y del Caribe) (SELA) 222
League of Arab States 6

Learning 31–32, 39, 55, 90, 92, 96, 106, 110–111, 115–117, 134, 150, 158, 166, 170–172, 180, 182, 204–205, 208, 212, 275, 295
  Lifelong 106, 115, 130, 134, 151, 155
  Outcomes 90, 95, 97–8, 111–112, 115, 155
Left-wing 276, 290
Lisbon 31, 59, 69
  Agenda 24, 31, 33, 68
  Convention 34–35, 56–57, 60, 93, 154
  Strategy 30, 32–33, 59, 156
  Summit 30–31, 92
Lula, President (Luiz Inácio Lula da Silva) 254, 256, 260–261, 266–267, 272

Maastricht Treaty 28–29
Malaysia 83, 103–104, 108–109, 114, 116, 119, 126, 130, 134, 138–139, 141, 169, 171–172, 174–175, 178, 181–182, 300
Market-making
  World 13, 25–26, 33, 39, 43–44
Metagovernance 212, 214, 216–221, 223–224
Mittelman, James 9
Mobility 2, 4, 14, 18–19, 28, 34, 53–54, 65–66, 69–70, 74, 88, 90, 94–96, 103, 105–111, 113–117, 119–120, 130–131, 133–134, 137–138, 147, 149, 151–155, 157, 159–160, 166, 168, 184, 209, 230, 232–233, 234–241, 243, 245–250, 259, 264, 265, 278, 297
Monetary Community of Central African (CEMAC) 95–96
Monetary Union of Western Africa (UEMOA) 95–96
Mutual Recognition Agreements (MRA) 129, 134, 136, 141
Myanmar 104, 108, 120, 127, 130, 139, 141, 172, 176

Neighbourhood Policy 38
Network for the Excellence of the Higher Education of Western Africa (REESAO) 95

New Regionalism Approach (NRA) 50–53, 274–275
Neofunctionalist 8–9, 230
Neoliberalism 6, 9, 19, 29, 31, 58, 69, 257, 266–267, 293, 299
New Zealand 35, 88, 134, 137–138, 141, 161–162
North American Free Trade Agreement (NAFTA) 1, 5–6, 229
Norway 12, 150

Oman 289–290
Open Method of Coordination (OMC) 32, 92, 247
Organization for Economic Co-operation (OECD) 8, 85, 87, 91, 97, 209, 294–295

Pacific Alliance 229, 248, 250
Pan-African University (PAU) 94
Paraguay 11, 232–236, 244–245, 250, 257, 266–267, 279, 287
Paris Chamber of Commerce 297
Peru 229, 231, 247–248, 264, 266, 287
Philippines 103, 108, 114, 119–120, 126, 130, 134, 138–139, 141, 172, 174
Polanyi, Karl 9, 255
Power 1, 8, 11–12, 19, 26–27, 31, 39, 41, 43–44, 54, 67, 72, 82, 83, 86, 93, 99, 124, 131, 145–146, 148–149, 152–159, 161, 167, 169, 183, 242, 245, 251, 256, 267, 273, 276, 286, 292, 296, 298
  Agenda Setting 1, 14, 152–159, 242
  Soft 72, 169
  Rules of the Game 1, 14, 152–159, 242
Privatization 260–261, 265, 280
Putin, Vladimir 191–192

Qatar 289, 299–301
Qatar Foundation (QF) 300
Quality Assurance 1, 2, 7, 19, 34, 39–40, 54, 60–61, 67, 92–97, 105–111, 115–116, 118, 120, 128, 134–135, 137–140, 147, 151, 153–155, 157, 215–230, 235, 240, 242–243, 245

Regions
    Cultural Political Economy 24–48
    Definitions 4–5
    De Jure Regionalism 4
    Extra-regional 17, 18, 25, 26, 38–40, 44, 86, 108
    Hegemonic Regionalism 19–20, 228–229, 247, 254, 259, 265–266, 274, 276, 279–280
        Post- 19, 229, 266
        Counter- 19–20, 229, 247, 254, 265
    Hybrid Regionalism 5, 54, 143–165, 228–229
    Hybrid Inter-regionalism(s) 5, 54, 143–165, 228–229
    Immature Regionalism 19, 211, 224
    Informal Regionalization 53–54, 61
    Inter-regionalism xiv, 2–3, 5, 15, 17, 52, 298, 299
    Mature Regionalism 19, 211–214, 216–219, 222–223
    New Regionalism 7–13, 16, 49–53, 61, 148, 221, 228–230, 240, 272–288, 296, 302
    Old Regionalism 7–8, 10–11, 212, 219–20
    Region-building 2, 9, 14, 18–19, 25, 30, 51, 139, 143–145, 160, 230, 243, 249, 291, 296
    Regional Society 10, 52
    Regionness 3, 10, 19, 296, 302
    Regionalizing xiv, 2–3, 7, 11–13, 15–16, 18, 20, 24, 27, 58–61, 125, 143, 146, 161, 197, 198, 221, 236, 250
    Theories 1–23, 25, 49, 144–145
        Functionalists 7–9, 15, 50, 107, 212, 219–220, 223–224, 230, 232
        Social Constructivists 14, 50, 148
    Trans-regionalism 5
    Types 4–5
    Variegated Regionalism 14–21
Regional Accreditation Mechanism (RAM) 215, 219
Regionalization 3–5, 10, 13, 16, 18, 49–64, 106–107, 124–127, 131–134, 138–140, 150, 289–304
Regulatory Regionalism 12–13, 16, 19, 27, 44, 183–184, 217, 223, 228–252

Rentierism 291–293, 302
Robertson, Susan L. 1–48, 55, 57, 59, 67, 86, 98, 103, 156, 184, 217, 223, 228–230, 295
Rosamond, Ben 14–15, 58
Russia 5, 12, 19, 34–35, 56, 95, 161–162, 191–210

Santos, Boaventura de Sousa 261, 275
Saudi Arabia 289–290, 297, 301
Sbragia, Alberta 15, 50
Scale 4, 6, 12
    Global 3, 52, 57–58, 70, 265
    Local 266
    Regional 3, 9, 12–13, 15, 27, 43, 107, 256, 291
Schumpeter, Joseph 33
Silk Road 171
Singapore 2, 5, 103, 108, 130, 139, 141, 149, 161, 169, 172, 178, 181–2, 300
Social exclusion 31, 275–276
Soft power 72, 169
Söderbaum, Fredrik 9, 15, 49–51, 144, 254, 274, 298
Sorbonne Declaration 3, 53, 58, 68
South East Asian Treaty Organization (SEATO) 125–126
South–South Cooperation 3, 19–20, 253–257, 264–267, 281
Southeast Asian Ministers of Education Organization (SEAMEO) 106, 109, 121, 147
Southeast Asian Ministers of Education Organization–Regional Institute for Education and Development (SEAMEO–RIHED) 18, 105, 107–108, 110, 114, 118, 124, 127, 130–139, 141
Southern Common Market (Mercado Común del Sur) (MERCOSUR) 3, 5, 6, 11, 12, 19, 26, 221, 222, 228–252, 253–259, 261, 263-7, 272, 277–9, 287, 290
Sovereignty 1, 17, 27, 42, 86, 89, 91, 93, 96, 104, 106, 111, 144, 167, 174, 212–3, 219–21, 239, 262, 279
State 1–288
    Transformation 12
    Topography 12, 13
    Core Problems 13

Students 2, 11, 14, 18, 20, 28, 34, 37, 39–40, 58–59, 61, 65–67, 69–72, 74–76, 78, 81–83, 93, 95–97, 106, 109, 111–115, 117–121, 131, 137, 149, 153, 159–160, 162, 178–184, 193, 198, 200–201, 203–205, 234–236, 248, 260–261, 263–264, 272, 282, 284–287, 289, 297–299, 301, 303
    Graduates 29, 34, 67, 77, 112, 114, 128, 298
    Unions 15, 154, 162
Supra-nationalism 220

Tariffs 6, 128, 170, 289
Tempus 29, 87, 298
Tuning Programme 39, 94–95

UMAP Credit Transfer Scheme (UCTS) 117–118, 141
United Arab Emirates (UAE) 289–304
United Kingdom (UK) xiv, 3, 28, 34, 76, 108, 134, 178, 209, 217, 298
University Mobility in Asia and the Pacific (UMAP) 117, 121, 141
Union of South American Nations (UNASUR) 222, 229, 232, 248–249, 254, 255, 266, 277

United Nations Educational, Scientific and Cultural Organization (UNESCO) 35, 51, 54–57, 62, 85, 91, 130–137, 140–141, 232, 242, 260–261, 280
United Nations University (UNU) 297
University Network of the Peoples of ALBA (UNIALBA) 248
University of the Arctic 193
University of the West Indies 213
Uruguay 232–236, 238, 244–245, 250, 257, 261, 266–267, 279, 287

Venezuela 11, 19–20, 229, 231–232, 234–236, 243, 248–250, 253–271, 277, 287
Vietnam 18, 103–104, 108, 114, 120, 127, 130, 134, 139, 154, 162, 166–168, 179–184
Violence 174, 276

Warleigh-Lack, Alex 15, 51
Washington Consensus 279
Westphalian 8, 51
World-class universities 290
World Trade Organization (WTO) 5–6, 30, 133, 177, 180, 274, 280

Zgaga, Pavel *xiv*, 34, 37, 57, 86